GLOBAL METAL

CW00543088

GLOBAL METAPHORS
Modernity and the Quest for One World

Jo-Anne Pemberton

Pluto Press

LONDON • STERLING, VIRGINIA

First published 2001
by PLUTO PRESS
345 Archway Road, London N6 5AA
and 22883 Quicksilver Drive,
Sterling, VA 20166–2012, USA

www.plutobooks.com

Copyright © Jo-Anne Pemberton 2001

The right of Jo-Anne Pemberton to be identified as the author
of this work has been asserted by her in accordance with
the Copyright, Designs and Patents Act 1988.

British Library Cataloguing in Publication Data
A catalogue record for this book is available from
the British Library

Library of Congress Cataloging in Publication Data
Pemberton, Jo-Anne.
  Global metaphors : modernity and the quest for one world / Jo-Anne
Pemberton.
     p. cm.
Includes index.
  ISBN 0–7453–1654–9 — ISBN 0–7453–1653–0 (pbk.)
   1. Civilization, Modern—20th century. 2. World politics—20th
century. 3. Globalization—History—20th century. 4. Technology and
civilization. 5. Intellectual life—History—20th century. 6.
Rhetoric—Political aspects—History—20th century. 7. Postmodernism.
I. Title.
  CB427 .P39 2001
  909.8—dc21

                                                        2001001054

                 ISBN 0 7453 1654 9 hardback
                 ISBN 0 7453 1653 0 paperback

Designed and produced for Pluto Press by
Chase Publishing Services, Fortescue, Sidmouth EX10 9QG
Typeset from disk by Stanford DTP Services, Towcester
Printed in the European Union by TJ International, Padstow, England

CONTENTS

ACKNOWLEDGEMENTS

Many people have helped me in the preparation of this book. Special mention must be made of Roderic Pitty who warmly supported this project from the beginning and whose detailed comments on an earlier draft were crucial to the completion of this book. Thanks go to Ephraim Nimni for his enthusiasm and support and Conal Condren, Professor of Politics at the University of New South Wales, whose work has had a deep and lasting influence on my intellectual development. I am indebted to Richard Falk, Albert G. Milbank Professor of International Law and Practice, Princeton University and Richard Little, Professor of Politics, University of Bristol for their wise and sympathetic comments on my proposal for this study. I am also enormously grateful to Cavell and Attilio Fomiatti, Joyce Pemberton, Dr Gregory Pemberton, Mark and Sally Pemberton, Gail Burke, Christian Pemberton and Tony Palfreeman, all of whom have helped, in all manner of ways, to facilitate the research and writing of this book. Special thanks to the staff of the League of Nations Archives and Historical Collections Unit, United Nations Library, Geneva. In particular, I would like to record my appreciation of the invaluable help of Dr Ursula-Maria Ruser, formerly Chief of Archives, and Alfred Guindi. Thanks also to Jens Boel at the UNESCO Archives and Peter Carman and Jean-Michel Ageron-Blanc of the Paris American Academy for their great efforts on my behalf. I would also like to express my gratitude to Rebecca Wise who carefully read through and corrected my manuscript and to Roger van Zwanenberg for encouraging me to undertake this study and urging me to complete it. A few sections of this book have appeared in earlier incarnations and I would like to acknowledge the opportunities given me to test some of my ideas. Versions of parts of Chapters 1 and 2 have appeared in *History of Political Thought*. Chapter 7 contains material that has appeared in *Review of International Studies* and Chapters 4 and 6 further material that is due to appear.

INTRODUCTION

Modernity is an amazingly elastic notion. In temporal terms, it can be made to span 500 years. Writing in 1938 Stefan Zweig sought to convey the sense of excitement aroused among early sixteenth century audiences by news that Magellan's fleet had circumnavigated the globe: with that feat modern times arrived:

> What sages had suspected for thousands of years, what learned men had dreamed, was now certain, thanks to the persistent courage of this one man. The earth was round, for a man had rounded it...The news...spread like wildfire across Europe, rousing immeasurable astonishment and admiration...Other bold discoverers could and would fill in numerous details in the world-picture, but the basic form of our planet had been ascertained by Magellan, and persists for all time to come...Thirty years had taught more about the place of man's habitation than had thousands and thousands of years before. Though half unwittingly, the generation which had had this intoxicating, this stupendous experience, realized that a new age, the modern age, had begun.[1]

Here the beginning of the modern is commensurate with the expanded spatial awareness engendered by the age of exploration. (Note, however, that Zweig also depicts Magellan's achievement as the realisation of an age-old awareness. As we shall see, the new is often presented as being no more than the triumph of an older perspective.) Others would have the modern era emerging out of the late seventeenth and eighteenth centuries, treating it as if it were coextensive with that almost equally swollen concept the enlightenment project. Modernity here means bringing to bear on experience the bright light of reason, especially scientific reason. Celebration of the modern and its identification with a kind of global consciousness and forms of rationalism has been a recurring feature of intellectual life over several centuries.

Yet the repetition of certain terms and the presence of conceptual parallels between ideas articulated at various junctures does not entitle us to group them under a single rubric. The term modern has been enthusiastically employed for a variety of ends and invested with manifold significations. That words such as rationality and utility have been its frequent travelling companions suggests some circumscription of meaning. To be modern might be coldly to assess and manipulate reality in the cause of efficiency. It might

1

be to conquer the universe. Yet the modern can also connote hedonism, voluptuousness, a pagan revival. It might suggest leaping into unknown realms beyond the horizon of everyday meaning. Modernity is thus not to be taken as some glutinous conceptual essence running through and binding together the thoughts of a myriad of thinkers. It is not some extra layer of reality, some macro-historical fabric, hovering above us; there is no modernist metaphysic of which individuals are but terminal expressions. Clearly, it is problematic to place tendencies of thought expressed at any particular time under one heading and this holds all the more when we are dealing with arguments put forward at various moments over the centuries and in vastly different rhetorical contexts. Intellectual historians should and do seek to uncover resemblances or even relationships among the range of concepts thrown up across the ages. They can shock us by revealing unexpected lines, whether madly zig-zagging or faint and meandering, connecting the old with the new. Yet caution must also be exercised when charting the course of ideas, lest special nuances and shades of meaning be lost amidst the drive to establish conceptual lineages.

This study is a work of conceptual history. Drawing on the work of philosophers, historians, scientists, writers, artists and political actors, it examines thoughts about world order, about the political and social configuration of the globe, throughout the twentieth century. Most importantly, it relates these to ongoing metaphysical speculations as to whether nature favours form and fixity on the one hand or fluidity and flux on the other. These metaphysical and aesthetic issues are also reflected in that dazzling complex of ideas called modernity and discussions of world order are placed against this backdrop. The continuing identification throughout the century of modernity with a global sensibility and with global phenomena warrants this move. In this study, the word modernity will be used most particularly to refer to certain tendencies of thought which captured the early twentieth century imagination. Many writers at this time felt they were being confronted by unfamiliar phenomena and in the light of this, the idea of what it meant to be modern required reexamination. Paul Valéry, for example, would argue that in the years after 1913 especially, modernity had come to signify, above all, conceptual fragmentation and confusion. In this light of this, I will argue that modernity in the early twentieth century acquired dual implications; it had both a dynamic and deterministic side. It implied both riotous colour and scientific uniformity, both creative intervention in, and submission to, nature. Many of the thinkers I examine slid, more or less with ease, between these poles of meaning. I will be arguing that intellectual debates during the last couple of decades concerned with the question of whether we are to describe the world as universe or a multiverse or whether the future lies with one or multiple world orders are in many ways developing and enlarging upon early twentieth century themes. This is the principal reason why emphasis is placed on this period in this study. In addition, I am going to argue that the concatenation of ideas that we call postmodernity is actually modernity itself, or at least a further elaboration of one of its major tendencies. Peter Conrad draws a similar conclusion in his wonderfully literate and exquisitely written *Modern Times, Modern Places: Life & Art in the Twentieth Century* (1998). He states at the outset that in this he will be focussing on modernity and avoiding the 'abstruse and academic category of the "post-modern"', explaining that while the 'term comes in handy when defining architectural fashions' he has found it of 'limited use' in other areas as 'the idea is already latent in modernism'. I would develop this point by saying that postmodernity is not so much latent in modernity as it is one of its more striking dimensions.[2]

Numerous themes explored in this study well pre-date the twentieth century. The worship of the new is one example as is the idea of a scientific commonwealth. It is in their blending with one or more motifs drawn from a multifaceted semantic arena that included such items as crisis, speed, futurity, mass organisation and international rationalisation that these ideas acquire a peculiarly twentieth-century complexion. To give one example, Robert Brady, the author of a major study of the interwar phenomenon called rationalisation (rationalisation being a term which as we shall see bore many of the significations carried by the word globalisation), remarked in 1930 on the arrival of a 'new rationalism', one of the chief denotations of this expression being expert control for the purposes of social coordination. Brady distinguished this new rationalism from the 'old' rationalisms of the seventeenth and nineteenth centuries because the latter, he maintained, were by contrast concerned mainly with 'matters of personal, social, and economic freedom and equality'.[3]

I should also note that many of the notions I address were discussed by writers, scholars and artists in the second part of the nineteenth century. Contemporary modernity was certainly beginning to take shape by then as Peter Gay has so elegantly detailed.[4] Indeed, Geoffrey Barraclough in his *An Introduction to Contemporary History* (1964) describes the period beginning around 1890 and ending around 1960 as marking the transitional period between the modern and 'post-modern' eras; Barraclough used the 'provisional name' postmodern to refer to a period which had yet to form definite contours and features.[5] He goes on to suggest that a degree of form-lessness, a slightly unsettled appearance, might well be a key aspect of contemporary history. If there were to be a common culture in the future, it would have to be more inclusive and multicultural than in the past for the postmodern age is a post-European age. (A point which neatly parallels the overlap between contemporary postmodern and postcolonial theory.)[6] Barraclough argues that it was at the close of the nineteenth century that one can discern the first glimmers of the new world to come. The important changes intimated included the 'transition from a European to a global pattern of international politics', the rise of mass society and the 'challenge to liberal values'. These trends, he wrote, became more pronounced after 1918, proceeding to maturity in the years following the end of the Second

World War.[7] Barraclough describes the years between 1880 and 1914 in the literary and artistic spheres of activity as one of 'reaction against the tradition of the past four hundred years'; this period of revolt overlapped with and was succeeded by an era of bold experimentation. Barraclough saw intellectual challenges to the old order as reflected in the ideas of Henri Bergson, who was renowned for elevating intuition above intellect and the mathematician Henri Poincaré whom he believed, somewhat erroneously, had denounced the idea that scientists could speak of an objective reality. He saw the dissolution of the old humanist outlook and an attendant individualistic ethic not only in the artistic work produced by cubists, dadaists and surrealists but also in modern physics. He thought physics had unveiled a universe that was 'unintelligible, senseless and accidental', and portrayed 'man...[as]..."no more than a fortuitous concourse of atoms"'.[8] The new rationalism was an attempt to re-establish an ordered and public realm of meaning. Its adherents sought to organise and channel in constructive and collectivist directions all the energies the times had unleashed. While in a sense predicated on the idea of active willing, the notion that human beings were capable of intervening in and reconstructing reality, it also had a deterministic cast; there was also a very strong sense that rational planning was an induction from certain social and psychological facts of which the individual was but a function.

So modernity had in the first part of the twentieth century a double and tensive meaning. The term frequently signifies scientists in white coats rigorously planning streamlined, standardised new orders founded upon physical facts and laws. Yet already by the late nineteenth century there was profound questioning of the objectivity of science. Scientists and philosophers asked whether the principles and data of science were anything but inventions of mind, artifices to help us make sense of and mould the rich and confusing flow of experience. Whereas an austere positivism might suggest there is a final resting place for humanity once social life had come to reflect in its design and operations, the structure of the physical universe, the new thinking about science was seen as suggestive of a world of indeterminacy and mobility. Those who favoured the latter image also tended to promote a doctrine of action. In the midst of an open and fluid experience it was left to human will to shape the future. This idea would be forced in more or less explosive directions. It could point to madness and commotion no less than scientific mastery and control. Indeed, we will see how the erosion and questioning of the foundations of science in conjunction with celebrations of will, action and disruptive energy informed challenges to the rationalist quest for social blue-prints.

I will add further flesh to these points by briefly discussing ideas and events in post-revolutionary Russia. In that fulcrum, the contrasting tendencies of modernity came clearly into focus. Lenin, who as we shall see deplored science's questioning of its foundations, fantasised about a technical utopia, a 'mechanised world of proletarian dominion' centred on the ideas of 'rationalism' and 'systematised industrial organization'.[9] The worship of the machine was a central feature of Bolshevik thinking; minds and matter were to be rationally organised along its lines. The result was such bodies as the Institute for Psychotechnical Research into Human Labour Force and the Time League, a Taylorist organisation with individual cells located in branches in government and industry, its members pledged to 'Fight for time', committed themselves to economy of effort, iron discipline, mental hygiene and to communicating with clarity and brevity.[10] There was much that was fantastic about this devotion to the mechanical image as indicated by H.G. Wells's description of Lenin as the 'dreamer of electrification'.[11] Yet it was no less crazed than the fury of grand destruction that for a period existed alongside it. I am talking here of the Russian futurists, a movement which believed in the ultimacy of movement and change and which sought to bring to bear all the militancy of the political revolution on the cultural realm.[12] Certainly the construction of a scientific socialist order demanded the smashing of old forms, the clearing away of all the 'old rubbish'. Yet there is a sense that some of the cultural revolutionaries were excited by the constant electricity of crisis, by relentless, unyielding negation. Compromise between the order-dissolving and order-building impulses are apparent in the 'dynamic-monumental architecture' as advocated by Vladimir Tatlin and which upheld the idea of forms in movement. Tatlin drafted a plan for a Palace of Labour comprising three 'vertically stacked' glass chambers, one cubical, one pyramidical and one cylindrical, each revolving at different speeds. Peter Conrad finds it significant that the chamber housing the bureau of propaganda was placed at the summit of the building: 'Tatlin's decision...revealed the aspirations of the new state, committed to promulgating a universal faith.'[13] (We might note here that the founder of the futurist movement, the Italian Felipo Tomaso Marinetti, had earlier rejoiced in the idea of the 'house in construction', a complex of steel equipped with an airplane landing platform it symbolised for him movement, open-endedness and becoming.) The tension between the aesthetic of flux and the principle of machine order is particularly evident in Russian town planning debates of the late 1920s. In a fascinating essay S. Frederick Starr notes that while there was broad agreement that the wonders of science should be distributed across the whole landscape rather than concentrated in a few grand metropolises there were differences among antiurbanists as to what form the decentralised future should take. Some theorists favoured the 'construction of numerous collectivized settlements' that would be fixed at certain points along an 'integrated' national electricity grid.[14] Yet the spread of the electricity grid in conjunction with modern means of transportation as also believed to make possible a 'wholly "destationized"' existence; individuals and functions would be 'free to move anywhere' and operate anywhere. They would be liberated from ties of place; instead of stationary, collectivist housing individuals would live in mobile 'housing cells' in the midst of a '"linear city" consisting solely of continuous bands of parallel transportation lines covering the entire country without beginning or end'.[15] These competing visions of town planning and of the social function of electricity, with one valorsing concrete order and large-scale organisation and the other valorising fluidity of movement and individual liberation, parallel exactly the two tendencies of modernity I have identified. Both of these versions of disurbanism were defeated by the Communist Party in mid-1931 in favour of the 'hard-headed and "scientific"' centralised planning favoured by Stalin. Yet for a brief and heady period, the notional tension between the understanding of modernity as flux and the understanding of modernity as rational order became manifest and with breathtaking clarity.[16]

Attempts to reconcile modernity, understood as mobility and multiplicity, and modernity as scientific, rational order were apparent in debates in the intellectual and political arena in Europe and the United States in the 1920s and before the war. I will be demonstrating that prior to the war and in the interwar period the ideas of multiplicity and flux were often seen as the defining features of modern thought. At the same time, and especially after the disaster of the Great War, these ideas were increasingly associated with the crisis of the twentieth century. If ideas current at the turn of the century and the decade following had a postmodern look, the interwar period saw a reassertion of scientism and rationalism, albeit versions of these which incorporated to some degree notions of variety and temporality.

Great emphasis will be placed on how these overarching themes were played out at the level of debates about world organisation. In regard to this matter, I will be suggesting that the trend of thought from the early twentieth century onwards was in the direction of a planetary commonwealth. It should be apparent that I will be drawing attention to the scientific framing of this goal. But I will also be attempting to show that the idea of a planetary commonwealth often reflected a spiritual yearning for wholeness however much it was defended in technical-rational and utilitarian terms. But no matter which format it came in, social monism on a world scale encountered resistance. Intellectuals of a pluralist temperament believed it was inconsistent to attack monism at the state level while supporting it at the world level, as many proponents of world organisation did. The one world scenario, it would be claimed, was at odds with the *Zeitgeist*, one which favoured the multiform and irregular. In an effort to accommodate this sort of critique, deference was paid to the principle of diversity in unity and I will be arguing that this see-sawing problem of the one and the many is something with which international relations theorists are still attempting to grapple.

I have suggested that modernity was also defined in relation to the notion of crisis. Crisis, particularly where that term is used to denote the breakdown of the foundations of knowledge and belief, has often been portrayed as a peculiarly twentieth century phenomenon. José Ortega Y Gasset in *Revolt of the Masses* (1930) wrote of the shallowness of mass man's preoccupations, his worship of speed and delight in the proliferation of commodities. These modern advances were merely quantitative; believing in the intrinsic superiority of the new, and proud of his technological capacity, modern man had cut himself off from the past, 'recognizing no classical or normative epochs'.[17] The result was a moral and intellectual drift towards barbarism; given the absence of standards to which appeal could made, it was not surprising that in Europe 'strange things' had begun to happen. Here he was thinking not only of a general decline in manners, but also the movements of syndicalism and fascism. and their belief that force is the '*unica ratio*'; it was the triumph of the doctrine of 'direct action' over reasoned discourse, a development reflected also in the descent of public life into a war of opinions, that defined the modern epoch, the beginnings of which he traced to around 1900.[18] Several years later, the problems Ortega identified were said to have 'enveloped virtually the whole world'. Louis Wirth wrote in the preface to the English edition of Karl Mannheim's *Ideology and Utopia* (1936) that in response to intellectual chaos and attendant social *anomie* there had 'arisen an extensive literature which speaks of the "end", the "decline", the "crisis", the "decay", or the "death" of Western civilization'.[19] Wirth's comments are testimony to the continuing sense of crisis and a convergence on the theme, as I discuss in what follows, that social disorder had as its source the erosion of intellectual foundations. They are indicative of the increasingly self-conscious nature of the crisis literature which swelled in the interwar period. Those pondering the ills of the century became acutely aware of the fact they were contributing to a particular genre of social commentary, seeing themselves as adding to an ongoing conversation.

In dealing with the issue of crisis, Mannheim too gave expression to the varying tendencies of the modern. Conscious of the potentially frictional relationship between them he sought to elaborate a sociology of reconciliation. Mannheim can be read as an archrationalist, and certainly that was the view of him entertained by liberal polemicists such as Friedrich Hayek in the 1930s and 1940s in the context of debates about planning.[20] In *Ideology and Utopia* Mannheim insisted that the trend of modern life is the growth of the 'sphere of the rationalizable and of the rationally controllable'; the political element, which he identified with irrationality, with the flash of emotions, especially mob emotions and uncontrolled will, is reduced as institutions of detachment expand. Social problems come to be regarded as technical problems, as though they were mere maladjustments in the social machine.[21] In *Man and Society in an Age of Reconstruction* (1940) he wrote: 'A hygienic or sanitary problem is usually solved by non-political means, it is a question of the best scientific methods available and political differences are inconceivable.'[22] In keeping with his fear that mass emotions could clog the wheels of planning, he accorded a special role to the intelligentsia whom he branded as the 'thinkers and forerunners of a new society' and urged them to retain their faith in the power of reason.[23] Despite his seemingly extreme advocacy of conscious control, Mannheim stated he did not believe that society can be utterly rationalised, that the presence of irrationality and

evaluation could be utterly extinguished. On this score, he wrote, the Enlightenment was shortsighted; the counter to irrationalism is not merely
rationalism but also, as John Dewey put it, 'refined passions'. He followed
William James and Henri Bergson in emphasising the creative aspect of the
self; it is this that ensures the individual, as James put it, 'escapes predicabil-
ity'; the aim of social planning should be to liberate this creative self, hence
Mannheim's formula planning for freedom.[24] Mannheim called his
attempted resolution of the opposition between collectivism and individualism, of organisation and spontaneity, the 'Third Way'; he offered it as a
mid-way course between the anarchy of *laissez-faire* and a suffocating total-
itarianism. The label may be viewed as a rhetorical device, a means of
obscuring how one-sided his social philosophy was; certainly, it was a
slippery notion and it is worth noting that in the early 1930s fascism was
described similarly. Yet Mannheim was genuine in his acceptance of the
many-sidedness of the self and the mutability of reality. He did not endow
truth with an objective quality, rather, it is the 'unified perspective' of an
age, which it is the duty of intellectuals to discern and promote for the
purpose of achieving maximum social cohesion and individual happiness.
Whereas there were those who thought Mannheim's sociology of knowledge
was no more than a type of cloudy relativism. Charles Frankel, while noting
and critiquing the pragmatic aspects of Mannheim's thought also considered
that Mannheim came 'perilously close' to thinking 'about social planning in
terms of a society organized and controlled by a select group in possession of
the One True Doctrine'.[25]

  After the Second World War the other, wilder side of modernity was
obscured and this term became largely identified with hard-headed
positivism, mass-organisation and rigid, angular shapes. Barraclough wrote
that in the postwar era there was a retreat from 'experimentation' which
marked much of the first half of the century. This was not to be regretted
because he thought writers and artists of that era had nothing but
destruction on their mind and no desire to construct a new world. It was also
well, he thought, that other features of early twentieth-century intellectual
life, the introspective speculations on the nature of consciousness and the
'mood of pessimism and despair and resignation, of wandering helplessly
without moorings in a world without hope' had been left behind. Attitudes
were now more upbeat.[26] Sociology, he enthused, had stimulated a change
in outlook:

...from an egocentric and ultimately tedious preoccupation with the individual's
personal fate and the malady of the European soul to the problems arising out of social
relationships within the new, technical, industrial mass societies in which the change
of the last sixty years had plunged the world. The literature of protest and revolt – the
characteristic product of an old order in decline – seemed to have shot its bolt, and a
movement began away from subjectivity in the direction of objectivity.[27]

Yet while perhaps less central to intellectual debate, talk of crisis did not end with the Second World War. The Cold War provided further grist for the mill, although typically, like the hot wars and social convulsions which preceded it, it was treated as only an outward manifestation of deeper intellectual or spiritual problems. While not concurring with this last view and believing that the Cold War, another mark of the twentieth-century transition, was drawing to a close, Barraclough nonetheless portrayed his own times as precariously poised. The advent of the nuclear bomb had exploded all the old certainties. This along with enormous breakthroughs in science and technology mean we live in a 'world with unparalleled potentialities but also with sinister undercurrents of violence, irrationality and inhumanity'. Invoking Valéry, he then warned that whatever the future might be it will be nothing like what is expected or predicted. Barraclough knew that Valéry perfectly understood the condition which he referred to as postmodern. More so than Valéry, he was optimistic that we could learn to live and work with uncertainty.[28]

The postmodern turn of recent decades can be seen as a reawakening of the other side of modernity described by writers such as Valéry in the first part of the twentieth century. Barraclough's foray into contemporary history reveals that a consciousness of modernity as postmodernity never entirely faded away; indeed he sees the unfolding of the postmodern as the key to understanding the period from the late nineteenth century until the early 1960s. This is not to say that his use of the term is wholly commensurate with its academic usage today. His understanding is not particularly theoretically sophisticated nor highly nuanced, further, he evinces a longing for synthesis and this might be questioned by contemporary audiences. It is interesting that the rich profusion of theory coming under the heading of postmodernism has appeared in a period in which Western peoples feel secure and are less susceptible to warnings of social collapse. It was observed after the First and Second World Wars that a sense of crisis explained why notions of discipline, security and control came to predominate in intellectual and political discourse. Let us note too that in the interwar years science was seen as standing above the strife and anarchy of the times. Where spiritual foundations of society had crumbled, it was only the scientific sensibility that was seen as standing between civilisation and a return to the jungle. There certainly was a consciousness after the First and during the Second World War, that science, due to its lethal inventions, had become associated in the public mind with death and destruction. There was, as a result, especially during the Second World War, a deliberate campaign by natural scientists to align the scientific estate with the matter of social welfare, although it should be noted that this welfarist orientation was largely defended in scientific terms. Social scientists pursued a similar strategy, both to add to the authority of their political recommendations and to fend off the charge of socialism. We are scientists not socialists planning advocates such as Julian Huxley would say.[29] Thus, despite concerns about some of its tech-

nological fruits, science was generally a venerated and prestigious discipline
in the first half of the century. It was above all a magic word. Science was
seen as a key element of both the 1920s and 1930s, the new order in both
the domestic and international spheres. It is also important to note, as well,
that throughout the twentieth century scientific concepts and practices were
said to recommend internationalism as will be shown in my discussion of
the League of Nations. Scientific reason was subject to wider and more
intense criticism in the 1960s, it being argued that positive science, priding
itself on its value neutrality, had become a willing tool of the state and
commerce and had thus helped facilitate the nuclear arms race and environmental breakdown. An ecological paradigm which emphasised
integration and interdependence was favourably contrasted with the spatial
divisions of the state system which some treated as a deduction from the
atomistic world-view of the physical scientist. Increasingly, we find planetary
thinking being promoted as a happy alternative to this system. As we shall
see, the planetary model was cited in the early part of the twentieth century
in the course of promoting one world order and then as now it had both
scientific and spiritual resonances. Yet, as I argue, images of the world which
emphasise oneness do not play as successfully in the present as they did in the
past. Models suggestive of ultimate harmony and completeness encounter
audiences educated into a postmodern sensibility, and a postmodern
universe is loose-ended, it has spots and jumps, gaping holes and tears.

The relation between modernity's dual implications was not systematically explored in the first half of the twentieth century. In one sense it did not
need to be for as I have indicated crisis made fashionable the ideas of order
and discipline. As we have seen there were varying attempts to incorporate
the themes of spontaneity and multiplicity into rationalist political
narratives. But in general we are dealing with a situation in which philosophies that spoke of active wills at play in an open and untidy universe claimed
a diminishing number of adherents. The concept of a scientific order had an
air of chill splendour. The new rationalism succeeded in the political and
intellectual arenas; modernity understood as mobility and swirling energy
dissipated in influence. Yet the intellectual tension between these two understandings was no less real for modernity's wilder side being submerged
amidst a welter of enthusiasm for scientific technique. We now live in an
intellectual environment in which the concepts of multiplicity and becoming
reign and in which rationalism is very much out of vogue. We might say
that the other side of modernity is now in the ascendant. Yet there are those
who still devise formulas for salvation along rationalistic lines or who dream
of differences ultimately merging into unity. And there are those who, aware
of the grip on the contemporary imagination of the multiplicit, seek to find
room for the many inside the one. I will argue that social theories that
challenge the established order, while making use of ideas of difference and
multiplicity, are typically unable or unwilling to confront the possibility that
the world can only ever be one in a very bare or strained sense. Although

there are, to borrow the words of William James, numerous hangings together of its various parts and of various degrees of intensity, much form-lessness pertains and is indeed willed. Approaches to the politics of the one and the politics of the many in the second half of the twentieth century in respect to the issue of world order, as well as the growing and conscious hardening of the distinction between these two categories in recent decades, are discussed in the concluding section of this work.

1 UNKNOWN FORCES

For much of the Western intelligentsia the coming of the twentieth century marked the world's slide into chaos. The new century brought with it increased social confusion. It was thought to be riven with mental discord due to a collapse in belief in an ordered and knowable cosmos. Experience was no longer seen as fundamentally harmonious. It was ruptured, encircled by strange multiplicities.

Portrayals of social and intellectual disarray presaged calls for the creation of a rational society devised in accordance with scientific principles. A chaotic world cried out for the imposition of order. The dissolution of established social forms and categories of thought highlighted the plasticity of experience, its openness to injections of human will. Experience could be seized and moulded into a happier shape. Armed with positive knowledge man could become, as H.G. Wells would put it in 1926, a 'master of the universe'.[1] The move to modernise social life at the national and world levels in the early twentieth century was based on such a philosophy of action. In a speech at Leeds in 1909 the scientist Arthur Balfour foretold that the '...motive power' which was 'really going to change the external surface of civilisation' and 'add to the material well-being of mankind...lies after with science'.[2]

A philosophy of action need not have as its goal the building of grid-like structures. Where will and experience are conceived as ever restless it might favour disruption and anarchy. An aesthetic of disorder might be preferred to that of order. Early twentieth century modernity valorised the latter while also being informed by the former. Confidence in human ingenuity demanded a belief in the plasticity of things. In *Literature and Revolution* (Allen & Unwin, 1924) Trotsky's description of a communist future in which people would be 'trained to be "more plastic," and become accustomed to considering the world as a flexible clay for the modelling of ever more perfect forms of life' is an affirmation of faith in humanity's capacity to alter the 'map of nature', to correct and reform nature 'in accordance with his image or at least his taste'.[3] However, this emphasis on human freedom is potentially subversive of new order schemes. Just as we have freedom to create in an open universes we also have the freedom to destroy. Acts of destruction must be undertaken before the building of a new order can proceed. But if its construction is not to be haunted by negations and if its contours are shaped according to plan then a shift of emphasis may be necessary. Humanity's freedom may be said to consist in our ability to work in accordance with scientific laws. We need to consider that the persuasiveness of programmes for social change in the early twentieth century greatly depended on their possession of an air of scientific necessity. For these reasons, what might be the governing premise of proposals for social change, namely a faith in the ability of human will to intervene in and shape a relatively malleable experience, may in the end be suppressed. After its realisation especially, a new order loses its air of contingency and acquires an aura of permanency. The idea of a new world both before and after the Great War was imbued with a sense of drama and energy while also conveying the promise of stability and discipline. Designs for a new world order continued both to feed on and be shadowed by the twin spectres of will and multiplicity.

Early twentieth-century modernity contained two contrasting tendencies. Modernity denoted rational organisation based on objective social knowledge but it also implied an enthusiasm for waywardness and indeterminacy. These tendencies meet at the point at which they embrace a doctrine of action be it of a technical or intuitionist nature. Both are reflected to varying degrees in positivist philosophy, so an examination of its nuances helps us understand better the dual character of modernity. This in turn will illuminate the thinking behind, as well as the ambivalence expressed about, the construction of a world order in the years after the Great War.

THE FLOW OF SENSATIONS

The label positivism conjures a world comprising elemental units, the behaviour of which detached minds observe and map. From this they attempt to induce regularities or laws. The objective character of knowledge acquired through the application of positivist method is believed to arise from its being grounded in hard, granular facts. Richard Rorty thus describes positivism as empiricist foundationalism.[4] To sum up the range of ideas which come under the heading of positivism in this way is to risk falling into caricature. It is to accept the myth perpetrated by those students of man and society who promoted the cult of science, passionately embracing the language of the laboratory, not least as a means to enhancing their own intellectual status. Beyond this, and due to its 'magnificent and overwhelming success', science came to stand for a creed and a way of life.[5]

Ralph Barton Perry, a Harvard philosophy professor, explained that science had become an object of worship because of the ambiguous nature of science itself. He wrote: 'Science both belittles man and magnifies him. When science puts man where he belongs in nature, man looks very small and very feeble.' At the same time, in so far as science affords humanity greater control over its environment, it instils in it an enormous sense of pride. In reducing and enhancing the human being's stature at the same time, science resembles religion.[6] To put this paradox another way, science seems to accord limitless power to human beings to control their destiny yet the truths proffered in its name are also said to command humanity. In a partial synthesis of these two viewpoints we might say that humanity's power derives solely from its obedience to those axioms which science reveals. The French scientist Henri Poincaré expressed this point in stating:

To-day we no longer beg of nature; we command her, because we have discovered certain of her secrets and shall discover others each day. We command her in the name of laws she can not challenge because they are hers; these laws we do not madly ask her to change, we are the first to submit to them. Nature can only be governed by obeying her.[7]

Poincaré appeared to be advancing the standard idea that science disclosed an objective reality governed by deterministic laws. However, turn of the century positivism was potentially subversive of this notion, it being a crude version of the ideas put forward in the mid-nineteenth century by August Comte. Comte posited an ordered world which existed beyond sense perceptions and was not subject to human intervention. For him, humanity's 'principal merit consists in perfecting as much as possible the natural sub-ordination of man to the world so that our brain becomes a faithful mirror of the external order'.[8] Later positivist thinkers, working under the rubric of empiriocriticism, swerved in the direction of radical empiricism according to which the basis of knowledge is contained in that space encircled by the senses. In contrast with Comtean positivism, the implications of *fin-de-siècle* positivism were, in Leszek Kolakowski's terms, 'psychologistic and subjec-tivist'.[9] Given empiriocriticism's focus on the immediately given it is not surprising that questions concerning the nature of reality and ultimate truth were seen as belonging solely to the realm of philosophical or religious speculation. To apply this approach rigorously, however, was to undermine the objectivity of science itself. The foundations of scientific knowledge were softened where the transitory character of sense impressions was emphasised. Science could help us understand and conceptually organise sensory experience but it could not tell us about reality. Nor could it assert what was true. Truth was what scientists agreed worked in the course of experiment and such agreements were always open to revision.

One of the driving influences behind this sensationalist turn was the Moravian-born physicist Ernst Mach. In an essay published in 1890 he rejected the 'monstrous idea of a *thing of itself* claiming that things, bodies and matter are complexes of sensations. For Mach the world is constituted only by our sensations, percepts and thoughts and it was unnecessary to suppose, as the realist did, that behind 'moving phenomena' there must be permanent nuclei. It was Mach above all who justified the charge that empiriocriticism was mentalist or subjectivist in its implication.[10] What is also interesting is that Mach sometimes represented the data of science in a fluid and heterogeneous fashion. As Kolakowski observed, Mach seemed to reduce matter to motion which itself was nothing more than a process of sensory elements such as 'colour, sound, space, time'.[11]

The British geometrician Karl Pearson in *The Grammar of Science* (1892) agreed with Mach that we cannot get outside of our sense-impressions and meet reality as the metaphysicians conceive it. He wrote:

The mind is absolutely confined within its nerve-exchange; beyond the walls of sense-impression it can logically infer nothing. Order and reason, beauty and benevolence, are characteristics and conceptions which we find solely associated with the mind of man, with this side of sense-impressions. Into the chaos beyond sense-impressions we cannot scientifically project them...Briefly chaos is all that science can logically assert of the supersensuous – the sphere outside knowledge, outside classification by mental concepts.

What holds for characteristics and conceptions also holds for physical objects and effects. For Pearson, what we call real in everyday life is more properly termed a *phenomenon*; that is, it is something we project outside of ourselves – a *construct* created out of our sense-impressions both immediate and stored.[12] Pearson argued that science deals with an interior realm rather than a material world under the sway of natural laws. This privileging of the mental is evident in his contention that the chief objects of investigation are conceptions and constructions derived from sense-impressions rather than raw, immediate perceptions.[13]

Pearson's empiricism would be destructive of the scientific enterprise, which depends on common understanding and coherent explanation, were we to view mental constructs as unstable and varying dramatically from person to person. However, for Pearson the part of the world which science investigated appeared much the same to all; our sense organs are 'machines of the same type'. Further, the world revealed to us by these machines displayed relatively stable sequences and constant facts. The 'routine nature' of sense-impressions he largely attributed to the 'structure of our perceptive faculty'; it is on this basis that we develop the notion of law.[14] Pearson thus offered us, on the one hand, a radically subjectivist interpretation of science which has mind imposing order on an ever-changing, dissolving experience. In upholding the worth of positive knowledge as against 'undisciplined imagination' he wrote of the wonderful mystery to be found in the 'chaos of sensations' and science's 'capacity for containing those little corners of consciousness which project their own products, of order and law and reason, into an unknown and unknowable world'.[15] On the other hand, he also pointed to an ordered and predictable physical universe existing beyond the senses and which is coercive of human thought and behaviour. The sense-impressions which he makes the basis of consciousness are in fact the result of 'physical impresses'; likewise, the 'sequences of sense-impressions' or 'the routine nature of our perceptions' are an effect of physical stimulation of the nervous system. In addition, he tells us that the organs affected by physical impresses, as with our capacity of reason, have evolved to aid the individual and race in the 'struggle for existence'.[16]

In so far as Pearson treated consciousness as science's proper domain, he would seem to be limiting it to just a small portion of the universe. His insistence that the supersensual realm must remain unknown to us indicates a narrowing of the scientific estate. However, in making these seemingly modest claims Pearson was extending the reach of science. He made its scope coextensive with the 'whole content of the human mind'.[17] Yet Pearson defined the expression contents of consciousness in relation to certain special criteria. The respect he accorded sense-impressions, to which he attributed regularity and structure, and his disdain for imaginative flights of fancy, underline this point. Citing Mach's principle of economy of thought, Pearson moved to limit the range of permissible experience and concepts by denying the intellectual and social utility of that which ultimately cannot be validated by the senses. In doing so, Pearson was not merely eliminating from science 'shadowy unknowables' such as God, will and mind-stuff. He was also suggesting that physical science provided the model that other forms of inquiry should emulate if they were to be seen as serious and useful disciplines. Pearson's positivism was ultimately expansive. He urged that it is scientific method, through the verification of physical hypotheses, which brings us closer to truth and best equips the race to survive. Disturbed at the flourishing of spiritualist movements, he wrote that mystical contemplation and ecstatic states, because they turn people from the 'long experienced routine of perceptions', are not a basis for knowledge; they undermined belief in the 'uniform order of phenomena' which is the mark of the rational person and is necessary for social stability and victory in the battle for life. In the context of these wider claims any distinction between a conventionalist and foundationalist understanding of truth seems to disappear:

> There is no short cut to truth, no way to gain a knowledge of the universe except through the gateway of scientific method. The hard and stony path of classifying facts and reasoning upon them is the only way to ascertain truth. It is the reason and not the imagination which must ultimately be appealed to.[18]

In Pearson's hands, a project which began with the aim of carving out a distinct realm and method for scientists developed into the physicalist dogma that whatever can be said must be said in the language of science. This dogma would triumph in the field of social thought in the interwar period. Pearson himself recommended a scientific approach to social policy and training in science as the soundest basis for citizenship. Fabian reformers such as Sidney and Beatrice Webb echoed these sentiments. The idea of scientific government would inform thinking about international organisation after both World Wars as is discussed in later chapters.[19]

Poincaré was almost as ambiguous as Pearson on the issue of scientific certainty. In the *Value of Science* (1902) he acknowledged that recent scientific discoveries appeared to be subversive of science's truth claims. He wrote that there were 'indications of a serious crisis' in physics and not only because 'radium, that grand revolutionist' was challenging the principle of the conservation of energy. He added that '...all the other principles are equally in danger'; one response to this apparent crisis was to insist that scientific principles were simply constructions of the intellect and not provable in any ultimate sense. Of space and time he wrote '...it is not nature which imposes them upon us, it is we who impose them upon nature...All that is not thought is pure nothingness.'[20]

Poincaré appeared to endorse the conventionalist understanding of scientific truth implied by empiriocriticism:

What, then, are we to think of the question: Is Euclidean geometry true? It has no meaning...One geometry cannot be more true than another; it can only be more convenient. Now, Euclidean geometry is, and will remain, the most convenient.[21]

On this matter, his position appears to be very close to that of Edouard Le Roy, a Catholic philosopher and mathematician disturbed by the 'idolatry' surrounding science.[22] Le Roy insisted on the 'entire artificiality or conventionality of science, both in respect of its facts and its laws', and argued that: 'Science is an invention for the purpose of action; and cannot, therefore, be regarded as a revelation of reality.'[23] Like his mentor, the philosopher Henri Bergson, Le Roy appreciated the efficacy and utility of scientific knowledge but held with Bergson that analysis, and its instrument discourse, deformed a reality composed of fleeting impressions which vanished upon being touched. He followed Bergson in insisting that reality could only be truly penetrated through acts of intuition and poetic appreciation. Poincaré admired Le Roy and thought they had similar views of science, but he criticised the latter for embracing Bergson's supposed anti-intellectualism and rejected Le Roy's claim that all science was conventional and thus could tell us nothing about truth. As Poincaré noted, Le Roy's nominalism was tactical in that he sought to knock science from its pedestal only in order to elevate a realism based on faith.[24]

While Poincaré denied the possibility of knowing a reality 'completely independent of the mind which conceives it, sees or feels it', he nonetheless endowed with the quality of objectivity that world which was identical for scientists. He argued that while scientists intervene in the world, in that they choose the facts to be observed, they are not the creators of facts.[25] While conceding that facts move more quickly than we do and so we 'can not catch them', he gave them a sufficient amount of determinacy so as to permit the production of certainties by means of repeated experiment. Further to this, Poincaré disputed the precedence given to action in Bergson's and Le Roy's thought, arguing that the instrumental value of science was dependent upon the prior validity of its hypotheses. Science was useful but only because it was true.[26] For Poincaré, the goal of science is to build an ordered edifice out of multiplicity, to seek sameness under diversity; this was no distortion of nature but the revelation of its refined, architectural beauty.[27]

Pearson and Poincaré made statements open to the charge of subjectivism; yet they also implied that the sensory realm was ultimately a reflection of an ordered, external realm which science could accurately portray. The main difference between the two was that Pearson at times tended towards a physicalist account of reality, whereas Poincaré placed greater emphasis on the constitutive role of reason.

Mach's sensationalism stands between these tendencies. Although seemingly reducing reality to the contents of consciousness, he rejected the dualism which was the 'opposition of body and spirit'. His position was *monistic* in the sense that he saw the distinction between the real and the perceived worlds as being a function of different ways of viewing the same experience.[28] For Mach the physical and mental universes were a 'manifold of neutral elements' which were neither physical nor mental in nature but equally composed of things, bodies, matter, perceptions, ideas, volitions and emotions.[29] It was because Mach was concerned that the use of the word sensations carried with it too much subjectivist baggage, thus undermining the neutrality of his account of experience, that he preferred to 'speak simply of *elements*'.[30]

Kolakowksi noted that Mach's aim was to arrive at 'pure experience' into which the ego and external world were dissolved. Yet, as Kolakowksi's paradoxical description of Mach's empiricism as 'subjectivism without a subject' indicates, it is questionable whether Mach had reached a neutral psycho-physics.[31] A thoroughgoing conventionalist might view pure experience simply as a construct of scientific thought. It is testimony to the conflicting interpretations to which positivism is open that Mach was charged with physicalist foundationalism since he attempted to reduce heterogeneous experience to 'a small number of homogeneous elements'.[32]

It was Mach the subjectivist who most excited and antagonised his philosophical peers. In Lenin's rather plaintive work *Materialism and Empirio-Criticism* (1908) he branded the ideas of Mach (which were being advertised by Lenin's counterpart A.A. Bogdanov), as well as those of Pearson and Poincaré, as 'subjective idealism'; aware of empiriocriticism's fashionable appeal he dismissed it as a rehash of the ideas of David Hume and Bishop Berkeley.[33] Lenin's depiction of Machism might be seen as a perversion of Mach's thought given the latter's submergence of the self into a more extensive experience. Yet Lenin viewed this move as deceptive. Pure experience lacked a stable and independent basis. He wrote: 'If the "sensible content" of our sensations is not the external world then nothing exists save this naked I engaged in empty "philosophical" acrobatics.'[34]

Lenin was correct in perceiving that 'modernist' philosophies such as empiriocriticism, in conjunction with the scientific dissolution of matter into energy, challenged the materialist interpretation of history and hence the authority of communist doctrine. In seeming desperation Lenin cited discoveries such as X-rays, Becquerel rays and radium claiming that these only confirmed Engels' view, expressed in *Herr Eugen Dühring's Revolution in*

Science (1877–78) that in nature 'there are no irreconcilable contradictions, nor forcibly fixed boundary lines and distinctions' only one moving substance. By contrast Lenin noted:

...you cannot take up any of the writings of the Machians or about Machism without encountering pretentious references to the new physics, which is said to have refuted materialism...Whether these assertions are well-founded is another question, but the connection between the new physics, or rather a definite school of the new physics, and Machism and other varieties of modern idealist philosophy is beyond doubt. [35]

Lenin, in a somewhat selective reading of Poincaré's *Value of Science*, noted that with the atom having dematerialised, matter having disappeared and its old laws having been overthrown, there had appeared a 'crisis in modern physics'; the essence of this crisis consisting in the rejection of an objective reality and the retreat into 'idealism and agnosticism'. [36] Empiriocriticism was further condemned for being 'conceptualist' or 'energeticist', that is, for upholding the view that thought, freed from matter, was still in motion. This suggests that mind is not only able to imagine the world as it wishes but actively to shape it. Intriguingly, Lenin perceived that while empiriocriticism tended in the direction of subjectivism, it could also flower into metaphysics and in so doing render individual minds as particular aspects of a larger energy current. Mach described consciousness as a shifting, 'multiplex' of interconnections and he went on to suggest that pure experience should be conceived in a similar fashion. Mach might thus be seen as pouring on to a wider screen his conception of the contours and qualities of private sensory experience. Radical empiricism could thus be fashioned in a way that brought sensory experience back into communion with the cosmos with being characterised as both pluralistic and mobile. To the extent that empiriocriticism could be seen as upholding the supremacy of will in an untidy and open universe, it posed a challenge to political doctrines, the compelling power of which was derived from a form of historical determinism. Certainly, as we shall see, radical empiricism came to inform a metaphysical and political pluralism which would serve as a counterpoint to rationalist philosophies and social schemes. [37]

METAPHYSICAL PLURALISM

In a 1907 commentary on Pearson's *Grammar* the American man of letters Henry Adams pondered the wider significance of the so-called crisis in science. He wrote that history, although curving and accelerating at certain junctures, had been continuous from the beginning of time. However he added, cleverly alluding to Poincaré's conventionalism, that:

...in 1900, the continuity snapped. Vaguely conscious of the cataclysm, the world sometimes dated it from 1893, by Roentgen rays, or from 1898, by the Curies' radium; but in 1904, Arthur Balfour announced on the part of British science that the human race without exception had lived and died in a world of illusion until the last year of the century. The date was convenient and convenience was truth. The Child born in 1900 would, then, be born into a new world which would not be a unity but a multiple.[38]

Adams thought that while Pearson and others had attempted to keep looming chaos at bay by confining the scope of science to a rigorous analysis of sense data, their efforts had proved futile. Chaos had penetrated the realm of the senses. Adams saw Mach's account of sense-impressions as convincing evidence that a supersensual fluid had seeped into the sensory domain. The view of mind as motion had appeared just at the same time as novel conceptions of matter were emerging from the laboratories. The turn of the century, Adams concluded, saw the reality of 'Multiplicity, Diversity, Complexity, Anarchy, Chaos' become starkly apparent. He wrote that 'the mind could gain nothing by flight or by fight; it must merge in its supersensual multiverse, or succumb to it'.[39]

The period around the turn of the twentieth century was what we might call, although somewhat anachronistically, a postmodern moment. Images of cosmological multiplicity predominated and these were derived from parallel pictures of mind and matter. Adams treated representations of consciousness as a moving feast of percepts and ideas as a cosmological template. He reinforced his picture of a manifold and fluid cosmos by making references to scientific descriptions concerning the enigmatic nature of matter and energy. Adams was making a move similar, albeit conceptually more promiscuous, to that of Mach who spun out of the contents of consciousness the wider idea of pure experience. We can also observe the same line of thought unfolding in the work of Bergson and the American philosopher William James. These philosophers are of interest as they are most credited with making intellectually fashionable the notion of reality as flux. They are also significant because they elaborated a voluntaristic philosophy of action. These two ideas are crucially interrelated and featured prominently in the thinking of both proponents and opponents of the idea of world order in the interwar period. A discussion of these authors also reveals how radical empiricism may blur into mysticism.

In his *Principles of Psychology* (1890) James used the expression 'stream of consciousness' in order to challenge the depiction of consciousness as a compound of 'separate, independent parts'. For James consciousness is one, although only in the sense that it is felt to be continuous; we have, he wrote, a 'feeling' of relation between states of consciousness and so our thoughts, while distinct and fluctuating, are unbroken, melting into each other at their margins. He depicted conscious activity as a 'teeming multiplicity of objects and relations'; it was an image that he would later transpose to experience and the universe in general.[40] For James true reality was to be found in that 'theatre of simultaneous possibilities' which is the 'river' of consciousness. As his theatre metaphor implies, James thought mind played an active role in shaping a primordial flux, creating a 'world full of contrasts, of sharp accents, of abrupt changes, of picturesque light and shade'; giving an intimation of the pragmatist epistemology he later developed, he likened minds to sculptors producing a variety of statues from the same piece of stone.[41]

James was familiar with the work of Mach, Pearson and Poincaré, and he drew attention to the similarities between his philosophy of pragmatism and their empiricism, conventionalism and instrumentalism. In his *Pragmatism* (1907) he declared that the pragmatist turns 'from fixed principles, closed systems, pretended absolutes and origins, He turns towards concreteness and adequacy towards facts.'[42] Further, he claimed that the experience we select is based on considerations of what is 'worthwhile', has 'cash value', 'pays' and is 'practical'; he wrote that notions such as 'thing', 'minds', 'bodies', 'one time', 'one space', 'causal influences' are simply 'extraordi- narily successful hypotheses...sublime tricks of human thought, our ways of escaping bewilderment in the midst of sensation's irremediable flow'. James likened the methods of the pragmatist to the experimental scientists' technique of verification. This comparison, however, is somewhat misleading. More telling is his depiction of pragmatism as an expression of 'democratic' and even 'anarchistic' sentiments, something which he thought was shown by its flexibility and openness to variety.[43]

James was aware that his psychological theory could be seen as solipsistic and so like Mach he expanded the mental contents examined in his *Principles* into something larger called experience. He made it clear that by experience he did not mean just conscious experience. Pure experience, as James now called the 'immediate flux of life', includes thoughts and things but privileges neither. It might be thought that James' view of pure experience was also monistic as if he held that thoughts and things were actually derived from the same neutral stuff. Yet James denied there was a '*general* stuff of which experience at large is made...There are as many stuffs as there are "natures" in the things experienced.'[44] James's empiricism did coincide with Mach's to the extent that he too placed an emphasis on relations as well as particulars. When using the word radical in order to describe his empiricism, James meant that, in contrast with what he called 'bugaboo' empiricism, it accorded conjunctive relations the same respect as particular elements.[45]

James endorsed the view he attributed to Mach that the only reality was 'the flux of our sensations and emotions as they pass'; yet we should recall that Mach emphasised economy of thought and sought to pare back the flux of experience to its fundamental elements. James, however, preferred philo- sophical 'profusion' to 'economy' and this is reflected in the fact that experience, as he described it, included a much wider range of contents than it did for the strict positivist. His idea of what constituted verification was equally expansive. He included desires, will and temperamental preferences among the criteria of the test of utility. In *Pragmatism* he developed the argument that one had a right to believe in that which one felt to be true if such a belief had, in a more or less free-wheeling sense, 'practical consequences'. He wrote that both truth and right are '*made...in the course of experience*'; they are what is '*expedient in the way of our thinking...*[and]...*in the way of our behaving*. Expedient in almost any fashion.' On the basis of this test of expediency James defended private 'mystical experiences' and even universals.[46]

James thought his empiricism radical because it did not conceive of experience in atomistic terms but allowed that each element was surrounded by fringes connecting them, perhaps only in the vaguest manner, with other elements. However, this should not obscure the point that James was sympathetic to empiricism precisely because it went to particulars, a move which he contrasted favourably with that understanding of philosophy as the 'quest or vision of the world's unity'. James did allow that a more unified world could evolve either spontaneously or as a result of decisions made on the part of humankind. He wrote that:

Human efforts are daily unifying the world more and more in definite systematic ways, we found colonial, postal, consular, commercial systems...The result is innumerable little hangings-together of the world's parts within the larger hangings-together, little worlds, not only of discourse but of operation, within the wider universe.

Yet James maintained that whatever unity might appear in the world would never be all-encompassing. Manyness would continue to exist and not merely and discreetly inside oneness but also alongside or outside it.[47] Pluralism, he wrote, demands:

...*some* separation among things, some tremor of independence, some free play of parts on one another, some real novelty or chance...How much of union there may be is a question that she thinks can only be decided empirically. The amount may be enormous, colossal; but absolute monism is shattered if, along with all the union, there has to be granted the slightest modicum, the most incipient nascency, or the most residual trace, of a separation that is not 'overcome'.[48]

In order to make his picture of experience unambiguously independent of mind James converted his radical empiricism into metaphysics. As Charles Morris pointed out: 'The cosmos as a whole became simply the totality of "pure experience".'[49] In *A Pluralistic Universe*, the metaphysical reality James outlined exhibited the same pattern of heterogeneous continuity and qualities of process and transition which he ascribed to experience and before that to consciousness. The universe at large is depicted as an ongoing stream of multiplicities and their relations. More so than in his account of pure experience we witness an attempt to reconcile the one and the many. He depicts the universe as a picture of 'manyness in oneness' just as he had seen in mental states a pattern of 'complexity in unity'; while insisting on the 'distributive' character of reality he also uses words like 'coalescence' and 'compenetration', allowing that pieces of reality and individual minds may be 'confluent' with each other. He goes as far as to accept, in the spirit of Fechner's panpsychism, the possibility that 'finite minds', or at least the spiritual part of selves, are 'simultaneously...coconscious with one another in a superhuman intelligence' even though they might not as yet know it. Nonetheless, it is important to stress he treats this higher spiritual being as finite and locates it within a wider stream; in a genuinely pluralistic universe 'nothing includes everything'. Things may be 'with' one another and 'in many ways', nonetheless something is always left out of any relation and remains 'unreduced to unity'; thus, the type of 'oneness' that exists in our world must be partial and 'strung-along' rather than 'rounded' and 'complete'. Hence *many and one* (rather than many *in* one) would be an accurate description of a 'multiverse' in which particulars are in 'mediated connection' with each other without ever being enveloped by a larger whole. Using a political metaphor he described his pluralistic universe as being more like a 'federal republic than like an empire or a kingdom' because no matter how much is gathered up: 'Something always escapes' and remains 'self-governed'.[50] James' anti-monistic bias was calculated. He preferred a world in which there was a real element of wildness as he wanted living, morally speaking, to be 'what we make it' and wanted the fight against evil to be a real fight rather than one in which the outcome was preordained.[51]

THE VITAL FORCE

James was enchanted by Bergson's philosophy. He hailed him as a 'magician' and applauded his injunction to: 'Dive back into the flux'.[52] Bergson sought to break down the 'mechanistic and materialistic' beliefs of the previous generation by stressing liberty of action, contingency and the reality of change and his efforts captured the imagination of not only philosophy students but also 'poets, theologians and social revolutionaries'.[53] Charmed by his ideas people clamoured in Paris, London and New York to hear this 'prophet of the New Philosophy'.[54] Following the war, he would play a key role in establishing the intellectual arm of the League of Nations.

Bergson's attitude to science was mixed. He conceded that it was necessary to spatialise nature in the interests of action. Yet such was the worship of science in the early twentieth century that the useful constructions of scientists had come to be embraced as the sole truth about reality. It was not merely the deification of science that perturbed Bergson. His real argument with science was the way in which it chopped and pruned manifold experience, reducing it to spare geometrical forms or dividing it into nugget-like facts. Bergson saw in this 'cinematographical' approach an actual distortion of reality.[55] By contrast, in his *Creative Evolution* (1907) he described 'true positivity' in terms of 'undivided flux', 'unseizable multiplicity' and 'becoming'.[56] Curiously, many of Bergson's criticisms of the scientific world view drew upon biological and psychological observations. The success of his assault on scientific discourse was partly attributed to the supposedly rigorous scientific nature of his arguments.[57] Yet Bergson's ideas were generally dismissed by the supporters of *scientisme* as mystical. Paul Valéry underlined this in writing that in the early twentieth century intellectuals were 'divided between two widely divergent schools: Poincaré with his Kantian ideas opposed to those of Bergson which were highly ideological'. He contrasted the biological dimension of Bergson's philosophy with Poincaré's intellectualism although it was Bergson's very naturalism that placed him on common ground with the Machian branch of empiriocriticism.[58]

Unlike James, Bergson seemed little affected by the empiricist turn of the later positivism. The philosopher A. Boyce Gibson wrote that he 'never quite shook off the simple materialist view about science.' Yet both he and empiricists converged on the point that phenomena do not need support, although it should be noted that Bergson's reason for arguing this was not out of disdain for metaphysics but because he thought the changing does not need support from the unchanging. Further, his notion that reality could only be approached by intuition and surrendering of the self to duration, by which he meant time as lived and perceived, might be seen as complementing Mach's sensationalism. It should be recalled that Mach had depicted sensory experience in terms of transitory spatiotemporal relations.[59] Bergson, however, was much more explicitly metaphysical than were the positivists and in this regard he, like James, revealed a preference for the lush over the spare. Just as James had with the stream of consciousness, Bergson began to objectify the psychological sense of the flow of time. *La durée* came to refer not only to a felt quality of experience but to a cosmic process. Duration came to be identified with that process of 'continuous but heterogeneous development' which is creative evolution.[60]

Bergson claimed that evolution has its source in and is impelled by a fluent essence he called the *élan vital.* All the living can trace their roots to this impulsion and are united by the same life-giving fluid that runs through and animates them, endowing them with a forward urge. He wrote that evolution 'goes on for ever in virtue of an initial movement' just as it is by virtue of an original act of creation that evolution keeps on creating.[61] Yet we need to know exactly how it is that the great variety of life forms which one witnesses on this planet emerge out of this vital fluid. Bergson wrote that the history of evolution is like a 'shell which has immediately burst into fragments, which, being themselves species of shells, have again burst into fragments destined to burst again, and so on for a very long time'.[62] It is the need to adapt to the external environment which explains 'the sinuosities in the movement of Evolution', although not its actual beginnings.[63] To sum up then, we can see that for Bergson evolution is whole to the extent that it is derived from and excited by the vital force. It is continuous or enduring as, whatever happens to its specific manifestations, the vital impulse itself presses on. It is pluralistic because from the fluid of life there emerges a multiplicity of life forms. In giving expression to the principles of novelty and differentiation in nature he wrote that: 'Harmony is rather behind us than before: it is due to an identity of impulsion rather than a common aspiration.'[64] It follows from his open-ended account that as well as great achievements in nature there can be in nature 'terrible setbacks, periods of retrogression'.[65] Bergson suggested that one can neither predict what sort of forms shall emerge out of the evolutionary process nor what particular course evolution might follow.

According evolution an indeterministic quality was important to Bergson because of the bearing this had on humanity's freedom of action. In order to approach this issue we should recall that for Bergson life is a forward movement and to the extent that it is expressed in individual entities they too partake in this forward push. However, individual creatures come up against all sort of obstacles which block their path and this results in the process of adaptation. In the case of plants and vegetables their development is significantly arrested; members of the animal kingdom are forced to rely on their instincts and their bodily sense-organs to help them on their way. Humans, however, develops their intelligence. It is they above all who are best able to break through those barriers which hold life at bay. It is through their intelligence that humans draw lines in nature – lines along which we can act. It is for this reason that Bergson claimed that intellect is originally an instrument of action. We are then essentially tool-making animals; our intelligence being the tool of tools. Indeed, it is in the course of practical activity that one finds the crude beginnings of mathematics, science and geometry, each being empirically founded, practical in origin and based on likeness and repetition. Bergson wrote that human beings were only 'geometricians' or thinking animals because they are first 'artisans'.[66]

It is due to our immersion in practical activity that we lose consciousness of the vital force. We come to forget that intelligence and science are originally instruments of life. Instead we reify the categories produced by intellect, treating them as universally correct and coercive of human behaviour. Human beings subject themselves to the conceptual structures they have created and refined. Bergson's representation of human beings as individuations of a vital force was developed so that individuals would cease to believe their destiny was hostage to a set of abstract principles. Inserting human beings back inside the vital current was a way of getting them to understand that the divisions they impose on nature are provisional for action. 'Freedom', he wrote, 'brings back matter to the condition of a mere instrument. It is as though it had divided in order to rule.' In recognising its transformative energies, humanity thus acquires 'more power to act and to live'.[67]

POLITICAL TENDENCIES

At this juncture I want to tease out some of the political implications of the strains of modernist philosophy I have highlighted. That the new positivism was seen as having political significance should be clear from Lenin's reaction to empiriocriticism. The position of the positivists themselves as regards the political ramifications of their philosophies was less fraught. Poincaré appeared to think that scientific method, with its quest for sameness and constancy, could not be extended to the study of social affairs. He noted the embarrassment of the sociologist when confronted with the complex, capricious and variable material which is human nature and a history which never repeated itself. Poincaré drew a distinction between the realm of science and the inquiries of those concerned with social and moral issues; science was of great practical advantage to society although its social utility was a happy by-product of the aesthetic quest to reduce manifold experience to simple facts and harmonious relations. He claimed that the intellectual preference for simplicity among Europeans had aided them in the struggle for survival. He contrasted this with the sensual culture he associated with primitive peoples, what he saw as their indulgence in an excess of colour and sound:

If the Greeks triumphed over the barbarians and Europe, heir of Greek thought, dominates the world, it is because the savages loved loud colors and clamorous tones of the drum which occupied only their senses, while the Greeks loved the intellectual beauty which hides beneath sensuous beauty, and that this intellectual beauty it is which makes intelligence sure and strong.[68]

Pearson thought that the sphere of social activity could be scientifically studied, believing that the unity of the sciences rested on the methods employed rather than the material investigated. He was more confident than Poincaré that science could be used to discipline human behaviour. It is thus not remarkable that this geometrician would take the chair of eugenics at University College in London. Pearson feared social collapse. The times in which he lived he claimed were characterised by 'rapid social variation', 'restlessness' and decadence. In view of this, he sympathised with those writers heralding a coming golden age where 'new knowledge' would replace 'worn-out customs'. In particular, he thought it important that citizens be trained in science so that their judgements would be 'free from personal bias'; he considered that minds 'trained to scientific methods are less likely to be led by mere appeal to the passions, by blind emotional excitement to sanction acts which in the end may lead to social disaster'.[69]

Scientific mastery of the social realm demanded that society be finely regulated by the state. This was crucial, in addition, if the state were to survive in the international struggle for markets, minerals, land and food. Pearson also thought that mastery and survival implied organisation on a world scale. He wrote of the benefit to:

...humanity at large from common organization against organic and inorganic foes. The interdependence of mankind throughout the world is becoming a more and more clearly recognized fact. The failure of human beings in one part of the world to master their physical environment may lead to a famine at their antipodes...This solidarity of humanity in the struggle with its environment is no less a feature than Individualism and Socialism of the law of evolution. We may perhaps term it *Humanism*.[70]

The solidarity of humanity is presumed to arise out of the common struggle against nature. Related to this, in Pearson's view, is the partial solidarity brought about by the struggle between the civilised and uncivilised. Pearson wrote that it was a

false view of human solidarity, a weak humanitarianism, not a true humanism, which regrets that a capable and stalwart race of white men should replace a dark-skinned tribe which can neither utilize its land for the full benefit of mankind, nor contribute its quota to the common stock of human knowledge.[71]

Pearson's humanism did not equate with cosmopolitanism where that is taken to mean, as Ralph Barton Perry defined it, that 'there are bonds between man and man more fundamental and more significant than those of state and race'; rather, he gave the imprimatur of science to the *territoria nullius* justification of colonial seizure as well as competition between nations. Although widely repudiated in its aftermath, social darwinism in this form was an accepted current of thought in the years prior to the Great War in Europe and in the English-speaking world.[72]

Mach's comments on the wider implications of his epistemology are sparse. He did not attempt to legislate methods outside the domain of science arguing that no one point of view had final validity as each was important for 'some one given end'. He thus described his empiricism as tolerant and this attitude was further reflected in the decomposition of the ego attendant upon his notion of pure experience. He thought this would encourage greater toleration of and sense of interdependence with others. He further considered the dissolution of the self liberating. No longer an 'unchangeable, definite, sharply-defined unity', its breakdown underlined the individual's capacity to alter their way of being in the world. He wrote that with his concept of pure experience:

We shall in this way arrive at a freer and a more enlightened conception of life, which will exclude the neglect of other egos and the over-estimation of our own. The ethical ideal founded on this view of life will be equally far removed from the ideal of the ascetic, which is not biologically tenable for whoever practises it, and vanishes at once with his disappearance, and from the idea of an overweening Nietzschean 'superman', who cannot, and I hope will not be tolerated by his fellow-men.[73]

In his emphasis on human spontaneity, the purposive nature of human thought and in his openness to variety, Mach was spiritually closer to James, with whom he was personally acquainted and whose psychology greatly informed his analysis of sensations, and Bergson than to the rationalist Poincaré and Pearson, the proponent of scientific social control.

James and Bergson did not reflect at great length on politics although they both considered that their philosophies had definite political implications. Their ideas and vocabulary were drawn on and adapted by a surprising range of political thinkers and actors. James sometimes used political analogies in describing his philosophical outlook. This was not a frivolous exercise. James was as particularistic in his ethical and political thought as he was in his empiricism and metaphysics. That he mixed the language of philosophy and politics so freely flowed from the fact that he saw philosophical and political pluralism, as with their monistic counterparts, as correlates which sprang from the same cast of mind. Following Mach, James stated that the practical consequence of the philosophical position that there 'is no point of view absolutely public and universal' was a 'democratic respect for the sacredness of individuality'.[74] Merging political and philosophical sentiments he wrote:

I am against bigness and greatness in all their forms, and with the invisible molecular moral forces that work from individual to individual, stealing in through the crannies of the world like so many soft rootlets, or like the capillary oozing of water, and yet rending the hardest monuments of man's pride, if you give them time. The bigger the unit you deal with, the hollower, the more brutal, the more mendacious is the life displayed. So I am against all big organizations as such, national ones first and foremost; against all big successes and big results; and in favor of the eternal forces of truth with always work in the individual and immediately unsuccessful way, under-dogs always, till history comes, after they are long dead, and puts them on the top.[75]

James' views on international politics are coterminous with his robust individualism and his belief in the toleration and enjoyment of 'differences'. Just as he opposed bigness and greatness at the national level so too did he oppose it in the international sphere and hence he became a champion of the principle of national self-determination. The continuity between his politics and philosophy, as well as his individualism and anti-imperialism, is further revealed in his declaration that he 'went in for small nations and small things generally'. 'Damn great Empires! including that of the Absolute...Give me individuals and their spheres of activity.'[76]

Such sentiments led James to wage a public campaign against the American military expansion into the Philippines. While expressing appreciation for the passion for adventure stirred by the Spanish-American war in 1898, when the American drive for a greater national destiny manifested as the appropriation of the Philippines, James' attitude changed sharply. For a start he was indignant about the way imperialism, which he said sprang from the biological desire for mastery, was dressed up in pious talk of 'raising and educating inferior races', as though what was to be created was a 'Philanthropic empire'. In a letter to the Boston Evening Transcript on 1 March 1899 he caustically voiced his objection to the masking of imperial expansion as civilisation:

We are to be missionaries of civilization, and to bear the white man's burden, painful as it often is!...The individual lives are nothing. Our duty and our destiny call, and civilization must go on! Could there be a more damning indictment of that whole bloated idol termed "modern civilization" than this amounts to? Civilization is, then, the big, hollow, resounding, corrupting, sophisticating, confusing torrent of mere brutal momentum and irrationality that brings forth fruits like this![77]

It was not just the hypocrisy of portraying imperial ambition as philanthropy that annoyed James. James was of a cosmopolitan outlook but it is important to emphasise that this expression connoted for him, in a way similar to the expression pluralistic universe, the idea of many worlds as much as one world. It could be argued that the word cosmopolitan meant for him, above all, the generous acceptance of the multiplicity of world society. His was as Perry described it, an 'individualistic internationalism'. James's temperamental preference for national manyness over imperial oneness says something about his ambivalence towards modernity where that involves the uniform spread of industrial civilisation. Crucial however, is the ethical and rather Kantian reason for his defence of national self-determination. He objected to the imposition of one country's ideals on another with a different set of traditions. He charged that in seizing the Philippines the rulers in Washington had 'destroyed...the one sacred thing in the world, the spontaneous budding of a national life'; they were able to do this because of their failure to conceive of the Filipinos as 'psychological quantities' with their own type of 'inwardness'. For the American leadership they were instead 'mere matter in our way'.[78]

The issue of international aggression continued to involve James. In an essay called the *The Moral Equivalent of War* published in 1910 by the American Association for International Conciliation, he argued that in an age when 'whole nations are the armies' and are perfecting the 'science of destruction', war had become 'absurd and impossible from its own monstrosity'. The period between wars called peace was hardly less horrific such was the intensity of the competition to prepare for it. This state of passive war among nations, he wrote, '*is the real war*, permanent, unceasing' with battles being but the 'public verification of the mastery gained during the "peace" interval'. This grim analysis was, however, accompanied by pointed criticism of the pacifist movement's effort to win converts by stressing war's horrors and cost. Although himself a pacifist, James thought the movement failed to recognise war's glamorous, stirring pull. Contemporary individuals exhibited all the 'innate pugnacity and...love of glory' of their predecessors; given this, highlighting the 'irrationality and horror' of war was of limited value. James perceived that for many it is precisely the 'horrors' of war that compelled attention. War is fascinating because it 'is the *strong* life; it is life *in extremis*'; more greatly reviled perhaps was the 'image of pacific cosmopolitan industrialism' that pacifists proposed as an alternative to the fear-regime.[79]

Its [wars] 'horrors' are a cheap price to pay for rescue from the only alternative supposed, of a world of clerks and teachers, of co-education and zo-ophily, of 'consumer's leagues' and 'associated charities' of industrialism unlimited, and feminism unabashed. No scorn, no hardness, no valor any more! Fie upon such a cattleyard of a planet![80]

James was parodying the outlook of the war-party but he was making a serious point: that proponents of peace had to appreciate the 'aesthetic and ethical' viewpoint of their opponents. Pacifists had to learn to respect martial values and appreciate their social utility. He thought that no peace would be 'permanent on this globe, unless the states, pacifically organized, preserve some of the old elements of army discipline. A permanently successful peace-economy cannot be a simple pleasure-economy.' He approvingly noted H.G. Wells's observation that in entering the 'barrack-yard' men left behind the superficial, self-regarding and capricious world of commerce and stepped 'to a higher social plane...They are fed and drilled and trained for better services. Here a man is at least supposed to win promotion by self-forgetfulness and not by self-seeking.' If we were to have peace in the 'socialistic future' to which humanity appeared to be moving then states should harness military sentiments and direct them towards constructive ends. James put a cosmopolitan spin on social darwinism in proposing his own moral equivalent for war; he called for, on this 'only partly hospitable globe', the conscription of the young for a period to an 'army enlisted against *Nature*'; its task would be to reduce inequality in the conditions of life and, more generally, improve the lot of humankind.

The military ideals of hardihood and discipline would be wrought into the growing fibre of the people; no one would remain blind as the luxurious classes now are blind, to man's relations to the globe he lives on, and to the permanently sour and hard foundations of his higher life.[81]

One can discern in James's argument his own aesthetic and ethical preference for a world in which manly types sweated and endured in order to win their freedom without the promise of final victory. One senses that James was appalled by the idea of a world in which a life of struggle and strenuous exertion were absent and unrequired. Yet he was sincere in his attempt to counter the menace of war, polemicising at a time when peace proposals could still be dismissed as 'mawkish and dishwatery'; it would take the Great War to make the public expression of such sentiments unacceptable. The League of Nations would be heralded as a moral 'substitute' for war in the Jamesian sense, although those sharing James's distaste for imperial, bureaucratic bigness were wary of it becoming a superstate.[82]

Bergson's connection with the League was direct. It was he who dreamt up the idea of a 'committee of thinkers to "represent the deeper spirit of the League"'; the result was the International Committee on Intellectual Co-operation (ICIC) which was established by the League Council in 1922. That Bergson should attempt to foster something approximating a planetary mind might seem odd given that, like James, he was so often identified with modernity's wilder side. For him the tendency of evolution was not towards unity but towards differentiation. While not thinking that all changes were good or endorsing utterly wilful behaviour, Bergson's conception of nature as an 'immense inflorescence of unforeseeable novelty' was crucial to his belief in human freedom. His philosophy was seen as recommending a society in which individuals were able to express themselves fully.[83]

One of Bergson's most noted political meditations was a speech he gave entitled 'Life and Matter at War' in front of the *French Académie des Sciences Morales et Politiques* on 12 December 1914. Bergson asserted that philosophers and philosophy could not stand apart from international strife and in his speech he registered his support for France's war effort. One of his expositors, Herbert Wildon Carr, insisted that Bergson's pronouncements on the war were 'grounded not in simple patriotic fervour'.[84] Bergson saw the war against Germany as fundamentally a philosophical struggle between freedom and matter; that is, between the vital impulse embodied by the allies and the forces of mechanism, determinism and uniformity represented by the Germans, all this despite their past love of art, metaphysics and poetry. His ultimate message was an optimistic one in that he argued that life would triumph over the 'powers of death' and elsewhere he emphasised the shape of their future was up to the will of the French people.[85] He declared: 'The France of tomorrow will be what we will it to be; for the future is dependent upon us, and is that which free human wills make of it.' Importantly, he emphasised that whatever was willed would be the result of 'pure caprice' and elaborated on his meaning in saying that: 'Our will is the faculty that we possess as men, of decision by the consideration of ideal values.'[86]

One can question Carr's judgement considering Bergson's diplomatic missions on behalf of France to America and Spain during the war, however the important point here is the social philosophy hinted at in Bergson's comments. The end of the war coincided with his growing interest in sociology, as Bergson was seeking to free the human will not only to express its own individuality but also to move towards social unity. This is also true of James. However, Bergson struck a more holistic note in urging us to find unity through returning to the life principle, 'the impulsion which comes from the deep' and which is the common source of our being.[87] Yet the point here is not to revel in occult experience. Imbibing the life force not only makes us more sympathetic towards others, it also leads us to appreciate our creative potential. We realise that we can actively build a happier, more cooperative world. In *Mind Energy* (1918), a collection of essays based on lectures given over the previous decade, Bergson stated that society, which he defined as the 'community of individual energies', can only 'subsist' through the subordination of the individual, while progress requires that the individual be free. The task ahead of us is to reconcile these contradictory needs and achieve both improved social efficiency and greater individual freedom. Bergson actually invests in conflict and war, in a way similar to Kant, a hidden function which is to resolve the contradiction between individual desire and the common good. Merging biological description and ethical prescription, Bergson said that societies are:

Struggling among themselves and at war with one another, they are seeking clearly, by friction and shock, to found off the angles, to wear out antagonisms...to bring about that individual wills should insert themselves in the social will without losing their individual form and that different and diverse societies should enter in their turn into a wider and more inclusive society and yet not lose their originality or their indepen- dence. The spectacle is both disquieting and re-assuring, for we cannot contemplate it without saying that, here too, across innumerable obstacles, life is working both by individualization and integration to obtain the greatest quantity, the richest variety, the highest quality, of invention and effort. To conclude, then, the aspirations of our moral nature are not in the least contradicted by positive science.[88]

So the tendency of evolution is not merely towards differentiation but also towards compenetration. Bergson like James deduced from a cosmology which gives room to both diversity and unity a social philosophy which permits both manyness and oneness. As with James, genuine unity can only be willed and never coerced into being. This belief was reflected in Bergson's conception of the ICIC's role, a body which he saw as the common will in embryonic form. Yet achieving peace is not a wholly communal enterprise as it will come about, he added, only with the aid of genius. It is equally telling of Bergson's understanding of the function of the ICIC that he accorded the 'moral man', whom he described as the 'culminating point of evolution', the unique role of revealing to the rest of humanity the secret of the life principle. The moral man is one 'whose action itself intense, is also capable of intensi- fying the action of other men'. Bergson added that it is the 'men of moral grandeur', especially those possessed of 'inventive and simple heroism', who opened 'new paths to virtue' and revealed 'metaphysical truth'. James' had a less regal moral outlook. In addition, we can say that Bergson went further than James in presenting a picture in which particulars are more completely absorbed into the whole. He came close to investing a telos in history, one which is propelling us towards harmony even though, in *Creative Evolution*, he objected to radical finalism which has things being realised in accordance with a 'programme previously arranged'. Bergson always emphasised that nature was a scene of novelty and surprise, yet it may also be telling that he held that life, in all its variety, had at the outset poured out of the one spiritual source be it called God or the Super-consciousness. To balance this point, it should be stressed that for Bergson to commune with the super-conscious- ness, or understand its work, is not to ascend to a static, eternal realm; to know the super-consciousness, or what issues from it, is to identity with the creative, condensed energy of a temporal process.[89]

CONCLUSION

Twentieth-century modernity grew out of a conceptual arena in which science, social theory, aesthetics and philosophy interpenetrated. It was an admixture of ideas. Yet it is often thought of in terms of sharp, geometrical shapes and complex grids, all concrete blocks and mass organisation. It is associated with a crisp, scientific rather than poetic sensibility. However, modernity should be viewed as having a dual significance. In the early twentieth century the term suggested both rational organisation and a conception of experience as an indeterminate rush. These two tendencies are reflected in the positivist-empiricist spectrum of thought. Pearson sought to isolate for science a sensual arena hospitable to notions of sequence and regularity. Yet the ideas that came under the heading positivist-empiricism could be interpreted in a very different fashion. Scientific notions which might assist in the rearrangement of social and intellectual priorities were readily seized on by non-scientists. Ideas associated with positivism and empiricism were pushed in strange and explosive directions. This was not mere opportunism as positivist notions such as pure experience and the theory of conventionalism were intrinsically slippery. There was some justification for seeing positivism and the philosophies spun around the ideas of immediacy and flux as convergent. Both scientists and philosophers converged in their naturalism, their determination to strip thought of unnecessary intellectual ornamentation and return to the primitively given. This naturalism could be pulled in more or less subjectivist directions and some philosophers would build out of pure experience a pluralistic universe. Empiriocriticism was also seen as tending towards voluntarism and this last featured prominently in philosophies of flux and becoming. Kolakowski wrote of the intellectual emphasis on '"activism"…"Pure experience"', he wrote, '…was not conceived of as a kind of mirror in which reality is reflected, but as the active life of a man as natural, spontaneous organizer of all data'.[90] It was because they were seen as denying the existence of a hidden metaphysical order and valorising human will that the movements of pragmatism, intuitionism and positivism were frequently tied together and dismissed as symptomatic of modernism's confusion and irrationality. Moves by positivists and pragmatists to shake off this charge and reassert the objective quality of scientific knowledge will be addressed in following chapters.[91]

2 FROM PLURALISTIC UNIVERSE TO SUPERSTATE

Bergson thought the spatial categories of the scientist failed to capture an overflowing reality. Yet he recognised that scientific freeze-frames were born of necessity; they were a sophisticated expression of the biological process of adaptation. Bergson thus allowed for the existence of an external environment which partly determines human behaviour. Creative energies come up against resistant elements and it is through such encounters that the faculties are developed.

Bergson's view intersects with Pearson's contention that our perception of repetition and sequence in nature is prompted by physical events and the requirements of survival. Although there are intriguing points of overlap between them, the ontologies elaborated by late nineteenth and early twentieth century positivists differ in crucial respects from philosophies of becoming. For one thing, the latter accord reality a greater degree of plasticity so as to give reign to human creativity. In seeking to centre the language of philosophy around terms connoting flux and fluidity and displace those suggestive of the static, the final and complete Bergson, and this is true also of James, was seeking to emphasise liberty of action. Pearson's positivism translated into a social philosophy which, while calling for action and assuming that it would not be in vain, imposed notional constraints on behaviour. Progress resulted from our behaviour being in accord with the dictates of science.

The more we emphasise the plasticity of experience the more politics may be seen as an artistic enterprise. The more we accord it hardness of texture the more politics is likely to be seen as a matter of calculated adjustment. Bergsonian philosophy tends towards the former view while positivism tends towards the latter. Pragmatist philosophy, however, can be pushed in either of these directions which is why it could be construed as both a lyrical hymn to activism and a theory of scientific social control. Further complicating the matter, pragmatist philosophy permits that active willing may be undertaken on either an individual or collective basis. There is scope for this also in Bergson. In what follows, I examine political translations of all these tendencies of thought, focussing on Georges Sorel, Benito Mussolini, Mary Parker Follett and Harold Laski. In particular I address the question as to what extent the philosophies of James and Bergson were seen as favouring the idea of one world or many, a universe or a multiverse.

THE POLITICS OF ROMANTICISM

Let us begin with those social theories which we might classify as belonging to the unashamedly activist category. My first example is the explosive revolutionary syndicalism advocated by *La Nouvelle Ecole* of socialist thinkers whose most prominent member was Georges Sorel. Sorel who, along with Hubert Lagardelle, published regularly before the war in *Le Mouvement Socialiste*, rejected the gradualism and moralism of the orthodox European socialist movement and the supposedly futile parliamentary route it had taken. He insisted instead that if the Fourth Estate wanted control of its destiny they had to seize it themselves. War, he wrote, 'is not made under the direction of talking assemblies'.[1]

Distinctions were drawn between Sorel and his calls for 'fine and heroic' proletarian violence in order to awaken proud sentiments in the workers and the more mundane and flexible operations of the industrial groups he sought to inspire.[2] Harold Laski, who had flirted with syndicalism as a student and continued to exhibit hostility to *étatisme*, complained that people had been 'greatly misled by the attractive glamour' of Sorel and ignored the actual programmes devised in the workshops. One of the more repeated syndicalist phrases was: 'Do the humble and humdrum syndicate work', a major element of which was the grouping process which involved the routine recruitment of new members to the point where the industrial groups achieved numerical superiority.[3] Of more significance in terms of the syndicalist association with Sorel was their practise of direct action, as typified the French railway strike in 1910, which brought them much of their initial success and notoriety. The syndicalist employment of violence, whether in the form of sabotage or mass-strikes, as with their withdrawal from the political process, was a tactical rather than an aesthetic choice. Sorel was enchanted by the poetry, the 'sublime fanaticism' of revolutionary violence – although he meant by this an energy finer and nobler than mere brute power; he also had the intellectual aim of asserting the primacy of force and social life. Nonetheless, Sorel's name was indelibly linked to this revolutionary movement and it was largely as a result of his writings that syndicalism came to be associated with the intuitionism of Bergson and the activism of James. Critics savoured the notion that the philosophy of Bergson and James encouraged social theories which promoted violent action over rational discussion.[4]

It was Bergsonism in particular that was named as the ideology responsible for the revolt against the state; syndicalist theorists were sometimes referred to as 'Bergsonians'. Sorel drew from Bergson's ideas about the desirability of voluntary action and constant motion, and the view of reality as ceaseless change. The political world was full of potentialities which could be seized by brave adventurers; one had to immerse oneself in reality rather than sit back and wait for the fulfilment of divine edicts or latent patterns in history. The revolutionary should rupture history and break its steady course by swift and sudden action. Sorel's rejection of socialist visions of utopia was in line with his rejection of the scientific belief in progress which was so current in France in his student days when he was training to be an engineer. Bergson's rejection of rationalist conceptions of historical development impressed him.[5] Sorel did not object to all imaginings about the future but only those which posited the certain realisation of a final and ideal world. He wrote that one cannot predict the future scientifically. Yet Sorel granted that one has to think about it in some way if one is to act. He preferred to call musings about the future social myths. These myths were less forecasts than tools – tools which were useful to the degree that they excited action.[6] This is apparent in his claim that the myth of the General Strike, the exhilarating vision of the 'catastrophic regeneration of society', was to be judged as a means of 'acting on the present' rather than 'taken literally as future history'; the future, it would seem, '...must be left to the *élan vital*'.[7]

It was Bergson's theory of precognition that was most associated with the intellectual wing of syndicalism. In according a primary role to intuition, the syndicalist Largardelle was seen as revealing a deep 'fondness' for Bergson's philosophy. In a challenge to political formalism he declared:

No more dogmas or formulas; no more vain discussions of the future society; no more comprehensive plans of social organization; but a feeling for the struggle, a feeling which vivifies itself by active participation, a philosophy of action which give the first place to inutuition, and which proclaims that the simplest laborer engaged in the combat understands it better than the most learned doctrinaire of all the schools.[8]

Sorel similarly drew on Bergson's idea that genuine understanding was achieved intuitively rather than through the medium of discourse and its linguistic symbols. In explaining the appeal of the myth of the General Strike in *Reflections on Violence* (1908) he married the *élan vital* to the *élan ouvrier* and in doing so contrasted the power and clarity of immediate insight with the distant glimpses of reality achieved through intellectual reflection and discussion:

Strikes have engendered in the proletariat the noblest, deepest, and most moving sentiments that they possess; the general strike groups them all in a co-ordinated picture, and by bringing them together, gives to each one of them its maximum of intensity; appealing to their painful memories of particular conflicts, it colours with an intense life all the details of the composition presented to consciousness. We thus obtain that intuition of Socialism which language cannot give us with perfect clearness – and we obtain it as a whole, perceived instantaneously...[this is] the 'global knowledge' of Bergson's philosophy.[9]

Sorel saw at the core of James's philosophy a celebration of a 'mystic *élan*' and the apprehension of the supernatural. In the second edition of *Illusions of Progress* (1911) he wrote that numinous experiences, of which vulgar bourgeois society was increasingly bereft, ennobled human beings.[10] James's pragmatism meshed with Sorel's instrumentalist appreciation of the role of myth and gesture in social life. Yet it was in a later work called *De l'utilité du Pragmatisme* (1920) that Sorel announced his qualified acceptance of this philosophy. He thanked James '...for the important part he took in the struggle waged against the servants of *scientisme*', by which Sorel meant those sociologists who would '...seek to *know* how the general lines of the past are organized with a view to foreseeing the future forms of civil order – which suit [their] present aspirations'.[11]

Sorel approvingly cited James's perception that the 'Yankees not only "consent to live on possibilities"...but they even seek out the hazardous in their enterprises', a perception which he identified with his own injunction that the future should be left to the vital force. His insistence on the '"Right to believe" in a Myth of one's choosing' is highly suggestive of James's own doctrine of the will or right to believe. In the wake of criticisms of this doctrine's seemingly limitless flexibility, James sought to anchor it to codes of rational discourse and Sorel reproached James for endorsing, following Poincaré, the scientific test of truth which is the method of verification. To do so was to limit expressions of belief to those which conformed with the protocols of empirical narration and to downplay the role of volition. Calling on Bergson, Sorel stated that it is not a 'description of things' that we seek but rather an 'expression of the will' just as politically we do not formulate utopias but 'prepare...for a combat to destroy what exists'. He boasted that in order for the full force and 'fecundity' of James's doctrine to become apparent it was necessary for it to be rethought by a 'European brain'.[12]

Neither Bergson's nor James's philosophy, while generally seen as favouring movements for social change such as feminism, were intended as incitements to anti-state violence. Bergson confessed that he had a 'high esteem' for Sorel's thinking and recognised that Sorel embraced some of his views and always cited him attentively. Yet Bergson denied Sorel was his 'disciple' and declared as 'false' the asserted connection between his 'disin-terested' speculations and syndicalism. As Melvin Radeer put it: 'The "intuition which he [Bergson] exalts is "instinct become disinterested", and is much more akin to pure aesthetic contemplation than to political pragmatism. It is Sorel who reinterprets Bergsonian intuition so that it becomes a faculty of political action.'[13] James died in the same year Sorel's remarks on his work first appeared. Nonetheless, the mobilisation of spiritual energy against the absolute, as James's own use of political imagery indicates, could be easily converted into a celebration of group agitation against the state. Yet the activist spirit can just as equally be harnessed by the state and its military machine. Revolutionary syndicalism, as evident in the language of war used by Sorel and Largardelle, had adopted the philosophy of militarism regardless of its anti-military stand in relation to the state.[14] And we saw in chapter one that Bergson projected the societies at war with Germany as articulations of the current of life. Michael Howard reports that the doctrine of the offensive, which stresses the importance of having a 'proud and violent army' and which sees small losses in war as a sign of weakness and lack of patriotic fervour, was explicitly associated before the war in France and elsewhere with Bergson's well-attended lectures at the Sorbonne on the vital force.[15]

FUTURIST NATIONALISM

I have argued that voluntarist politics may encourage the flowering of local units of political autonomy but that it can also sponsor the construction of larger entities. Here we might consider fascism a brand of activism which, like the syndicalist theory, conceived of an energetic élite reshaping mutable social conditions. Yet the fascists sought to capture and regenerate rather than destroy the state. In respect to the state it was a monistic rather than fragmentary movement. While accommodating within its structure a section of the syndicalist movement it did so only to the extent that the syndicates neatly dovetailed into the whole. The difference between socialist and fascist syndicalism according to Mussolini was that 'Fascist Syndicalism accepts the national idea...It means "the subordination of the masses to the peace and war exigencies of the nation".'[16]

Bergson's, Sorel's and James's ideas were debated in Italy in the first decade of the century as part of an anti-positivist (positivism being equated with materialism in the that context) reaction on the part of neoidealism and which would feed the elaboration of fascism. As Zeev Sternhall has argued, fascism was not simply an outgrowth of the interwar era. It was very much a product of prewar intellectual currents. Pragmatism was promoted in Italy by Giovanni Papini who, along with Giuseppe Prezzolini and Giovani Amendola, was part of a small discussion group existing in Florence between 1903 and 1907 known as the 'Pragmatic Club'; James met members of the club in 1905 on a visit to Rome and was impressed by Papini's enthusiasm.[17] There were a number of approving references to 'the young Italian pragmatist' in James's *Pragmatism*, especially to his notion that the pragmatist seeks to 'unstiffen' established categories and forms.[18] Papini became known in America due to an article he wrote called 'What Pragmatism is Like' (1907–08); therein he highlighted the pluralistic nature of pragmatism, its possession of the characteristics of a *thing not yet finished* and described the pragmatist as one who incites 'men to act more than to talk'.[19]

Mussolini probably began to read James before 1910 due to his acquaintance with Papini, the 'Pragmatic Club' and its publication *Leonardo*. When *Leonardo* ceased publication in 1907 Papini and Mussolini became contributors to its successor *La Voce* with Papini continuing to blend the ideas of

Bergson, with whom Papini was also personally acquainted, Nietzsche and James in the course of advocating the renewal of Italy under the auspices of a strong and vigorous state.[20] By the end of 1914 Papini was involved in the effort to get Italy involved in the war entertaining 'heady visions of an Italy regenerated and modernised through the war experience'. He became close to Mussolini who was also supporting the interventionist cause through the *Popolo d'Italia*. This cause gained the support of prominent syndicalists prepared to surrender their notional internationalism.[21]

Papini is significant because of the connections he forged between pragmatist philosophy and fascism. Papini referred to pragmatism as a corridor philosohpy because it could lead off in so many different directions. He was especially conscious of the distinction between the 'puritanic' utilitarian and instrumentalist side of pragmatism, which seeks to control the environment, and its luxuriant, ecstatic side which elevates the principles of movement and vitality. He distinguished between a social and magical pragmatism and he saw himself as standing alongside James at the latter end of this spectrum of thought.[22] The ideas of pragmatism, Papini wrote, seemed made to 'stimulate the poets and dreamers of the world'.[23] The fascist state however, was said to reflect both aspects of control and vitality under the influence of the French legal theorist Léon Duguit in the case of the former and James in the case of the latter.

Papini was intimately associated with the futurist movement, the founder of which Felipo Tomaso Marinetti, had gone over to the nationalist side in 1914. This was curious given the anarchist and internationalist temper of his early Futurist Manifestos, the first of which was published on the front page of *Le Figaro* on 20 February 1909. In that piece, Marinetti bathed rapid means of transit in an aesthetic light, announcing that the splendour of the world was suddenly enriched by the new beauty, the new religion of speed: 'Time and Space died yesterday. We already live in the absolute, because we have created eternal, omnipresent speed.' He continued with this theme in subsequent manifestos and conjured a world wrapped in flashing transportation and communication networks.[24] There is a similarity between the portrayals of modernity issued by the futurists and those appearing in Gerald Stanley Lee's *The Voice of the Machines: An Introduction to the Twentieth Century* (1906). Lee wrote that in the electric vehicle he saw 'the infinite' represented. Like the futurists he endowed electricity with an ethereal quality. 'ELECTRICITY', Lee declared, was 'the archangel of matter' and he endowed it with a moral significance: 'Out of all the machines that [man] has made the electric machine is the most modern because it is the most spiritual...The electric machine fills him with brotherhood and delight.'[25] Marinetti's depictions of a world showered in electricity were not intended to promote the sentiment of brotherly love. In line with the metaphysics of flux which he drew from Bergson, Marinetti celebrated in a 'cosmopolitan nomadism'; he decried the idea of a 'friendly fusion of peoples' arguing instead that humanity was 'marching toward anarchic individualism'.[26]

For Marinetti the war was not just a fight between great powers to dominate 'markets of a superabundant production'; it also represented a struggle between modernity, progress and the future on the one hand and the dead weight of tradition on the other. Like Papini, he urged Italy to side with the modernist states of Britain and France against the pedantic, '*passé*-ist' countries of Austria and Germany. Yet his concern was not so much to further the international advance of modernity but rather to modernise Italy. He saw in war the means of its liberation. War, he declared in 1914, is

...the world's only hygiene...Only war can rejuvenate, accelerate, stimulate human intelligence...War is the only measure of altitude for the the new aeroplane life which we are preparing. War, intensified futurism, will never kill war, as the *passé*-ists hope, but will kill *passé*-ists War is the culminating and perfect synthesis of progress.[27]

This declaration is reminiscent of Sorel's idea of the catastrophic regeneration of society through revolutionary violence. However, unlike Sorel and even before Mussolini, Marinetti hailed the nation-state as the unit of velocity and aggression in international society. Still, there is a strong parallel between the syndicalist picture of the group as the key unit of political action operating in an anarchical environment and Marinetti's brand of state-centrism. Bergson, by contrast, allowed that through will and genius we could advance towards a great society of humankind.

Marinetti acknowledged the apparent strangeness of his fusion of patriotism with the glorification of the 'Destructive Gesture of the Libertarian' as the last was usually accompanied by anti-patriotism. Marinetti explained that he sought to 'separate the idea of the Fatherland from that of reactionary, clerical Monarchy' and unite it with notions of 'daring Progress and of anti-police revolutionary democracy'.[28] A libertarian, modernising ethos thus meets patriotism where the two combine to destroy the old order and achieve 'liberty and every progress within the great circle of the nation'. Yet conceptual tensions resulted from this union of ideas. Marinetti's invocation of the ties of blood and soil imparted a primal mien to his patriotism and stands in seeming contrast with his hymn to a new race of airmen whose 'flesh' had come to 'resemble the...steel' which surrounded them. The temporal flexibility implied here was not wholly unconscious. Peter Conrad notes that Marinetti and his fellow futurist Umberto Boccioni 'hoped that the future might bring back the savage, war-mongering past' and happily referred to themselves as 'primitives'. Equally war, which could be seen as springing from ancient instincts and which involves the spilling of blood, was to be celebrated because it initiated 'the dreamt-of metallisation of the human body'.[29] Less open to resolution is the tension between his enthusiasm for the idea of the circle of the nation, one which suggests closure and containment, and his earlier idea of cosmopolitan nomadism; the latter conjures an image of constant, unrestrained mobility across unbounded space. Marinetti had written evocatively of his orientation 'toward[s] boundless fields of the New and the Future' and one of his explicit reasons for denouncing those who sang of 'ideal and universal peace' was precisely that they denied the 'absolute principle of futurism' which is 'continuous becoming'.[30]

There is also ambiguity in his representation of war. Naming the Great War the 'first electric war' he thought it would act as a lightening rod in the cultural battle between futurists and *passé*-ists Yet Marinetti had also explained war as an expression of what could be regarded as ancient sentiments and impulses. In a manner reminiscent of James, he had written that the internationalists ('the false tomorrow-ists') in their exaltation of peace had failed to appreciate that without 'the noble bath of heroism' that war provides the races would 'fall asleep in the idle egoism, in the economic urge to "arrive"'.[31] It is worth noting here that the standard opposition between internationalism and war was transcended by the idealist Giusseppe Prezzolini who, reflecting on Woodrow Wilson's war against Mexico in the name of international peace in April 1914, argued that war made internationalism possible – war was 'a form of the world's activity'.[32]

Marinetti's conception of futurists, after Bergson, as mystics of action did not blend altogether happily with the heavy shape and style of the mature fascist state. Certainly, Marinetti had proposed rule by elected technical experts should parliamentary government fail. The futurist belief that X-rays had exposed the immateriality of the human body, that it was no more than, in the words of one physicist, 'transparent, colourless tissue', could reinforce the anarchic conception of the individual as a nomadic wanderer, fluid in identity. Yet it could equally support the right of an élite cadre to treat individuals as anonymous and interchangeable cogs in a vast social machine. Nothing if not inconsistent, Marinetti also warned that a top-heavy, administrative state could lead to that 'fixed, restful uniformity' he discerned at the heart of communism; its dream of peace was founded on the idea of a 'single type of world man', a man stripped of that 'aggressive virility' that led to war. He early warned of the 'bureaucratic cancer' eating away at the post-revolutionary Bolshevik state, a state which he had initially welcomed as futurist. It is not surprising that Marinetti, while staying loyal to the regime unto the bitter and squalid end, felt ill-at-ease as dreary, vulgar and toneless monotony came to infuse the fascist state.[33]

NATIONALIST VITALISM

In an interview appearing in the *Sunday Times* in April 1926 Mussolini discussed his intellectual affiliations, declaring that it was above all Sorel who captured his imagination. He stated that his 'rugged theories on revolutionary tactics contributed most decisively to the forming of the discipline, the energy and the power of the fascist cohorts'. Like Sorel, Mussolini admired American society and culture for what he saw as its dynamism and unremitting realism and he too was seen as seeking out 'these "American" traits' in embracing pragmatist philosophy.[34] He announced:

The pragmatism of William James was of great use to me in my political career. James taught me that an action should be judged rather by its results than by any doctrinary basis. I learnt of James that faith in action, that ardent will to live and fight to which Fascism owes a great part of its success...For me the essential was to act.[35]

In the style of the pragmatist he insisted that the opinions he expressed should 'not be considered as dogmas, but as expression of the needs of today, which may tomorrow become relative...Every program should be carried only to the right point.'[36] Mussolini and his education minister the philosopher Giovanni Gentile persistently denounced systems as errors and theory as prisons and upheld action against doctrine.[37]

Both syndicalism and fascism placed will at centre stage and insisted on the malleability of things and in these respects they intersected with pragmatist thought. The commonality between them may seem odd given that syndicalism had a polyarchic complexion and fascism was ultimately monistic. Fascism in its postrevolutionary stage was more associated with Gentile's philosophical idealism, than to pragmatism given the latter's decided particularist tendencies. It was the idea of a universal mind that provided a basis for the conception of the state as an organic whole. Gentile's philosophy was likened to that of James as well as Bergson for the reason that Gentile described mind in terms of activity rather than knowing. Gentile's description of the doctrine of 'Thought and Action', which he discerned in Sorel and sourced back to Mazzini, bore a resemblance to James' will to believe. Gentile himself dismissed such comparisons stating that he rejected the conception of mind as pure will, which he thought denied the quality of ideality, as much as he rejected the idea of mind as pure intellect. He complained further that pragmatism had failed to unite particular minds with the universal. One critic wrote that Gentile would find offensive the notion that he was a 'pragmatic Hegelian'.[38]

That said, it should be apparent that although a voluntarist philosophy might inspire a politics of fragmentation it can also lead to divine rule whereby the will of the active few is institutionally enshrined as the will of all. Discordant wills may agitate for an autonomous space in which they can express themselves but they may also seek to conquer and absorb others because they imagine themselves to possess the one true will. Roberto Michels explained how fascism, 'the party of the *élite*', under the pressure of political necessity was compelled to 'solicit, secure, and conserve the sympathy of the masses'. Fascism, blessed with the '*élan vital*, snatched the power from weak hands and called to itself, in the name of the country, the minority of active and energetic men' all the while proclaiming it wholly represented 'the authentic and autochthonous popular will'.[39] Ralph Barton Perry conceded that there was a certain logic in the development of fascism from a pragmatist to an idealist political movement. Yet the logic he outlined was of a political rather than philosophical kind, a consequence of the transition from revolutionary agitation to rulership;

Pragmatism of the type represented by the youthful Papini encourages the individual or casual group to become heroes and martyrs on behalf of *any* cause. Its tendency is disruptive and anarchical. But when a revolutionary movement has seized upon the agencies of the state it becomes automatically the champion of the state. For the subjective principle of freedom it is now necessary to substitute the objective principle of common action. For a plurality of militant loyalties which ennoble life diversely, it is necessary to substitute one loyalty, and to give that an exclusive title to nobility.[40]

Others thought that there was a more direct link between political absolutism and James's pragmatic pluralism. It was argued that any philosophy which encourages the idea that success depends not on right reasoning but on swift and sudden action, will lead to chaos and then tyranny as the individualistic doctrine of the will to believe is transformed into a totalising will to power. Identities within the state which cannot be absorbed will be crushed and the state will then seek to impose on the world the national idea.[41] Although vehemently rejecting any association between Italian politics and James' philosophy in 1935, Perry did note a few years later that romantics felt themselves irresistibly pulled towards a form of unity infused with their concept of a higher being. Romantic individualism or syndicalism, this point suggests, was thus a pause on the road to absolutism. Perry wrote that this explains why their romantic adherents can be seen pursuing either a 'ruthless subjectivism' or immersing themselves in nationalist movements.[42]

Explanations of the metaphysical basis of fascist state were also partly derived from scientific speculation as to the nature of the physical universe. The fascist state, according to the national syndicalist Angelo Olivieri Olivetti, found support in an image of matter which, in contrast with the atomic point of view, portrays nature as a set of complex but stable organic relations. Olivetti's metaphysics was centred on the principle of association. Herbert Schneider in 1928 summarised it as follows:

Matter is not a congeries of atoms, each of which is a simple independent entity. For the atom itself is a very complex organization of electric charges, an organic unity of energies...The atomic concepts of biology have given place to organic ones. In psychology too, thought has been discovered to be a product of 'social man'; and in place of the older analysis of simple ideas being mechanically associated, modern psychology has revealed the mind as a function of society, of intercommunication, language, and association. In short, 'everything in the universe is association and association implies not the casual agglomeration of entities according to their chance proximities, but a union of entities in a fixed manner, which union determines their state of equilibrium, their forms, and figures'.[43]

Now from the point of view of the universe disclosed by science, state forms which cut across nature's networks can be seen as irrationalities. To replicate in a political sense the patterns science discloses is to construct global forms. Yet the organic depictions of matter and mind that fascist thinkers drew from science and blended with religious conceptions were applied primarily to the national domain. According to the 'spiritualized view' of fascism the world is an '"organic whole" in which culturally and metaphysically speaking, the nation-state becomes the smallest authentic unit'. It is the state, rather than individuals, groups or humanity as a whole, which acts and makes history.[44] Karl Mannheim later argued that fascism had no commitment to the idea that world affairs could be improved; its approach was thus one of 'reckless exploitation of the immediate chances' for the benefit of the state. If it were recognised that the common good demanded 'a new order be planned on a world-wide scale' but that autarchy paid more in the short-term the fascist would choose autarchy and 'exploit' its opportunities even if it meant the 'ruin of mankind'.[45] For many identifying with the communist cause, and perhaps taking more seriously the universalistic pretensions of science, the organic unity to which the interest of the individual or nation must be sub-ordinated was, in principle, the wider society of humankind. Gentile applauded Mussolini for exposing as an 'illusory' fancy of 'proletarian inter-nationalism' the belief that individuals would be ready to forsake their native land in the name of humanity; this last abstraction paled against the 'infrangible integrity...of the national organism'.[46] Mussolini early expressed disillusionment with the League. In a speech he gave at Trieste in September 1920 he claimed he could not rule out the possibility of the evolution towards a supranational organism if he was to keep faith with the idea of an open universe. His defence of the subordination of human solidarity to the national ideal was in a sense political and practical rather than ethical or metaphysical. At the same time he confessed to being dismayed at the prospect of a world without storms, shocks and clashes. Paying tribute to Heraclitus he declared:

Strife is the origin of all things, for life is full of contrasts; there is love and hate, white and black, night and day, good and evil, and until these contrasts are reduced to an equilibrium strife will always remain at the root of human nature, like supreme fatality. And on the whole it is well that it is so. Today strife is possible in war, in economics, in ideas; but the day in which there should be not more strife would be a day of melancholy, of the end of things, of ruin. For the present this day will not come. For history always presents itself like a changing panorama. If one pretends a return to peace, calm and tranquility, one is refuted by the current tendencies of the present dynamic age. One must be prepared for other surprises and other strifes. There will never be a period of peace until the peoples shall have abandoned themselves to a Christian dream of universal brotherhood and shall be able to extend their hands to each other across the oceans and the mountains. I, for my part, have no great faith in their ideals, but I do not rule them out because I rule out nothing: everything is possible, even the impossible and the absurd. But to-day, seeing how things are to-day, it would be a blunder, a danger, a crime, to build our house on the shifting sands of Christian Socialist-Communist Internationalism. These ideals are worthy of respect, but they are still far from realization.[47]

Mussolini could thus contrast Fascism's pragmatic realism with the 'lyric...mysticism' prevalent at the League. The fascist looked with repugnance on supranational organisms like the League. Such organisms lacked 'vitality' and were obstacles to the uninhibited action of the national organism thus threatening to sap its strength and energy. But imperialism was 'based on the vital forces of every people that naturally tends to expand economically and spiritually' and maintains the state's vigour.[48] The fascist dogma of 'nothing outside the State' did not preclude participation in international government.[49] It was an Italian, M. Mauro, who represented the Geneva-based International Institute for Scientific Management (IMI), which was established by the League and private American interests in 1926 in order to facilitate rational organisation of industry and agriculture at the World Economic Conference (WEC) of May, 1927. Mauro announced in that forum that fascist organisations were vigorously promoting scientific management through central bodies such as the *Ente Nazionale Italiano per l'Organizaziare Scientifica de Lavoro*. The fascist state was depicted as a state organised in accordance with scientific principles and in this respect it was likened to the Soviet Union and similarly accorded the title 'New State'.[50] But the fascist state remained the centre of active willing and it was asserted that its contribution to international organisation would be circumscribed by the national interest. When it touched their vital interests the Fascist government was renowned for treating the League with 'thinly veiled contempt' fearing it 'not as a super-state but as a machinery for directing powerful alliances of their natural enemies against them'.[51] Just a few months before the WEC R. Forges-Dalmatia, a fascist propagandist, denounced Wilsonian and League 'ideology' as imperialistic albeit veiled by a corrupt and 'corrosive' moralism; the pretensions of what Mussolini referred to as the Holy Alliance of Western nations, as well as an 'anarchic Russian universalism', were 'repudiated only by the serious and suffering manliness of fascism'.[52]

FUNCTIONALIST THEORY

I have pointed out that pragmatism had a scientific dimension as revealed by its declared affinities with the methods of the empirical sciences. This version of pragmatism gave rise to a social positivism centred on the idea of satisfying maximum demand through scientific organisation. This was the philosophy which inspired the creation of the IMI and some of the key economic policies promoted and pursued in the interwar era at the international level. I have suggested that it was also a feature of fascist thinking. While conjuring with the cloudy idea of an energetic national will competing with other multiplicities in a chaotic universe, fascist leaders also presented themselves as the engineers of a technical futurist state. Here we should note the influence of Léon Duguit whose administrative syndicalism or pluralism was inspired by the controversy in the French Civil Service before 1914 over its claims to autonomy from the arbitrary acts of political authorities. He saw the evolution of self-directing boards and commissions in the civil service to deal with particular issues as the most objective means of ensuring social well-being and harmony.[53]

Administrative syndicalism, which involved calls for the decentralisation and independence of the public service, was at a great distance from revolutionary syndicalism with its calls for the overthrow of the capitalist state and Sorel's gestural politics with its emphasis on the permanence of conflict. Despite the greyness of his theory Duguit is important as he greatly inspired thinking about the public service state and, as George Modelski confirms, supranational organisation.[54]

Duguit billed himself as as a nominalist and a functionalist; he argued that the state had no personality of its own, it being no more than a 'group of individuals having in their control forces which they must employ' to secure public services and that social interdependence, the 'jural principle' to which the governed and governing must submit, was derived from the necessary division of social labour. For Duguit the only wills were individual wills.[55] Duguit was noted, above all by the pluralists, for reviving the notion that there were laws that existed beyond the state, that its behaviour was conditioned by a higher social purpose. He spoke of the requirement that the state obey what he called 'objective law' (*droit objectif*). Duguit described his approach, however, as positivist or realist. Rather disingenuously dismissing natural law as an outdated metaphysic, he claimed that objective law was derived from those things that are necessary to ensure the survival of the social organism and thereby its constituent elements. Duguit's doctrine is grounded in what he calls the fact of social interdependence or social solidarity, a fact which exists independently of individual wills. It is this fact which obliges the state and its functional institutions to act in the public interest. Government cannot 'infringe' objective law; the laws governments issue will only be obeyed to the extent that they give expression to the objective law. Note that the efficient cause of Duguit's objective law lies with another crucial social fact: that individuals are psychologically impelled to seek the realisation of social purposes. Hence he wrote: 'Statute is the expression of a rule which social needs are elaborating in individual consciences.'[56] Just as the government has a function to perform so too does the fact of social interdependence commit individuals to certain obligations. Each citizen will uphold the law so as not to threaten social security and to preserve and promote those benefits which one gains in becoming a member of a community. Public law thus ceases to be based on either autonomous sovereign will or subjective right but upon the idea of a social function imposed on every person.[57]

Obviously, when Duguit insisted that the state and individual must or will conform to objective law he was actually being prescriptive. Rather than being scientific as he had claimed, Duguit's objective law is an abstraction derived from the fusion of organic analogy with psychological supposition which have solidarity in the interests of survival as their governing idea. Duguit's social positivism was directly imported into fascist thought. Sergio Panunzio, a syndicalist theorist of long-standing, wrote in *Popolo d'Italia* in 1923:

Duguit, the first exponent in France, beside Sorel, of integral syndicalism, had already defined a class in precise terms, as 'a group of individuals among whom there exists an unusually close interdependence because they exercise the same function in the division of social labor.' This is an idea which derives from the sociological theory of Durkheim,...a theory which differs, I believe, very little in essence from the organic theory of Plato's *Republic* (*i.e.* of the strong and hierarchical state which is today the aim of fascism). It is obviously but a short step from Plato's *Republic* to the corporationalist theory of fascist syndicalism.[58]

The term function frequently appeared in fascist writings. Despite its mechanistic and positivistic cast, the functionalist model of social organisation well suited the organic metaphysics which underwrote the fascist conception of the state. It should also be recalled that the notion of social solidarity was grounded in biological imagery. Both the organic analogy and Duguit's theory were charged with debasing political thought. Their effect, according to certain critics, was to substitute for the representative state-person a functional state which, in the name of objective social needs, would deny the existence of subjective rights. The National Fascist Party's programme of 1921 stated: 'The nation...is an organism embracing an indefinite series of generations in which each individual is but a transient element.'[59]

We have seen that pragmatic pluralism could swell into absolute idealism where the state is posited as the transcendent one. We have also seen, in discussing Duguit, that it can be transformed into a theory of functional organisation at the state level. I want to discuss here both of these conceptions in respect to their application to the international sphere. As we have seen, there is no logical obstacle to going from the idea of a group will to that of a national or world will. Equally, functional organisation can be applied at local, national and international levels. Kung Chuan Hsiao condemned pragmatic pluralism arguing that its voluntaristic side encouraged strife among the interests or the attempted seizure of the nation by bands who would mould it in their own image. It was when it was rendered as a cosmopolitan international theory that he thought it reached its most constructive phase.[60]

THE WORLD AS ONE AND MANY

At this point we shall look at two authors: the American Mary Parker Follett and the Briton Laski. Both are useful for my purposes as the former was strongly influenced by James and Bergson and the latter by James and

Duguit. Follett was enamoured of the spiritual dimension of pragmatism whereas Laski ostensibly preferred its empirical side. There is nonetheless some overlap between them and both discussed the other's ideas. Crucially, both sought to deal with the matter of the one and the many at the international level.

In *The New State* (1918) Follett accused the radical pluralists of denying the rational basis of the social contract and the existence of a state based on anything but force. In addition, she was concerned about the contribution that crowd theory had made to the discrediting of the state its adherents having depicted it as being the captive of an irrational mass. The Great War had done much to reinforce this view. The most famous of the crowd theorists Gustave Le Bon, whose psychology informed fascist thinking, had pointed, in the midst of that conflict, to the reawakening of basic impulses. He wrote that: 'All nations possess an aggregate of inherited feelings, which are determinative of their mental orientation' and added that one of the chief causes of the war was 'inextinguishable race-hatreds'.[61]

Like Leonard Woolf and Graham Wallas, Follett challenged those who, on the basis of crowd psychology, invested a mystic will in the nation and denied the possibility of transcending that form of particularism. She objected to the idea that Germany was imbued with an ineradicable lust for power and praised President Woodrow Wilson for refusing to regard that nation 'as a thing-in-itself'.[62] Follett's goal was to see groups incorporated within the state and for the state to be similarly accommodated within the wider community of humanity. This was to be achieved, not through the building of large and coercive institutions but through the friendly absorption of lesser by greater wills, albeit without any particular losing its individuality. Metaphysically speaking Follett sought to reconcile 'irreducible pluralism' and what she called the self-unifying principle and she drew on James and Bergson in order to do so.[63]

Follett argued that the extreme pluralists (she was referring to those syndicalists who 'apotheosize[d]' the group) who had based their political theory on pragmatism had not paid close enough attention to the development of pragmatism beyond its earlier phenomenalistic phase. Where they did so (as in the case of Laski) they had accepted only a partial account of its metaphysics, that is its pluralistic cosmology, and had ignored its tilt towards panpsychism, the idea that every individual may be part of a wider self. She claimed that James had shown that an ethical community and state could be willed into being.[64]

As I pointed out, James had moved beyond his earlier particularism by making a macrocosmos out of personal immediacy. Further, he did not exclude oneness from this enlarged conception of experience. While there is no transcendent One, numerous interconnections obtain among the world's parts. In line with Bergson he emphasised the continuous aspects of experience:

Our 'multiverse' still makes a 'universe'; for every part, tho it may not be in actual or immediate connexion, is nevertheless in some possible or mediated connexion with every other part however remote, through the fact that each part hangs together with its very next neighbours in inextricable interfusion. The type of union, it is true is different from the monistic type of *Allenheit*. It is not a universal co-implication, or integration of all things *durcheinander*. It is what I call the strung-along type, the type of continuity or concatenation. If you prefer greek words, you may call it the synechistic type.[65]

It is a matter of emphasis as to how much unity and how much multiplicity we see as being contained within James's universe. Contemporary critics and sympathisers seemed to think that while he was drawn to a concrete monism it was the imperfect character of the world's unity that was most important to him. Yet Follett saw James as moving towards something akin to the idea of a general will. She claimed that James was much closer to Hegel than many pluralists realised; they had failed to realise this because they had misunderstood both, mistakenly attributing absolutism to Hegel and radical pluralism to James.[66]

James had said: 'Things are "with" one another in many ways, but nothing includes everything, or dominates over everything. The word "and" trails along after every sentence.'[67] This sentence was frequently cited by pluralists such as Laski who used it to support their contention that one can never have a unified state because all our differences can never be included in a single whole. For Follett, however, James's *trailing and* argument, rather than being the last word on the matter provided both the incentive and basis on which to form more profound unions between things. She argued that it is precisely because of the constant addition of the conjunction 'and' or the never-ending appearance of differences that we *must* seek to unify; otherwise differences might overwhelm us and our world would fall apart. Further, she argued that the *trailing and*, 'the deepest truth of psychology', is the very precondition of the unifying process. It is because of the presence of differences that we are able to enter into multiple new and intimate relations with each other; difference itself becomes the means by which 'infinite unrelation' can be transformed into an infinite variety of relations.[68]

Follett's argument is flawed in that she hails difference for compelling us to solve and as the means of solving the problem which is difference itself That aside, Follett's solution to the problem of the one and the many in social life was to pose a situation in which all our differences are swept up into a unified whole, a whole that encompasses and is enriched by the inclusion of these differences.[69] It is not surprising that Bergson figured prominently in this modification of James's pluralistic empiricism. The conception of life that I have just outlined echoes his understanding of life as a great evolutionary army containing all sorts of novelties. Follett explicitly adopted Bergson's vocabulary in order to stress both the continuous and open-ended aspects of life. She wrote that each *durée* does not come to an end but rolls on into 'the new *durée* endlessly' and insisted that the world must remain open to growth, that the *élan vital* must have 'free-play'. Curiously however, both time and the vital force would seem to be bearing us toward a destiny which is wider unity.[70]

On her interpretation Bergson's metaphysics suggests that community is a process but that it is also a unifying process. How is this continuing expansion towards unity to be achieved in the social sphere? We should recall here Bergson's argument that it is by an act of will that we can reconnect ourselves with the life force and rediscover our vital energies. Similarly for Follett, personal freedom can only be enhanced by active willing; in this case, willing oneself into wider and wider communities by blending or interweaving our consciences. Thus individuality is not in the first place a question of difference but of 'each finding his own activity in the whole'. 'True individualism is this moment pierced through the soil of our new understanding of the collective life.'[71] The act of willing for Follett ensured not only unity but also growth that is rich, diverse and vibrant. 'Unity, not uniformity, must be our aim. We attain unity only through variety. Differences must be integrated, not annihilated, nor absorbed.'[72] Yet the scene she paints is a rather picturesque one in which differences sit happily alongside and in intimate relation with each other. This compels us to doubt whether she wholly kept faith with James's ideal of a genuinely loose-ended universe.

That pragmatic pluralism became metaphysical monism in her hands becomes very apparent when she attempts to draw out its political implications, especially in respect to international relations. In her eyes, it was a means of reconciling all political or social differences – differences between public and private or collective and distributive interests; between the interests of capital and labour and more grandly, differences between nations. She insisted that we could will a family of nations. Indeed, she wrote that it was such willing was behind the creation of a federal League of Nations and would put an end to international conflict.[73]

Follett wrote that the world was 'growing more spiritual'. The war had performed the task of revealing all the

inner forces bursting forth in fuller and fuller expression. The Great War has been the Great Call to humanity and humanity is answering. It is breaking down the ramparts to free the way for the entrance of a larger spirit which is to fill every single being by interflowing between them all.

While emphasising the federal or international nature of the League she also urged countries such as France, Germany, England and Russia to merge into a true community in the form of a 'world-union'.[74] She called for an end to national sovereignty while also insisting at the same time that by delegating the sovereign power the nation would not become less sovereign or free but more so. The League, she wrote, should be an institution in which no country had to make 'sacrifice' of its sovereignty '...but where each gains by the fullest joining of sovereignty' in order to achieve that intermingling of national wills. She argued that such an intermingling would amount to a 'genuine common will' and that this in turn amounted to the same thing as a '"real" personality'; taken together, these notions imply creative power, authority and sovereignty on the part of the whole world community. The individual nation would only miss out on freedom to the extent that it refused to participate in this unity. While she argued that even the most fervent supporters of the League would not abandon their nation she expressed the hope that should differences arise between nations and the League these would not prove insurmountable and that 'true integration' could be found. Such an integration would involve mutual, cooperative adjustment of wants to achieve an 'inter-individual' mind on a world basis. Such an effort would be premised on the belief that: 'Not the "reduction" to unity but the expansion towards unity is the social process. That is, the expanding process and the unifying process are the same.'[75]

For Follett the League was a phase in the overall movement of world history in the direction of oneness. The teleological dimension of her account becomes even clearer when she too suggests that the war was part of a hidden plan to foster a greater sense of human solidarity. She urged people to elaborate on this plan by reason of the moral law and social utility. Her exhortation was backed by the empirical claim that social life was in any case becoming 'internationalized. Socially, economically, in the world of thought, national barriers are being broken down. It is only in politics that we are nations.'[76] The ultimate aim was thus for individuals to evolve a loyalty higher than the nation, a loyalty to all humanity; a world league with its own constitution and legislature backed by a collective will of this kind would not require powers of enforcement. At the same time, and potentially in contradiction to the previous claim, it would have machinery for not only arbitrating but also preventing the eruption of disputes.[77]

Despite her use of the inspired language of Bergson and James. Follett asserted that the unifying process was a psychological rather than rhapsodic event. Here she appealed to Freud as well as James in arguing that we are self-unifying centres – we constantly integrate our impulses, experiences, desires and wishes. This provides the basis for what she called the law of inter-penetration and it is a law that applies to us in our relations with both groups and the wider community. It is only this law which makes world federalism possible.[78]

One should not take this pretension to social psychology and 'disclaiming of mysticism' too seriously. The British neo-Hegelian Bernard Bosanquet, who described the *New State* as one of the 'most sane and brilliant works on political theory', did not. He wrote that Follett's arguments sounded like those of the ethical idealist T.H. Green. He saw her idea of active willing as being closer to his own conception of the general will than to the philosophies of James and Bergson which he argued privileged difference over organic unity. He followed her in projecting the League as a 'World-state' grounded in a 'daily self-renewing...world-will'.[79] Follett herself spoke of

Bosanquet as a true interpreter of Hegel and observed how paradoxical it was that at the same time as so many English commentators were 'raging against Hegelianism' they were making grand efforts to 'establish on earth Hegel's absolute in the actual form of an International League'.[80] Follett's Hegelian interpretation of pragmatism which had disparate experiences combining so as to form an integral whole was not completely impertinent given that James had accepted that finite minds can share some form of identity in the one.[81] Yet she was more enchanted with the idea of the 'many becoming one' than James ever was; Follett was *perhaps* on stronger ground in drawing out the spiritual monism that underlay Bergson's account of evolution.[82]

Laski also claimed the pragmatist mantle. His ultimate commitment was to the freedom of the individual conscience and this drove his opposition to political monism. He had as one of his primary targets the neo-Hegelian school of philosophers and their theory of the common will which he saw as giving justification to colonialism and to state oppression of individuals and groups.[83] His distaste for this school of thought intensified with the onset of the war, the causes of which he linked to the state-worship monistic theories encouraged. Laski's was not the only nor the most compelling voice protesting along these lines. L.T. Hobhouse wrote that Hegel's idealistic theory, in elevating 'the state above men', had contributed to such military abominations as Ypres and the Somme. But he was the first to use the expression pluralistic state and to make explicit the politics of James's controversial philosophy.[84]

James's student Horace Meyer Kallen claimed he began to develop the notion of 'cultural pluralism' in 1905, although the expression did not appear in print until 1924 in his *Culture and Democracy in the United States*. Kallen put forward cultural pluralism as the only alternative to the vicious schemes of the Ku Klux Klan. James's influence is apparent in his claim that: 'In manyness, variety, differentiation, lies the vitality of such oneness as they [cultures] may compose.' Kallen anticipated this line of argument in a 1915 essay called 'Democracy Versus the Melting Pot'. In that piece he likened ethnic groups to orchestral instruments each with its own 'specific *timbre* and *tonality*' – the 'harmony and dissonances and discords of them all make the symphony of civilisation'.[85] Ross Posnock argues convincingly that Kallen's cultural pluralism, with its emphasis on the persistence of ethnic distinctiveness, suggests a 'static separatism' at odds with James's belief that the 'each-form' is in 'inextricable interfusion' with 'its very next neighbours'.[86] Follett thought Laski had committed a similar error. Laski himself wrote, in defending his use of James, that he liked to use the word pluralism because he 'badly' wanted to emphasise the 'lack of all-togetherness in' and 'barriers between things, not their unity' which he saw as a defining feature of the immigrant society which was America.[87]

When Laski first grafted James's pluralistic cosmology on to political life he implied that it supported a polyarchy of groups, albeit a rather unstable one.

In his early writings Laski followed James in describing individuals as 'bundles of hyphens' in their allegiances; it cannot be assumed that any one group will automatically command a person's support. It followed from this that power should be divided with the state being regarded as just one group among many competing 'Darwin-wise' for our loyalty. As the last remark suggests, political manyness in Laski's view could not stand still; Laski emphasised not only the 'essential plurality' of our loyalties but also their fluid character.[88] Citing James's pragmatism he emphasised that all institutions had to be constantly tested against experience or events and this would seem to make for a state and society resting on foundations no more solid than our shifting desires.[89]

The early Laski was notorious for invoking James's pluralism and pragmatism to privilege the role of groups against the state and for this Laski's thought was condemned. Yet Laski always left open the possibility of giving loyalty to the state, that is, as long as it served as an instrument of happiness.[90] Indeed, in *Studies in the Problem of Sovereignty*, Laski put forward a functionalist or 'pragmatist theory' of the state, an approach that became more prominent in his writings as groups began to decline in importance and Laski came to see the 'value of the routine' that the state gave to people's lives.[91]

It was because of his move towards admitting the state on pragmatist grounds that Follet praised Laski, claiming that he had started to draw a distinction between the cold, strained sovereignty that existed in the present and the rich and vital sort in which, once our energies were released, she hoped we would 'grow'.[92] Follett was referring to views expressed in *Studies*. However, in his *Grammar of Politics* (1925) this reading would becomes even more plausible because there Laski refers to Follett's *Creative Experience* (1924) and speaks of the legal and political community as process; as an organisation which cannot be imposed but which grows in people's minds as interests are interwoven.[93]

In *Grammar* Laski did not present the same picture of bare political manyness that he embraced during his syndicalist period. In that work he attempted, as James did, to strengthen continuities. While depicting society in terms of profusion and multiplicity Laski also allowed for the formation of a legal and political community; he too referred to a process in which finite selves are compounded and accepted that individuals could will into existence some form of unity. In this regard, Laski developed a social theory in the *Grammar* that owed much to the picture of diversity in unity that James offered in his discussion of the continuity of experience.[94]

Follett made the point that, as in James' universe, the unity Laski spoke of was enriching rather than devitalising. We do not lose ourselves in or reduce ourselves to unity, rather each of us adds to the common pool that which is 'distinctively myself'. This is why Laski said, citing James, the state must be '...federal and not imperial in character'.[95] At the same time, even if these distinctive selves combined most harmoniously the unity we would have made would remain incomplete and external; following James, Laski insisted that we are never 'wholly included in any relation. About us is always an environment which separates us from others, or, at the best, makes our union with them but a partial one.'[96] This means that however much one contributes to the social synthesis something of oneself is 'omitted'; borrowing from James, Laski wrote: 'Men will never be content to be syllables in the mouth of Allah.'[97] Laski makes it clear the compounding process refers to nothing more than the gradual lodging in finite minds of common experiences, feelings and beliefs. No new level of personality is created, in contrast to Follett's idea of the inter-individual mind.[98]

The *Grammar* can be viewed as an attempt by Laski to establish a compromise between freedom and authority. In this respect it parallels James's own struggle to reconcile the distributive and the collective aspects of reality. Unlike Follett, Hsiao thought James had failed in his attempt to reconcile the one and the many, even assuming such a reconciliation were possible. Since Hsiao thought Laski's political world was a copy of James's pluralistic universe he was not surprised that Laski too had provided readers with glimpses of a monistic ideal in the form of a social will; equally however, he thought Laski was unable to develop this notion because of his own pluralistic and empiricist tendencies.[99] Laski's partisanship revealed itself in the *Grammar* when, calling on James's terminology, he explicitly endorsed the 'multiverse' over the universe and the distributive over the collective.[100] Laski's pluralism was not merely an aesthetic choice. He recognised that if living was to be what we made it then one must deny that experience came with any guarantees or even offered the possibility of final harmony; one must permit the universe a real and irreducible element of wildness. What he liked about *A Pluralistic Universe* was its 'perpetual question-mark', its message that: 'We have to take the world of sense as we meet it, its losses and gains, its struggles and victories, and assume that...it is a real world in space and time. We have to treat evil as genuine and not merely an appearance capable, otherwise, of being harmonised into good.'[101]

Laski was genuine in his pluralism and he would continue to affirm his preference for political arrangements that were experimental and 'untidy'. Yet it needs to be noted that for him it was first and foremost a weapon against the state, especially the sovereign bourgeois state. That his main concern lay with monism at this level rather than monism in general is revealed by his endorsement in the concluding section of the *Grammar* of the idea of a world policy. In subsequent years he would move to endorse the collectivist state. As part of his assault against the state, Laski depicted a world scene in which loyalties were diversifying as geography ceased to determine interests; concomitantly, new forms of integration and social organisations were appearing which cut across state borders. World life was more complex and indeterminate but Laski was not happy to leave matters in this condition. He favoured a more settled environment which would see the state, along with various other social groupings, enfolded in the great society which he thought was emerging however much national rivalries obscured its nascent presence. He wrote: 'Amid passion and differences, and, also, the passion of differences, we are able dimly and yet securely to discern interests of mankind that make them one and indivisible'; Laski saw the task ahead as one of adding to and deepening these relations.[102]

Laski's emphasis on the open-ended and shifting nature of experience meant that he had to surround the state with a fringe of anarchy. However, the picture of world unity that he elaborated seemed much more secure and tidy that this. In the fashion of T.H. Green he wrote that individuals and nations alike could only find freedom and flourish in the context of the whole. Attempting to keep faith with his pluralism, he added that in joining a richer totality we would not lose ourselves. Like Follett, he argued that the creation of world unity was an expansive rather than reductive exercise. Still, there seemed less room for separateness and randomness in this instance; his world picture seemed to leave room only for 'wise diversities' which could sit comfortably sited inside the one. He wrote that the modern world of steel ships and aeroplanes was an integrated whole in a 'sense so compelling that the only question before us is the method by which we represent its unity'; he called for the League to give expression to an emergent common will.[103] Despite technological adornments, Laski's observations concerning growing world intimacy sound as though they emanate from someone who believes we are all of us ultimately bound together by a spiritual glue. Laski was conscious of the charges of idealism and teleology and made a point of denying that he believed that humanity possessed a communal soul. He also denied that he was investing a purpose in history which would unfold regardless of what we did; he insisted that '...unity is not there, but has to be made'.[104]

Laski was at pains to stress he was a pragmatist of the scientific type and distanced himself from some of James's more poetic imaginings. Before going up to Oxford, first to study zoology and then history, he worked in Pearson's eugenics laboratory. Laski had been influenced by Duguit and it was in part due to the latter's 'pragmatic positivism', to use Laski's description, that he ended his flirtation with the idea of group personality, a notion which only had to be inflated in order for it become that common will to which Laski so objected. Duguit seemingly provided a basis for solidarity grounded, not in metaphysics, but in social facts, the most important being the fact of social interdependence born of the natural impulse towards and demands of survival. Individuals had to work together in order to serve their joint interests and from this arose a necessary sense of solidarity. As we saw, the role of government was to organise society so as to maintain this solidarity and serve common purposes.[105]

Laski argued that it was the common interest in survival and development that provided the basis of world solidarity. Thus unity was not spiritually 'indwelling', but arose from the biological compulsion to adapt to changed external conditions. The sovereign state was in a 'process of disappearance' because it could no longer serve social purposes either within or without; the 'scientific fact of interdependence' commanded organisation on a much larger scale, one over which the state could have 'influence but not ultimate power'.[106] Laski wrote of the League in functionalist terms urging it to build up methods of international administration in the areas of economics, health and the management of resources in order to ensure these issues were decided on the basis of 'technique' rather than 'prestige' in the hope that this would dilute and overcome conflict.[107]

In his transition from pluralist to internationalist Laski was following a route which Kallen had already navigated. Kallen had sought to rally public opinion in favour of Wilson and against the '*Realpolitiker* of the public press and the interests it guards' who denounced discussions of the League as disloyal and utopian. In the *Structure of Lasting Peace* (1918) Kallen had potrayed the League as the extension of the United States' system of governance into the international arena. He imagined the League as a federation of democratic states which had voluntarily agreed to limit their sovereignty. At the pinnacle of world governance would be an International Congress made up of states, ethnic minorities, subnational political parties and individuals of an international mind. It would determine the levels of armaments and ensure industrial integration, proper food distribution, health standards, free movement of persons and goods, the 'equality of all men before the law of any land' and the internationalisation of education. Kallen believed internationalism flowed naturally from the democratically-minded philosophy of pragmatism. The pragmatist sought to liberate the energies and creative powers of the mass of people. This meant escaping the warped and stultifying condition of exclusive national sovereignty. Like James he recognised how much war whetted the appetite of people. The lust for war dulled the 'sense of repression' and gave people a temporary emotional stimulus; but the 'universal enterprise of self-expression and self-realization' must ultimately tend in the direction of peace. Echoing James he insisted against the tired nostrums concerning an eternal human nature that the world was becoming 'more and more what we choose to make it'; just as there are no limits to the growth of civilisation, to creative striving, so too there are no limits to internationalism.[108]

In the *League of Nations Today and Tomorrow* published in 1919 Kallen tempered his view of the League as some sort of constitutional superior. Laski went much further than the likes of Kallen and Leonard Woolf in explicitly vesting sovereignty in the LON. Laski did state that the League would not be based on compulsion because states would come to appreciate that they could only serve their needs and be their best selves through working together. Nonetheless, he also stated that he thought the League should become a 'superstate' with the capacity to bind the wills within it.[109] In the manner of Duguit, he argued that groups such as states must not be able to inhibit the delivery of public services. He thought the League should have representatives in each state reporting to Geneva on breaches of its rules.

Such control by the League was not a frightening prospect. It was the state that was the locus of the irrationality and the will to power was manifest in its wasteful economic competition, stupid and bloody wars, imperialism abroad and oppression at home. Forecasting that the League would become a more democratic and inclusive institution he thought that it should be empowered to prevent states from indulging in acts of folly and cruelty. As a result of criticism from other League supporters, the 1928 edition of the *Grammar* qualified his claim about the League's superstate status. Nonetheless, and despite his functionalist pretensions, Laski strongly wanted to believe that the League could be the authentic voice of humanity. He came very close to admitting at the international level what he denied at the national: a 'plane of which the differences can be coerced into unity'.[110] Laski was aware, in the same way as James, that visions of the world's oneness seemed feeble in comparison with the passions excited by the idea of national struggle. He thus emphasised that the prevention of conflict by an international government would not '...deprive life of its colour or romance'; it was perhaps a reflection of the shift in sentiment on the question of war that he added that the 'glamour of war is as unreal as the bought affection of the prostitute'. Modern warfare, involving the use of poison gas and bombing aeroplanes, was communal suicide. The choice facing humanity was not between a life of valour or one of bland security but between world government or disaster.[111]

CONCLUSION

We can see from the accounts of Follett and Laski how easily pluralism expanded into monism in the form of a universal legal order. Recitations of empirical evidence pointing to transnational association and the painting of threat scenarios were all intended to aid the establishment of this goal. It was in deference to the principle of multiplicity that pluralists, rather than speaking of world government, preferred to speak in terms of world federalism. However, as fashioned by Follett and Laski, a federal republican model of governance. a model which James had cited in order to make clear the contours of a pluralistic universe, began to resemble a universal empire or kingdom.[112]

I have sought develop the political implications of some of the intellectual strands which I have designated modernist. I noted that the philosophies of will and becoming associated with James and Bergson informed anarchistic celebrations of social chaos although these were often only a prelude to the attempt to construct an order of some kind whether in the form of fascist corporatism or a world state. I have also explained that, however homogeneous and disciplined it was made to look on the inside, the fascist state often represented an irreducible and wayward will in the international context. Rational organisation at both the state and world levels was dictated by the perceived need to respond to eruptions of explosive energy variously represented by the syndicalists, the Great War and in some contexts fascism; these phenomena featured prominently in the discussions of intellectual and social collapse in the postwar period. That the resultant new orders presupposed to some degree the mutability of things along with a pragmatic instrumentalism was soon forgotten. New orders generally came to be seen as the by-products of impartial reasoning upon social facts and came to acquire that hard, objective cast that radical empiricism had denied the natural sciences at the beginning of the century. While prewar thought described a world with the lid off the interwar period, against a background of crisis rhetoric, saw increasing attempts to put a clean and shiny lid back on intellectual and social experience.

3   A WORLD WITH THE LID ON

I have argued that intellectual life prior to the war exhibited many of the characteristics which are identified with postmodern thought. Scientists and philosophers vigorously questioned the foundations of belief and were preoccupied with the notions of immediacy and becoming. What we might call a postmodern idiom, that is a vocabulary centred on terms such as flux, fluidity and difference, was already being shaped. As we have seen, these allegedly anti-intellectual tendencies were associated with an explosion of what were deemed irrational political creeds, running the gamut from revolutionary syndicalism to fascism. Yet the ideas of James and Bergson, these being the names most identified with the twentieth-century celebration of will, action and multiplicity, were also incorporated into social theories which spoke of an emerging league of humanity. As depicted by Follett and Laski, this league comprised the qualities of both oneness and manyness, although I have suggested that the former ultimately prevailed over the latter. It says much about the intellectual temper of the times that both these authors, to varying degrees, sought to defend the idea of a common will by appeals to science. It is this manner of argument, and more generally the notion that only science offered a means of making a cosmos out of chaos, that I explore in this chapter.

TOWARDS A SCIENTIFIC UTOPIA

Marinetti was not alone in depicting machines storming into the future. Henry Adams too described modern machinery as a symbol of 'infinity...vertiginous speed...[and]...ultimate energy'.[1] Yet Adams looked upon contemporary life, with its thrusting materialism and exploding multiplicity, with a shudder. Of a pessimistic temperament, he premised his philosophy of history on the second law of thermodynamics which maintains that '...the tendency in all creation is toward decay or degeneration'. It was gross delusion to think that through our scientific inventions we could stall or reverse this tendency. Every supposed conquest of nature only further depleted the earth's energy stocks and accelerated the rate at which we hurtled towards our doom. Nature, he insisted, was exhausted by the constant assaults of man; she had '...educated herself to a singular sympathy for death'. Adams did provide a faint ray of hope, venturing that if we were not to be the sport of chance in the modern era of 'acceleration' what was needed was a 'new social mind' – one which could absorb the complexity of modern existence and impart to it coherence and purpose.[2]

H.G. Wells also surveyed the modern landscape with a measure of unease. His early novels have the earth reeling under the pressure of population growth and industrialisation. The culture of the time is presented as shallow, its emptiness masked by its meaningless variety.[3] John Carey writes that as a man of science Wells knew that 'Entropy, not evolution' was the ultimate destiny of all life.[4] Yet Wells was also very much a man of the twentieth century in that he held out the possibility of a rationally organised world. In his *A Modern Utopia* (1905) the narrator describes a situation in which the old order has been 'smashed up and scattered and mixed discordantly together'; as an alternative to the resultant confusion he recommends a 'world-wide synthesis of all cultures and polities and races into one World State'. This, the narrator states, was the ultimate objective of 'all civilising efforts'; a World State would bring the 'forces of unrest and disorder' under control. Yet what is intriguing in the light of what I have said about the dual nature of modernity, is that the narrator points out that 'synthesis' need not mean 'fusion' nor 'uniformity'. Wells was keen to stress that there is a fundamental difference between the Utopia dreamt up by modern minds and those designed 'before Darwin quickened the thought of the world'; past utopias 'were all perfect and static States' but the 'Modern Utopia must be not static but kinetic, must shape not as a permanent state but as a hopeful stage, leading to a long ascent of stages.' A modern Utopia for Wells (and here we should note Wells had already outlined a kind of pragmatic-pluralist philosophy called 'Scepticism of the Instrument') does not transcend time and history; rather than utterly subduing experience, it floats 'upon the great stream of things'.[5]

Wells' pluralistic sympathies are further shown by his insistence that the World State would be characterised by an 'evolving interplay of unique individualities'; 'all our Utopias', he wrote, should be 'no more than schemes for bettering that interplay'. The attempt to accommodate diversity and unity is further apparent in the description of the language of Utopia. The narrator announces that this language will be 'a coalesced language, a synthesis of many'. Philosophical themes that would surface in Follett's and Laski's versions of political pluralism were threaded through Wells's writings. His social philosophy was grounded on a conception of experience as a 'universal becoming of individualities' and interrelations; believing the whole of metaphysics to be an account of the interplay of and opposition to the 'One and the Many' Wells modelled his conception of a '*finite*' God, 'struggling and taking a part against evil' and 'synthetic in relation to men and societies' on that of James. Yet the Utopia sketched by Wells was characterised by homogeneity and hierarchy. It was not profoundly pluralist. Individuality, he insisted, cannot have free play; he argued in the manner of the ethical idealist that real freedom can be had only by adherence to common rules of conduct. The State, he wrote, will chip away 'just all those spendthrift liberties that waste liberty'. It should also be recalled that Wells's modern Utopia progresses towards a higher and final destiny Most revealingly, in a modern Utopia government is to be undertaken by a specially trained elite, a 'voluntary nobility', who on behalf of the World State administer 'land...natural objects or products', control reproduction and record on index cards at the 'universal register in Paris' the social, physical and mental histories of citizens.[6]

In later examples of what Wells would refer to as his 'fantasias of possibility' he depicted flying machines as benign forces weaving minds together as they glide swiftly and noiselessly over the surface of a planet. In the *War in the Air* (1907) the airplane is an ominous machine 'dripping death' as it bombs in the night. In this story the primitive economic interde-pendence that the world had evolved rapidly dissolves under the pressure of a metallic onslaught. Yet the way in which Wells describes the scope and character of the war can only be meant to compel a fuller appreciation of the oneness of the planet and its people. For with air power war ceases '...to be an affair of "fronts"' and becomes 'an affair of "areas"; neither side, victor or loser' was 'immune from the gravest injuries, and while there is a vast increase in the destructiveness of war, there is also increased indecisiveness'. He tells us that the real possibility of escalating air wars ending in mutual destruction make a mockery of our 'silly old flags' and our 'silly unmeaning tradition of nationality' and underline the need for an 'orderly, scientific and secure' world republic.[7]

The scenes of disaster and attendant utopias that Wells sketched also featured in non-fiction works urging global organisation. William Archer's *The Great Analysis: A Plea for a Rational World-Order* (1912), which included a forward by the classical scholar Gilbert Murray, later to become a prominent figure in the International Committee on Intellectual Cooperation (ICIC), urged that given the limited 'resources of the planet' there was a need for a major mental adjustment. In order to bring 'cosmos out of chaos' the mind, aided by scientific learning, had to encompass and organise the world as a whole:

In one form or another, a world order must one day arrive. It may come as a benefaction or it may come as a calamity; and, assuredly, the best way to avert the latter alternative is to study, from a planetary point of view, the conditions and poten-tialities of life for the crew of sentient creatures who have somehow been marooned on this island in space. The human intellect, organizing, order-bringing, must enlarge itself so as to embrace, in one great conspectus, the problems, not of a parish, or of a nation, but of the pendant globe.[8]

Appealing to natural interrelations, Archer called for the elimination of 'artificial' spatial divisions. Although sounding more monistic than Wells in insisting on a reduction in differences his proposal was essentially the same. What was needed, he wrote, was 'collective thought from a collective brain consciously organised for inquiry and reflection on a planetary scale'; such thought would not be dictatorial but would command the critical attention of a scientifically educated world community which would be equipped with a world language.[9]

CRISIS AND COLLAPSE

The themes of social chaos and scientific organisation continued to be inter-related with even greater frequency and urgency following the shock of the war. Whereas Henry Adams pointed to 1900 as the date of our slide into confusion, in the postwar period 1914 was often held up as the date which marked the beginnings of humanity's fall. 1913 was described as an age of security. The postwar period, by contrast, was painted as a period of dreadful insecurity. The prewar era was described in the 1920s as an one of great optimism due to the belief in the possibility of social reform and because of the 'advance of civilisation' (manifest in the spread of culture, education, commerce and democracy) and 'assumed growth of feeling of fellowship among the world's races'.[10]

Such portrayals were partly exercises in myth-making. Evocations of a golden age before the war were part of a strategy of persuasion, just as before the war images of crisis were conjured with in order to compel acceptance of particular formulas for salvation.

Yet the psychological impact of the war was profound, leading to a widespread perception of social collapse evident in the large body of crisis literature that appeared in its wake. Perhaps the most notorious examples of this genre was Oswald Spengler's *The Decline of the West* (1918). In the preface to the first edition Spengler claimed that he had conceived of the title in 1912 although he had extensively rewritten the text in the midst of the 'storm and stress' of the war years.[11] It apparently caused an enormous 'sensation' in Germany on its release, encapsulating the 'dreary mood of pessimism' which so absorbed the German people.[12] What Spengler referred to in the preface to the revised edition in 1922 as the 'misery and disgust' of the early postwar period only seemed to provide additional confirmation of his earlier diagnosis: that Western man was witnessing the agonising death of Western culture.[13]

Spengler did not regard the crisis of Western culture as a crisis for humanity the world over. He dismissed the term mankind as a mere 'zoological expression, or an empty word'; there was no such thing as mankind in the sense of a collectivity which progressed along the same timeline. History was not a single and linear movement, there was 'no ageing Mankind'. He saw instead multitudinous cultures springing from the earth 'each in its deepest essence different from the others' blooming, thriving and withering in the process of traversing their own particular and finite timeline.[14] The belief that the West was the main bearer and generator of world history, according to Spengler, was a defining feature of Western culture. However, he thought it was an extraordinarily conceited perception as was the notion that modern life was lived at a more rapid pace and more vividly experienced than life in ancient times. He sought to undermine such self-aggrandising by emphasising Western civilisation's particular and ephemeral nature.[15] He wrote:

....world-history is our world picture and not all mankind's...We have to thank that conceit for the immense optical illusion become natural from long habit whereby distant histories of thousands of years, such as those of China and Egypt, are made to shrink to the dimensions of mere episodes while in the neighbourhood of our own position the decades since Luther, and particularly since Napoleon, loom large as Brocken-spectres. We know quite well that the slowness with which a high cloud or a railway train in the distance seems to move is only apparent, yet we believe that the tempo of all early Indian, Babylonian or Egyptian history was really slower than that of our own recent past. And we think of them as less substantial, more damped-down, more diluted, because we have not learned to make the allowance for (inward and outward) distances.[16]

Crisis, according to Spengler's biological interpretation, was a cyclical phenomenon. The ongoing cycle of life decreed that every 'creation ... every thought ... every deed' was foredoomed to 'decay' and 'oblivion'. So it was with cultures and their decline began at the same time as they reached their highest stage. Civilisation is the point at which cultures are at their most refined, structured and intellectually sophisticated. Yet Spengler contended that when a culture reaches the pinnacle of its development the vital force which animates it dissipates. The culture declines and atrophies into the 'dead Nature of Newton'. A civilisation is thus the life-force congealed and hardened:

Civilizations are the most external and artificial states of which a species of developed humanity is capable. They are a conclusion, the thing-become succeeding the thing-becoming, death following life, rigidity following expansion, intellectual age and the stone-built, petrifying world-city following mother-earth and the spiritual childhood of Doric and Gothic.[17]

Spengler thought the only culture on the planet at that time which had reached its pinnacle was the Western Europe American one.[18] It had achieved such an intense level of mechanical activity that the earth quaked under it. But it was not enough to conquer nature: it had to be almost physically transcended. Western civilisation was seeking to escape the earth, the 'bonds of the body' and to 'fly above space and time'.[19] Aeroplanes and radio allowed Western people to 'rise above' the sea-lanes, railways and roads. Spengler notes how these machines appeared more 'mystic' and 'esoteric' than steel ships, steam engines and motor cars. He depicted them as weaving the '...earth over with an infinite web of subtle forces, currents, and tensions' with their bodies becoming 'ever more and more immaterial, ever less noisy'.[20]

For Spengler technological devices and their operations are initially overseen by a priestly caste of engineers. However, as nature becomes more strained the engineers desert the machines which are then seized by a dictatorial plutocracy. The 'dreams of world-improvers' he writes, turn 'out to be but the tools of *master*-natures'.[21] Machines become the instruments of the money-power. It weaves around the world a vast network of commercial relations. Loyalties to culture and place which inhibit the flowing movement, the mobility of currency and things are branded reactionary. Yet money civilisation soon reaches the climax of its success and is challenged by that 'purely political will-to-order' called Caesarism which springs out of the dark undergrowth which is blood tradition; it seeks out and thrives on formlessness. At this point the final conflict 'is at hand in which the Civilization receives its conclusive form – the conflict between money and blood'. As suggested by his depictions of the sterility of the civilisation wrought by intellect and money, and the attendant mechanisation and organisation of the earth, it is a conflict which blood will win.[22]

CRISIS OF THE MIND

The French man of letters Paul Valéry also believed that the Great War was a manifestation of a crisis, one that was essentially European in nature and which had been a long time in preparation. Yet his aim was not to puncture Europe's pretensions to uniqueness. To the contrary, he wanted to reawaken a sense of Europe's unique destiny. Valéry thought the war had served to accentuate and hasten the European 'decadence', a phenomenon which was ultimately intellectual in origin. He wrote in his 1919 essay 'The Crisis of the Mind':

The military crisis may be over, The economic crisis is still with us in all its force. But the intellectual crisis, being more subtle and, by its nature, assuming the most deceptive appearances (since it takes place in the very realm of dissimulation)...this crisis will hardly allow us to grasp its true extent, its phase.[23]

To explain the nature of this crisis we must note Valéry's comment that the idea of the modern as denoting a single and secure pattern of thought had reached its limit in 1914. Strange philosophies and faiths had proliferated and were jostling, in tandem with 'two dozen kinds of positivism', for attention; the war had only aggravated this situation. Science was toppled from its shaky throne. Having already lost its epistemological foundations, its moral claims, due to the 'cruelty of its applications', were now being shot to pieces; meanwhile philosophy was being denounced for its otherworldly 'dreams'. A great carnival of contrasting and contradictory ideas succeeded the illusion of a united and well-founded body of knowledge. Valéry thought conceptual heterogeneity, superabundance, proliferation and dissonance were now the key characteristics of the '*modern* epoch'.[24] Valéry likened such conceptual cacophony to the 'insane displays' of city lights. Yet he also perceived that a contemplative life of rich abundance could be fatiguing and disturbing. For these reasons people might choose to forget passionate questioning and lose consciousness. They could then, aided by science, concentrate on the task of collectively organising a safe and comfortable existence. He forecast that once the remaining confusion was cleared away Europe would 'witness at last the miracle of an animal society, the perfect and ultimate anthill'.[25]

The anthill society was already, according to Valéry, being extended across the globe. Scientific research which began as an artistic activity, a source of aesthetic pleasure in itself, had become an instrument of European domination. Material wealth had flowed to Europe through its exploitation of the resources of the planet. The demonstrable utility of science had seen it turn into a commodity and one which was sought by increasing numbers of people. In order to satisfy growing demand science was 'turned out in more and more manageable or consumable forms...it was to become an article of commerce, an article, in short, that can be imitated and produced almost anywhere'. The spread of industrialisation meant a world in which qualitative difference disappeared; the only important means of differentiation were physical size, population levels and raw materials. Valéry's chief concern, however, lay not with the threat to planetary social diversity posed by the spread of industrial civilisation. Rather, he worried that the wide dissemination of European culture, and he regarded Europe as the mother of invention, would serve to weaken it. As a result of its mass adoption European culture would become trivial and superficial. Related to this was his concern that the wider distribution and application of science meant a reduction of the inequality between Europe and other regions of the world, as shown by the rise of Japan and America. He wrote that a world based on the principle of superiority of technical power, in which mind and genius little mattered, would see international hierarchies flattened in the same way that meritocracy and democracy had upset social hierarchy within the state.[26] He asked:

Will Europe become *what it is in reality* – that is, a little promontory on the continent of Asia? Or will it remain *what it seems* – that is, the elect portion of the terrestrial globe, the pearl of the sphere, the brain of a vast body?

Valéry called for the preservation of those conditions which fostered individual European genius in order to preserve Europe's special place in the world.[27]

Valéry continued to write of the 'terrible uncertainty' pervading all areas of human affairs. In 1922 he observed: 'We ponder what is gone, we are almost ruined by what has been ruined; we do not know what is to come, and have some reason to fear it.' As we have seen, one of the possible futures he depicted was that of a homogeneous order based on the principles of economic and technical efficiency. In 1926 he expressed sympathy for those who believed that the scientific conquest of things is leading us on, or back, to barbarisms, though in laborious and rigorous form; yet more to be dreaded than the older kinds of barbarism, being more exact, more uniform, and infinitely more powerful. We are returning, they say, to the era of fact – but of *scientific fact*.

Yet Valéry argued that while society was advancing ever more and more in the direction of precision, history suggested that it was not amenable to such a framework. Society, he wrote is based on '*Vagueness*'; it needed its sense of the 'mysterious' and 'irrational' as this restrained the impulse to revolt. Freeing the mind from dark fears of anything that cannot be seen or measured, as well as the comfort that order brings, only makes the mind bold in its questions, mockery and criticism. Respect for old certainties fades away.[28] This was the condition of Europe in his day and hence the explosion of intellectual contrariety and the doubts raised about the foundations of science. In 1929 he again likened modern life to an 'orgy of electric lights' which he had symbolising not only heterogeneity but also superfluity. He wondered whether the war, which he saw as a modern war in its 'scope, intensity, duration', was but a concentrated expression of all the overflowing energy that modernity generated and whether irrationality and excess were the destiny of Europe.[29] Yet these qualities also explained the counter tendency towards precision. Valéry placed in dialectical relation the idea of 'extreme order, which is automatism' and which compels instinctive striving or incites revolt, and its antithesis 'extreme disorder' which makes us seek either obligatory organisation or oblivion.[30]

Valéry's conceptualisation of the relation between order and freedom parallels Bergson's thoughts on the matter. As well as counting Bergson as his greatest influence, Valéry would follow him in serving on the ICIC which was Bergson's idea; he too would attempt to encourage the 'co-operation of *minds especially dedicated to the mind*'.[31] We have seen that Follett had earlier detected in Bergson's philosophy precisely this notion of conceptual harmony among peoples and this significance of the ICIC is assessed in the following chapter. Here I want to discuss the criticism levelled at philosophies of freedom in the postwar period: that they had encouraged moral and social degeneration.

THE CULT OF TIME

In 1919 the philosopher F.C.S. Schiller complained of the amount of 'poison gas' being let off on the topic of Nietzsche and the extravagant talk of the 'Euro–Nietszchean War'. That the war had profound intellectual roots, specifically that it was a result of the different philosophies embraced in those countries taking part, was commonplace among members of the Western intelligentsia. It was as though embodied philosophical systems had been firing from the trenches. Nietzsche was not the only target of those seeking to expose the intellectual causes of the war. Idealism was condemned for encouraging a reverence for state power. Positivism stood accused because of its moral scepticism. Bergson's thought enjoyed renewed currency after the war. With its emphasis on contingency it provided a hopeful antidote to the belief that war and social misery were the result of inexorable forces. It suited well the atmosphere of postwar reconstruction. Yet Bergson's theory of creative will, as well as James's notion of the will to believe, was also linked to international strife. (It is telling in this regard that Bergson's creative will and James's pragmatism were seen as resembling Nietzsche's theory of truth.) In the postwar period, Bergson's philosophy would be portrayed as socially subversive and a reflection of modernity's frantic dimension.[32]

The philosopher S. Radhakrishnan wrote that it seemed as if the universe Bergson disclosed was utterly unintelligible, capricious and arbitrary. In it there existed nothing but flux. Where there are no laws, no ends nor even any moments of 'rest and stability', he wrote: 'Chaos is God'; Bergson's philosophy, he added, was a 'mirror of the twentieth century soul, who lives in an atmosphere of constant hustle and excitement, in a perennial maelstrom of events'.[33] For religious thinkers, the superficiality of modern existence and social disarray derived from a destructive immersion in time, conceived as endless process, accompanied by an ecstatic worship of the future. Without an appreciation of atemporal values, a sense of cosmic destiny, social life would be poisoned at the source and would descend into disunion and strife. The emptiness of modern life and intellectual and moral nihilism were attributed to all those trends in modern science and philosophy which denied the higher purpose of human beings and their special relation to God. This was held to be as true of positivism, neo-realism and Freudianism as it was of Bergson's philosophy. Western men and women would continue to live under the sign of the collapse of civilisation until they embraced the perspective of eternity.[34]

The notion that the foundations of knowledge and belief had been eroded was fuelled in the 1920s as new theories about the macroscopic and microscopic physical universe developed by scientists attained a wider impact. Discussion of a crisis in science was more intense than it was before the war. Herbert Carr, who sought to make the theory of relativity 'talk Bergsonianism' claimed that Einstein's physics constituted a crisis in the history of ideas, one which falsified and rendered 'useless' all the old ways of thinking about and arranging practical, scientific, social, political and religious affairs.[35] Mattoon Curtis noted in the *Philosophical Review* in 1925 that the 'chaos of irrationalism' which reigned in philosophy and social theory was complemented by the state of quantum physics. He wrote that a leading physicist had declared that: 'The sole concept of modern physics, energy...is above all things immaterial. The theoretical structure of our science is left without material means of support. The twentieth century so far is a century of bewilderment.'[36]

Creative interpretations of physics were issued by philosophers in order to reassert the importance of their own discipline. Physical theories were interpreted in ways that supported a variety of pet metaphysical schemes. For some, they underwrote a type of organicism which emphasised complexity in unity, the idea of an absolute identity possessing different and finite expressions. They were also believed to endorse the Heraclitan hypothesis that 'life was eternal becoming', continuous 'flux and change', Bergson's conception of reality as essentially psychic activity or mind energy and the belief in fundamental indeterminacy. These understandings were used for political purposes. As we saw in chapter two, the notion that the atom was becoming an organism (or that the self was but a congeries of atoms), was used to underwrite the corporate fascist state. Somewhat in contrast with this use of physics, Sarfatti would boast that Bergson's *élan vital* and Einstein's relativity were merely restatements of Vilfredo Pareto's doctrine, one imbibed by Mussolini, of the imponderability of things, a doctrine which presaged the celebration of the energy of the act. It should also be recalled that the new physics was cited by John Dewey in support of a tolerant, liberal pluralism at both the state and international levels. Then there were those for whom the supposed crisis in science and mystical readings of modern physics only made more apparent the need for spiritual and moral renovation.[37]

Bergson and Einstein were conscious of how different their theories were. At a meeting of the *Société de Philosophie* in Paris on 6 April 1922, just several weeks prior to Einstein's acceptance of an invitation to join the ICIC, the two engaged in a debate over the meaning of time. Bergson argued that the only real time was the time of minds and he favourably contrasted the psychological awareness of temporal passage with the measured time of the physicist which he said was truly 'the ghost of space haunting the reflective consciousness'. Physical time was not time at all, it was really only motion in space.[38] Einstein asserted emphatically that there was no 'time for philosophers' which was more real than the physicist's time; there was he asserted 'only a psychological time which is different from a physicist's time'.[39] Einstein would also denounce the belief that modern physics favoured subjective idealism and philosophical relativism.

Yet in the broader intellectual arena popular stereotypes held fast. In *The Rediscovery of America* (1929) Waldo Frank complained that Bergson and that 'Child of dissolution' which was modern science had between them made a God of motion. All that was once stable and fixed, the molecule, the atom, State, spirit and mind was now moving. Frank believed that relativity theory had joined Bergson in infecting time and space with subjective will. The universe was not only in motion, the world of events had become largely a function of our desire. This was reflected in the promotion of the doctrine of action by positivists and pragmatists. This, he explained, was the 'rationale of Europe's dissolution'.[40] Science was not content merely to blow up the cosmos of old and replace it with a multiplicity of wills and objects in motion. For he added:

It had to bring a monster in our midst; an anarchic mindless master in place of God, to trammel and rule us. It put upon disrupted modern man the embodiment of his own dissociate will. The Machine...the machine is action, particularised and dissociated into a body. It symbolises the final break of a universe, wherein the personal will and every object had been theoretically fused within the Will of God, into a multiverse made up of independent wills and of insulate objects.[41]

For Frank the machine, which contains within it an energising power, brings nature within the dominion of the subject and bathes its possessor in its lustrous glamour. It encourages the cult of self and the desire for mastery. The multiplication of machines parallels the multiplication of self-regarding wills. Levels of social integration are dissolved even though at the same time we are enveloped in the one industrial civilisation. Indeed, for Frank this civilisation is best characterised as 'regimented disarray' and he believed this was reflected in the dissonant sounds of jazz and the awkward movements of modern dance.[42] While the machine does appear to 'compensate for this apartness of each personal will, by bringing men closer together in time, in space and in communication', this is only a superficial intimacy. The linkages are extensive as we race feverishly into the future but they are not deep. Depth is to be found in the will to wholeness and the machine can only be an instrument of spiritual growth where it becomes subservient to the impulse towards oneness.[43] Unfortunately, the more we speed the more empty and tired we feel; we become passive and inert. He declared: 'We start as hard expositors of Power; we become soft consumers of comfort' and with this our impotence increases. The world, he announced, is succumbing to 'the disease' of 'Americanisation' which is the 'cult of power' and turpitude and soon the human race will not even have the energy to seek comfort.[44]

The English literary critic Wyndham Lewis (a leader of a group sympathetic to but also rivalling the futurists called the Vorticists in prewar London) in his confused and contradictory *Time and Modern Man* (1928) similarly lamented the contemporary loss of faith in absolute forms and denial of the soul. Modern men were revolting against the authority of Greece with its hard, classical forms. They were embracing instead the cult of flux the two high-priests of which, he imagined, were Bergson and Einstein; both, he claimed, gloried in the dynamic immediacy of the present moment.[45] He was also disturbed by the cult of action reflected in the widespread popularity of Bergson's philosophy of becoming and James's pragmatism. He held the doctrine of action, with its celebration of struggle, responsible for the war and the rise to power of Mussolini. He noted Marinetti's description of the futurists as the mystics of action observing also that fascism was at its inception involved in an 'exclusive glorification of the Present...*fascism* is an adaptation, or prolongation, only, of *futurism*'.[46] As with Frank, Lewis saw the doctrine of action as being concerned only with the realm of exteriority, with transitory wants and appearances. Science too had now been cast into the 'zone of chance and externality' with contemporary empiricists depicting nature as 'a sort of shimmying, contourless, metis' on which we pressed our desires.[47]

Lewis claimed the thought of Bergson and James, as well as modern empiricism, were perfectly suited to the likes of Mussolini. To the extent that they denied a stable self these philosophies could have been especially designed for comedians and magicians; the former love volatility and mayhem while the latter are masters of vanishing tricks. For Lewis, Mussolini exhibited exactly such actorly impulses and talents, possessing '...all the instincts bred behind the footlights, the apotheosis of the life-of-the-moment, of...display and make-up; and of an extreme instability' – he was like the advertising man for whom words need to have style and cash-value but not substance.[48]

Mussolini was but one element in Lewis's strange picture of a violently oscillating and temporally saturated modernity. Big business, motor cars, Atlantic 'hops' and Wall Street all conspired to send people into a '*trance of action*'. Yet it was action devoid of meaningful purpose. Like Frank he too saw, underlying a glittering kaleidoscope of styles, forms and fads, a stultifying conformity warning of the physical and cultural uniformity which would be attendant upon scientific advance. He wrote that: 'Everywhere the peoples are more and more alike. Local colours, which have endured in many places for two thousand years, fade so quickly that already one uniform grey tint has supervened.'[49] For this reason and due to fear of world hegemony the cosmopolitanism resulting from the mobility of modern life had engendered a nationalist backlash. Lewis thought the fascist movement showed, and we have canvassed this already in relation to Marinetti, that the subjective orientation of the philosophies of time and action could be translated not only into anarchic individualism but into nationalism, regionalism and ideological distinctiveness.[50] Nonetheless, Lewis thought these forms of difference were only cosmetic. He wrote that all over the world people were merging into the same futuristic mass in which individuality will be suppressed and each person will be converted into a mechanical function in the service of the state.[51] To convey his picture he cited Rene Fülöp-Miller's *The Mind and Face of Bolshevism* (1927) in which the latter followed Le Bon in describing the mass psychology of 'collective man' a 'reassertion of the old instincts of the primeval horde'. The mass was likened to a primitive beast and a lifeless production machine, its empire being most firmly established in Communist Russia. He wrote:

It is only by such external functions as the millions have in common, their uniform and simultaneous movements, that the many can be united in a higher unity: marching, keeping in step, shouting 'hurrah' in unison, festal singing in chorus, united attacks on the enemy, these are the manifestations of life which are to give birth to the new and superior type of humanity. Everything that divides the many from each other, that fosters the illusion of the individual importance of man, especially the 'soul', hinders this higher evolution, and must consequently be destroyed.[52]

It is further testimony to the undisciplined nature of Lewis's polemic that, despite his evident distaste for the cultural uniformity engendered by industrialisation and collectivist social forms, he recommended that the inchoate, undifferentiated and dumb mass of people be ruled by a concentrated, intellectual elite. This was less a scientific utilitarian vision of the future than a reflection of Lewis's enchantment with the idea of lean, muscular leadership. John Carey writes that Lewis later became drawn to nazism, not only because of its racist dimension (he despised the idea of the 'melting pot') but because it 'promised a strong leader to halt this drift into chaos', a political disposition which perfectly paralleled his aesthetic passion for 'classical authority and marble rigidity'.[53]

A NEW ARISTOCRACY

The Russian self-styled philosopher-prophet Count Hermann Keyserling, who counted Bergson, Walther Rathenau and Arthur Balfour among his intellectual associates, concurred with Spengler and Lewis that 'all the old culture on the face of the earth is perishing', that technical progress was liquefying life. He wrote in his *The World in the Making* (1927) that cinema, radio, motor-cars and aeronautics had made us into both virtual and real 'globe-trotter[s]' who could no longer remain tied to social forms such as the nation which depended on 'narrow inner and outer boundaries'; technical life had produced a mass of 'new, traditionless and unburdened people' who with a more developed psychic sense of humanity would carry forward the task of the subjugation and transformation of nature and the clearing away of old modes of living.[54]

He also noted the transition from a society in which ancestral lines mattered most to one in which the social service or function a person performed, both of which may change over time, determined status. He saw the functionalist approach as akin to Bergson's idea of becoming, just as he saw the notion that blood ties should determine one's social destiny as springing from a philosophy of being. Liberated from a pre-determined identity people would be free to become their best selves. In the Soviet Union, he asserted, such freedom had not caused 'disruption' but had instead tremendously intensified the power of the country. For this same reason, he argued that the universalistically conceived League must be constituted on the basis of the principle of the self-determination of peoples and groups. He wrote that:

The spirit of the time is precisely *not* international; it is super-national, resting still on the basis of an extremely assertive individuality of the peoples. At the same time the nations will...no longer play a decisive rôle in the future, and just as little will the states. New forms of socialization are arising irresistibly. Among the many possible, one finds its futuristic pattern shadowed forth in the Soviet Union...in its form of free association of peoples.[55]

Keyserling declared that until a 'more modern general condition' arose the future belonged to the Bolsheviks.[56] This general condition was the world or 'ecumenic' state yet one must question how much freedom would be permitted under Keyserling's world state; conceived along functional lines he imagines it as a larger version of the supposedly futuristic states constructed by the fascists and bolsheviks. It is a state in which individuals will be differentiated according to their performance. The decision as to what functions are important and necessary would rest on the needs of the community for it is a general condition of life that the 'pre-existent whole conditions' the parts and determines the well-being of the whole; the parts must embrace the whole if they 'wish to retain their own being and to go on living'.[57] Under this situation, the world state would be a service state providing for the welfare of the peoples and forging a common culture; the nation and state would cease to be seen as the 'ultimate expression of the human community' and national wars between peoples would become as unthinkable as religious wars.[58] Curiously however, this new age of functional meritocracy will also mark a return to aristocracy; an 'expertocracy', made up of those born with the right talents to run the new total order, would after a time come to be seen in a charismatic light. Keyserling viewed fascism and bolshevism as aristocratic systems in this sense. He treated them as temporally Janus-faced, for the birth of these new orders also marked the 'rebirth of the caste ideology of ancient India'.[59]

We can see that the very fluidity of identity that Lewis believed Bergson, James and the positivists valorised can serve to loosen existing structures. Yet very quickly disruptive vital fluid congeals and is fashioned into organisation which then becomes hierarchy. Flux hardens into function and functional identities become fixed. Tasks and roles are distributed and controlled in accordance with the principle of organic solidarity. I have pointed to this general tendency in relation to fascism at the state level and I would also argue that it holds in relation to some of those theories of the world state current after the war. As we have seen, Laski used the Jamesian theory to unseat the sovereign state but the functional superstate he suggested in its place had the potential to become a structurally rigid and all-pervading institution. Yet I want to put this matter aside for the moment and say investigate developments in postwar epistemology and their translation into social thought.

NEO-POSITIVISM

I have suggested that a common feature of political and intellectual debates in the interwar period was the notion of crisis. Crisis was manifest in the massing in cities of undisciplined crowds, economic waste, social friction and war. What made modern crises much worse than in the past was that humanity was now armed with extremely powerful instruments. This was at a time when there no longer seemed to be any ultimate confirmation of those virtues which form the basis of a civilised existence. The cause of moral doubt was sheeted home to the neutral and even sceptical stand taken by positivists on questions of value. Yet science went even further in dissolving its own foundations. Where once science had promised to rationalise the cosmos – providing an accurate description of the structure of the whole as well as accurate predictions of the workings of its parts – it was now revealed as a world of indeterminacy and chance. Science thus could no longer even offer a rational and coherent interpretation of the world and nor could irrationalist philosophers. Science might provide material comfort but not spiritual satisfaction and confidence. Philosophers and religious thinkers warned of the need to return to an ultimate point of view. The renunciation of the synoptic view threatened society's hold on civilisation. It was thought that Western society risked descending into purposeless materialism and barbarism.

Modernity risked turning into a nightmare. This helps explain the renewed emphasis on the part of postwar philosophers of science on the rationality of scientific explanations as well as on the distinction between science and metaphysics. The postwar positivists, such as those philosophers who established in 1922 an association called the 'Vienna Circle' (it became the Ernst Mach Society in 1928) insisted that science had 'nothing to do with metaphysics'. As one commentator noted:

This declaration of independence, epitomized under the word "positivism", assigns to science a narrow but definite and autonomous sphere. Science must cleave to particular facts and, eschewing speculation concerning their ultimate nature and destiny, must confine itself to a description of their definite relations and constant laws, capable of mathematical statement and experimental proof. The whole business is relative and its adequacy is to be tested with reference to its self-imposed limitations and by its own exact methods.[60]

Strictly speaking, these stipulations did not amount to a denial of any role for metaphysics; rather, their thrust is that metaphysics simply falls outside the domain of science. Certainly this was the view of the leader of the logical positivists, Moritz Schlick, a Professor of Philosophy at the University of Vienna. When Schlick stated that only that which could be 'measured is real' he only meant to deny the idea of a universe governed by invariable laws. Positing such laws required postulates which were themselves unverifiable.[61] More so than their prewar counterparts, the postwar positivists sought to 'unite empiricism with a sound theory of logic' and it was on the basis of the high level of analytical rigour claimed for scientific method, rather than simply its inductive foundations, that the superiority of science over other forms of knowledge was asserted. Yet it was not enough to affirm the distinctiveness of scientific method thus conceived; one also had to announce the possible demise of philosophy. Metaphysics was dismissed by adherents of logical positivism as meaningless or even 'ideological' to the extent that it sought to convey an ultimate reality; propositions about the nature of reality were simply not capable of verification.[62] While in principle from a metaphysically neutral school of thought, Schlick's colleague Rudolph Carnap claimed that the 'logic of science' should replace the 'inextricable tangle of problems which is known as philosophy', a position that Schlick himself thought was based on the erroneous belief that logical positivism was derived entirely from science and 'owed nothing to traditional philosophy'.[63]

The position of the logical positivists was still regarded as potentially self-destructive given their continued affirmation that scientific laws were statistical and their refusal to speculate on the ultimate nature of facts. Scientific realists continued to react against the empiricist denial of the objective reality of science's truths. Bertrand Russell, while accepting that the 'old glad certainty' had been banished from science, worried that scientists had gone too far down the path towards scepticism. He wrote that:

Eddington, in expounding the theory of relativity, tends to the view that most so-called scientific laws are human conventions. Some of the leading authorities on the structure of the atom maintain explicitly that there are no causal laws. This skepticism is a canker at the heart of science...capable, in time, of paralyzing the activities of the whole army of scientific workers.

Yet Russell thought the 'practical pragmatic attitude', which is concerned with the success of a theory rather than its abstract truth, would triumph over the mood of doubt encouraged by radical forms of empiricism and further the advance of scientific civilisation. Epistemological realists demanded more than this; they wanted scientific laws and facts to maintain a measure of independence, believing this was crucial to overcoming the crisis in both science and society.[64]

Positivists and realists did however converge on the point that science could produce a saner world. We can understand the triumph of this position, despite the attacks on science because of its lethal technological fruits, given that in the main it was philosophical ideas of a metaphysical kind, such as the idealist theory of the state and the notion of creative will, which were variously blamed for war, social upheaval and domestic oppression. What I want to draw particular attention to is the fact that philosophies which promoted freedom, like that of Bergson, were superseded after time by theories centred on the idea of specialised expertise.[65] I should stress however, that those who advocated the application of scientific methods to society showed little awareness of the complex epistemological debates that had taken place about the scope of science at the end of the nineteenth and into the twentieth century. Sometimes being scientific amounted to no more than insisting on the need to face the facts. Despite the attempts by the more careful positivists to peg out a limited domain for science, its idolaters claimed its method was universal in scope whether the objects under investigation were electrons, earthworms or ethics. The aim was to provide the same kind of proven facts in the the the social fields as were found in the natural sciences.

THE REVOLT AGAINST ANARCHY

Not all writings which appeared between the wars were drenched with fear and pessimism. Social crisis was mysterious, defying accurate description and understanding. But on the scientific view, the cause of crisis was not bewildering or obscure. Aided by scientific methods one could pare away the cataclysmic and emotive resonances of crises and expose their real character as maladjustments in the social machine. William Kay Wallace embraced this spirit in *The Passing of Politics* in 1924 in which he wrote that despite the 'prevailing pessimism, as reflected in the work of novelists and writers in general' one of the outstanding features of the age was 'Faith in the possibility of social regeneration'.[66]

For Wallace war, social strife and economic competition were expressions of egoism, which is the 'philosophy of politics'. While through politics people had sought to 'regulate social intercourse without immediate recourse to force' over the previous few centuries, it had become apparent in the twentieth century that politics was a 'wasteful and expensive luxury'; politics' modus operandi was reckless and haphazard. Wallace blamed philosophy for fostering the spirit of egoism. Philosophy had spawned metaphysical systems which advanced the claims and ambitions of the nation-state; more recently, and in order to fill the void left by the relentless assault on science's foundations, philosophies based on feeling had proliferated and were fuelling an assault on the social order. Wallace thought the voluntaristic doctrines of James and Bergson, in the form of the 'will to believe' or ' will to live', marked the decadence and final 'dissolution' of the political age. He was happy to report that the 'increasing complexity of social life' and an attendant reliance on 'scientific regulation of social intercourse', had seen 'politics and political method...[rise]...to the top like a light and frothy scum, beneath which the new technique' was making itself ready.[67] This technique was derived from methods employed in industry to improve efficiency and from the physical sciences and was concerned with material forces and conditions; denying the metaphysics of will. the new technique would render politics and the state 'superfluous' their substitutes being a 'materialist moral code' and transnational a 'functional economy' designed to promote 'health and public welfare'.[68]

Wallace provides us with another example, so common in the first half of the twentieth century, of a doctrine of social mastery being presented as neutral scientific prescription. The social reorganisation he recommends is not about the imposition of a particular will but is rather a matter of adjusting social behaviour in line with disinterested scientific insights. The technocratic thrust of his argument is apparent when he declares as urgent the need to further work in the area of group psychology. He predicted that in the new cosmopolitan order democracy, which permits eruptions of passionate will on a massive scale, would be superseded by rule by engineers, technicians and, more intriguingly, people of genius whom he called Caesars.[69]

One of the sub-themes of crisis literature was the danger posed to civilised values by mass society. It had once been hoped that democratic reform would see the growth of an enlightened and educated citizenry. However, some argued that the extension of democratic rights had seen the entry into political life of great numbers of people who had little sense of political obligation or identity. When such types were massed together they became a crowd governed by emotion rather than reason. The Great War, because of the eruption of nationalist fervour during that conflict, had focussed attention on crowd behaviour. Increasing industrial conflict, and most especially the Bolshevik revolution, aroused further debate about the mental quality of the masses. Anxiety about social pathologies helps explain the interest in the new fields of social psychology and psychobiology. Assertions were made that the democratic movement was exhausted and that the properly equipped should take the place of the untrained mass. William Tait, a McGill University psychologist, asserted that democracy should progress to an 'aristocracy of worth' so that the 'stupid, or those unable to exercise the right of citizenship will not have a voice in control'.[70]

In the light of this shift from a prewar emphasis on freedom to a postwar preference for social control it is instructive to look at the development of Walter Lippmann's thought. In *A Preface to Politics* (1913) Lippmann had rejected the fatalism of Le Bon whose psychological theories of crowds he thought reflected a melodramatic sensibility and 'contempt for current effort'. He drew on James, Bergson and Wells, all of whom he saw as advocating that the intellect was an instrument of action and that truths, whether scientific or social, were experimental in character, designed to help us cope with a world full of creative possibilities. He discerned in their writings a call to revolt against routine and mechanical habits; one should seize life and shape it.[71] It was thus for humanity to decide whether in the midst of this 'rich and varied age of generous passions' it would be the victim or master of life. Lippmann was a socialist but his socialism was stirred up by James's 'romantic cosmology' and his notion of the will to believe as well as Sorel's paeans to the role of grand myth. In this work he expressed sympathy for constructive syndicalist energies as opposed to the gradualism of Fabian scientific socialism. He rejected that type of positivism that held that only those 'ideas that mirrored external nature' were worthy of study. Sounding like a pasteurised Sorel, Lippmann offered the view that scientific socialism was an attempt to mask socialism's reality as 'a living force…a product of the will – a will to beauty, order, neighbourliness, not infrequently a will to health'. The Fabians' gas and water socialism seemed dull and rigid. It assumed a human personality fit for a society dedicated to social utility. Yet the passionate and intuitive sides of human psychology, as Sorel

recognised, are no less real and important. He admired the complex psychological portraits in Graham Wallas's *Human Nature in Politics* (1908) and
approved of Wallas's socialism precisely because it was grounded in human
nature in all its variety.[72]

Lippmann's next work *Drift and Mastery* (1914) continued with the
themes set down in *A Preface to Politics*. Principally, it upholds the notion
that life is there to be shaped. In particular, he places the future in the hands
of energetic inventors.[73] Yet there are telling differences between the two
works. In *A Preface* the act of moulding life is almost an artistic exercise. The
world is awash with sparkling jewels, splashed with loud colours. In *Drift
and Mastery* he again upheld James's pluralistic philosophy against the
notion of the 'One, the All Embracing, the Permanent' and denied the
possibility of a fixed picture or golden ideals; visions are to be amended in the
course of experience.[74] Yet there is a greater emphasis on the need to create
unity out of multiplicity and in this respect he is closer to Wallas, who was
a leading Fabian, than James.[75] Lippmann stressed the need to discipline
social energies. The times, he wrote, had seen the rejection of old authority
and the rejoicing in novelty and change, yet this transition held danger. The
erosion of traditional structures of thought and patterns of obedience had
caused a sense of drift. Modern man had become, psychologically speaking,
a nomadic wanderer.

All of us are immigrants spiritually. We are all of us immigrants in the industrial
world, and we have no authority to lean upon. We are an uprooted people, newly
arrived, and nouveau riche...The modern man is not yet settled in his world. It is
strange to him, terrifying, alluring, and incomprehensibly big.[76]

For Lippmann the real 'battle' was not 'against crusted prejudice but against
the chaos of a new freedom'.[77] The key to overcoming the sense of drift did
not lie with a return to 'eternal forms of justice and moderation'.[78] Lippmann
was still Jamesian enough to refuse fixed and final schemes. Further, while
he emphasised the role of the intellectual in giving guidance to a society
mired in uncertainty, he also portrayed scientific endeavour as a natural ally
of democracy because it was a cooperative enterprise productive of public
meanings. He wrote that:

For the discipline of science is the only one which gives any assurance that from the
same set of facts men will come approximately to the same conclusion. And as the
modern world can be civilized only by the effort of innumerable people we have a right
to call science the discipline of democracy. No omnipotent ruler can deal with our
world, nor the scattered anarchy of individual temperaments. Masterery is inevitably
a matter of coöperation, which means that a great variety of people working in
different ways must find some order in their specialities. They will find it, I think, in a
common discipline which distinguishes between fact and fancy, and works always
with the implied resolution to make the best out of what is possible.[79]

He once more dismissed a narrow positivism which believes 'rigorous,
classifying method where each color is all one tone' in favour of a science

involving 'the blendings and interweavings of reality' but never with the end of achieving a static order. Scientific mastery to this extent does indeed seem like a creative and adventurous exercise on the part of an energetic community. He wrote: 'To escape from barren routine...this must be the endless effort of democratic people.'[80] Yet it is telling of his more technocratic bent in this work that he made no mention of Sorel. The American syndicalists of the International Workers of the World are written off because they prefer 'revolt to solidarity' and are 'quite ready to destroy union for the sake of militancy'.[81] Further, although he had succumbed to the vogue for Bergson which had gripped his peers in 1912 (the year of Bergson's traffic-stopping visit to New York) in *Drift and Mastery* he invoked science against vitalistic philosophy seeing it as too emotive, fanciful and obscure to generate confidence in social progress.

A mere emotion of futurity, that sense of 'vital urge' which is so common to-day, will fritter itself away unless it comes under the scientific discipline, where men use language accurately, know fact from fancy, search out their own prejudice, are willing to learn from failures, and not shrink from the long process of close observation. Then only shall we have a substitute for authority...The scientific spirit is the discipline of democracy, the escape from drift, the outlook of a free man. Its direction is to distinguish fact from fancy; its 'enthusiasm is for the possible'; its promise is the shaping of fact to a chastened and honest dream.[82]

Despite the attempt to marry science and democracy, his account of a scientific society unavoidably had elitist implications. Freedom was to be gained by embracing the wisdom of technical experts whose role it was to channel our lusts in positive directions. Members of juvenile gangs, and here we might recall James's idea of a youthful army doing battle with nature, thus might be converted into 'Boy Scouts'.[83] Lippman's bias towards instrumental intelligence, which he contrasted favourably against submersion in the 'ebb and flow of sensation', became more prominent after the war.[84] In the *Public Opinion* (1922) he called for 'trained and unprejudiced fact-finding bodies and for adequate avenues of dissemination to the public'; only a period of expertocracy could save democracy from itself. Although something of a caricature, Harry Elmer Barnes likened Lippmann's proposal to Comte's idea of a 'Positivstic commonwealth' guided by science and governed by 'highly trained sociological priests' devoted to 'social betterment'.[85]

For Wallas too the main problem facing modern life was that of drift. He wrote in the *Great Society* (1914) that the most striking phenomenon of the new age was that people were now 'working and thinking and feeling in relation to an environment which, both in its world-wide extension and its intimate connection with all sides of human existence' seemed to hold out the promise of a cosmopolitan world order. At the same time there was also the fear that 'the civilisation which we have adopted so rapidly' would bring with it neither harmony nor stability. There was a fear of blind forces and questioning of whether society would spontaneously evolve towards harmony.[86] Wallas, however, was a social optimist. He took Le Bon to task for arguing that people massed together 'were of "inferior mentality"', 'unconscious', more easily prompted by 'fashion, prestige, party spirit' than people living in 'simpler and earlier forms of social organisation'. To the contrary he thought that, generally speaking, people living in cities were much more conscious and alert, given the cacophony and activity surrounding them, and no more prone to irrational outbursts than were villagers.[87] Yet he supported the need for a 'science of social psychology...to forecast, and therfore to influence, the conduct of large numbers of human beings organised in societies' and prevent large-scale organisation losing loyalty through becoming impersonal.[88]

Le Bon's crowd theory was not Wallas's only target. The preface to the *Great Society* was written in the form of an open letter to Lippmann who had attended his lectures at Harvard in 1910. He indicated therein that he was concerned that *Human Nature in Politics,* in attacking 'nineteenth-century intellectualism', had given too much ground to irrationalist philosophes. These gave encouragement to disintegrating tendencies. The *Great Society,* by contrast, he saw as an argument 'against certain forms of twentieth-century anti-intellectualism' and he sharply indicated that he hoped Lippmann in his next work would take the same tack. As we saw, Lippmann obliged.[89]

In the text Wallas made it clear that the anti-intellectual trend he is referring to stems from the work of James and Bergson. The line of attack was predictable. Their privileging of instinct and feeling over reason threatened social solidarity; such a doctrine could only inspire syndicalist revolts and sabotage, predatory behaviour on the part of power hungry corporations and lust for war. He also saw James and Bergson, to the extent that they promoted a metaphysics of difference and multiplicity, as encouraging social particularism manifest in growing racial and class identification.[90] He wrote:

...the loose anti-intellectualism which now threatens to take the place of the old intellectualism may prove to be infinitely more dangerous in the twentieth century. An internecine European war is the one enormous disaster which overhangs our time; and such a war is made more possible whenever thought is represented as the mere servant of the lower passions.[91]

Wallas's point was that the vast and all-penetrating network of world social relations both demanded and provided the grounds for social administration on a large scale. Presumably, what was need were philosophies more sympathetic to the ideas of rational organisation than were those of James and Bergson. Wallas pressed the case for a world collective plan and the machinery with which to put it into operation. He spoke of a world organisation grounded in a world will.[92]

Wells ceaselessly promoted the idea of a world state. In *The World Set Free* (1914) he begins by defining humans as essentially 'tool-using, fire-making' animals and it is the constant quest for power over the external environment that sees, in quick succession, steam, electrical and atomic energy unleashed upon the world. The 'Age of Energy' permits humanity to soar above the earth. However, in a world filled with tribal hatreds and political jealousies, it also allows the construction of monstrous atomic war-machines. Yet the devastation wrought during the Age of Energy at the same time brings about the end of the era of sovereign, warring states. A council of the wise set about planning a 'new common social order for the entire population of the earth'. As in *A Modern Utopia* the proposed World Republic, which he sees not only as the realisation of the twentieth-century idea of a state planned 'upon scientific lines' but also the Christian dream of an ethical commonwealth, accommodates a degree of difference. There is a universal language, in order to facilitate 'common understanding', which is English although it does come to include countless foreign nouns and verbs. Accompanying this development are 'certain minor acts of uniformity'. We are also told that the collectively planned world, which lifts the masses out of the realm of necessity, gives rise to a period of enormous artistic creativity, a 'phase of history...termed "Efflorescence"'. The same interplay of the one and many and identity and difference is apparent in a subsequent work called *The World of William Clissold* (1926) in which the eponymous central character goes as far as to anticipate the development of a 'collective human person', a 'common mental being of our race', however the rider is added that this being will not replace individuals. We will, he stated, be 'different' but 'enlarged'.[93]

This last point recalls Follett's attempt to unite the one and the many at the world level and, like her, despite the nods in the direction of diversity, Wells was really elaborating a form of social monism. Yet Wells is in another way closer to Wallas than Follett. Wells was less sure that spontaneous harmony would arise, hence the prominence given to central direction in his visions of the future Note also Wells's concern that a culture liberated from dirt and sweat might become trivial, lazy and juvenile. By becoming too luxuriant, indulging in 'childish sexual love' minds would soften; the intelligence that saved us from disaster would dissipate. Progress must be vigilantly pursued and at full speed. In the *World Set Free* Wells has the dying philosopher Marcus Karenin pronounce that: there is no limit to humanity's capacity for 'self-modification'; he adds: 'Man lives in the dawn for ever...Life is beginning and nothing else but beginning.' Yet Karenin is not celebrating in sheer fluidity and profusion, in an 'ecstasy of waste'. Freedom is married to a stern doctrine of forward striving. If humanity is to delay its appointment with death, energies must be disciplined and directed towards exploring space, 'the immense and awful future of our race'.[94]

Wells's postwar writings would further underline the trend towards monism induced by a sense of crisis. He would continue to assert the need to design an integrated 'world machine' exercising control in the educational, scientific, transport, economic and biological fields.[95] Following the war, there was less pressure to make concessions towards the principle of difference. Laski and others invoked it against the sovereign state only to advocate the replacement of the state system with a superstate. Yet there were those who were wary of the superstate ideal as it raised on a grand scale all the problems seen as besetting national sovereignty. In 1919 the American scholar and James sympathiser Lewis Mumford, impressed by Laski's analysis of the domestic implications of sovereignty, painted the Western state as essentially a military organisation which imposed on its subjects a 'mechanical unanimity of purpose' while seeking to 'disintegrate lesser nationalities' beyond its borders. For Mumford the state was by nature an oppressive, imperial institution which justified its 'own existence by denying the existence of a common humanity'; it was only by asserting its 'exclusiveness' that the state could 'maintain its own sacred union'. Mumford was also at one with Laski in believing that the League should be more than a league of sovereign states. A league constituted by sovereign states could only maintain its 'authority...by promoting the interests' of its individual members. He added that:

In this case it is plain that if the League have any reality apart from the constitutions of the Great Powers this international state will have the same characteristics of an exclusive, territorial association. Thus its members eschew to some slight degree the privilege of waging warfare among themselves only for the purpose of obtaining dominion over the rest of mankind. Such a coalition will not rid the world of wardom. The underlying native populations of the subject territories are too large, too self-conscious, too disaffected, and in the end too powerful. Universal peace on such terms would be synonymous with universal exploitation. To break through the obscene crust of such an arrangement the volcanic eruption of war would be a welcome release.

For Mumford, countering the possibility of the League becoming a means for the larger powers to lord it over the rest of the world necessitated the further expansion of transnational association. Only the 'great industrial, professional, and civic associations' could counter the military organisation which the League seemed destined to become.[96]

It was the American pragmatist John Dewey who offered a critique of the vision of world order most in keeping with the spirit of James. This was even though Dewey liked to present himself as a pragmatist of the empirical rather than esoteric kind. He sought to prevent pragmatism from collapsing into nominalism and subjectivism, by putting it on a more realistic basis and not simply grounding it in sensations. The objectivity of his pragmatism derived from an asserted continuity between the energies that are expressed in the habits and behavioural patterns of living organisms and the energies of nature.[97] For this reason there is also a continuity between the study of nature and that of society and hence the possibility of disinterested social knowledge. Dewey liked Bergson's description of man as a tool-making animal and he, like James, viewed knowledge as an instrument of action. However, its function in this regard was to serve, not personal whims nor desires, but objective social needs and purposes. Dewey wrote after the war:

...while we have been reasonably successful in obtaining command of Nature by means of science, our science is not yet such that this command is systematically and pre-eminently applied to the relief of the human estate...[This is]...the specific problem of philosophical reconstruction at the present time. For its emphasises the larger social deficiencies that require intelligent diagnosis, and projection of aims and methods.[98]

Dewey was conscious of the damage to philosophy's reputation resulting from its perceived social irrelevance and the weirdness of some philosophical doctrines. He wanted its practitioners to turn from introspection (he rejected Waldo Frank's 'revolt against the of machine' and embrace of 'private estheticism') and develop its experimental intelligence so as to plan a better future.[99]

The distinction between Dewey's social instrumentalism and James' acceptance and embrace of the loose-endedness of things was frequently noted. Dewey, like Ralph Barton Perry, depicted the war as a conflict between the democratic, pluralist spirit and an iron-clad absolutism and supported America's entry into it. Their call to arms seemed perfectly to reflect James's moral activism. However, Dewey's former student, the social critic Randolph Bourne, expressed disappointment asking whether James would have accepted the 'war-situation so easily and complacently' and supported a peace that promised a 'league of benevolently-imperialistic nations'; he saw in the prowar stand of Dewey and other American new liberals a reflection, not of James's tolerant philosophy and 'poetic vision', but of the desire of instrumentalists to discipline and mould events.[100] While favouring intelligent control, Dewey was Jamesian enough to deny knowledge the qualities of finality and completeness. He acknowledged the restless and creative aspects of experience. He was in such a Jamesian mood when in 1921 he raised metaphysical objections to proposals for world government. He was a more consistent Jamesian than Laski seeing, as did Follett, the contradiction in attacking monism within the state but proposing it without in the form of a world state. Dewey railed against Wells's conception of a 'new world history' quoting with disapproval Wells's assertion that: 'History is no exception amongst the sciences; as the gaps fill in, the outline simplifies; as the outlook broadens, the multitude of details dissolves into general laws.' For Dewey this was a 'unitary and absolutistic' view of science based on a theological analogy. Popular in the Victorian era, it was an outlook Dewey thought had been superseded by the relativity theory of Einstein as it had substituted for 'the neat, smooth, well-ordered world of Newton a world which is full of puckers and skews...'. Dewey added that the Wellsian interpretation of science was a 'rationalization' of social absolutism and monism.

One may sympathize with a longing for some state which shall reduce international anarchy to order, and enable harmonious intercourse to take the place of war. But even here it makes a mighty difference whether the super-state is something into which the multitude of nations is to 'dissolve', or whether it is a descriptive formulation under which the multitude of local states, provinces, towns, villages, and other human groups may follow more securely their own careers and voluntarily engage in undisturbed and fruitful conversation with each other. For the only conversation in which participants 'dissolve' is the one in which some tyrant bore monopolizes discourse, while voices melt into monotony...a state which shall give play to diversity of human powers is a state in which the multitude of of human groups and associations do *not* dissolve.[101]

For Dewey a real internationalism, and he certainly hoped that the technological age would lead to greater social and political integration, accepted the 'infinite plurality of purposes for which men associate themselves' and consequently was an internationalism tolerant of national differences. He saw Wilson's policy of blockading Russia as springing from an absolutist temper which rivalled that of the Bolsheviks. He wrote: '...if we believe in democracy we shall believe in the right of that vast group of human beings known as Russians to make their own experiments, to learn their own lessons in their own way'.[102]

In progressive circles Dewey's definition of internationalism was somewhat unusual. The cultural disaster which was the Great War gave rise to a strong desire to scientifically organise social life. Philosophies which emphasised the indeterminacy of experience were overwhelmed by a vigorous social positivism and were even depicted as dangerous. It was unfortunate that one of the most prominent champions of the metaphysics of becoming in public life in the 1920s was the leader of a fascist state. The League of Nations would not become a superstate, although for reasons of prudence and *realpolitik* rather than any widespread allegiance to cosmological pluralism. Yet the belief that a world society and state were evolving continued to be strongly entertained up until the early 1930s. The main agent of this process was a phenomenon called rationalisation and it is the various discussions and analyses of rationalisation at the League and in related contexts that I discuss in the next chapter.

4 NEW WORLDS FOR OLD

A LEAGUE FOR PEACE

The League of Nations was portrayed as the culmination of a century-long process of world unification. It was as if, below the surface of international anarchy, fed by economic interdependence and communications links, a consciousness of international interests had slowly developed. Functional integration accompanied these advances as typified by the creation of the Universal Postal Union in 1874. Thus the Great War had only made more apparent the need for an institution which had long been in the making. Such an explanation of the League's origins served to naturalise the institution, to render it less foreign and revolutionary. It was also necessary to relay this account so that the League would not be seen merely as a victor's institution. While the idea of world government was in the air in the decade before the war, the League itself was very much a product of the Great War. Its initial cast was significantly determined by this event in combination with a particular strain of American exceptionalism.[1]

In a speech he gave on accepting the Nobel Peace Prize in 1910 Theodore Roosevelt recommended the formation by the great powers of a 'league of peace', not just to 'keep the peace among themselves, but to prevent by force if necessary, its being broken by others'. It was this idea which was at the core of the programme of the League to Enforce Peace which was established in America in 1915 as was the League of Nations Society in London. Already in the autumn of 1914 President Wilson had announced that: 'all nations must be absorbed into some great association of nations whereby all shall guarantee the integrity of each so that any one nation violating the agreement between all of them shall bring punishment on itself automatically'; this was a cause he would vigorously prosecute over the next few years. On 8 January 1918 he elaborated before Congress his programme for enforcing peace.[2]

Wilson did not think a harmony of interests would spontaneously arise. While believing that enlightened opinion was converging on the notion of a common humanity, the war encouraged in him the view that states might sometimes have to be compelled to fulfil their legal obligations. Although rejecting the French idea of a League with a 'standing army with commander-in-chief and permanent general staff' as 'international militarism', he did go so far as to suggest an international army controlled by

84

a small group of powers.[3] William Rappard, as Rector of the University of Geneva and member of the Mandates Commission, explained that for Wilson the League was less a forum for conciliation and arbitration and not even a 'medium of peaceful co-operation'; rather, it was 'essentially the instrumentality through which a just peace should be permanently guaranteed by the concerted will and power of its member states'.[4]

Wilson imparted to the League a somewhat austere, punitive mien. The word League itself was suggestive of an army of the righteous which is why some professed a preference for the French description *Société des Nations*. When Wilson said the League had to be 'made to work' and it would be made to work 'by the organized major forces of mankind' he was not only referring to the pacifying effect which he attributed to public opinion.[5] We might also consider the conditional nature of Wilson's commitment to the principle of sovereign equality. At one stage he stated that the League 'sends autocratic governments to Coventry' and while this injunction was ignored it is indicative of his belief that the democratic states were truly worthy of respect.[6] Wilson seemed to picture the League as a somewhat exclusive club of missionaries to the world. By contrast some Britons advocating or directly engaged with the construction of the League, such as Sir Robert Cecil, General Jan Smuts, Leonard Woolf and Alfred Zimmern, suggested the League should centre its activities on functional cooperation.[7]

Wilson had dreamed that the League would be a 'wider union of the United States type'; although this did not come to pass either. When he announced in 1919 the birth of a 'new order of things' he was in many ways, as his preference for a League of democratic states similarly indicates, projecting the new world onto a larger canvas. After all, he had declared that the flag of America was the 'flag...of humanity'.[8] Wilson was extending themes he had deployed before the war in the domestic context; he declared in his *New Freedom* (1913) that with economic life increasingly dominated by large business enterprises what was required was a 'new order' in which government legislated to protect individuals and foster their flourishing. He declared: 'Now this is nothing short of a new social age, a new era of human relationships, a new stage-setting for the drama of life.'[9] At the end of the decade such sentiments caught the social imagination. Wallas, who advocated a form of Fabian socialism at both the domestic and international levels and thus was politically at some distance from Wilsonian liberalism, began the *Great Society* with the above quotation because he saw it as an antidote to social fatalism.[10]

Here it is important to recall the sense of temporal disjuncture that followed the Great War and the crisis literature that flourished as a result. Visions of despair and warnings that the social and intellectual foundations of Western civilisation were disintegrating featured prominently in philosophical and social commentary and were often a prelude to meditations on the devitalising impact of modernity. There were calls for spiritual and cultural renovation. Nonetheless, in the interwar period it was futurophilia, strongly manifest in the intertwined cults of science and internationalism, that shone most brightly in public discourse. Reflecting this, we find the expression 'new order' continuously being invoked by dominant and less prominent members of the League up until the early 1930s and acquiring fresh nuances in the process. It came to connote science in the service of world solidarity. The League soon drifted from its Wilsonian moorings. While initially seen as a political body, by the mid-1920s supporters such as Harold Laski were emphasising the need to multiply its cooperative functions in the economic and technical areas. Wells, who propagandised in favour of the League during the war, argued that Wilson's conception of the League had proved too narrow; what was needed was a more detailed plan for reconstructing the world. This was to be the wave of the future.[11]

TEMPORAL AMBIGUITY

While interwar internationalism drew principally on evocations of new worlds it also incorporated forms of patriotism. The *Song of the League of Nations and International Brotherhood*, published in 1921 in both Esperanto and English and officially approved by the League of Nations, opened with the lines 'Ye sons of all nations join hand in hand, sing mid acclamations, "One Brotherland"!' Yet the lyrics of this hymn to peace are curious, for while through them their author John Malham-Dembleby sought to engender an enlightened spirit of internationalism, at the same time and to this end, he toyed with patriotic and martial sentiments of old.[12] The song continued:

> The hatred and madness
> Men would divide,
> Together in gladness
> March side by side!
> Ye soldiers fraternal,
> God in Command!
> Singing united of
> 'One Brotherland!'
> Singing united of
> 'One Brotherland!'

As well as revealing the culturally specific character of the myths surrounding the League's creation, these lyrics illustrate the sometimes temporally ambiguous nature of the rhetoric of new orders. In this instance, aspects of a projected future, otherwise seen as involving a sharp break from tradition, are woven into the fabric of the past. Just as a discontinuity between past and present may be exaggerated in order to sharpen the appeal of proposed futures, it may also be smoothed over in order to win assent from audiences disturbed by the spectre of the unfamiliar. This helps explains why the League was represented by its supporters in Britain and the Dominions as the Commonwealth of Nations writ large.

For much the same reason the League was treated as the outcome of historical processes that had been underway for at least a century. Indeed, H.R.G. Greaves, a London School of Economics (LSE) colleague of Harold Laski's, traced its origins back further, grounding it in medieval religious and political thought. In introducing his 1931 study of the League he wrote that once again, 'beckon[ing] from the future', was the pre-Reformation ideal of a Christian 'doctrine of world governance...[one] which comprehended the whole human race'.[13] Greaves thus placed the mechanical notion of functional cooperation on spiritual foundations. Christian cosmopolitanism might have been an inappropriate way to brand a League which included numerous non-Christian members, Mussolini derided the institution as an expression of exactly that illusion. Further, and as we have seen with Laski, there was some tension between the attempt to bathe the League in a religious light while also presenting it as a technical institution.

Salvador de Madariaga, a Spanish citizen who served as head of the Disarmament Section of the League Secretariat and then as a member of the ICIC's Committee on Arts and Letters, acknowledged the problems associated with religious representations of the League. While accepting Christendom as the model for world society, a model which strongly informed Arnold Toynbee's efforts on behalf of world peace, he also realised that this model would have to be reworked so that it seemed less exclusive, superstitious and imperial. To this end he attempted to secularise the idea of world society, render it a product of intellect rather than feeling. Yet the spiritual pull was still in evidence, for Madariaga appeared to invest a purposive life force in the waves of electricity and electrical machinery which he believed were binding communities together. He wrote that:

...forms of vital circulation gradually [are] drawing together into a single living organism all those organisms that not so long ago were proudly independent nations. And like living nerves galvanizing the whole, the cables and the ether are continually transmitting waves of news, sentiment, hopes, and fears, more and more common to all humanity. Thus under our very eyes a new society is taking shape, a wider Christendom, a *civitas mundi* less theological than medieval Christendom, less sentimental and abstract than the 'Humanity' of our ancestors. It is not based on the beyond but on the here and now; it draws its strength not from sentiment and opinion but from facts and necessities. Its domain is 'nothing but the earth'; its constituents are men, races, and nations; its creative moral force is culture; its creative natural forces are place and climate; its guide is reason; its fate is the intuition of order.[14]

The League was mostly presented as a creature of modernity. Rappard told the audience at a symposium organised by the Geneva Institute of International Relations in 1926 that: 'Like motor-cars, wireless telephony, aviation, prohibition, fluctuating exchanges, Russian bolshevism, Italian fascism, American opulence and European impecuniosity', the League was a 'fact' which the 'student of contemporary affairs' could either praise or damn but simply could not ignore. Rappard was imputing to the times a degree of wildness. As I have highlighted, speed and friction had been widely presented as defining features of twentieth-century life. Zimmern noted in the same context that since the war the world was moving even faster, that it danced to a different 'rhythm'.[15] Yet modernity also signalled scientific control of social development and the peculiar gyrations of the modern world only further underlined the need for this.

A LEAGUE OF MINDS

Unlike publicists such as Wells, Laski and Greaves, all of whom wanted to leap into the new world, Rappard, Zimmern and Sir Arthur Salter, the last being Director of the League's Economic Section until 1930, rejected the notion that the League should become a superstate as had Sir Robert Cecil before them. They were aware that governments and communities remained jealous of their independence and suspicious of international institutions. At the Geneva symposium Rappard took issue with Laski's conception of the League's destiny. While conceding that extreme or 'popular' interpretations of sovereignty 'had done a great deal of harm in recent times' he insisted that these should be distinguished from its juridical meaning. Further, he thought entirely unhelpful Laski's idea of the League as a world state controlled by a two-thirds majority of its members and able to 'defy the Great Powers'; the League he insisted had 'no existence apart from the states which composed it; it was a League of States' and it was hardly likely that the Great Powers which founded it would accept defeat at their own hands. Such clear-eyed analyses of the League's constitutional status aside, these 'civic monks', to use Madariaga's expression, still subscribed to the belief that social and economic frictions and waste could be reduced through the application of intelligence by international bodies of specialists.[16]

The ICIC encouraged this view with both Zimmern and Arnold Toynbee promoting, under its and the LSE's auspices, the 'scientific study of international relations' and special programmes to train people for international careers. There was even the suggestion that the ICIC should coordinate all such study and training seeking to ensure that it led to the 'development of "the international mind"'. The international mind, as Zimmern saw it, was fundamentally a religious notion which upheld the essential oneness of the universe, but it was also invested with scientific nuances; while some writers produced a smooth blend of spiritual and scientific images of harmony, others tended to emphasise one or the other.[17]

The ICIC was not only the brain-child of Bergson who was its first director. It included among its members some of the great minds from the field of arts and letters. Thomas Mann, Paul Valéry, Murray and Zimmern would all serve on the ICIC at various times, as well as such scientific luminaries as

Einstein, Marie Curie and H.A. Lorentz. Léon Bourgeois claimed that the ICIC had in a sense parentage of the League of Nations for it was only the existence of a well-established 'international intellectual life' before the war that made the institution possible.[18] Bergson pointed out that due to the war and its economic consequences civilisation was menaced by a grave danger which was precisely the erosion of intellectual life, and it was this that the ICIC was charged with restoring both within and among nations. This involved not only improving the conditions in which intellectuals worked and promoting foreign translations of academic works but also, in keeping with Bergson's belief that humanity in all its variety springs from the same source, seeking out amidst dissent matters of fundamental intellectual agreement. At its first meeting in August 1922, Bergson stated that while he accepted that ideas are necessarily distinct from one another, there was nonetheless interplay among them. At the same meeting, Bergson also implicitly privileged the role of philosophical reflection in bringing about concordance. He stated that he recognised that above all the League sought to promote the scientific world view and that the promotion of the interests of international science was an important basis for the ICIC. Yet he also emphasised the ICIC's role in furthering the moral end which was the 'realisation of the grand ideal of fraternity, of solidarity and of agreement among men'; this was a notion he thought more easily appreciated in the upper intellectual echelons but it was one that the ICIC could cause to be progressively absorbed by nations.[19]

Follett's detection of strains of ethical monism in Bergson's philosophy and her belief that it implied the growth of a world will are further supported by a remark Bergson made in the following year. He told a meeting of the ICIC that it should seek to make real the dream of a 'supra-national intelligence' and establish for itself a moral ascendancy in world affairs. Bergson retired from the ICIC in 1925 on grounds of ill-health although he would continue to concern himself with the progress of the League and the issue of war and peace.[20] In his 1932 work *The Two Sources of Morality and Religion* Bergson described his as a democratic mysticism, one which entailed an enthusiastic embrace of all humanity and the will to introduce harmony where there is discord. He contrasted this with a false, imperialist mysticism which excludes and suborns those outside the privileged circle of the nation. The first type of morality is open and dynamic whereas the second is closed and static. The sovereign state, itself a compromise between fraternalism and tribalism, had to give way to a more cosmopolitan international order, indeed to a cosmopolitical state. He called for a League of Nations with the 'authority to intervene in the legislation of the various countries, and even perhaps their government'. A move to world government was not just commanded by morality; worldwide population growth, leading to ongoing conflict over resources, could only be managed by international institutions. As we have seen before with Bergson, there is more than a glimmer of teleology in his account of the destiny he wished upon human race; yet it is but a glimmer for here again he advised that the future lay in humanity's hands.[21]

Bergson's meditations on morality were well-received in English-speaking countries. The racially exclusive Nazi regime, which quit the League in 1933, was seen as epitomising his notion of 'closed' morality; societies supporting the League, however, were practisers of the 'open' variety.[22] Arnold Toynbee, a prominent commentator on and supporter of the League, extensively quoted Bergson's *Two Sources* in his three volume *A Study of History* (1934), reaching the very Bergsonian conclusion that civilisations are like 'rock-climbers...the several climbers, though they are certainly separate individuals, are also representatives of a single species and are all engaged upon an identical enterprise' albeit with varying degrees of success. Toynbee elaborated on his meaning in likening the civilisations to seeds dispersed by a sower some of which 'fall by the wayside', on 'stony places' or 'among thorns'; others fall on rich, soft earth, germinate roots and eventually flower. Despite their different destinies, the seeds are all of the one type and all serve the 'sower's purpose'. Toynbee challenged Spengler's social fatalism and also his cultural relativism.[23] He shared Bergson's belief in the mind's capacity to feel 'Life' and feel it 'as a whole' and he drew on the philosopher in arguing that in culture as well as nature diversity is contained within a wider uniformity. While the unity of humanity is in one sense given at the beginning it is also a process and Toynbee again called on Bergson in expressing the hope that democracy, the political expression of 'Christian intuition of the fraternity of all Mankind' and propelled by love, would burst forth from its various tribal vessels and realise its ecumenical purpose.[24] Toynbee then goes on to elaborate on Bergson's perception, one which he also discerned in Smuts, that it is the mystical genius, the possessor of intellectual *élan*, who is above all the lover of humanity and whose role it is to shake the social kaleidoscope thus causing new ways of being and patterns of living to emerge.[25] As Toynbee noted, Bergson saw society as being divided along psychical lines with some falling into the category of leaders and others into the category of followers. Toynbee thought Bergson was giving a certain degree of support to earlier theses which divided 'a breed of natural-born masters' and 'natural-born slaves'; yet Bergson rejected social philosophies suggestive of rigidity, hierarchy and immobility. He was not proposing social structures modelled on insect life as Toynbee complained of Wells. As Toynbee further noted, Bergson's mystics do not compel concordance but seek to inspire or rely on the 'faculty of sheer mimesis'; they create conceptual environments the contents of which pour into minds of men. Like Bergson, Toynbee thought that in '...the new age, the dominant note in the corporate consciousness of communities' was their feeling that they were 'parts of some larger universe' (which he too saw as a revival of medieval thought), and it was this that explained the willingness of states to shape their sovereign independence to fit international institutions and procedures.[26]

Despite the brevity of his tenure as president, there is no doubt Bergson left his imprint on the ICIC. Valéry, who served on the ICIC's sub-committee of Arts and Letters from the mid-1920s, would repeatedly refer to its goal of begetting and supporting a '*League of Minds*'; he regarded this as not only essential to but also the basic premise of the League. All the treaties and conventions signed by nations would prove to be mere ephemera unless they were 'animated by a sincere and profound *spirit of agreement* – not written agreement but an agreement of minds on certain fundamental points of human thought'. This perception is wholly in keeping with his previous contention that a crisis in the mind, manifest in intellectual unrest and dissonance, was the source of the world's ills.[27] Valéry continued to maintain that this condition was 'the very essence of modernity' and that it made it very difficult, perhaps even impossible, to represent the 'world on a single plan and a single scale'.[28]

One means of overcoming intellectual and social disarray pursued by the sub-committee was the organisation and publishing of correspondence between celebrated intellectuals of the day, most famously an exchange of letters between Einstein and Freud on the question *Why War?* (1933). The first such exchange, however, took place between Valéry and Madariaga and was published in French as *Pour une Société des Esprits* and in English as *Toward a League of Minds* (1933). In his reply to Valéry, Madariaga stated that he too believed the job of the ICIC was to gather under its umbrella those minds best able to uplift world consciousness, élite consciousness especially, as well as each other. This was necessary, he later wrote, if the League were to become a 'more permanent and efficient' body than was indicated by 'its English name'; he declared that '...for a society of nations actually to come to life, a society of minds had first to be fostered'.[29] Madariaga wrote to Valéry that it was they above all who appreciated that intellectual cooperation was the 'soul of the Covenant'; it was an idea, he thought, which might seem to future historians 'the most fertile of all the ideas elevated into general law by the first World Charter'.[30]

What type of understanding did Valéry and Madariaga think provided the basis for a society of minds? Whereas Bergson elevated mystical apprehension, Valéry and Madariaga placed a great deal of emphasis on scientific knowledge. Valéry had long admitted a profound interest in science, its discoveries and inventions, and was very concerned about the apparent collapse of its intellectual foundations. He wanted the idea of disinterested science maintained because intellectual scepticism undermined attempts in the political field to replace 'selfish scheming and disorderly passion' with the rule of reason.[31] For Valéry the demands of scientific research had given rise to an international order which the League should strive to emulate in terms of its structure and organisation as well as in terms of its intellectual practices. Indeed, the seed for such a development had already been planted as the League was founded on the same faith in disinterested intelligence. Scientific researchers, he wrote:

...have defined and given birth to institutions that form a sort of intellectual 'city' covering the whole world. The interests of science, the intellectual interests of men of science – that diffuse nation, which is yet more solid and compact than many political entities – are felt, conceived, organized, and defended with remarkable vigor and lucidity. The League of Nations has done much in this field...In this task it has been aided by the strong connections that hold researchers together as a group, though they may be scattered over the whole planet: connections constituted by shared disciplines, specific techniques, and clearly defined needs. Laboratory research, just as much as the milling of metals, implies division of labor and standardization of instruments – both being expressions of deliberate agreements and a common order.[32]

Valéry denied that harmony among minds implied 'uniformity' for this would 'be monotonous, and certainly undesirable'; variety and novelty were necessary for 'vitality', yet he added the rider that prized differences 'should not turn into obstacles, should not harden in isolation and become inaccessible to exchange'.[33] Given his respect for Bergson, we should not dismiss Valéry's concession to variety as mere gesture, and we should recall that Bergson's philosophy charts a course towards conceptual oneness through urging us to plunge back into the common fluid which is the vital force. Yet the harmony that Valéry evokes reflects the sharp contours of scientific rationalism rather than the fuzzy, glow of esoteric understanding.

In Madariaga's reply to Valéry, the notion that one world order is dictated by the fundamentally harmonic structure of nature, or rather the mind which analyses it, was clearly spelt out. He reflected on the contemporary disarray observing: 'What a vast insane asylum is our world! What discordant gestures! What cacophony of opinions!' As with Valéry, Madariaga was disturbed by the thought that science might have reached the 'limits of the knowable', that it had declared that it was 'helpless to explain the caprice in the soul of atoms'; he worried that science was fragmenting into a series of lesser disciplines, each offering only partial truths rather than a description of the whole. He detected in the realm of art also a destructive psychology; artists, sensing a void at the heart of things, sought 'originality on the periphery, in bizarre and irresponsible gestures'. Such intellectual anarchy had its political manifestation in the form of a wayward individualism and the equally dangerous dream of national sovereignty.[34]

Madariaga privileged the role of mind in the universe claiming for it an architectonic role. Mind was the grand 'organizer of Nature'; in the fashion of Poincaré he stated that mind 'felt' as necessities the principles of order and hierarchy. Conceived as such, mind had the whole of the earth as its field of action. Its major task at that juncture being to develop codes of behaviour that would render the 'human race one vast family'.[35] In using the term mind to refer to a type of agency Madariaga was referring to conscious beings in general; still, he certainly believed there was a place for intellectual leadership and he saw it as the ICIC's task to organise knowledge of the social world, to offer as an alternative to anarchy a 'precise and vigorous scene drawn in clear lines'. He added:

I like to think of the organization for Intellectual Co-operation as the mother cell of a whole field of fermenting minds drawn toward unity, order, and hierarchy...Under its continuous and methodical influence, we should witness the gradual growth of a powerful structure of ideas, a solid framework of freely accepted duties and undeniable obligations, which would bind individuals to nations and nations to organized humanity.[36]

There existed a natural agreement between a putative scientific holism and a virtuous internationalism. William Kay Wallace wrote that science offered a 'pattern of a well-ordered universe', one which favoured humanity over national ideals. Science was also an important symbol of internationalism because of the cultural neutrality of its methods. Science knew 'no language'; scientific workers were blind to matters of class, race and nationality, their sole interest being finding the one best way. Scientific workers were thus especially equipped to assist in the rational control of social and economic life.[37]

The preceding discussion reveals the shifting ideas about the qualities which were imputed to an international mind and the thinking behind representations of the League's Geneva headquarters as a scientific 'research institution' staffed with trained experts devoted to international service and uninhibited by 'issues of nationalism and state sovereignty'.[38] The idea of an international mind, especially when discussed in relation to the League's functional activities, acquired a sharp, technocratic cast; the Economic Organisation, above all (which was assisted by an Economic Intelligence Service created by the Council in 1921 to research and analyse economic statistics), was likened to a laboratory where medical scientists were developing a formula for international salvation. Variations on this theme were offered by Salter and others and it was hoped that one day the Organisation's Economic Committee, seen as the economic equivalent of the ICIC, would be transformed into a comprehensive and technical authority to devise the 'world's economic policy'.[39]

RATIONALISATION AND THE QUEST FOR A NEW ECONOMIC ORDER

In the mid- to late 1920s the spirit of optimism in League policy circles stood in stark contrast with the dreary mood of pessimism which Cecil detected in the work of the Western intelligentsia and literati. Only the League, Cecil observed in 1928, stood between 'civilization' and the abyss; he stressed, in particular, the importance of the ICIC's work in fostering intellectual relations, believing moral disarmament was a necessary prelude to fiscal and military disarmament.[40] Salter had already signalled impatience with the continued preoccupation with themes of social collapse. At the Geneva symposium he spoke with enthusiasm of the forthcoming 1927 World Economic Conference (WEC) complaining that: 'During the last eight years there has been too much ill-founded talk about the "ruin of civilization"';

talk of crisis, an appropriate response in the immediate aftermath of the war, had become 'improper' given that Europe was well on the road to recovery.[41]

Salter's comments suggest a specific understanding of crisis. As we have seen, for Valéry and many others crisis had an elusive and enigmatic quality because its source lay in the depths of the human psyche. However, the League's Economic Committee tended to approach crisis as a technical matter. From at least 1924 the term had been defined in the work of the Committee and the Intelligence Service in economic terms, the changing shape of which these bodies sought to observe and measure. This definition gained increasing currency thereafter so that by the early 1930s the expression 'the crisis' in League policy circles typically referred to economic crisis. What was distinctive about this interpretation of crisis, as well as discussions of its social manifestations, was precisely that it was seen as amenable to control given the application of the correct knowledge as well as a rational appreciation of the need for concerted action. It is telling of perceptions of faltering public enthusiasm for the League (and that it was failing in its patently political role) that the Swiss statesman Gustav Ador, during his period as President of the Economic Committee, stated in 1926 that the League's destiny would lie with the 'new paths...opening out before it' in the economic field.[42]

In the following year the International Institute of Scientific Management (IMI), established in Geneva in 1926 and combining private and official efforts, reported to the Economic Committee that public opinion recognised the existence of a 'world-wide movement of economic thought destined to substitute for the "hit and miss" of laissez-faire economics a planned and sci-entifically ordered progress towards higher levels of material prosperity'. The name ascribed to this movement was rationalisation and it was chiefly in order to study and publicise this approach that the IMI was created. The prominence accorded to rationalisation is worth exploring because it shows that the economic policies of the League were not simply 'guided by the philosophy of liberalism of the English type'.[43] This concept should be of con-temporary interest because although some hailed it as the wave of the future, others viewed it dimly seeing it as a threat to national autonomy and an agent of destructive cultural levelling.

The doctrine of rationalisation achieved prominence at the 1927 WEC. This was considered the signal event in a year that saw the League convene the International Press Conference and the Third General Conference on Communications and Transit, the latter dealing with such as issues as the removal of 'artificial obstructions to transit raised by political boundaries' and the 'speedy transit of news'.[44] The premise underlying the Conference was that the idea and practise of economic solidarity was the gateway to prosperity and peace and the Conference agreed on this principle and on the 'impossibility of national self-sufficiency'.[45] Nonetheless, a return to the old order of *laissez-faire* was discounted. Scientific organisation, its proponents claimed, was based neither on protection nor free-trade; its governing principles were future needs and technical progress. It is significant that these requirements were invoked at the Conference in support of tariff stabilisation and definiteness in classification and terminology of duties, rather than an actual reduction in trade barriers.[46]

The Economic Committee and the 35 members of the Preparatory Committee appointed by the Council worked over 18 months to ensure the 'unity of view' and public interest deemed necessary for its success. For these reasons also, it was decided that the Conference be composed of individuals, appointed by governments and the League Council, with experience in the areas of economics, trade, industry and scientific management. It was thought that 'experts' would approach the Conference agenda more impartially than would government plenipotentiaries and command greater public respect. Conscious of resistance to economic reform from national governments Committee members hoped that through 'propaganda and persuasion...a body of public opinion in favour of...[their] work of international co-operation' could be formed.[47]

In addition to the issue of trade barriers, matters which vexed WEC members were industrial disorganisation, waste and duplication and, in connection with these, the question of how to raise standards of international production and consumption. At the Conference, as well as at the Preparatory Committee meetings, 'great importance...[was]...attached to' rationalisation as a solution to these problems; rationalisation was viewed as one of those 'new conceptions' which if absorbed by international public opinion would help give 'practical effect to the idea of the economic solidarity of the world'.[48]

Because of its innovations in the fields of mass production and scientific management, its huge markets and businesses the size of the General Electric and American Telephone & Telegraph Companies, rationalisation was often identified with contemporary America. In the early 1920s the Bolsheviks raved about American civilisation's 'rationalized industry', 'mechanization' and 'complete automata'; one of their poets, Mayakovski, wrote ecstatically of Chicago, that 'Electro-dynamo-mechanical city!'. Another poet, Gastev, whose Institute for the Scientific Organization of Work and the Mechanization of Man worked on the same lines as American Taylorism, urged his comrades to 'take the storm of the revolution in Soviet Russia, unite it to the pulse of American life, and do our work like a chronometer!' (The Bolsheviks, however, believed that Soviet practice would soon supersede that of the Americans as they were seeking to imbue the whole social machine, and not merely the factories with the 'mechanistic-technical spirit'.) The United States was also regarded with admiration, albeit expressed less effusively, in League economic circles; members of the WEC were 'clearly impressed' by the scale and organisation of economic activity there. In particular, it was a conventional wisdom that attempts to adapt to the 'technical necessities of modern times' foundered in Europe because countries of the continent were stifled within their own narrow markets. For some years, the American state and market would be cited as models for pan-European 'rationalisation' in the form of either a Customs Union or a federation of European States with common coins and stamps.[49]

The concept of rationalisation continued to evoke the dynamism of American enterprise. However, the term actually gained currency and was elaborated in postwar Germany with the International Labour Organisation (ILO) noting in 1929 the 'speed at which' rationalisation has been carried out there; importantly, in that context, rationalisation was an instrument of the state and not just private commerce.[50] The economist W.F. Bruck claimed the term was coined during the Great War by the industrialist and scholar Walther Rathenau and the engineer Wichard von Moellendorff (along with the term *planwirtschaft* from which the word planning was adapted) whose job it was to 'regulate production and consumption at the War Office' and that it originally meant industrial efficiency.[51] However, in a review of a major study of the phenomenon in America and Europe by Robert Brady, the Oxford economist D.H. Macgregor explained that the word *Rationalieserung* was first widely used to refer to a period of state directed 'Rationing, viâ a period of "cleaning up" *(Sanierung)*' of industry as part of a process of economic rehabilitation. (It was used in this sense in connection with the policy of cartelisation of the coal and steel industries.) Whatever the exact timing of its appearance, it is certainly clear that the term rationalisation soon acquired a grander meaning, coming to stand for the 'positive and futuristic reorganisation' of entire industries by the state so that they would function in the national interest; the state, because of its commanding view of society, was best able to articulate rational purposes.[52]

The WEC's *Final Report* reflected German thinking on the topic, presenting rationalisation as a systematic pattern of ideas and techniques conducive to efficiency and human betterment. It was because of its larger significance that the ILO insisted that the term should not simply be confused with what the Americans referred to as 'taylorism' where that simply meant waste elimination. The *Final Report* of the Conference defined rationalisation in a way that was, as Sir Arthur Balfour put it, 'fluid and progressive'. This was necessary to make clear that the term did not imply sterilisation and to accommodate different national approaches, in particular an emphasis was put on its application either by the state or by private enterprise. The *Final Report* thus commended to governments:

...the methods of technique and of organization designed to secure the minimum waste of either effort or material. It includes the scientific organization of labour, standardisation of material and or products, simplification of processes of improvements in the system of transport and marketing...Its judicious and constant application is calculated to secure...[for]...the community greater stability and a higher standard in the conditions of life.[53]

CARTELISATION

Rationalisation was discussed as a development taking place in the international and not just the domestic arena and in this regard it too it had a commercial and governmental significance. The expression '*internationalised rationalisation*' was used at the 1927 WEC to refer to international industrial agreements institutionalised in the form of cartels and syndicates; examples cited included the International Incandescent Lamp Agreement, the *Société anonyme internationale de télégraphie sans fil* and the London-based International Rail-makers Association. Some delegates urged governments to remove barriers to cartelisation putting the view that in cutting across state boundaries cartels could render customs barriers 'partially useless' and political opposition to tariff reform pointless.[54] The vogue for international cartels also sprang from the belief that they would serve to break down cultural and intellectual parochialism; cartelisation entailed standardisation of materials, parts and products of 'international importance', agreements on the definition of terms, the methods employed and the scope of statistics used in industrial research and the harmonisation of national scientific research efforts.[55] For these reasons the 'great federations within industries' were seen as 'much more truly conducive to real internationalism'.[56] This benign view of cartels, as well as their scientific aura, was reaffirmed at the Inter-Parliamentary Commercial Conference held at Rio de Janiero in August 1927, which issued a resolution calling for the establishment of responsibly governed international cartels in the hope of intensifying 'the world's moral, political and social solidarity' and promoting 'rational concentration and co-operation'.[57]

Scepticism about the benefits of rationalisation in this form was clearly articulated at the WEC and after. Even supporters of the formation of international ententes noted that there was immense opposition to them; some governments worried that they could undermine the sovereignty of states while public opinion feared that industrial concentration would lead to monopoly pricing and ruthless economic exploitation. Because American trusts had abused their positions in these last two respects the American delegate H.M. Robinson attempted to dampen European enthusiasm for rationalisation in the sense of industrial concentration. Grigori Sokolnikoff, representing the USSR, declared that cartelisation was a 'further enforcement of the tyranny of the great international capitalistic organisations of the world market'.[58] Delegates speaking on behalf of consumer groups and workers' organisations in capitalist countries did not rule out cartels altogether; however, they were insistent that combines be brought under 'uniform' national and international supervision in order to prevent the growth of a 'new and economic tsarism'.[59] Mme Freundlich of Austria proposed that cartels should be watched over by a 'permanent institution' made up of men and women representing every class; such a 'world economic centre' could control the process of organising the world market to ensure that it resulted in secure living conditions for all.[60]

International supervision was deemed necessary in order to discourage rationalisation on a purely national basis. While it was emphasised at the Conference that the state should play an important part in advancing ratio-nalisation in the domestic sphere, as well as ensuring that its benefits were dispersed among the wider community, the concern was raised that the term might become a euphemism for economic nationalism. Moderate protection had been defended as an adjunct to the rationalisation of domestic industry and was often described in a neutral fashion, much to the annoyance of orthodox economists, as scientific protection or safeguarding; in these guises protection was distinguished from *tarifs de combat*. Nonetheless, the concern was expressed that rationalisation, if regarded solely as a means of improving the technical and industrial capacity of a state or group of states, would be perceived as an economic weapon by others and would become, according to a Polish delegate to the WEC, a source of 'jealousy' and friction.[61]

In any case the representation of cartels as agents of beneficent interna-tionalism was not sufficiently persuasive and the Conference was unable to reach a 'conclusion of principle' on international industrial agreements. A cautiously worded resolution in the *Final Report* of the WEC simply requested governments not to place obstacles in the way of the 'benefits' that such agreements 'might secure'. International supervision of international agreements was also rejected with a number of delegates claiming that it would entail unacceptable political interference in states. The Conference instead recommended governments forestall abuse by means of publicity, a position reaffirmed at the Inter-Parliamentary Commercial Conference, and that the LON should study the 'operations and effects' of such agreements.[62]

FROM RATIONALISATION TO WORLD PLANNING

The 1927 WEC was regarded as an enormous triumph for the League and its economic agency. This not only because there was unanimous agreement, albeit non-binding, to reduce tariffs and address the issue of customs nomen-clature. After listening to an account given by Salter at Chatham House of the WEC's achievements in respect to commercial and industrial policy, Major Leigh Aman declared that 'in the near future the tariff question would occupy a position of comparatively little importance and that the Economic Conference itself would live by reason of the publicity it had given to the question of rationalisation and reconstruction of industry as a whole'.[63] Soon after, the newly established Economic Consultative Committee, which was in its make-up a microcosm of the conference and seen as a breakthrough in functional representation, delightedly reported to the Economic Organi-sation that the word rationalisation was being used with striking frequency in Anglo-Saxon countries; its general usage indicated a 'profound "mental revolution"' was underway. The IMI, which published in its bulletin information on private and public developments in the area, hoped one day to establish a universal definition of rationalisation.[64]

Overall, the WEC was said to have shown that nationalism was dead and that the prevalent idea of the twentieth century would be international collaboration. The WEC came to be portrayed as an important step in the direction of scientific control of world economic affairs. Sir Herbert Samuel told a conference of the League of Nations Union in London in December 1927 that all around the 'world...the old individual system of competition' was 'giving way' with 'centralization, amalgamation, rationalization' taking its place. He proclaimed:

...because I believe that the future lies along the lines of international co-operation rather than international rivalry, because I believe that the lines of scientific development can be developed by international conference...I say God speed to the economic movement inside the League of Nations.[65]

Projecting a significant role for the League in coordinating the economic and social fields was even more crucial as it became clear that the LON could not effectively fulfil its explicitly political functions. In 1931 Greaves counselled against focussing on the 'dramatic' but 'negative' question of disarmament and the activities of the Council and the Assembly; he insisted that much more crucial in eliminating the underlying causes of war was the empowering of the League's 'organs of international disinterestedness' by which he meant bodies like the Economic Organisation and the ICIC.[66] A universalising telos continued to be invested in science, with Bertrand Russell writing in 1932 that it had already made the world 'one economic unit' even though political institutions, due to the play of passions and prejudices, lagged behind.[67]

While at the 1927 WEC the words international and world were often used interchangeably, the organisers of the Social Economic Congress in Amsterdam in 1931 (which comprised both government and non-government participants, members of the 1927 WEC and representatives of international institutions) emphasised that they had deliberately chosen the word 'world' rather than 'international' for the title so as to highlight the intensity of the 'growth towards unity'.[68] Against the background of economic crisis, speakers from Britain and Europe condemned the 'national egotism' of governments and their adherence to the dated principle of economic self-sufficiency; citing a 'new awareness' of the historical trend towards unity, they lamented that governments were not fully conscious of this fact.[69] Speakers also complained how little the League and its Economic Organisation had done to realise the goal of a world economic centre. Lewis L. Lorwin of the Institute of Economics of the Brookings Institution stated that as 'political sovereignty must and is being modified' it was logical that the League and the ILO should expand into a 'world planning board' and armed with a 'Five-Year World Plan'.[70]

The words rationalisation and planning were often used synonymously. Major L.F. Urwick, director of the IMI from 1931 to 1933 and a participant in the Amsterdam Congress, wrote in *Management of Tomorrow* (1933) of the application of the 'scientific point of view' to world economics, describing this as both rationalisation and international planning.[71] Although the concepts would continue to be conflated, planning was used increasingly to refer to a more comprehensive and detailed programme of state action with rationalisation as one of its foremost techniques. The symbolic impact of the First (1928–32) and Second (1932–37) Russian Five Year Plans greatly accounts for this terminological switch. At the 1927 WEC Russian delegates, insisting that rationalisation undertaken in the absence of socialism could only harm workers, claimed that the Soviet state was applying science to and rationalising its economy in all its component parts.[72] In the early 1930s in Anglo-Saxon countries Russian endeavours to construct a rationalist economy were reported with awe in mainstream publications. The Five Year Plan, Paul Einzig claimed, was a 'household word in England'. Compared to the energy and sweep of the Russians plans, capitalist rationalisation could seem hesitant and colourless, although the vaunted international dimensions of the latter project meant it could be described as being of 'vaster magnitude'. It was understood at the 1927 WEC and in the years following that Moscow and Geneva stood for competing myths of peace and prosperity.[73]

At the same time, Soviet experiments in rationalisation were recorded dutifully by the IMI and discussed by the League's Economic Consultative Committee as examples of a more general push to intellectualise experience; the key issue from the perspective of these bodies being the application of scientific methods to industry rather than ownership. Urwick cited approvingly Obolensky-Ossinski's statement to the Amsterdam Congress, which the latter attended as a Member of the Institute for Economic Research of the State Planning Commission (Gosplan), that the 'one general premise for social economic planning' was that the 'plan...cannot base its methodology on anything else but science – the quintessence of social thought and experience'. Soviet electrification schemes could be thus treated as instances of rationalisation alongside private sector initiatives such as the Paris-based Commercial Radio International Committee, the International Standardisation Association and the Advertising Research Institute in Vienna.[74]

MACHINERY AND THE METAPHYSICS OF RATIONALISATION

As the preceding examples underline, rationalisation was strongly associated with the techniques and devices of modernity, especially those which could be seen as challenging physical and conceptual boundaries. In *Forward From Chaos* (1933), the British engineer Allan Young anticipated some of the themes which feature in contemporary discussions of globalisation. He rendered rationalisation as a metaphysic which he called 'Industrial Flow' and treated electrical machinery and scientific methods as its congealed expressions. Young also endowed the industrial flow with a telos, writing that it had an '...all-embracing sweep; recognises no frontiers of country or creed and in a steadily increasing degree is becoming the very life-blood of our civilization...[and is]...ultimately leading to...a world family animated by a common interest and purpose'. But what he found most fascinating about the freshly dawning 'Electric-Machine-Power-Age' was that it was greatly '"speeding-up" world activity'; the effect of this was ever more rapid flows of money and, most importantly, the flow of knowledge, especially in the form of industrial research:

The advent of radio art has provided a revolutionary change in the method and rate of thought dissemination. The human voice is now able to encircle the globe in the twinkling of an eye, and this was forcibly impressed on all of us who were fortunate enough to 'listen-in' to that truly wonderful 'Empire Broadcast' arranged by the B.B.C. last Christmas Day. It is thus possible for me to project my thoughts instantly into the mind of someone living on the opposite side of this planet, and possibly by the establishment of such contact through the medium of the human voice, to cause immediate action to be taken, having far-reaching consequences. The evolution of the radio machine, which makes all this possible, seems to be one of the very biggest happenings in our civilization...I stress the importance of the great acceleration we are witnessing in the whole process of translating thought into action...Before very long it is certain that man, in addition to being able to project his thoughts around the globe, will have his vision similarly extended...It will definitely bring Man to a position where his voice and his vision can encircle the globe. The world is practically becoming a very small place, and this process of virtually reducing the physical dimensions of our planet is being accelerated by the evolution of three machines – the aeroplane, the radio machine and the television machine.[75]

The parallels between Young's conception of electric flows annihilating the distances breaking between states, symbolised especially in the workings of the radio and the aeroplane, and the contemporary rhetoric of globalisation should not require elaboration. Another striking continuity is Young's grounding of his metaphysic of flows in the vitalistic conception of reality which some philosophers were ascribing to quantum physics. Young cited a 1931 address given by Jan Christian Smuts, who was intellectually drawn to a vitalistic interpretation of holism, on the 'Scientific World-Picture of To-day' wherein the latter claimed that scientists had forsaken mechanistic and materialistic explanations, having established that 'electronic energy' underlay and formed the world of matter. Drawing on this notion allowed Young to bathe internationalisation in a naturalistic light. He claimed that since matter had dissolved into electricity, reality for the scientist, as Smuts put it, was now a 'seething state of material flux', and he used this conception to underwrite the claim that social experience should be viewed as a 'seething economic and political flux' activated by the streams of energy unleashed through scientific invention. In the midst of a world characterised by 'movement and change', where 'Nothing is quiescent, and finality is unknown' national borders seemed anachronistic.[76]

While Young sought to evoke a sense of excitement with his emphasis on the fluidity and indeterminacy of modern existence he was not singing a paean to chaos. To render experience as plastic is usually to insist on its malleability. Young hoped that a new generation emerging from the universities and trained in the fields of engineering and scientific management would seize and mould the flux of life, that they would embrace that marriage of technics to doctrine of social progress which the scientist R. Plank, in a 1931 address called 'Engineering and Modern Culture', named 'metatechnics'. Young wrote that while the 'crisis in world affairs' was grave it also offered an opportunity to use scientific knowledge to undertake a 'planned thrust' just as was being done under the Five Year Plan and President Roosevelt's New Deal. The crisis thus marked the beginning of a 'new era' in so far as humanity was now in a position to master the machine environment, free itself from fear and accelerate progress towards a 'world state'.[77]

In relating the themes of crisis and science Young was continuing and elaborating on a story that had been told since the beginning of the century. Wells was telling it well before the war and would continue to do so into the 1930s. I observed that the ideal of one world was promoted in *A Modern Utopia*, *War in the Air* and *The World Set Free* and it appeared again in his 1933 science fiction work *The Shape of Things to Come*, a work which Lawrence Wittner writes 'inspired the formation of small "Wellsian societies" in various parts of the world'. (It was turned into a motion picture called *Things to Come* [1936].) *The Shape of Things to Come* canvassed themes Wells had already touched on in *The World Set Free*. It is the tale of a civilisation breaking down as a result of decades of relentless warfare, involving the use of bombing aeroplanes and poisoned gas, and consequent pestilence. Humanity regresses to tribal forms existing amidst a state of nature; the main preoccupation of the various national chiefs being military security, hence the nations are described as Combatant States. Yet elsewhere, as well explained in the 1935 film script based on the book, civilisation is being renewed under the stewardship of engineers, mechanics and airmen working under such rubrics as World Communications and Wings over the World and sharing a belief in the 'freemasonry of efficiency' and the 'brotherhood of science'. The airman John Cabal asserts of his selfless crew: 'We are the natural trustees of civilisation when everything else has failed.'[78] This brotherhood dispensed from their aeroplanes an anaesthetising 'Gas of Peace' thereby rendering the nation-state extinct.[79] Cabal then declares: 'And now for the World of the Airmen and a new start for mankind'; humanity enters a 'New Amazing World', a great, gleaming, hermetically sealed technopolis.[80] Yet, as in *The World Set Free*, a melancholy note was struck at the denouement for Wells again raised questions about the notion of perpetual progress which was represented by the construction of an awesome space gun intended to shoot men and women to the moon. The same ambivalence was reflected in the invocation of space as a symbol of human freedom on the one hand, and the dismissal of it as 'that outer horror' on the other. Wells had a character called Passworthy ask in the final pages whether there is 'never to be rest' for humanity from all this endless effort and striving. The response comes from a descendent of Cabal and it echoed the previous work, for the choice would seem to be between unending and strenuous attempts to master the universe or a descent into decay and 'nothingness'.[81] The later Cabal warns his fellows against the temptation, a warning wholly in keeping with James's point that a peace economy should not merely be a pleasure-economy, to become 'indolent, fantasising, idlers and pleasure-seekers', nothing more than a 'planet-load of holiday makers, spinning to destruction. Just a crowning festival before the dark...' Such could be the path to ruin. Yet Wells had Cabal make the the very Jamesian point that to live to the 'best effect' is to live 'nearer the bone'; the 'best of life', Cabal adds, 'lies nearest to the edge of death'.[82]

The meanings attached to machinery in the interwar years swung between the exultant and the ominous. As we saw with Young, radio was seen as a means of harmonising thoughts and some urged that the League should utilise more extensively wireless technology to inform the world of its activities and promote the cause of moral disarmament. In the face of the 'misuse of wireless facilities for propagandist purposes' on the continent of Europe international control of broadcast propaganda was also proposed.[83] Aircraft too were portrayed as mystical vehicles melding minds together. The British League of Nations Union, which followed the ICIC in seeking to foster an international mind, in its broadsheet *Headway* in 1933 gave Esperanto the happy description the 'Aeroplane of Language' and likened it to those 'distance-annihilating' inventions which were rendering nationalism an anachronism. (Bergson at the ICIC had earlier rejected suggestions that the League should promote Esperanto or any other universal language. To do so would be an artificial imposition. It was thought much better to encourage spontaneous exchange among and an intermingling of the world's various tongues.) At the same time there was considerable talk of the air menace. There were efforts to persuade states attending the ill-fated Disarmament Conference of 1932 and 1933 to accept international control of civil aviation and the organic internationalisation of air forces. There was a Wellsian science fiction aura surrounding the revived proposals for a League Police Force made in this context. David Davies, founder of the first chair in international relations at the University of Aberystwyth, advocated in early 1932 that the League should be the world's policeman, stating that members of such a force must 'be relatively small in numbers' comprising only 'highly trained technicians and experts' such as 'airmen, chemists, engineers'. A plan to internationalise aviation and establish a League Air Force was put forward by the French government in November 1932 following Germany's first departure from the Conference. The notion of arming Geneva, however, in the interest of disarmament was widely dismissed as ludicrous by governments and newspapers.[84]

Brady too used the word rationalisation to refer to those technological and economic processes which he thought were annihilating the 'age-old physical barriers of time and space' and dissolving distinctions between nations as well as metropolitan and rural zones. Like Young he used the term flux to evoke the shattering effects of these processes as well as a more seamless conception of experience; yet more so than Young he emphasised the way in which rationalisation was also generating a uniform and rigid social space. The age of electricity implied a more standardised or '"streamlined" age'; further, rationalisation, in the sense of conscious control, was no mere expression of the will to power, precisely because it was a deduction from the solid knowledge generated by the natural science disciplines.[85] Brady defended moves towards political and economic integration and control at the state and international levels by pointing to a growing unity among the various branches of the natural sciences which itself was predicated upon a common embrace of an 'organismic conception of natural phenomena'. Actually, the conception of the universe Brady attributed to science was built from mutually informing biological and mechanical analogies, as revealed in his claim that the entire universe according to science was ultimately a 'single immensely elaborated and almost infinitely intricate and life-like machine'. The fusion of these analogies resulted in a picture which, while admitting complexity, pointed to a reality more rigid, structured and complete than was suggested by Young's metaphysics of flow. Brady asserted that rationalisation was grounded in pragmatism and radical empiricism but for him these terms signified scientific methods and objectivity rather than a voluntarist and mentalist conception of experience. Most importantly, Brady's social machine was not spontaneously adjusting and required intervention by technicians to keep it running smoothly. The biological notions of 'functional dependence and interdependence' and 'balance' similarly pointed to a need for 'harmonious coordination and integration of...separate parts and processes' in the interest of the whole. These metaphorical implications explain the presence of words like functionalisation, engineering and coordination in the '*patois*' of those urging rationalisation and planning of the social realm.[86]

Spengler in his *Man and Technics* (1932) persisted with his dire predictions concerning the mechanisation and organisation of the world. Eternal motion which is the ideal of machine civilisation was reaching a 'highly dangerous period of over-tension'. The natural world was being poisoned by an artificial one. 'All things organic', he wrote, 'are dying in the grip of organisation.' The march of the machine, according to Spengler, not only destroyed biological diversity, it flattened and sterilised social experience. That people were growing weary of endless conquest and the spread of gargantuan cities was apparent in the springing up of nature cults, occultism and spiritualism. Describing the same condition of *ennui* and unrest which so vexed the likes of Valéry and Madariaga, Spengler observed of the period: 'It is the spirit of Rome in the Age of Augustus. Out of satiety of life, men take refuge from civilization in the more primitive parts of the earth, in vagabondage, in suicide.' And it was the *taedium vitae* pervading the European world that greatly explained production shifting to non-Western countries. Spengler wrote: '*This* is the real and final basis of the unemployment that prevails in the white countries. It is no mere crisis, but the *beginning of a catastrophe*.' He joined another declinist Alexander Raven in predicting that an increasingly soft and degenerate Western culture would be eaten up from within; it would thus become increasingly susceptible to attacks by nomadic forces from without.[87]

It was not only defenders of provincial *Kultur* such as Spengler who saw rationalisation of Western life as culminating in a metaphysical turn towards death. Walther Rathenau, who was credited with providing the first example of 'mechanized trade and industry on a large scale' and whom Brady acknowledged as a father of German rationalisation, predicted in *The New Society* (1921) that the Age of Mechanism entailed a 'world-revolution' which materially meant the dissolution of class structures and transcendently the liberation of the human spirit. Yet he came to view the rational society of the future in a dimmer light. Mechanisation reflected a 'spirit of abstract utility and systematically futile thought, without wonder and without humour of the greatest complexity and at the same time of deadly uniformity'; mechanised life is a life of 'endless gyration' devoid of any deeper purpose hence 'in the depths of consciousness the world shudders at itself'.[88] Addressing Spengler's critique directly, Brady sought to respond to concerns raised about the cultural and spiritual implications of rationalisation. He accepted that the spread of electrification networks could see the emergence of a 'highly urbanized mass culture' of the American kind which would 'overflow national boundaries' and extinguish local and national variation; he accepted that it might lead to the suppression of individual spontaneity and the demystification of existence. The arguments Brady used to counter these fears are especially revealing in the light of current debates about the merits of globalisation. He argued first of all that the age of the masses necessarily meant a shift in emphasis from individual freedom to that of plenty, comfort and security, and rationalisation in the sense of economic planning was the means to this end. Standardisation of attitudes and modes of existence was a price that had to be paid. Yet he also acknowledged that differences must be respected, stating that, as with the Soviet Union, plans for a United States of Europe would only work if they allowed for 'cultural autonomy'.[89]

Brady pointed to the spiritually liberating potential of rationalisation, arguing that far from eliminating cultural 'diversity' and producing 'one dead level' once 'certain minimum levels of comfort' had been achieved positive differences and creativity would flourish. Brady argued international economic integration would facilitate cultural borrowings and thus the

appearance of new hybrid forms. As a cultural dynamic, he wrote, rationalisation had resulted in an unparalleled 'profusion, a luxuriance of forms,
styles and modes'. While in some respects it entailed uniformity, rationalisation also, when its more explosive side was emphasised, suggested: 'Speed,
kaleidoscopic change, size, color, variation.'[90]

Brady captured the optimistic and cosmopolitan spirit of rationalisation
depicting it as spreading outward from Germany, across Europe and around
the world. The state he considered to be an 'historical anachronism'
undermined by economic empires, international agreements and transnational association. He condemned it for standing in the way of further
international rationalisation, the culmination of which he believed was
centralised world planning. Turning Spengler on his head, he wrote of the
nation-state as a leftover from a dead past futilely seeking to repel the more
virile forces dwelling in scientific achievement and the organisational arts.
Brady doubted whether even 'the recrudescence of extreme German
nationalism under the Hitlerites' would impair the impulsion towards
integration.[91]

NATIONAL PLANNING

The influential Political Economic Planning (PEP) group in Britain was at
that time defending planning in a similar fashion to that of Brady. It
announced that planning was for liberty – it would result not only in greater
comfort but also more 'colour and variety'. (It is perhaps telling of its ultimate
tendency toward social monism, that the publication presented Britain's
Electricity Grid as the 'symbol and stimulus of efforts towards' scientific,
national planning. As a closed circuit the Grid had a social significance rather
different from the unbounded movement which the futurists saw in
electricity. Note that the ahistorical order of the Grid was opposed to the
'Chaos' and 'frictions' induced by private enterprise.)[92] Just when elabora-
tions of rationalisation had reached their most sophisticated stage the notion
was being subsumed by the rhetoric of planning. As I have indicated, this
development owed much to the air of vast promise which had gathered
around the Five Year Plan; the grand projects which came under that rubric
were juxtaposed with images of democracies in chaos. David Mitrany wrote
in 1937 that although initially derided, the Russian programme of national
economic planning (*planovie khoziastvo*) soon elicited almost universal
'worship'. While this is an exaggeration it is telling that, as was commented
in the early 1930s, even liberals were finding it 'worthwhile to steal from
the Russians the word plan'. Against the background of the mass economic
insecurity it also mattered that planning was conceived as an instrument of
social justice. Despite attempts, especially in Britain to make it bear the stamp
of social welfare, rationalisation continued to be associated with the
conception of men as machines.[93]

It should be remembered as well that during its rhetorical heyday the concept of rationalisation was often presented as a process and policy of international proportions; planning, however, was discussed largely in relation to the national domain. Reduced interest in the concept and practise of international rationalisation was also reflected in the demise in 1934 of the IMI which had struggled for years to obtain financial support from governments. In 1931 Zimmern warned that national planning was but a short step away from the 'Economic Nationalism' which lay at the 'root' of the crisis. He urged governments to return to the goals set by the 1927 WEC and embrace a

...common policy of economic internationalism. The devotees of 'planning' must learn to think internationally and the devotees of the free movement of goods, capital and labour must be ready to interpret *laissez faire, laissez passer* in a new sense – as a command by the organized peoples of the world. For the re-establishment of confidence involves international political policy as well as international economic policy.[94]

Zimmern was involved with other members of the ICIC at that time in an effort to counter the potent force of nationalism, urging the use of wireless and cinematography to transmit fraternal feelings and encourage pride in world civic duty, as he would continue to do up until the late 1930s. The ICIC also persisted with attempts to foster scientific relations in an effort to provide an enlightening contrast to political and economic autarky. When it came to economic planning, however, nationalism was on the ascendant and the Soviet programme was seen as exemplary in this regard. Echoing statements made by Soviet delegates in respect to rationalisation at the 1927 WEC, Alexander Cohn, Director of Russia's Institute of Foreign Trade, announced at the Amsterdam Congress that scientific planning was possible only under socialism. However much it came under the cover of scientific policies, international planning was but a staging post on the way to a period of ultra-imperialism. More importantly however, he argued that the '...experience of the Soviet Union has shown that it is possible for planning to be carried out on a national basis'; proposals for capitalist planning through the League which had neither a 'power nor the function of planning', were thus pernicious, futile and unnecessary.[95] The Congress witnessed repeated avowals of the necessity and inevitability of world planning, however its organisers commented afterwards that national planning had been 'more clearly envisaged than world planning, which hovered like a will-o'-the-wisp before the Congress, eluding concrete expression'.[96]

Young continued to entertain the possibility of international economic organisation, expressing the hope that the 1933 WEC would be regarded in future as the first stage in the creation of an 'International Planning Control Board. A supreme international authority of this nature could concern itself with those world problems generated by industrial flow between Nations.' However, he also offered the modest suggestion that world planning could begin within the confines of the British Empire which was then being transformed from an imperial institution into a mutually beneficial arrangement among independent members of a Commonwealth. In this more utilitarian and egalitarian format, this body was deemed to be a candidate for rational organisation, and Young proposed the establishment of an 'Empire Planning Control Board' to act as the 'supreme industrial authority' and solve 'problems in accordance with scientific and ethical principles'.[97]

The prospects for so-called Empire Planning were greater in the early 1930s than they were for international planning. The League's Economic Section reported in October 1932 that the possibility of establishing a body to oversee the domain of economic activity should be discounted. As many expected, given the fraught nature of the Preparatory Committee meetings which preceded it, as well as the lack of success of international conferences in 1930 and 1931 on the tariff truce, the June 1933 WEC collapsed within two weeks. Sir Frederic Leith-Ross had told a meeting of the WEC's Preparatory Committee of Experts in January 1933 that the coming idea was national planning:

In the first place I feel that the situation has not improved. The fact is...*new ideas and conditioning* have developed which leave radically altered the pre-war situation. The international balance is definitely changed and throughout the world almost every country is taking steps *to organise its production...to create an economy on a nationalist basis.*[98]

Dr Charles Schrecker told a meeting at Chatham House in November 1933 that with the failure of the WEC the hope of solving economic problems in an international sense had to be abandoned. Some put this down to the triumph of politics over scientific rationality. However, Schrecker argued that science had now made 'relative autarchy' a viable policy, as was being demonstrated in Germany, Russia and the United States. He added that despite much conservative opposition to this 'phenomena of a new age', moves to render the 'British Empire an economic unit' through arrangements such as the Ottawa Agreements on imperial preference, (which was projected as international rationalisation and planning in embryonic form), especially if these were accompanied by increased domestic use of science would soon see Britain embrace this development.[99] PEP dismissed the 1933 WEC's goal of forging a trade agreement arguing that as long as states were a 'mob' rather than a 'team' the time would not be ripe for 'world planning'; it announced that the dreadful failure of the WEC had not only put national planning 'on the map' but confirmed the PEP's position that 'planning begins at home'. This outlook was defended as 'realist' although the publication added the rider that domestic stabilisation through an enlargement of purchasing power was a necessary precursor to the expansion of international trade and thus the best contribution Britain could make to international planning.[100]

The Economic Organisation sought to accommodate determinedly nationalist approaches to planning by extending its coverage of domestic standard of living issues, including the economics of consumption and nutrition, in the mid-1930s. The Economic Organisation thought that these moves reflected an important 'change in the politico-economic outlook': the belief that solving war and political turmoil demanded the satisfaction of wants within national communities no less than an improvement in international commercial relations. The Economic and Financial Committees, which were adjourned in in 1939, kept this point in view when they met in 1942 to address the question of postwar reconstruction. By that stage, excited discussions of plans for a new social order were well under way in democratic countries. But again, as an ILO report underlined, the idea of a new order in the sense of economic planning was conceived by many political actors and commentators within a national framework and branded postwar reconstruction. Advocates of government intervention framed wartime planning as a patriotic necessity; due to its conduct of a battle economy the state had acquired much prestige in the area of economic administration. These sentiments did not preclude support for international economic agreements and institutions and on a more extensive basis than in the interwar years, but their prevalence suggested that any such agreements and institutions would have to operate within defined limits.[101]

CONCLUSION

The rhetoric of new orders is a way of responding to perceptions of crisis and an attendant sense of social insecurity. However, predictions of dramatic social transformation coupled with attempts to generate excitement about possible tomorrows are also strategies of persuasion with the aim of rearranging intellectual and political priorities. In the wake of the Great War promises of a new dawn in world economic affairs were a means of addressing social anxieties. Yet they also marked a determined effort to deliberately produce a harmony of interests. Proposals for rationalisation or planning on an international basis, by which was often meant Europe and the British Empire, were grounded in pictures of a planet crisscrossed by streams of energy. While there are limits to historical comparisons the parallels between the meanings accorded rationalisation and those attached to globalisation are instructive. Both terms have a dual significance. As with rationalisation before it, the commercial and technological manifestations of globalisation are evoked through metaphors of flux and fluidity which are in turn often grounded in a metaphysical interpretation of science. At the same time, the disorder generated by globalisation is seen as facilitating and warranting further global governance. Rationalisation was represented as a set of commercial flows yet it was also argued that the 'spread of rationalisation' in this sense opened up people's minds to the possibility of rational organisation of world economic life through intergovernmental cooperation.[102]

The overlap between the political rhetoric of the interwar period and that of today in respect to world afffairs underlines the point that vaunted new directions in history are just as likely to reflect past imaginings and yearnings as the actual contours of unfolding events. To make a related point, to draw pictures of tomorrow is less to engage in induction than to attempt to direct debate and remould the course of events. The comparison between the rhetoric of rationalisation and that of globalisation is also valuable in that it underlines the interested and historically contingent nature of tales of things to come. Rationalisation lost much of its sociological and international significance by the mid-1930s. As many perceptive commentators noted, despite its cosmopolitan wrappings governments had always negotiated its meaning in line with their national interests. If only subconsciously, in the minds of nations international economic cooperation was sought in order to enhance their capacity to 'live more intensely the national life that belonged to them'.[103] In the sense of industrial reorganisation, the word rationalisation continued to be used in connection with national planning schemes into the 1940s although in later decades its meaning would contract to techniques of industrial efficiency. Globalisation is not quite the shimmering fantasy that rationalisation was, although it is regarded with a comparable measure of ambivalence. If indeed it is deeply rooted in experience it is likely to prove more coercive of social behaviour; on the other hand, to the extent that globalisation interpreted in an expansive fashion is also something of a will-o'-the-wisp the term could well, depending on the tide of events and rhetorical fashions, meet an equally inglorious linguistic fate. It is the emergence and elaboration of the rhetoric of globalisation, as well as the composition of further new world order scenarios in the postwar era, that I explore in subsequent chapters.

5   COLD DECADENCE AND PLANETARY UTOPIAS

THE RETREAT FROM MOBILITY

The beginning of the twentieth century marked the dawn of a new age, one of complexity and confusion. Science proffered odd, elliptical accounts of the micro and macro worlds. Philosophy, art and literature were entranced by the polymorphic and bizarre. The ideas circulating in all these fields were believed to spring from the same source – the temporally bound, discontinuous mindset of the modern. The idea of temporality, interpreted as velocity and ferocious change rather than a languorous unwinding of events, was manifest in the commotion of city life, the crazed behaviour of crowds and the proliferation of consumer goods. Experience no longer offered moments of rest or stability. It had become a mad rush into unknown realms. Revolutionary syndicalism and fascism, revelling in iconoclastic destruction, were seen as the sharpest political expressions of the time doctrine. Yet we have seen that images of chaos were generated by those who embraced a form of activism which sought to regiment flux. The impulse to organisation, operating at both national and international levels, was apparent from the first decade of the century. The Great War greatly reinforced this trend. It revealed the possibility of state control of disruptive and wasteful private forces but it also led to calls for the control of the state itself to the extent that it was seen as a vessel out of which poured baser instincts. A rational world system would be stripped of competitive excesses and national egotism. It should be recalled that those designing world orders drew on representations of science according to which it was a solidly grounded, intellectually coherent and unified body of thought. Prewar radical empiricism, by contrast, had phenomenonalistic and particularistic tendencies.

Fantasies of world order in the interwar period were not solely cast in mechanistic and futuristic terms. The notion of a world mind was discussed as though it were a viscous fluid penetrating and fusing together individual minds. The triumph of the notion of world unity was also seen as the revivification of an earlier cosmopolitanism. At the same time, it was the very tools of modernity, such as the radio and aeroplane, which were seen as propelling humanity, although somewhat mysteriously, towards its common and happy destiny. To the extent that the task of mind is to gain an appreciation of the rational order of the cosmos and translate this into social forms, such conceptual and temporal ambiguities can be resolved. The movement towards oneness denotes a shared awareness of the laws of the universe which dictate our rational and moral natures.

In public debate the prevailing tendency was to highlight the rationalist and forward-looking credentials of world order plans; but whether in its mechanical or millenial guise the new world order can be seen as a response to the disruptive side of modernity and not just to the persistence in social life of primal instincts. I have pointed to the two-sided character of modernity; the term implied both organisation and ungoverned energy. The general drift in the interwar period was towards conscious control. This was the commanding principle of the new world order. Yet there were forces abroad which this order could not tame. Fascist Italy gave expression to modernity's chaotic side in the field of international politics, although its futurist nationalism exuded a primeval air. A milder example of the confrontation between modernity's two major tendencies in the context of debates about international politics is provided by Dewey's critique of Wells's idea of a world state. For Dewey, Wells's scheme was a recipe for a dead and dull universe lacking in spontaneity and genuine variety, principles which he thought were underwritten by the new physics.

Adherents to the League ideal, especially those who wished it to become a superstate, sought to address this concern by conceiving of it as an institution that was flexible enough to accommodate these qualities and even a degree of vagueness. So here we have an attempt to reconcile that side of modernity which elevates the many with its other side which tends towards technocratic uniformity. Yet many in one can be a deceptive formula in that it may allow only for harmless or officially sanctioned forms of otherness. Wells made this clear in stating that the unity of human society, which he regarded as an inescapable condition, '...must be politically organized. Internationalism must not merely link diversities, but govern them'; this sentiment found substantial support in official League circles.[1]

By the early 1930s the dream of one world order had begun to disintegrate. E.H. Carr has been accused of exaggeration in painting the 1920s as a period a great optimism which abruptly collapsed into grim despair in the 1930s. Yet this perception was evident several years before Carr wrote the *Twenty Years' Crisis*.[2] The Secretary General of the League, Joseph Avenol, speaking at a meeting at Chatham House chaired by Gilbert Murray in December 1933, stated:

From 1924 to 1930 the world experienced a period of prosperity such as it had never known before, and this engendered a feeling of optimism and led to the hope that human possibilities would be fully realised. In the economic field we looked forward to limitless prosperity; in the political, in that of the League of Nations, there seemed to be a certainty of peace, assumed automatically and permanently on a juridical basis. This period came to an end with the approach of the economic crisis, and immediately the optimism of previous years gave way...to a feeling of pessimism and often of excessive pessimism.[3]

In the light of the changed circumstances, Avenol wondered to what extent Geneva could be said to represent international public opinion. He stated that while prior to the crisis 'currents of thoughts and feeling passed beyond national frontiers and spread themselves...throughout the world', public opinion was now taking a 'nationally-concentrated form'; governments in the 'new political systems' especially, were 'imbuing the whole populations of the country with a community of ideas and feelings, so that they vibrate...in unison...one might compare public opinion in such countries to a whirlwind revolving within their frontiers'.[4] Avenol's observations complement a previous point: that however much a corporate state like fascist Italy was seen as ordered from the inside, it appeared more like combustible fuel to its critics on the outside.

Avenol's explanation for the trend to national inwardness might be usefully compared to comments by Valéry who, characteristically, offered an obscure account of the same development. In 'Our Destiny and Literature' (1937) he wrote of the appearance in the modern world of a 'new type of nomad', one who 'sits astride five or six hundred horsepower, and flies over territorial boundaries, ignoring frontiers and Customs'. He went on to elaborate, in keeping with his earlier meditations on crisis, that this condition of intense physical mobility reflected the uncertain state of knowledge. Indeed, indeterminacy was perhaps the essential characteristic of the modern mind. He illustrated his point with a puzzle:

You would think it ridiculous if someone should answer you, on being asked his name: 'My name? Whatever you like!' You find the answer absurd. And if he should add: 'My name is whatever you like, and that is actually my name,' you would think him mad. And yet, that is perhaps what we shall have to get accustomed to: indeterminateness as a positive fact, a positive element of knowledge.

There is a faint hint of Bergson here. Bergson identified real positivity, not with the realm of the concrete and definite, but with flux and becoming. (Although this does not mean he conceived of experience as all whirling storms.) There are shades of Marinetti in his description of zooming nomadism, yet Valéry's tone is anxious rather than gaily mischievous. (Nor is there any recognition here of the attempts to marry futurism and state-centrism.) The modern world, according to Valéry, was being remodelled along the lines of the shifting, kaleidoscopic consciousness of modern man. He wrote: 'Man has sought in Nature the means and power to make things around him as restless, as unstable, as mobile as himself.' He put the argument, one which was reminiscent of Wyndham Lewis's explanation of the rise of the fascist state a decade earlier, that it was in reaction to the condition of 'complete mobility' that nations had sought to become 'an autonomous system, a closed economy, an autarky'. Thus contemporary international conflicts could be seen as a struggle between 'rooted man' and the 'ancient framework', of the nation, and 'mobile man' and our 'increased power of movement'; put another way, they can be seen as a struggle between tradition and modernity with the latter referring to the unpredictable and dislocated.[5]

Valéry's reflections are further testimony to the persistence of crisis literature throughout the interwar period. It was as if the same forces that had caused the Great War continued to zigzag across time causing all the difficulties and cataclysms which followed. It was complained in the mid-1930s that the term crisis was much over-used and sorely abused, but it seemed to lose none of its dramatic appeal. In the midst of the Second World War the Harvard University sociologist Pitirim Sorokin, of the University of St Petersburg until banished by the Soviets in 1922, published *The Crisis of Our Age* (1941). He stated gravely that in the world of the present: 'Red human blood flows in broad streams from one end of the earth to the other.' Yet this dreadful condition was but an outward manifestation of a deeper crisis. Sorokin had argued in various works since the 1920s that what humanity was really undergoing in the twentieth century was a period of cosmic transition, one which involved the death of sensate culture, the breakdown of four centuries of materialism, and the birth of a new ideational culture, one founded on the principle of the basic spiritual unity of all the world's parts. For a time it was thought that there would be an end to war and bloodshed; opinion leaders believed 'in international good will and cooperation led by the League of Nations; in the economic, mental, and moral improvement of mankind and in "streamlined" progress'. But it was not enough, as the social engineers had thought, to make adjustments to economic and social mechanisms. The crisis did not abate; misery, suicide and gloom spread throughout the culture and then there was the bloodiest war of the bloodiest century.[6]

In the theoretical sphere Sorokin saw crisis apparent in the way in which science, the materialist culture's intellectual citadel, was undermining its own foundations. Poincaré, Pearson, Mach, James and Dewey, the doctrines of empiricism, neo-positivism, logical positivism and pragmatism, were all responsible for 'obliterating the boundary line between sensory truth and falsehood, reality and fiction, validity and utilitarian convention'.[7] As many philosophers had earlier insisted, the scientific culture had made the physical senses the principal or sole means of evaluating truth; but the senses proved to be a fragile base on which to establish reality and eventually science, aided by contemporary philosophy, proceeded to eat itself, to undermine its own foundations. In the worlds of art and musical composition too the modernist, deconstructive mood prevailed.[8] The conditions were thus created for a decline into moral atomism and nihilism. Hence, Sorokin wrote, the rising tide of criminality, apparent not only in the increasing numbers of racketeers, kidnappers and murderers, but in the political gangsterism represented by the governments of Hitler, Mussolini and Stalin. Despite this grim assessment, Sorokin did not think the situation was as dire as Spengler had predicted.[9]

The road to salvation could be found were we to recognise the nature and depth of the crisis and move to reembrace the synoptic view, to restore coherence to and reintegrate knowledge and in so doing bring individuals and communities together. He wrote: 'The time of isolated states is past and mankind is already one interacting community.' But for Sorokin the principle of integration demanded much more than the reconstruction of the League; it meant 'making man again an image of the Absolute on this planet'.[10]

POSTWAR PLANNING

President Roosevelt and his advisers, in reponse to the crisis in Europe, had set about designing the second new world order of the twentieth century in the late 1930s. The Atlantic Charter, which Gilbert Murray thought made extravagant promises to the world's peoples, was issued in 1941.[11] Andrew Williams writes that American plans for the postwar world were global in scope and emphasised 'liberal democratic forms of government and capitalist economic structures'. Federalist sympathies were also articulated by Washington policy-makers. John Foster Dulles questioned the sovereign state system, because at best it promised negative peace, and urged in its place '*structurally* porous and elastic' borders. In Britain, Arnold Toynbee and others, who had participated in discussions surrounding the new world order of the 1920s, supported the American proposals and, in opposition to E.H. Carr, the principle of federalism. Given Williams's fine study *Failed Imagination?: New world orders of the twentieth century* (1998) it is unnecessary for me to describe here the detail of the blueprints for the world developed in the first half of the 1940s. What is important is that the enthusiasm for a new world order (as described above) was greater in Washington than in Britain, France and Commonwealth countries.[12]

While postwar planning meant international planning in Washington it had meant national planning in Britain. The PEP group announced in 1943 that it had modified the view it held around the time of the 1933 WEC that planning was essentially a national matter. From the late 1930s it came to the opinion that it was too difficult to separate national from the international questions adding that there was a need to look not just at the trade issue but also the matter of international welfare as specified in the Atlantic Charter. Yet PEP interpreted the Charter in especially statist terms. It saw it as advocating the 'progressive use of the State...as an instrument of public welfare'; an editorial in *Planning* applauded Churchill's endorsement of the 'idea of a Four Year plan' for reconstructing Britain and improving the 'economic security of the British people'. It is telling that PEP upheld wartime economic mobilisation as a model for peacetime development, singling out for praise, in particular, Russia's rapid conversion to a battle economy.[13]

There were those in Britain, as Andrew Williams points out, who were at first suspicious of the new world order fearing it as a 'plot against socialism';

yet the Atlantic Charter won the support of the Labour Party precisely because it could be interpreted as a 'mandate to transform British society'.[14] Richard Crossman touched on the question of whether emphasis should be placed on international or national planning in an essay published in 1940 by the Fabian Society. He branded as disastrous the interwar 'cult of "Internationalism" in progressive circles in Britain and America' and the attendant 'sweeping condemnation of nationalism'; sheeting home responsibility to the Left, he claimed that the effect was confusion and ill-preparedness in the face of aggression. Most importantly, he added that socialists, if they were to 'plan the future', had to recognise that their first duty was to their own country; until there was a recognition of the 'indivisible connection of nationalism', which League ideology was too weak to supplant, 'and a vital democratic socialism...all talk of Federal Union is futile'. For a federation (by which he meant an alliance of democratic states cooperating on the task of raising standards of living) to command support it should aim at reinforcing rather than destroying nationalism and the nation-state. The same held for democratic socialism; Crossman thought that for socialism to succeed in Britain it had not only to address the insecurities of the British people but also to harness patriotic feelings.[15]

The war years had seen a significant strengthening of such feelings and this, along with the expectation that the wartime promise of postwar social security would be fulfilled, was seen as favouring a closed economy rather more than economic internationalism. Robert Menzies, a conservative politician who would become Australian prime minister in 1949, observed at a conference on postwar reconstruction in 1944:

Whatever the tendency in pre-war years towards acute nationalism, and in particular economic nationalism, that tendency has been much accelerated during the progress of the war...those who regard as almost axiomatic the existence of a community of nations willing to subordinate their economic and national policies to a new world order are entirely ignoring it.[16]

Menzies saw proposals for federal union and the accompanying demands for an international police force and international control of finance and tariffs as well-meaning but utopian. Perfect schemes do not become reality simply by writing them down on paper. He endorsed Carr's objections to the world federalist project in the *Conditions of Peace*. In that work Carr, a proponent of the collectivist state, asserted the 'paramount importance of planning for the future' in the international sphere, notably in the areas of armaments, trade, resources and welfare. Perceiving President Roosevelt's 'four freedoms' placed too much emphasis on the removal of evils rather than the achievement of 'positive goods' he championed the idea of international public works, which he presented, following William James, as a moral equivalent for war. For all this he added the caution that people needed 'to be on guard against current well-advertised offers of ready-made systems of world organisation', against constitutional blue-prints with no grounding in public opinion.[17] Carr counselled a pragmatic, evolutionary approach to the creation of international networks of cooperation:

Until the body politic of a new order begins to take shape, it is premature to seek for elaborate constitutional vestments to clothe it...The new and broader commonwealth of nations can only be built up out of some such network of relationships, flexible in character and inspired by no undue itch for uniformity, to which it may some day be possible and convenient to give a more precise legal shape. At the present state inter-dependence is a practical, not a constitutional problem. It is a dangerous, if popular, illusion that it can be solved by a committee of ingenious constitutional lawyers to everyone's satisfaction and without impinging on anyone's interests. What we are required in fact to surrender is not a mythical attribute called sovereignty, but the habit of framing our military and economic policy without regard for the needs and interests of other countries.[18]

To express dislike for the formalism which characterised many new world order designs was not necessarily to rule out the establishment of international institutions and the possibility of international cooperation on a more extensive basis than in the interwar years. Nonetheless, the prevalence of objections to international economic planning suggests these would still have to operate within certain defined limits. Menzies, for example (who equally must have found Carr's ambitious proposals for international economic planning and his fundamental transnationalism, which he glided over, unpalatable), thought the day was far off when states would agree on that 'pooling of sovereignty' which the federalist Lord Lothian, otherwise known as Philip Kerr, had urged in his Burge Memorial Lecture of 1935 entitled 'Pacifism is Not Enough'. Lothian argued that the only way to end war was by applying the 'principle of the state...on a world-wide scale'. Echoing comments Rappard had made a decade and a half earlier, Menzies went on to state that no great power would give up a substantial part of its sovereignty.[19]

The priority given to reconstruction in Britain, moves towards a directed economy in France and the desire to include the Soviet Union in the postwar order meant that Washington had to accept national planning.[20] Popularly embraced in Britain, Australia, New Zealand and the Scandinavian countries it came to be regarded, according to Walter Lippmann (who in the late 1930s renounced his earlier belief in a society directed by a 'well-trained ruling class') as the 'dominant dogma of the age' among politicians, academics and bureaucrats, national planning nonetheless caused unease in some intellectual quarters. One argument, put by Lippmann among others, was that it could lead to the militarisation of society. Collectivism as a mode of social organisation fosters the martial spirit and encourages in people an obsessive concern for their physical security. Michael Oakeshott wrote in an essay in 1949 that it woult result in exactly what it anticipated: 'organised rivalry' and violence among states. It should be noted that planning had for some years been proffered as a moral equivalent to war, an activity which would soak up national energies and direct them towards the vast project of national reconstruction; further, it was presented as a continuation of the war effort except that the battle to be fought in this context was against enemies within: unemployment and poverty.[21]

In *The Road to Serfdom* (1944) Friedrich Hayek claimed that planning would, through engendering friction, endanger international peace. Yet Hayek went on to argue that the danger posed by state planning should not lead to the conclusion that planning controls should be undertaken by a supranational authority, a position ascribed to E.H. Carr among others. Hayek thought the practical implications of this proposal, which he saw as entailing international control over resources and development, were decidedly illiberal. First, given that in a world where there was minimal agreement over 'standards of value', such a central authority, however well-intentioned, would have to rely significantly on force in implementing its policies. The experience of colonial administration underlined this point.[22] Second, there was the danger that the great powers, while not themselves submitting to direction from on high, would use an international economic authority 'to impose their will on the smaller nations within the area in which they exercise hegemony'. Hayek agreed with those advocating world planning that the state should no longer have uninhibited sovereignty in the economic sphere. But the solution to the problem of sovereignty was not the creation of an intrusive international economic authority. Rather, what was needed was a superior political authority equipped with the 'powers of the ultra-liberal "*laissez-faire*" state'; the role of such an authority would be that of restraining states 'from action which will damage others'.[23]

The postwar international order is often described as a liberal order. Not only was one of its central planks free trade, it was an order which upheld the autonomy of states. It is argued that because of the value attached to the principle of state independence liberal internationalism does not like dense systems of governance. Yet in Hayek's view, the postwar economic order was illiberal to the extent that it preserved the sovereignty of states and in so doing licensed the great powers to bend the rules in their favour. Hayek's brand of liberalism, while recognising the instrumental value of the state by explicitly acknowledging the individual as the fundamental unit of political autonomy, takes us in the direction of federalism. (Hayek thought that the only type of federal union that was viable at that stage was one among Britain and the Dominions, the United States and the countries of Western Europe.) He noted that the 'idea of the world at last finding peace through the absorption of the separate states in large federated groups and ultimately perhaps in one single federation' was by no means new but 'was indeed the ideal of almost all the liberal thinkers of the nineteenth century'.[24] Hayek's supranational authority would be limited in its operations; it would be the night watchman state of legend. However, the potential for the mandate he accords such an authority to expand is revealed by the suggestion that prohibition against causing economic harm against other states might render certain forms of economic planning impossible. The fact that this might be seen by some communities as an oppressive application of the free trade principle and something that could only be implemented in a heavy-handed fashion, are not matters with which Hayek reckoned.[25]

FROM SPIRITUAL TO FUNCTIONAL UNITY

In his article 'The Biosphere and the Noösphere', written in Moscow in December 1943, the Russian scientist Vladimir Vernadsky told of how the First World War had caused him radically to alter his conception of nature. In the midst of the war he embraced 'a conception of nature, at that time forgotten and thus new' for himself and his colleagues, which had it as a 'geochemical and biogeochemical' phenomenon encompassing 'both inert and living nature from the same point of view'. For Vernadsky the planetary perspective was one of the chief markers of twentieth-century science, a perspective that had become even more compelling given the outbreak of war in the Far East in 1931 and the renewal of hostilities in Europe in 1939. The Second World War, a war of enormous 'power, duration and strength', was 'unparalleled in the history of mankind and of the biosphere at large'.[26] Vernadsky noted that in his twilight years A.P. Pavlov had begun to refer to modern times as the '*anthropogenic era*' by which he meant that humanity had become, almost imperceptibly, a 'mighty and ever-growing geological force'.[27] Vernadsky, elaborating on Pavlov's perception, wrote:

In the twentieth century, man, for the first time in the history of the earth, knew and embraced the whole biosphere, completed the geographic map of the planet Earth, and colonized its whole surface. *Mankind became a single totality in the life of the earth.* There is no spot on earth where man can not live if he so desires. Our people's sojourn on the floating ice of the North Pole in 1937–38 has proved this clearly. At the same time, owing to the mighty techniques and successes of scientific thought, radio and television, man is able to speak instantly to anyone he wishes at any point on our planet. Transportation by air has reached a speed of several hundred kilometres per hour, and has not reached its maximum.[28]

These developments were the result of 'cephalization', that is, the development of the human brain and the operations of this brain upon the planet. Vernadsky thought if human beings appreciated this fact and chose not to use their brains to wreak havoc and destruction then an 'immense future' would open up to them.[29] He claimed that his understanding of the biosphere underpinned the concept of the noösphere as developed by Edouard Le Roy in collaboration with Teilhard de Chardin. The term noösphere was introduced by Le Roy (whom Vernadsky, significantly, described as a Bergsonian philosopher) in lectures he gave at the Collége de France in 1927. It denoted the idea of a space in which human beings operated as powerful geological forces. The term noösphere was not intended to serve as a purely descriptive device. As Vernadsky's account implies, its prime function was normative and in this regard it served a purpose similar to that often attributed to the *élan vital*: it recommended concentrated efforts towards ideal ends. Vernadsky wrote that the idea of the noösphere indicated that:

[man] can and must rebuild the province of his life by this work and thought, rebuild it radically in comparison with the past. Wider and wider creative possibilities open before him. It may be that the generation of our grand-children will approach their blossoming.

Concerned at the physical and chemical changes wrought on land and water by the growth of human civilisation Vernadsky urged 'measures to preserve for future generations the wealth of the seas which so far have belonged to nobody'. On a happier note, the advance of civilisation was also witnessing the creation of 'new species and races of animals and plants...Fairy tale dreams appear possible in the future: man is striving to emerge beyond the boundaries of his planet into cosmic space.' The dawning of the age of the noösphere thus implicated resource conservation, the maintenance of biological diversity and the fanning out of human life into deep space. Above all, the concept of the noösphere implicated the '*reconstruction of the biosphere in the interests of freely thinking humanity as a single totality*'. And this in turn meant not only provision of material comfort but also the spread of democratic ideals, ideals which for Vernadsky were inscribed in nature. [30]

Vernadsky's thoughts were published in the *American Scientist* in January 1945, the month in which he died. The editor of the journal declared that Vernadsky's contribution presented 'the general outlook of one of the most remarkable scientific leaders of the present century'. Yet as I have suggested Vernadsky's piece was very much fired by social sympathies as evidenced by his communication that: 'I look forward with great optimism. I think that we undergo not only an historical, but a planetary change as well. We live in a transition to the noösphere.'[31] What Vernadsky did was unite to merge a democratic, ecumenical mysticism with the overall movement and pattern of nature. Bergson had already made this move in seeking to establish the moral and metaphysical bases of the League. Despite its provenance and perhaps because of the chastening effect of the interwar experience, the United Nations, however, was not to be similarly invested with a religious significance. L.A. Zimmern wrote of the pilgrimages made to Geneva by League devotees in order to see first hand the 'great international "stars"' who frequented the institution. Geneva's air seemed cooler, sweeter and more universal than that of other metropolises. [32] The United Nations, the name of the combined allied forces during the war, did not elicit the same zeal. Its atmospherics had a less ethereal quality and this is reflected well in the differences between the conceptualisation and operations of the ICIC and that of United Nations Educational, Cultural and Scientific Organisation (Unesco). The need to organise for postwar intellectual cooperation was under discussion from the early 1940s. Partially created from the residues of the ICIC, Unesco would continue the latter body's campaign for mental and moral disarmament and solidarity through encouraging improved education and communications standards, cultural understanding and scientific interchange. Yet it was intended to be a more practically engaged and less rarefied body. James Sewell reports that Joseph Needham, a member of the body's Preparatory Commission in 1946 and the first director of its natural sciences division, wanted to ensure that Unesco 'avoided' the ICIC's 'tendency towards "mandarinism," towards aims "too vague, academic and contemplative", toward affiliation with universities alone rather than governmental and industrial institutions'.[33] Needham was referring to the ICIC's scientific activities. He was conscious of how affronted the world's people had been by the use of scientific knowledge for destructive purposes and was keen to save its reputation and redirect it towards the positive end which was the welfare of all humanity. Yet the point he made had also been stated in relation to the totality of the ICIC's work. It is also telling that whereas the ICIC's founder and first director was the metaphysician Bergson, Unesco's Director General was the British natural scientist Julian Huxley. As befitted his office, Huxley was not a narrow specialist; he was very concerned with the social implications of science, both its benefits and its dangers. A member of PEP, he had argued since the early 1930s that the rate of technological advance demanded the scientific study of society and planning lest jungle governors seize the new forces and abuse them.[34]

In an essay written in 1947 he repeated this warning, while also asserting that the 'application of scientific methods in appropriate forms to human affairs' would 'yield results every whit as important and almost as revolutionary as those achieved by the natural sciences in the rest of the universe'.[35] Huxley insisted that Unesco must not be based exclusively on any particular world view be it 'existentialism, *élan vital*, rationalism or spiritualism, an economic determinist or a rigid cyclical view of history', yet Huxley was seeking to provide the institution with a guiding philosophy and it was one very much grounded in the scientific outlook. Through science, humanity could subdue nature and manage social development. Science was also conducive towards peace because it was an intellectually unifying force. In an article the year before, he stated, just as had many League officials and supporters in the interwar period, that:

Science and the scientific way of thought is as yet the one human activity which is truly universal. There is no single religious, aesthetic, or political way of thought which is as yet universal. We want, therefore, to encourage this universality of scientific thought and through it help to build the basis of general universalism.[36]

The 1947 essay continues in this vein with Huxley asserting that natural science was 'one of the fields in which two of Unesco's general principles – of thinking in global terms and of relieving the darkness of the "dark areas" of the world – are most obviously applicable'. While Huxley might be claiming too much for science these statements do not amount to scientism. Rather, he is saying that in so far as scientific outlook is the most widely embraced, it is the point of departure for the building of unity in other areas of human thought and endeavour. He described an authentic monism as one which considered the 'aesthetic and emotional foundations of a peaceful world civilization' to be equally as 'as important as the scientific and intellectual'.[37]

Huxley's 1947 Unesco essay was controversial. Sewell writes that its 'anthropocentrism shocked various kinds of theists'; his advocacy of population and birth control, eugenics and, more generally, his naturalistic account of social evolution also set alarm bells ringing. Huxley failed in his attempt to get 'a scientific world humanism, global in extent and evolutionary in background' accepted as the Unesco ideology.[38] In the light of this failure, Huxley began to prescribe 'the orchestration of cultural diversity within an advancing world civilization'; yet this prescription only served to underline that Huxley believed above all that humanity was one in a very profound way and further, that his evolutionary humanism, for all his lauding of scientific methods, was fundamentally of a religious character. A biological analogy is infused with the warmth of the sacred in his 1946 remark that:

Man must find a new belief in himself, and the only basis for such a belief lies in his vision of world society as an organic whole, in which rights and duties of men are balanced deliberately, as they are among the cells of the body. Economic values must yield in importance to social values, because the latter are the ones that are the most important.[39]

But Sewell adjudges that Huxley's concession to manysidedness only 'foreshadowed the Unesco retreat from "conceptual" approaches'. The fact that a shared moral philosophy could not be found only reinforced the need for the body to focus on achieving agreement on those concrete problems where there was a common interest in cooperation.[40] It had to take a functionalist approach because the world mind, which members of the ICIC had sought to imagine and foster, had failed to materialise. The second new world order reflected the same confidence in technical rationality and expertise as the first (Huxley saw Unesco as approximating H.G. Wells's idea of a 'World Brain') but seemed more conscious of the depth and resilience of national differences. The idea of a world mind, whether understood in intellectual or religious terms, was the dream of European philosophers and the European era was drawing to a close.[41]

Hans J. Morgenthau was not unsympathetic to the functionalist approach; for him the problem with Unesco was that, against David Mitrany's advice, it presumed too much when it came to social unity. Morgenthau thought Unesco was based on the same false premise that coloured the League: that there is ultimately one moral system, one correct way of seeing the cosmos, a point of view previously reflected in Wilson's promise to make the 'world safe for democracy', no less than Bergson's depiction of the First World War as a cosmic struggle between life and matter. That there was no clear connection between Unesco's diffuse activities and the goal of peace and security, laid down as its chief purpose in its constitution, was no accident. This lack of clarity flowed from another and related weakness in the philosophy on which Unesco was based: that international conflicts are in a sense imagined, caused by 'an intellectual deficiency, of ignorance and lack of judgement as to the qualities of other peoples' rather than being real fights over 'real stakes'.[42] Nonetheless, if we look at the rules governing the Security Council, we can say that the UN was certainly predicated on the belief, one which Wilson had also entertained, that a harmony of interests would not arise either spontaneously or easily. It was grounded in the realisation that in some circumstances certain states would have to be compelled to behave. Lord Lothian in his final speech to the American public as British Ambassador on 11 December 1940 offered a more hard-headed assessment of international politics, one with severely hierarchal implications, than he had in 'Pacifism is Not Enough'; in that lecture he had insisted that a peaceful world could not be built 'on a basis of the coercion of governments by governments, because that is trying to build a peace system on a foundation of war'. However, he now stated:

The plain truth is that peace and order always depend, not on disarming police, but on there being an overwhelming power behind just law. The only place where that power can be found behind the laws of the liberal and democratic world is the United States and Great Britain, supported by the Dominions, and some other free nations. The only nucleus round which a stable, peaceful, democratic world can be built after this war is if the United States and Great Britain possess between them more aeroplanes, ships of war, and key positions of world power such as I have described, than any possible totalitarian rival.[43]

Because of the powers accorded to the Security Council to police international peace and security the UN has been portrayed as a more realistic institution than its predecessor. That said, the UN Charter and the League Covenant were at one in making the sovereignty of the state the cornerstone of the international system. As we saw, this was seen by many as the League's chief deficiency; although seeking to facilitate international intercourse it kept intact a political arrangement based on dread. Nonetheless, Harold Laski and the lawyer Georges Scelle liked to imagine that the League was on its way to becoming a world state.[44] Like the Covenant of the League, the UN Charter was 'not a constituent act of the peoples of the United Nations' but rather 'an agreement freely entered into between governments'.[45] At the same time, there are those today who argue similarly to Laski and Scelle, claiming that the Charter is slowly being reconceptualised so that in the minds of many members the world community it is coming to approximate a world constitution. While this matter will be discussed in the next chapter it is worth noting at this point that Morgenthau countenanced the legal argument that the text of Article 27, paragraph 3 of the UN Charter which states that 'an affirmative vote of nine members including the concurring votes of permanent members', that is a majority vote, when read in conjunction with the law enforcement provisions under Chapter 7 (of the Charter) meant that the Security Council possessed 'supreme authority over the member states which are not permanent members' of the Council. Political conditions, not least the lack of agreement among the five permanent members, however, militated against the realisation of this legal possibility.[46]

THE COMING OF THE GLOBAL APPROACH

An exhausting, devastating Second World War and then the spectre of atomic war in the late 1940s saw a resurgence of intellectual and public interest in the topic of world government.[47] Ralph Barton Perry issued a work in 1945 called *One World in the Making*. The monism implied by the expression 'one world' might seem odd coming from someone who had done so much to explain William James's pluralistic cosmology. Yet a number of social philosophers cited James's influence in representing the world as progressing towards unity. I have suggested that James's own inclinations were more particularistic than those of his admirers, such as Mary Parker Follett and Harold Laski, both of whom cited his influence in explaining international politics. Yet the spirit of James was upheld in so far as the type of unity being promoted by these authors gave room to multiplicity, was primarily a product of active willing and was conceived as an ongoing, ever-unfinished project. Perry addressed all these points. He began his study by invoking Wendell Wilkie's best-selling *One World* (1943) in which the author explained how a 49-day trip around the world in the middle of the war, during which he took in vast expanses of the earth's surface, confirmed his belief that all nations, developed and undeveloped, had to unite in political and economic solidarity if the scourge of war were to be eliminated. Peace, he insisted, was indivisible.[48]

Perry saw the oneness of the planet as a pointer to humanity's social destiny. The appreciation of its essential oneness was a phenomenon of the modern era which he thought began in the sixteenth century. The age of exploration had witnessed the confirmation of the spherical shape of the earth. The sixteenth century was also the age of Galileo. It saw the beginnings of a scientific revolution which would reveal the unity of nature. Yet the relation between modernity and a global outlook is not straightforward. By means of ships and science humanity was actually recovering a perspective, that of the world as a single society, which arose in ancient times, specifically during the period of the Macedonian and Roman Empires. Perry went on to state: 'This idea, arising in antiquity, has never been forgotten. The Holy Roman Empire of the Middle Ages, and all the later dreams of world federation, are its revivals or lingering echoes.' So again, the contemporary pursuit of world unity is in a sense the reawakening of age-old reveries; yet it is a goal whose realisation owes much to the tools and methods of the modern era. Science permits the manipulation of nature. Science and its technological fruits have enabled humanity to spin an extensive and complex web of relations.[49]

Drawing upon l'abbé de Saint-Pierre's *Project for Perpetual Peace*, Perry argued, just like late twentieth-century advocates of global governance discussing globalisation, that there are two sorts of oneness existing in the world; there is the oneness which is interdependence, chiefly manifest in the 'planetary or global' extension of the world economy. This type of oneness can lead to comity but it can also result in friction; beyond this, there is the thicker kind of oneness which is deliberate, global organisation. Perry wrote that given the facts of interdependence it is something from which there can be no turning back. Yet interdependence can result in resentments and hostilities. It manifests as missiles and disease no less than mutually beneficial exchange. Managed oneness was thus not only possible but imperative.[50]

The delineation of the second new world order was aided by the production of new geographies just as Isaiah Bowman's *The New World: Problems in Political Geography* (1921) had been intended to illustrate and reinforce the recasting of the world entailed by Wilson's new world order. New geographies, Perry reported, revealed 'The Face of One World'; underlining terrestrial unity they were taken as signs of the 'coming age of the "global approach"'. The advent of the UN was the crowning moment of the new age; it was the spiritual and institutional expression of the emerging global outlook. Perry saw the UN as fundamentally democratic in character but he wanted it to be a democracy of democracies, with membership involving obligations to promote popular sovereignty and civil liberties, to eliminate racial prejudice and discrimination and to raise standards of living. Most importantly, he thought the wills which merged to form the UN, and upon whom rights should ultimately devolve, were individual rather than national wills. Perry questioned the use of the term international 'for the all-embracing human polity' although he welcomed the fact that 'when it is now used, it is with the emphasis on the "inter" rather than the "national"'. He mounted the pragmatist argument, one which Laski had used in the 1920s, that the sovereignty of the state was not absolute and given but was a mere instrument; respect for it wholly depended on the value it gave to peoples lives.[51]

In making this point Perry was not attempting to dissolve the distinction between domestic and foreign affairs and open the way to interference in the running of states by a higher authority. He was not urging the break-up of existing states. It was the association not multiplication of states that he wanted; for this reason he argued for a limit to the right of self-determination. If the cause of one world was to be achieved, the quest for autonomy was better answered by applying the principle of subsidiarity. In order to persuade states to take this cause, Perry also argued, as had Follett before him, that states would not lose their freedom through international organisation but would actually enhance it. They would exchange 'disorderly' for a greater 'orderly freedom'.[52] Perry's picture of world order featured the same Jamesian motifs as had those of Laski and Follett. As James might have insisted, for Perry the most important oneness that we achieve in this world is not that which happens accidentally but the one that we make ourselves; in keeping with James' philosophy as well, the one world he speaks of is always in the making, it is an ongoing process. Further, he saw the idea of a world forever in the making as at one with American sensibilities: 'It is more American to make a utopia than to dream of it or live in it. It would be American to improve and modernize Heaven rather than to enjoy it for a static eternity.'[53]

At the same time, Perry emphasised, as a Jamesian would, that the emerging global culture will seek to reconcile diversity and unity: Perry was not talking of a mosaic of distinct, frozen diversities; alongside the preservation of indigenous cultures he urged 'a cross-fertilization and an overlapping of cultures, with varying degrees of uniformity but no identical or static cultures'. Despite the homage paid to pluralism Perry's perspective, as he acknowledged, was above all universalistic. For Perry there existed an objective moral universe. 'Cultural relativism', he wrote, was 'in some sense an indisputable fact', although the significance of this fact had been blown out of all proportion by the aggressively tribal Fascist and Nazi regimes. This fact did not rule out the possibility of there being a 'foundation of sameness'. In one sense this foundation was something to be created in the future; 'world-wide and improved communication' would enhance spiritual, scientific and social exchange. Yet Perry believed humanity had always lived under the one moral law. Because it upheld the idea of a universal moral law, one which above all commanded peace, Christianity had 'prepared the mind of Christendom for world organization'.[54]

Perry explicitly considered new world order visions as Christian universalism in secular guise. He wrote that there was 'an agreement of the new world order with the teachings of Christianity'; Christianity was 'a source of strength of those who would unite and organize mankind'. As he conceded, he was not the first to traverse this ground. Bergson believed the League, conceived as a supranational body representative of all humanity, reflected the insights of Jewish and Christian mystics. (Mussolini, of course, had derided the League for perpetuating the Christian illusion of an ethical commonwealth spanning the globe.) Perry was not crudely proselytising on behalf of the Christian faith. His point was that Christianity was a 'universal religion'; it rose above the tribe and reached out to all humanity. Further it had aligned the principle of 'brotherly love' to the secular doctrine of social progress. Perry detected the same universalistic and progressive tendencies in the teachings of Judaism, Islam, Buddhism and Confucianism. These too approached the status of universal religions, faiths which gave rise to the 'ideal of morally unified mankind on a physically unified earth'; this was a cause which, given our common humanity, our propinquity to one another and occupation of the one and the same surface, would still be worthy and compelling if God were taken out of the picture. Perry foresaw a world in which atheists and theists of various denominations dwelt 'together in freedom, knowledge, and human kindness. Only cults which exalt slavery, ignorance, and inhumanity are excluded'; while there may not be a kingdom of God there could be a kingdom of man. Perry's liberalism, like his version of Christianity, was tolerant but muscular, something which was also apparent in his earlier defence of America's entry into the first World War. It has been suggested that like Dewey the vigorous tone of Perry's polemics in favour of American involvement in that conflict would have been too much for William James. Yet James's liberalism was often expressed in robust, even militant, terms. The idea of a liberal world order, which is the one world in the making, certainly seems to inspire in Perry a measure of zeal. Building the kingdom of man, he tells us, will be no easy feat; rather, an enterprise such as this, he wrote, required courage, it called for 'martial values, in combat against evil or against lesser good – against war, hate, prejudice, ignorance and misery, against the complacency of partial success, and the disillusionment of partial failure'.[55]

Perry's disavowal of the word international, and his repeated emphasis on the increasingly global dimensions of the world economy, signalled a shift in international discourse that would become more pronounced in subsequent decades. Certainly, there was in the interwar period, as we have seen, a consciousness that the words international and world might have different implications. In addition, the concept of the global was already being endowed with economic significance in the 1920s. In 1926 the Globocapital Association, based in Lugano, asked the ILO to air a plan at the 1927 WEC for the introduction of a universal monetary unit to be known, hilariously, as the Globo. As we saw, in the interwar years developments and policies similar to those discussed by Perry were typically placed under such rubrics as international rationalisation. Perry's argument parallels that of interwar advocates of rationalisation, but his use of the term global suggested an all-inclusive order rather than one confined to the industrialised world. Its resonance is humanistic rather than cold and technical.

ATOMIC PEACE

The predominant view up until the early 1930s was that one world would come about through a willing outpouring of fellow-feeling. Faith was still expressed in this notion in the 1940s. At the same time, those expounding on the theme of one world were by then doing so in a more thrusting and assertive manner. There seemed a greater acceptance that in order to make one world it might be necessary to make war. Even so absolute a pacifist as Einstein had increasingly come to the view that one had to be prepared to battle for peace. Einstein's pacifism was part of the reason why he felt uncomfortable about his association with the League. It was an institution that accepted the reality of war and, indeed, could do little about it. Yet Einstein also vested hopes for the future in the League and accepted in May 1922 an invitation by the League's Secretary General Sir Eric Drummond on behalf of the League Council to join the ICIC.[56] The addition of Einstein, whom Bergson described as making 'discoveries at a greater distance from the ordinary organs of human knowledge than any other man in history', would add enormous prestige to that body and to the League as a whole. When a politics scholar, Dr Enrst Jackh, put to him the view that the 'theory of relativity, and Professor Freud's psychoanalyses, the League of Nations and its World Court...are all an expression of the same revolutionary phase through which the contemporary world is passing', Einstein's response, curiously for one so empirically austere, was: 'You are quite right: I endorse your holism.'[57]

In any case, Einstein proved to be a rather itinerant member of the Committee. At first suspicious that it was a victor's institution, he felt ill at ease with its clubby atmosphere.[58] His main interest as a member was in seeing that education served as a means of eliminating national hatreds. It was this interest that resulted in his most substantial contribution to the work of the ICIC: the exchange of letters between him and Freud in July 1932 on the question of what can be done to to deliver humanity from the 'menace of war'.[59] Einstein's biographer Ronald W. Clark wrote that Einstein's God was not a personal God, rather the term denoted 'an orderly system obeying rules which could be discovered', a type of cosmology which finds its parallel in his conception of the social universe as fundamentally rational and harmonious.[60]

Writing as someone 'immune from nationalist bias', Einstein thought the simplest way of dealing with the problem of war was for every state to 'surrender in a certain measure...its liberty of action' and to accept the jurisdiction of an international authority; that no such body had as yet been established was due to the venality of the governing classes and the control by the ruling classes of the organs of opinion. Yet he wondered whether war had deeper causes, whether it occurred and recurred because 'man has within him a lust for hatred and destruction' and it was on this point that he asked Freud to elaborate. Freud tried to pen an honest response but his heart was not wholly in it; for one thing, the exercise involved broaching truths that were hard to bear. Freud thought efforts to 'replace actual force by the force of ideas' were, at that juncture, doomed to failure adding that it would be to make 'a false calculation if we disregard the fact that law was originally brute violence' and required the 'support of violence'; he accepted Einstein's view on the need for a 'supreme agency' but insisted that it must be endowed 'with the necessary power'. Freud endorsed rather than dispelled Einstein's suspicion that the cause of war lay in our instinctive natures. This diagnosis suggested the somewhat pessimistic conclusion that 'there is no question of getting rid entirely of human aggressive impulses'; nonetheless, Freud tried to strike an optimistic note in allowing that the war impulse might be checked in the future due to the combined effect of humanity's sociability and 'the justified dread of the consequences of a future war'.[61]

Clark remarks that the 'idea of peace by the threat of terror was not one which Einstein welcomed' adding, however, that seven years on Einstein would be pressing Roosevelt to spur research into atomic weapons in the light of Germany's seizure of uranium deposits from Czechoslovakia.[62] By the time the exchange between Freud and Einstein was published by the ICIC under the heading *Why War?* in 1933 Einstein had already quit the League. Expressing contempt for the goings on at the League's doomed Disarmament Conference, he called for the abolition of armaments and insisted that 'people must be persuaded to refuse all military service'.[63] At the same time, Einstein was dismayed by the League's impotence. The maniacal aggression of the Nazi regime, both internally and externally, had made it transparent that force had to be met by force.[64]

Einstein would urge the United States, Great Britain and the Soviet Union, 'the only three powers which possess great military strength', to agree to establish the United Nations as a world government. Einstein's attitude towards the UN parallelled his attitude towards the League. However, whereas Einstein had earlier been discomforted by the idea of a world government reliant on force, in August 1945 he openly called for a supra-national authority with the power to check aggression and ensure respect for human rights. A supranational body should have the 'secret of the bomb' committed to it. and be accorded the power 'to interfere in countries where a minority is oppressing the majority and, therefore, is creating the kind of instability that leads to war'.[65] The Emergency Committee of Atomic Scientists, of which Einstein was chair, in a public awareness campaign in early 1947 described atomic energy as a primordial force which made a mockery of national boundaries and demanded a new mode of thinking. The Committee stated that: 'this basic power of the universe cannot be fitted into the outmoded concept of narrow nationalism'.[66] Failing acceptance of the idea of world government, the Committee sought international control of atomic energy. (Although for most of the early opponents of the bomb the latter goal could not be dissociated from the former as underscored by the slogan 'One World of None'.)[67] Einstein thought Russian acceptance of such a proposal might be forthcoming given its previous support for the League; he would lament the fact that the scheme the Americans actually put to the Russians, the Baruch plan (the American State Department had utterly discounted world federalism), was framed in a way that was bound to prove unacceptable to them. His friend Bertrand Russell wrote to him later that year stating that he gravely doubted that the Russians would join a scheme to establish international control of atomic power under any cir-cumstance. He stated:

I have no hope of reasonableness in the Soviet Government...I think the only hope of peace (and that a slender one), lies in frightening Russia. I favoured appeasement before 1939, wrongly, as I now think; I do not want to repeat the same mistake.

Einstein was gravely mistaken if he had hoped that Russian scientists would publicly embrace his internationalism. In November 1947 in the Russian Foreign Ministry's magazine *New Times* four of Russia's leading scientists, unsurprisingly given official Soviet policy on the issues of arms control and disarmament, penned an open letter questioning Einstein's continued push for world government stating: 'And now the proponents of a "world super-state" are asking us voluntarily to surrender this independence for the sake of a "world government" which is nothing but a flamboyant signboard for the world supremacy of the capitalist monopolies.'[68]

In April of 1948 the Emergency Committee expressed support for the notion of world government while conceding that 'this cannot be achieved overnight'.[69] This was the same year that the Committee To Frame a World Constitution, comprising scholars drawn from American and Canadian universities, issued a *Preliminary Draft of a World Constitution*. (It was also published in the Committee's magazine *Common Cause*, the *Saturday Review of Literature* and the *Bulletin of Atomic Scientists*.)[70] The Preamble to this draft constitution mounts the broadly Kantian argument that the goals of spiritual growth and physical well-being can only be attained under conditions of universal peace and hence governments must surrender their weapons and unite in a pacific union. Yet Kant proposed only a federation of sovereign states in *Perpetual Peace;* the formation of the Federal Republic of the World, however, involved the relinquishing not only of the right to wage war, as was already specified by the UN Charter, but also sovereignty itself. Nation-states, 'driven by nature and tradition', had wrecked the League and were destroying the United Nations. Humanity could no longer afford the situation of 'competitive anarchy' which characterised the state system. The Preamble declared in Wellsian cadences: 'the age of nations must end, and the era of humanity begin'.[71] Arguing in the same vein as nearly all proponents of world political centralisation, the Committee stated that the choice was between a 'world constitutional order' and 'world destruction'. Committee members viewed dimly the routine Russian denunciations of world federalism; as indicated, Russia treated it as a 'camouflage of capitalist imperialism', specifically American imperialism. Hence, the Committee asked, in view of Russia's 'cult of the veto' and jealous protection of its sovereignty, '...is there any way of convincing...Russia that the One World we have in mind is not the One Empire of monopolistic capitalism?' Its way of grappling with this problem was to propose on a world-scale the sort of 'liberal-socialist mediation between communism and capitalism' which was then being undertaken in countries such as Britain.[72]

Such a mediation was framed as a deduction from natural law, that unwritten law which underpins all philosophies and religions and insists on the 'inalienable claims to life, liberty, and the dignity of the human person'. It was the role of the World Republic to see natural law 'universally written and enforced by positive law', and while this entailed a world police force under the direction of a Chamber of Guardians, it also demanded economic legislation and planning. In addition to the provision of social security, the world state would ensure careful management of resources. Foreshadowing the common heritage notion which gained currency in the 1980s, the Draft Constitution stated: 'The four elements of life – earth, water, air, energy – are the common property of the human race' and their control must be 'subordinated in each and all cases to the interest of the common good'. Clearly, the World Republic delineated here is the sovereign state, albeit the sovereign welfare state, writ large; granted all the formal elements of sovereignty, the world state would be adorned with its usual ornaments. A Federal Capital, an official language and common currency were all specified. Yet once again deference was paid to the principle of multiplicity; the World Republic will be a 'pluralistic unity'.[73]

The Committee had expressed confidence in the general movement towards world federalism. In Britain public figures such as Bertrand Russell achieved some success in organising a popular crusade for world government. In France intellectuals such as Albert Camus, André Gide and Jean-Paul Sartre endorsed a campaign initiated by American comedian Garry Davis, a bomber pilot during the war, for the spontaneous *mondialisation* of citizenship and territory. A registry of World Citizens was established and around 400 communities in France, Denmark, Belgium, West Germany and India declared themselves world territory. (Mahatma Gandhi and Jawaharlal Nehru both endorsed the idea of world government in the face of the threat of atomic warfare. The latter proclaimed that a 'world commonwealth' or 'One World' to be the goal for which 'free India' would strive.) In 1947 in America there appeared the United World Federalists, the same year that the World Movement for World Federal Government was formed at a meeting in Montreux in Switzerland. That opinion polls on the topic were conducted by Unesco in 1948 and 1949 is telling in itself, both of the mood of the times and the outlook of officials of that institution. Parliamentary groups in support of world government also sprang up in Britain, Western Europe and Japan.[74] Studies sceptical of the project of world government soon appeared. The theologian Rienhold Niebuhr, while allowing members of the international community an appreciation of their common interests and a sense of fellow-feeling, concluded in an essay called 'The Illusions of World Government' (1949) that there was still insufficient 'social tissue' at this level of experience. He wrote:

forces which are operating to integrate the world community are limited. To call attention to this fact does not mean that all striving for a higher and wider integration of the world community is vain. That task must and will engage the conscience of mankind for ages to come. But the edifice of government which we build will be sound and useful if its height is proportionate to the strength of the materials from which it is constructed.

Niebuhr was of course thinking about the Cold War ideological cleavage but he also conveyed the belief, one he would reiterate in the late 1960s, in the deep diversity of world society.[75]

Errol E. Harris, a long-standing proponent of world government, in looking back on the period in *One World or None* (1993), asserts that the decline of the movement for world federalism occurred because 'neither the peacemakers nor the mass of the people seemed able to grasp the crucial issues nor the conception of world unity'. In addition to a failure of imagination he cited the intensification of the ideological conflict between East and West and the continued presence of nationalist sentiments. The combination of these factors meant that the 'prospect of world government faded and the idea was castigated as visionary idealism throughout the Cold War era'.[76] Wittner records that in the late 1940s the Soviet regime would publicly warn against a creeping cosmopolitanism branding in *Pravda* in April 1949 as an 'Ideological Weapon of American Reaction'. Meanwhile in America, right-wing and supposedly patriotic publications would decry world federalists as members of a 'Communist Conspiracy'. It might be relevant, as Wittner notes, that the world federalist movement 'was actually rather divided'.[77] The dream did not evaporate entirely. While the Emergency Committee was disbanded in 1951 Einstein continued to campaign for world government until his death in 1955. The explosion of the H-bomb by the Americans in 1952 and by the Soviets in 1953 seemed to give added credence to the contention that nuclear weapons were poised to destroy civilisation. The escalating arms race was also decried for imposing an unsustainable economic burden on poor and affluent countries alike. Yet the first rallying of mass opposition to nuclear weapons did not take place until the end of the 1950s.[78] It was against this gathering storm of protest that a well-connected Wall Street lawyer Grenville Clark in *World Peace Through World Law* (1958) issued a detailed proposal for reform of the United Nations. He reworked the contractarian argument stating that in the light of the situation in which humanity now found itself, intelligence should lead us to reject tired maxims of realpolitik. Interest and intelligence should converge on the need to establish 'world institutions which will once and for all abolish war and utilize the great new discoveries of science for peaceful uses'.[79] Yet Clark also stipulated the need for a United Nations Peace Force; a 'full-time force of professionals' numbering between 200,000 and 600,000 as determined by an elected General Assembly it would be equipped with the latest weaponry and technology, including nuclear weapons. It would be the only military force allowed in the world, its role being that of ensuring states carried out their obligation to disarm and refrain from aggression. Lincoln Bloomfield in an article in *World Politics* in 1962 prophesised an even more exacting regime; his world government, membership of which would be mandatory, would be secured and policed by an international force 'compounded appropriately of ground, sea, air, and outer space elements' and consisting of half a million men clad in international uniforms. Nuclear missiles would be located and deployed in various zones for the purpose of deterrence. An international inspectorate would monitor nuclear testing through 'robot seismic stations', 'on-site inspections' and 'solar satellites'; indeed, because of the demands of disarmament, a large 'UN presence' would be needed in every country.[80] The scenario Bloomfield projected, one which he thought might become reality within 50 years, sounds much like a technologically sophisticated version of the world state described in H.G. Wells's *Things To Come*; certainly, Bloomfield appeared to place a premium on mechanisms of surveillance and discipline. He did countenance the 'nightmare prospect' that world government could transmogrify into 'world tyranny – a kind of global Holy Alliance to preserve the status quo'. This is precisely what Danilo Zolo thinks is the true character and purpose of the post-Cold War new world order, discussed in the next chapter. Bloomfield's response to the concern he raised was to call for a world authority sufficiently flexible and adaptable to manage change; it must be able to solve the problem which pervades 'modern history' which is how to 'accommodate dynamic forces making for change'. For all this, the centre of active willing remains an all-encompassing global institution possessed of overwhelming force.[81]

A less severe and more creative response to the risk of thermonuclear war was offered by Erich Fromm, although this was by no means the only issue which concerned him. He conceded that the balance of terror might indeed bring about stability, yet its maintenance would be at the cost of creating 'militarized, frightened, dictatorial societies'; not only peace but also democracy demanded a willing embrace of *'universal controlled disarmament'*. Fromm's analysis follows on from the thesis he had developed in his war-time work *The Fear of Freedom*: that the 'automoton conformity' engendered by the modern industrial system, through intensifying the individual's sense of 'helplessness and insecurity' had spurred the turn towards fascism and nazism. By identification with and submission to 'new authorities' individuals relieve themselves of their self-doubt. The nuclear arms race did not lead him to recommend a coercive world authority; rather, he emphasised the need for a 'material and spiritual reorientation' on the part of the West. In *Why War?* Freud had suggested that outward aggression resulted from the displacement of the organism's death instinct on to others. War could be seen as a means of suppressing the will to self-annihilation. Fromm presented a modified version of this argument in discussing the Cold War, presenting it as a case of bad faith on the part of West in particular; the West had embraced a kind of false consciousness as a means of coping with the discrepancy between its professed values and the reality of Western peoples' lives. The Western system was portrayed as prizing individuality and upholding 'religious or secular humanism' but the truth was that the West was a 'managerial, industrial society with a diminishing amount of individualism'; it was also a society without goals other than unlimited production and consumption. 'We are', he added, 'developing into faceless organization men, alienated from ourselves and lacking authentic feelings and convictions.' And it was this fact, or rather because of the difficulty of facing it, that the West projected paranoid fantasies onto the Soviet Union, representing it as a totalitarian monster bent on world domination. While Fromm was not suggesting that the Soviet Union was without malign intent, he was implying that anxiety about and detestation of the Soviet regime were really Western self-doubt externalised. The hard military shell concealed a deep neurosis and the 'doublethink' involved in suppressing and hiding this condition was proving debilitating. Fromm argued that if this situation continued:

...we and the West will not survive. We will lack the energy and vitality that are necessary for any nation or group of nations to live and to survive in a world that is witnessing the awakening of nations that have been silent for hundreds of years.

For disarmament to proceed, the West had to overcome its fear of freedom; that is, it had to take the risk of trusting its enemies and of accepting the new national energies which were then bursting forth. It had to show it was not afraid of competing with the Soviet Union on the socioeconomic front; it should seek to defeat communism, and this was really the only way of doing so, by demonstrating that at home and as well as in Asia, Africa and Latin America it was possible to achieve 'economic progress and individuality, economic and social planning and democracy'.[82]

DECLINE OF THE WEST?

Fromm thought this approach was more realistic than that of those who advocated nuclear deterrence. Walter Lippmann was in the latter camp of realists, although he was no unthinking proponent of this foreign policy disposition. In 1960 he asserted of the American nation that: 'On our success in achieving military security by arms and by an astute diplomacy depend our national existence.' Realism meant knowing when to exercise caution as much as when to act; for Lippmann, it dictated that America must overcome the yearning for 'isolation' while also avoiding the Wilsonian legacy of plunging 'into a new globalism which supposes we are omnipotent, and averts its eyes from the hard reality of the power of the Communist bloc'.[83] Lippmann marvelled at the way the Soviet Union, devastated at the end of the Second Word War and possessing technology which was backward by American standards, had gone on to make rapid strides in the scientific and technological fields as symbolised by the launching of the Sputnik satellite; while drawing comfort from the launch of the American equivalent Explorer, he nonetheless wondered whether the Russian lead in the science of rocketry was testimony to the declining quality and vulgarisation of American education.[84] Lippmann had already touched on this concern in 1954.

Situating himself as one who had had 'prolonged exposure to the continuing crisis' of Western society, to 'the crisis of democratic governments and of free institutions during the wars and revolutions of the twentieth century', to a world 'divided and frightened and full of hate' he emphasised that of most danger to the West was not those ideologies and political systems which challenged its hegemony but rather the failure on the part of Western free societies to promote the good life within.[85]

For Lippmann, the notion of the good society meant a society which invested and took pride in its public institutions and through its political and educational bodies promoted civil, reasoned discourse. Yet he found in the America of the 1950s a climate in which ignorance and demagoguery prevailed, the last most glaringly on show during the McCarthyist rampage, an affair which did so much to undermine the self-confidence and courage of American scientists and thinkers.[86] The masses were becoming increasingly indifferent to matters of state and the ideals underpinning liberal democracy, and were instead preoccupied with material consumption. Added to this was a fashionable revolt against the idea that there can be public standards of truth and falsity, of right and wrong. While there was no shortage of the 'will to believe', at least to believe in that which furthered private interests and desires, there was an unwillingness on the part of modern man 'to believe in the invisible, the intangible, and the imponderable' precisely because such belief might restrain action. Lippmann implicitly was rejecting the wilful philosophical pluralism, pragmatism and voluntarism, early identified with William James and with which Lippmann had initially been enchanted. He insisted on the need to 'stand on hard intellectual ground' and against the notion, now being perpetrated by Jean-Paul Sartre and his philosophical fellow-travellers, that the 'principles of the good society are...invented and chosen' in accordance with one's desires. Far from endorsing an unadulterated realism and against the prevailing mood, Lippmann sought to resurrect the natural law of tradition of thought, maintaining that hovering above the 'infinite number of contradictory and competing private worlds' was a higher law and that its content could be ascertained by reason.[87] Lippmann had denounced voluntaristic philosophies after the First World War in favour of a kind of rationalism; clearly, he saw the discontents of the 1950s as part of the same crisis that had been unfolding since 1914. Yet there is a greater sense of moral militancy in his Cold War writings, although this was driven by despondency about the condition of American society and culture rather than anti-communist fervour. Its moral and not just physical superiority under challenge, he wrote, America and other Western democracies would have to take the 'manly view' and accept that their failure, not only in the Cold War context but throughout the twentieth century, was 'due to the failings of the democratic peoples'; the West had lost its pride of place because its peoples 'lacked the clarity of purpose and the resolution of mind and heart to cope with the accumulating disasters and disorders'. He would go on to make the point, and it is a very Jamesian one, that the Soviet challenge could be a blessing in disguise, it might check America's slide into a life of ease and invigorate its soul.[88]

Pitirim Sorokin also saw the Cold War as another phase in the crisis of modernity. He had previously argued that the intellectual and political turmoil of the twentieth century was the outward marker of the decay of a sensate culture and the budding, as he put it in the foreword to the 1957 edition of *The Crisis of Our Age*, of a '*new – ideational or idealistic – sociocultural order*'. He saw such a new order abounding in numerous fields of thought and endeavour. Like many before him, he saw science becoming spiritual in the dissolution of the material atom into 'more than thirty non-material, "cryptic, arcane, perplexing, enigmatic, and inscrutable" elementary particles' or into 'the image of waves...waves of consciousness which our thought projects afar'. In philosophy the same tendency was evident in movement away from positivism and the upsurge of existential, intuitive, neo-Thomist and neo-Vedantist philosophies. Political life witnessed the gradual growth of social movements seeking the abolition of war and injustice. Whether the creative impulses would soon overwhelm 'the now largely outworn sensate order' was by no means certain; in an analysis of the Cold War situation reminiscent of Bergson's 1915 essay 'Life and Matter at War', Sorokin represented nuclear and bacteriological weapons as instruments of reaction on the part of the old, material order.[89]

The final outcome of this epochal struggle will largely depend upon whether mankind can avoid a new world war. If the forces of the decaying sensate order start such a war, then, dissipating their remaining energy, these forces can end or greatly impede the creative progress or mankind. If this Apocalyptic catastrophe can be avoided, then the emerging creative forces will usher humanity into a new magnificent era of its history. Which of these alternative courses is going to take place depends tangibly upon every one of us.[90]

Yet for Charles Frankel in *The Case for Modern Man* (1955), the work of Sorokin, as well as other writers of epochal history, however fascinating and prestigious, reflected a current 'malaise' as well as displaying an enormous 'audacity'. The malaise was in part caused by the apparent rise of East European and Oriental civilisations and their attainment of a measure of equality with the West. Western civilisation could no longer claim to be in command and as a consequence routine views on history were being 'shaken at their base'. Under assault was a liberal, secular humanism, the belief that through the application of reason and scientific methods social progress could be achieved. The 'revolution of modernity', as Frankel called the emergence and spread of this belief and which he dated back roughly 300 years, was a world revolution. Yet in the current period of historical self-doubt, scientific methods, which Frankel denied were 'culturally limited in their validity' however much there existed differences among people, were being dismissed as 'parochial and "merely Western"'; this for him marked the 'crisis of our time'. For him one of the most striking responses to this crisis was the attempt to forge a new philosophy of history, one which sought to overcome the limitations of and 'stabilize' Western culture 'by rising to a higher synthesis – a truly universal culture – which will absorb and transcend the differences between men'. As we saw, Sorokin saw crisis as caused by the pervasiveness of a scientific outlook which had sensory experience as its principal intellectual yardstick; once liberating he thought it had now come to impair social development. Indeed, it would lead us down the path of destruction unless it were informed by something approaching the religious perspective. Frankel conceded that the first half of the twentieth century provided many examples of scientific means being put to bestial ends. Despite the abuse of science's fruits, Frankel thought the scientific outlook had stronger ecumenical credentials than the religious alternatives to it. He thought it audacious and dogmatic for Sorokin and others to seek place at the summit of human understanding a supernatural Absolute. Others had sought to grapple with the issues thrown up by America's global extension in a more 'moderate' fashion; F.C.S. Northrop, for example, had discussed the possibility of a 'meeting of East and West' on the philosophical front.[91]

Such moves Frankel described as well-intentioned 'attempts to provide us with what might be called a metaphysics of global diplomacy, a sort of philosophic Esperanto, which might enable us to speak intelligibly to the rest of the human race'. Yet it was not on any mystical plane that we were likely to meet with other societies; rather, it was Western science which had been seized on most eagerly by other societies. The turn from modernity and quest for higher knowledge revealed more than a sense of historical disorientation brought on by the altered position of the West in the world, its sharpened sense of cultural difference and the self-questioning attendant upon that. As Lippman argued, the real source of the Western crisis lay within. With the doctrine of liberal progress and the principle of scientific reason having been abandoned, Western societies were in danger of becoming intellectual and moral voids; these societies were becoming bereft of common meanings, values and a shared sense of purpose. Feelings of confusion and alienation, a 'sense of the total flux and evanescence of things' had seen anxiety become a general psychosis. The quest for a 'universal point of view toward history', however dogmatic, was at least a morally serious response to this situation. Worse was its flipside which was the retreat into scepticism. Frankel saw the revolt against reason as a twentieth-century phenomenon and he associated it with the work of William James, popular versions of Freud and Karl Mannheim's sociology of knowledge. Frankel saw Mannheim as coming close to advancing that kind of rationalism which upholds the right to rule of an intellectual elite to the extent that it is armed with correct knowledge, and there is much to justify this interpretation in Mannheim's works. Yet he rightly discerns Mannheim's pragmatist, Bergsonian proclivities writing that Mannheim's work was 'part of the whole trend of modern thinking which has replaced the traditional notion of mind as a pure and disembodied thing with a conception of intelligence as something practical and creative, a tool by which a vital creature adapts himself to a changing environment'.[92]

Frankel's eulogising about scientific methods and insistence on their applicability to social affairs might lay him open to the charge of rationalism. Yet even accepting this description it must be emphasised that his was not a chilly, doctrinaire scientism. Rational techniques of inquiry and discussion were precisely those that were public and shared. It was because scientific methods involved public meanings that they could be described as modern. For Frankel modernity is an unambiguous phenomenon denoting the goals of the Enlightenment. It follows then that for him philosophies of flux and action are anti-modern, they place a premium on private determinations as opposed to public rules of verification. As numerous examples have shown, such philosophies often were seen as the *sine qua non* of twentieth-century modernity. Frankel recognised Mannheim was seeking to reconstruct liberalism; as with Laski, Mannheim summed up his programme with the slogan planning for freedom. Yet Frankel thought Mannheim was not able to realise this aim because he left the task of designing social policy to an intelligentsia, one which could arrive at a detached appreciation of the whole. Mannheim's scientifically planned state could thus be said to approximate rule by divine revelation. Discernible in Mannheim therefore, albeit in a highly diluted form, is that oscillating movement that for Frankel characterised contemporary intellectual life: the polar swing between scepticism and dogmatism.[93]

The issue of the West's loss of confidence was addressed at by a meeting of 'a small group of the finest minds in the world' sponsored by the Corning Glass Works Foundation from 18–20 of May 1961. The meeting's brief was to address the question of 'The Individual in the Modern World' and its proceedings were subsequently published under the title *The One and the Many* (1962). The issue of the West's sense of purpose came up because it was felt that communism at least had a clear end in view which was the raising of standards of living to a level comparable to that of the United States. By contrast it was felt that the West was losing its motive power, it had no goals, or at least, did not live up to those it proclaimed. The West preached individualism, perhaps too raucously at times, yet individuality was being suppressed under the weight of industrial civilisation, with its accompanying standardisation and uniformity. At the same time, because of the ease with which the material goods could be attained for many people, life had lost its bite; individuals were experiencing feelings of frustration and disappointment. The American literary critic Alfred Kazin thought this was 'surely part of the reason for the extraordinary vogue of irrationality in modern Western philosophy'.[94] Equally, when it came to international politics the West failed to live up to the principles set down in the UN Universal Declaration of Human Rights, itself honouring them, stated Salvador de Madariaga (who while initially working with Unesco had departed that body on the admission of Franco's Spain), 'in the breach' while also compromising with notorious regimes.[95]

These are arguments which are apparent in Fromm and Lippmann and were put with even more frequency and strength throughout the 1960s as we shall see. Here I would like to draw attention to the keynote address 'The Individual in Modern Society' given by Charles Habib Malik, a Professor of Philosophy at the American University in Washington D.C. and in Beirut and former president of the UN Security Council. His speech, delivered with a degree of fierceness, is breathtaking in its rebuttal of the one worldism that so captured the Western imagination throughout the twentieth century and which, despite the iron-clad enmities of the Cold War, continued to lurk on the side-lines of the postwar era. The expression Free World, from the point of view of its champions, only superficially denoted an alliance of like-minded states or set of geographic zones. Did not the Free World truly represent what the whole should be or would assuredly become? Malik rejoiced in the freedom afforded in modern Western societies, yet the type of freedom that he most valued was the freedom 'to be the deepest that there has been', to realise the 'possibility of a personal self-consciousness infinitely rich and infinitely true'. This freedom to realise one's deepest self carried with it the enormous responsibility not only to avoid harm and but to bear this 'wonderful epistle of freedom unto the ends of the earth. Itself the matrix from which all universalisms have sprung.' Malik saw the gospel of freedom, as described above, as the greatest gift of Western civilisation; it was for him its 'ancient, universal message' and it was through shaking off of its self-doubt and boldly affirming this message that the West, a term which stood for an accretion of traditions coming out of Greece, Rome, the Near East and Western Europe, would achieve victory in the ideological struggle with communism and reconcile itself with the less developed countries of the non-Western world.[96] Malik played a key diplomatic role in winning acceptance for the Universal Declaration on Human Rights; he saw it as embodying not only the West's belief in the individual but that of all the countries which had endorsed it. That the Russian representative Vishinsky did not vote against it, fearing world public opinion, he regarded as 'great victory...one of the few victories in the United Nations of that order'.[97]

That aside, it would seem that the virtue of this Declaration for him was precisely that it attempted to provide a framework in which individual self-expression, in all its multiformity, might thrive. Malik disliked all types of monism, seeing the individual mind as deep, labyrinthine. Equally, he said it was illusory to think that modern societies were all of the same type. Each modern society, whether African, Chinese, Russian, Indian, Moslem, Latin and Western, manifested a distinct way of being in the world. Thus Malik insisted 'that the notion that there is an univocal thing called "modern society" with an univocal being called "the individual in it" is a myth'. Pluralism was the only perspective which could bypass the ominous traps of a 'single world view'; that a pluralistic internationalism might give latitude to maleficent behaviour and indeed permitted the denial of that self-realisation he so cherished, he implicitly acknowledged.[98]

Malik was particularly scathing about the 'monism of materialism' which had become prevalent in both the capitalist and communist worlds and at the United Nations, where economic development had become the chief means by which countries were judged. The metaphysics of materialism had arisen because, gazing upon the world, modern individual was struck by the degree of physical unity that existed, through trade, travel and communications links. The mind craves unity. But the type of oneness which is sheer physical proximity is unsatisfying, it being merely external. Yet what more in the way of unity could there be? The members of the UN displayed 'so many sovereignties, a dozens religions, a score of cultures, a score or more of languages, a score of social orders, many different forms of government, and a dozen stages of economic development'. Further, it seemed as if access to and acquaintance with other societies only made communities cling more tightly to and proudly assert their own cultural origins. Torn by this dilemma, the mind turns to what seems the only obvious grounds for unity: material needs and desires. Particularity disappears amidst the emergence of a 'materialist brotherhood'; the persistence of cultural, political and moral variety is explained away in terms of differing levels of economic development. To deny this is to risk being branded backward or isolationist, unaccepting of our common humanity. Yet Malik regarded the notion that we all have fundamentally the 'same needs and interests, that we are all "human beings," that we are all "brothers"' as tender-minded and feeble. Look deep inside the hearts and minds of individuals and you will find the 'differences are far more significant than the similarities.'[99] Malik evinced scepticism about functionalism; that it rests on the presumption of difference but hopes that this can be put aside while attention is turned to common pursuits; at the same time, it harbours the hope that differences will gradually fade in the course of cooperative effort. Yet Malik's point would seem to be that differences cannot always be circumvented, let alone erased, by appeal to material wants or a common interest in peace; each community, like the individual, has its own very distinct and special story to tell and attention should be paid.[100]

Reactions to Malik's speech were mixed. Some thought he had failed to appreciate that the purpose of industrial civilisation was precisely human betterment, and indeed that the former was the precondition for the latter. Others expressed fascination but wondered how his 'offensive of the spirit' could be translated into policy. Malik accepted Walter Lippmann's contention that when it came to competing against communism in Asia, Africa and Latin America, providing development assistance and means of social improvement was a better alternative to that of propping up corrupt, client regimes. His point was that the resonance and resilience of the social structure, culture, religion, governing ideas and way of life of people in these parts of the world had to be appreciated. At issue was not just the matter of appropriate development, but also the issue of respect for the integrity of peoples who were otherwise seen, where they were not regarded by the Western mind as simply economic functions, as 'alien and different'. The theme of the need to avoid 'ethnocentrism', was vigorously asserted at the conference by the anthropologist Melville Herskovits. He objected to the view that developed societies were 'better' than those of the undeveloped rather than merely different. He concurred with Malik and Madariaga that people in such societies need have no less a rich interior life than those living in conditions of affluence, and thought there was no compelling reason why all societies must follow the path of industrialisation. The 'cultural modesty' he urged, one observer noted, was in a sense in abundance at the conference with Western participants indulging in lengthy bouts of self-criticism. Yet Herskovits wondered whether all this self-flagellation was simply a luxury enjoyed by those who were in truth comfortable with their 'snobbery and smugness', and for whom there was a psychic pay-off in scrutinising, in a knowing fashion, their apparent deficiencies; the psychiatrist Sibylle Escalona offered the insight that 'self-criticism can be an easy way out – almost a form of boasting'.[101]

THE CRISIS OF REASON

There was more to all these expressions of self-doubt than intellectual narcissism. Frankel was right to predict that the global extension of American power would prove psychologically confronting, that it would compel Americans to reconsider whether Western values were truly universal. Geoffrey Barraclough considered that the idea of a unifying liberal culture had had its day; he warned against thinking that a 'new unifying culture' would emerge quickly or that it would emerge at all.[102] The debate as to whether the West stood for anything other than the furtherance of its own economic and technological success was pursued relentlessly throughout the 1960s; it was a debate which, while causing discomfort in some quarters, had to be taken seriously not least because of the foreign policy implications it could have. Although diverse in their evaluations, Lippmann, Fromm and Malik all thought that for America and its allies to prevail in the bipolar conflict then the West had to be seen as standing for a set of ideals and a way of life worth defending and promoting. Yet many of those who continued to cast doubt on the foundations of Western civilisation did not see themselves as simply reflecting or responding to the paranoias generated by the Cold War and the rising tide of anti-Western rhetoric attendant upon the post-colonial transition.

Michael Harrington, for example, in *The Accidental Century* (1965) was disappointed that the new postwar order had not seen, as had been promised, the triumph of the masses but rather the triumph of technocracy; at the same time, for him this was just another chapter in the sustained crisis of the twentieth century. He observed that the Western world had 'haunted itself with rumors of its own death' for at least 50 years, beginning in August 1914 when the

very earth opened up under the feet of every Western social philosophy. At one and the same time, both *status quo* and utopia were in crisis...every nineteenth century hope, to use Sorel's phrase, became indeterminate.[103]

The crisis of the twentieth century was seen ultimately as a crisis of belief, that is a lack of faith in ultimate values; Harrington wrote that a fresh breeze of indeterminacy was already blowing through the fields of aesthetics and philosophy before the war, as reflected in Henri Bergson's notion of *l'élan vital* and William James's pragmatism. But after the war what had been an uplifting spirit of anarchy descended into full-blown scepticism. It troubled Harrington that so many in the twentieth century felt the lure of decay; there were many who were seduced by chaos, who would glamourise dissolution and delight in absurdity. But Harrington did not underestimate the enigmatic force of 'sophisticated barbarism'.[104] He described the likes of Spengler as architects of chaos; these were members of the Devil's Party, a 'major camp of modern genius. It is composed of those who could give aesthetic form to chaos, but not to order.'[105]

Harrington's analysis of crisis was a development of Valéry's; he noted that Valéry was among the first to discern that there were 'two decadences possible in the twentieth century'. The first concerned the decline of intellectual standards and a consequent abandonment of civilised values, while the second involved a deadening of the human spirit through the rationalisation of social life. Harrington argued that the first part of the century most expressed the former kind of decadence while the second half would be largely an instance of the latter. The first half of the century saw a 'violent apocalypse', with two world wars, economic collapse, class antagonisms, the rise and fall of vicious dictatorships 'and, finally, the discovery of a bomb which could annihilate mankind and render the world uninhabitable'. Adding to the sense of uncertainty, was the fact that the West was losing 'its unquestioned rule of the world' as symbolically signalled by the Chinese Revolution of May 1919. The dropping of the atomic bomb on Hiroshima marked the end of the period he referred to as the hot decadence. At a superficial level, postwar planning in the domestic and international sphere marked the triumph of the will to order over the will to chaos. Irrationalism was driven underground and the calm, cool face of technological reason shone upon the world. Yet technological reason had a darker side. The crisis of Western civilisation had not been overcome but had been submerged and in a sense deepened because it was now unseen. Harrington wrote:

a typical excess of the century emerges at the outset; that it has supported two, seemingly contradictory apocalypses, one gentle the other violent...In the thirties it was a question of a storm; in the sixties, it is one of a deep sea change below the social surface. And both moments are the expression of the same persistent turbulence of the twentieth century.

It is a turbulence induced by a technological revolution on a scale and at a rate unknown in history; Harrington calls it the 'accidental revolution' because it was under unregulated, private control and for these same reasons it was 'shaping an unstable new world'.[106]

Harrington's account of the twentieth century's technological transformation embraces the same polarity which had featured in discussion of the ideas of modernity and rationalisation in the years between the wars. On the one hand it means standardisation while on the other it signifies rupture and dissolution. These dual characteristics were apparent in the interwar period because in addition to witnessing much disarray, this was also an era which saw the growing corporatisation of industry; Harrington noted that this development had been forecasted by Walther Rathenau in *Of Coming Things* in 1917. It is a process which accelerated in the postwar period with the extending corporate colonisation and cybernation of economic and social life. For Harrington, it seemed the West was heading towards a situation in which technicians and skilled workers would be reduced to automatons, mere articulations of vast, centralised corporate machines. Below these categories, there would exist a new lumpenproletariat, confined to tasks of the most menial kind; disorganised and irregularly employed they would form an 'urban *jacquerie*'. Yet contrary to those who foretold the end of ideology, Harrington wondered whether these social trends might generate a renewed sense of the sacred, a feeling for utopia; they might give rise to a desire, if not in Karl Liebknecht's words to storm 'the gates of heaven', to make the accidental revolution conscious by seizing it and turning it towards ideal ends.[107]

The critical theorist Herbert Marcuse in *One Dimensional Man* (1964) lamented that people could not see beyond the apparent benevolence of postwar capitalism to the reality of crisis. For him too, it was not just the products of science that threatened humanity it was the scientistic mode of thought itself. a mode of thought which boasts of its rigour and objectivity but is ultimately vacuous because it is not concerned with the realm of value. Advanced industrial society, the latest phase in the projects of modernity, science and technology, had an increased capacity for 'domination', over both nature and the individual in both a conceptual as well as physical sense. The separation of Reason from questions of value, that is, the positivist 'denial of the transcending elements of Reason' and the projection of man and nature as mere instruments, as material to be rationally organised and administered, provided the academic warrants for this domination. Marcuse traced the curious, winding path taken by scientific philosophy from hard positivism to subjectivism, idealism and then on to pragmatic instrumentalism. His argument was that in quantifying nature, in seeking to explain everyting in terms of mathematical equations, science divorced reality from the question of final ends. Science's identification of reality with that which could be expressed in terms of measures not only had the effect of discounting the universe of values. The paradoxical consequence was that the status of reality became 'more and more dependent in its objectivity on the subject'. Reality takes on an ideational character where its imputed qualities are really 'only the results obtained' by mathematical or logical operations. The concreteness of the objective world thus dissolves, it becomes an effect of a constituting subject and acquires a form wholly reflecting the structure of the scientific mind.[108]

Lenin had expressed concern about the idealistic turn taken by philosophers of science because of the danger it posed to the materialist interpretation of history. Marcuse, however, thought contemporary philosophy of science, while 'moving dangerously close to an idealistic concept of nature', had managed to put 'idealism "on its feet"'; at least, reason imparts to nature scientifically conceived an air of objectivity. Matter almost slips from sight or becomes ethereal as it is rendered as a series of mathematical operations; such moves at the theoretical level have their practical parallel in the remaking and transformation of nature in the name of technological rationality. Marcuse wrote:

The science of nature develops under the *technological a priori* which projects nature as potential instrumentality, stuff of control and organization. And the apprehension of nature as (hypothetical) instrumentality *precedes* the development of all particular technical organization.

Gaston Bachelard described well the pragmatic enterprise in its scientific guise in observing of contemporary physics that: 'Nature is placed under the sign of active man, of the man who inscribes technique in nature.' Yet the point is that the forms and functions we engrave on extensive experience take on a given or necessary appearance, they are presented as 'pure objectivity' rather than as the constructions of subjectivities.[109]

It becomes rational to think of minds and nature as resources to be exploited in accordance with the demands of the economic system. They are reduced to being the means by which a self-propelling, self-reproducing productive apparatus maintains itself. In its debauched form, which is instrumental reason, theory serves the cause of all-pervading control. Yet while appearing to be the 'very embodiment of Reason' advanced industrial society was 'irrational as a whole'; it squandered resources, denuded the earth and denied the realisation of those human purposes which were real, historical possibilities.[110] Yet many people could not see through to the reality of their repression. This was not just because of the apparent effectiveness of the system on the economic front but also because of the 'one dimensional' character of people's thought. For Marcuse this meant that

...ideas, aspirations, and objectives that, by their content, transcend the established universe of discourse and action are either repelled or reduced to terms of this universe. They are redefined by the rationality of the given system and of its quantitative extension.[111]

It is for the reason that advanced industrial society integrates alternative sites of opposition, as well as because of our increasing enslavement and enclosure by the productive apparatus, that the system is 'totalitarian'. This description was justified on two other grounds. First, because the industrial system reproduced the same pattern of enslavement in the 'less developed' and 'pre-industrial areas of the world', and second, because it generated 'similarities in the development of capitalism and communism'. The struggle for existence, which involved the exploitation of man and nature, while becoming 'ever more scientific and rational' had become a 'total international struggle'. Marcuse posed the rhetorical question as to whether the 'threat of atomic catastrophe which could wipe out the human race' was not needed to maintain existence in this warped condition. One of the tasks of critical theorists therefore, was to redefine rationality in terms of such criteria as the 'pacification' of existence, at the individual, national and international levels, and the 'free development of human needs and faculties'. Marcuse declared: 'I believe that the very concept of Reason originates in this value judgement, and that the concept of truth cannot be divorced from the value of Reason.'[112]

What Marcuse saw as the positivist denial or derealisation of values, the American philosopher Stanley Rosen referred to in his essay on *Nihilism* (1968) as the 'denaturing' of reason by which he too meant the perversion of reason into 'rationalism'. Rosen also thought the 'crisis of reason' explained why the twentieth century had been a 'century of global convulsions'.[113] He repeated Henry Adams's notion that the dynamo had been substituted for God 'as the expression of human transcendence' and that in doing so we have transferred a 'psychic energy' and surrounded with a 'religious aura' merely 'the interactions of political and technological flux'.[114] He reflected on Valéry's 'Crisis of the Spirit' in which the latter, despite his pessimism, counterposed to Europe's confusion and debasement the cultivated intellect. For Rosen, Valéry's civilising intellect was too effete a construction to offer an effective barrier to either the poeticist politics of Sorel or those who would, in Spenglerian fashion, think with their blood.[115] He viewed as equally futile and pernicious the effort to escape the metaphysics of dynamism and the politics of nihilism attendant upon it through 'a neutral, universal scientific perspective', a solution which Valéry also tended to favour, as equally futile and pernicious.[116] With logical positivism Rosen wrote:

...the conception of 'reason' has been detached from its traditional affiliation with the conception of 'good'. It has become a virtually unanimous article of faith...that one may speak reasonably about logical patterns of inference of 'empirically verifiable facts'...but not about what is good...By detaching 'reasonable' from "good", the friends of reason made it impossible to assert the goodness of reason. Indeed, they made it all the more easy for the enemies of reason to assert the evil of reason. Reason (we are told)...will destroy us or enslave us to machines. Reason is a machine or machine-life; ultimately, a stultifying poem or human creation. Little wonder that so many are today searching for edifying poems in the regions of the nonsensical and the insane...Today philosophy and historical existence are both threatened by the nihilistic consequences of the denaturing of reason, which was ostensibly a purification of its nature. There is no time for melodramatic posturing before the abyss of nothingness, but neither is there time for an absurd refusal to take seriously the threat of absurdity.[117]

Wyndham Lewis saw the philosophy of becoming as apparent in, if not the desire to submerge oneself in the mass as well as the tendency to adopt the posture of the intellectual vaudevillian. Rosen made a similar point, explaining that in order to escape the anxiety and nausea attendant upon the embrace of spiritually empty ontologies, people have either become unconscious or descended into the superficiality of the comic consciousness as evident by contemporary '"black humour" and the ironical acceptance of one's own baseness and vulgarity'.[118] Indeed, the currency of ironic posturing is both a response to and defence against the more popular form of nihilism which is mental immobility and which is evident throughout the ages. It is this self-conscious glorification of nihilism which he described as an 'erotic perversion...similar to the worship of machines', which is largely a twentieth-century phenomenon. Rosen made the bold and sweeping assertion that: 'Only during the past one hundred years or less it has become *fashionable on a global scale* to say that it is abnormal to function normally.'[119]

Taken together the ideas of Harrington, Marcuse and Rosen amount to the contention that the positivistic denial of metaphysics, the refusal to admit notions of beauty, truth and justice into the domain of knowledge result in purposeless materialism and the treatment of individuals as mere quantities on the one hand, and nihilistic rebellion and hilarity on the other. The source and nature of the good or true reason varies from author to author. Harrington spoke of a spiritual resurgence, Marcuse's perspective was humanist and Rosen sought to defend Plato and classical philosophy. Yet they shared the belief that social life must be guided by something other than the pursuit of material satisfaction and sensual pleasure. Their observations were not completely fresh. The interwar period saw analyses of positivism and nihilism as well as the dialectical relation between them. We should also note the common tendency to project the peculiar anxieties of Western intellectuals onto the rest of the world. What had changed by the 1960s, and this point is most relevant to the observations of Harrington and Marcuse, is that criticism of positivism and rationalism, and the industrial systems these doctrines were seen to underwrite, had sharpened and widened. As compelling as some of the critiques of scientism and technocracy offered in the interwar years were, they had existed on the margins in an intellectual culture enchanted by the idea of technopolis and the chill splendour of the scientific estate.

A NEW VISION OF ORGANIC UNITY

It has been pointed out that in the geopolitical imagery associated with the Cold War, the idea of the global figured to the extent that this was the scope of the bipolar military orders being built by the super-powers as well as those weapons of mass destruction designed to secure these orders. It is tempting to contrast this with the generally happy connotations attached to the idea of the global in the early twentieth century, although we should not forget that a similarly deadly significance had once been been attributed to air power. I have shown that one worldism did not entirely disappear in the postwar period. Nonetheless, there is a telling contrast to be made between the interwar pictures of transborder flows entwining the world's people and Cold War depictions of a world divided into 'geostrategic regions', 'conflicting spheres of influences' and 'shatter-belts'; in its wording, the Antarctic Treaty of 1959 which designated Antarctica a scientific park to be used for peaceful purposes and in the 'interests of mankind as a whole' stands out against an otherwise bleak canvas.[120] In the light of the pictures of a spatially divided and armour-plated world painted by these expressions, as well as the mounting concern about the alienation induced by and destructiveness of machine civilisation, it is not surprising that the 1960s witnessed a revival of organic imagery. The organic analogy was deployed in the first few decades of the twentieth century to promote the principle of world unity, although I have suggested that more often than not it was electricity that was upheld as a uniting force. In the introduction to Kenneth Boulding's *Meaning of the Twentieth Century: The Great Transition* (1964) Ruth Nanda Anshen contended that there was at work in the world a new consciousness among spiritual and intellectual leaders, one which sought to break the bonds of Cold War prejudices and antagonisms and 'recapture the authority of truth and human totality'; people were beginning to sense 'the new reality of the World Age'. She wrote:

There is in mankind today a counterforce to the sterility and danger of a quantita-tive, anonymous mass culture, a new, if sometimes imperceptible, spiritual sense of convergence toward world unity on the basis of the sacredness of each human person and respect for the plurality of cultures...We stand at the brink of an age of a world in which human life presses forward to actualize new forms. The false separation of man and nature, of time and space, of freedom and security, is acknowledged, and we are faced with a new vision of man in his organic unity and of history offering a richness and diversity of quality and majesty of scope hitherto unprecedented.[121]

Again, we observe the diversity in unity motif, here given a naturalistic spin. We also observe a degree of temporal ambiguity for the new vision of humanity is evocative of the older conception of man existing in intimate relation with his fellows and with the rest of nature under cosmic law. This reintegration of man with nature might suggest for him the role of nature's steward rather than master. Boulding wrote of the enormous threats posed to our 'precious little planet, this blue-green cradle of life with its rosy mantle' by nuclear weapons and overpopulation. Man, he wrote, is 'captain' of a 'frail and delicate vessel' and he must take care that he does not destroy it. Yet technochratic and rationalist sentiments also colour Boulding's text, and inform his perspective on nature. An economist at the University of Michigan, he offered the view that the 'scientific and technological transition' the world was undergoing involved a

faith in the orderliness of the natural world, faith in man's ability to perceive this order and manipulate it for his own benefit, and faith in processes of learning which involve direct experience rather than mere acceptance of the received tradition from the elders.

He added, echoing views articulated by the interwar proponents of rationalisation, that in so far as 'atheistic communism' had served to undermine 'primitive animism' and replaced a 'belief in the arbitrary and wilful nature of the material world by a belief in its stability and orderliness' it too was part of the great transition. Boulding expressed confidence that by further extending scientific research into social matters ideological disputation could be reduced.[122]

Boulding depicted nature not so much as an all-encompassing organism but as a quietly functioning system. While the term system has an organic significance it also has mechanical overtones and Boulding wanted to allow some scope for the manipulation of the natural system. Boulding reintegrated the biological and mechanical viewpoints, and indeed these have a long history of interplay. In a way similar to Poincaré he saw scientific knowledge as mirroring nature's ordered structure. Also reminiscent of Poincaré, was his suggestion that the manipulation of nature can only be successful where it is done in accordance with nature's laws. Boulding continued to depict nature as a coherent system, although a growing sense of environmental crisis would lead him to underline further the need for careful management of the earth's resources. In 1966 he penned an essay called 'The Economics of Coming Spaceship Earth', the title of which was taken, wrote John McCormick, from a speech given by Adlai Stevenson, who was at that time the US ambassador to the UN, at a Unesco meeting meeting in Geneva in July 1965. Stevenson was canvassing the negative impacts of urbanisation the world over and described in his speech the 'earth as a spaceship on which humanity traveled, dependent on its vulnerable supplies of air and soil'. Boulding developed this idea, comparing 'the open "cowboy economy" (reckless, exploitative, romantic, where production and consumption were good things) with a future "spacemen" economy concerned primarily with stock maintenance'. McCormick notes that the idea of spaceship earth began to crystallise in the the public mind with the 'publication in 1966 of the first photographs taken by Lunar Orbiter satellites, which showed the planet as a lone, finite, and seemingly vulnerable oasis in Space'; he cites Arthur C. Clarke's claim that these photographs 'must have been the moment when the Earth really became a planet'.[123]

The image of spaceship earth is beautifully evocative in both organic and technological terms. Its appeal rests on its fusion of graceful nature with gleaming technology. While it is suggestive of a mystic monism it is also infused with the romance of scientific discovery and rockets to the moon. We might say that spiritual and scientific understanding meet in a quiet contemplation of the whole. Through its association with such images, science recaptured some of that air of cool neutrality which its role in the development of the nuclear strategies of the superpowers might have denied it. Space was a site of conflict. The space race was a form of passive wardom. Yet space signified stillness and calm. We might think here of the symbolic impact of the Treaty on Principles Governing the Activities of States in the Exploration and Use of Outer Space, including the Moon and Other Celestial Bodies (1967), also known as the Outer Space or Moon Treaty. Under this treaty, outer space, the moon and other celestial bodies were declared the common heritage of humanity and zones of peace. Astronauts were described as the envoys of humankind. At the same time, spaceship earth conveys a melancholic sense of our limitations and loneliness amidst a realm of cold, infinite darkness. To the extent that this significance is brought to the fore, it is intended to stir in people a willingness to cooperate in the interests of survival. In his *Principles of World Politics* (1972) George Modelski wrote:

> The primary referents of this analysis [of world society] are the planet Earth and nature, along with man and his works upon the planet In an era that has launched upon space exploration, what had already been known by astronomers for some centuries has become a property of public consciousness – namely, that the Earth is a small and fragile island of life in a vast and inhospitable expanse of space.[124]

We might recall here William James's suggestion that in order to overcome the problem of war humanity must unite in a war *against* nature on an only partly hospitable planet. In the era of space exploration humanity was urged to unite in a battle *for* the planet, our one and only home. Warnings of impending ecological disaster abounded in this context. In *Towards a Politics of the Planet Earth* (1971) Harold and Margaret Sprout, an American couple who did much to raise awareness of humanity's relation to the surrounding ecology in the 1970s, wrote:

> The ecological way of seeing and comprehending envisages international politics as a *system of relationships* among interdependent, earth-related communities that share with one another an *increasingly crowded planet* that offers *finite* and *exhaustible* quantities of *basic essentials* of human well-being and existence. Despite an appearance of abundance in a few countries, food and other essentials are in chronic short supply in many more countries, and the earth as a whole is being denuded, depleted, and polluted at rising rates that portend, unless arrested and reversed, a progressively degraded future for most of mankind, and the somber possibility of irreversible catastrophe for all...we are encumbered with an archaic, fragmented international system of jurisdiction and authority that survives from an era *when the human population of the earth was not one but many.*[125]

In invoking planet earth and representing nature as a system of relationships the Sprouts were seeking to promote a model of world politics in which
sovereignty was no longer an operating principle. Sovereignty is depicted as
a legal constraint belonging to another era and one which is hostile to
nature. The need to relinquish sovereignty is reinforced by the claim that
humanity, which from an environmental perspective is now one rather than
many, is living on the edge of disaster. The idea of system might be used in a
way that implies a need for technical management. Indeed, the possibility of
ecological doom was used to justify, as past crises had been, world planning
by trained experts. The Club of Rome, a group of scientists, technocrats and
politicians seeking to foster international cooperation on the issues of
economic development and population, argued in its report *The Limits to
Growth* (1972) that if society were 'to embark on a new course, concerted
international measures and joint long-term planning on an unprecedented
scale was needed'.[126]

At the United Nations Conference on the Human Environment in
Stockholm in 1972 and the 1974 Population Conference in Mexico the
questions of environmental and population management were sources of
tension between the North and South. This underlines the point that the
rhetoric of planetary oneness was largely a pet ideal of Western intellectuals.
Developing countries recoiled at any suggestion that they should curb their
economic growth, especially in the absence of serious moves towards the
New International Economic Order they were calling for during the 1970s,
while the push to curb population growth was seen as part of an effort to
curb further expansion in the numbers of non-Western peoples. William
Ophuls in *Ecology and the Politics of Scarcity* (1977) concluded that given the
limited achievements of such conference diplomacy, and the entrenchment
of the principle of national sovereignty in the form of Principle 21 of the
Stockholm Declaration, the only solution to the crisis of 'ecological scarcity',
one which threatened to erupt into 'Hobbesian turmoil and violence', was
planetary government. He wrote that the 'already strong rationale for a
world government with enough coercive power over fractious nation states
to achieve what reasonable men would regard as the planetary common
interest has become overwhelming'.[127] Ophuls's planetary government
would be placed in the hands of a body of 'natural aristocrats' who would
legislate temperance. Ophuls conceded that he was advocating a shift away
from democracy. He sought to deflect the charge of authoritarianism by
insisting that the rules of the steady state would be derived from values
established by common consent. He offered the classic ethical idealist defence
that compelling people to desist from intemperate acts does not make them
unfree, rather it is to deliver to them a higher freedom.[128] Others, however,
were promoting a system of world government which enshrined the principle
of popular sovereignty. A Constitution for the Federation of the Earth, drawn
up by the World Constitution and Parliament Association which had been
pursuing this matter since 1958, was agreed upon in 1977. As in the late

1940s, world government was needed to avert a global threat, in this instance the possiblity of global environmental breakdown. The Constitution announced that a new world was emerging out of the ashes of the old. A new age was dawning in which diverse peoples would come together as one in the cause of peace, prosperity and justice. The preamble read:

Realizing that Humanity today has come to a turning point in history and that we are on the threshold of a new world order which promises to usher in an era of peace, prosperity, justice and harmony; Aware of the interdependence of people, nations and all life; Aware that man's abuse of science and technology has brought Humanity to the brink of disaster through the production of horrendous weaponry of mass destruction and to the brink of ecological and social catastrophe; Aware that the traditional concept of security through military defense is a total illusion both for the present and for the future; Aware of the misery and conflicts caused by ever increasing disparity between rich and poor; Conscious of our obligation to posterity to save Humanity from imminent and total annihilation; Conscious that Humanity is One despite the existence of diverse nations, races, creeds, ideologies and cultures and that the principle of unity in diversity is the basis for a new age when war shall be outlawed and peace prevail; when the earth's total resources shall be equitably used for human welfare; and when basic human rights and responsibilities shall be shared without discrimination. Conscious of the inescapable reality that the greatest hope for the survival of life on earth is the establishment of a democratic world government; We, citizens of the world, hereby resolve to establish a world federation to be governed in accordance with this constitution for the Federation of Earth.[129]

It is useful to know that the thinking behind this proposal owed much to the legal monism of Léon Duguit who conceived 'of all law as belonging to one universal system, applying to the international (or better, world) community as well as to all subordinate communities included within it'. Further, it drew on the interwar supranationalism of Harold Laski and Georges Scelle, both of whom had subscribed to the natural law thinking of Duguit. Note also that this federal world state was to be endowed with powers of law enforcement.[130] World federalism was seen as a rather quaint enthusiasm in the postwar era. The critical theory, counter-cultural school of international relations scholars which emerged out of the 1960s and which included such prominent international relations scholars as Saul Mendlovitz and Richard Falk, preferred spontaneous, grass-roots cooperation to large-scale organisation. Mendlovitz and Falk were prominent in the World Order Models Project (WOMP) in the 1970s which set out to investigate the Clark-Sohn model of world government and propose alternatives to it. WOMP criticised the model on the basis that it glossed over the presence of authentic political cleavages based on issues of class and race and invested too much faith in constitutional engineering. A related criticism was that Grenville Clark, along with the Harvard law professor Louis Sohn, had focussed on the matter of war prevention to the exclusion of problems of social injustice, ecological breakdown, poverty and alienation. WOMP demanded that the new world order be a just world order. It emphasised the evolution of a world culture seeing in this fertile soil for functional governance and it contrasted this goal with that of world government with all its hierarchical implications.[131] Their position seems to be in contrast then with that of the proponents of the Constitution for the Federation of the Earth as it gave to the prospective world federation powers of law enforcement. Despite the emphasis placed by the WOMP team on social struggle, especially that of suffering peoples in the South, and local movements for social change, the same legal monism which underpinned this proposed Constitution was evident in WOMP's thinking. Further, one could argue, however, that world government was, in effect, the end point of just world order designs to the extent that they sought to overcome the sovereign state and institute world law. Mendlovitz, for example, announced in 1975:

> It is my considered judgement that there is no longer a question of whether or not there will be world government by the year 2000. As I see it the questions we should be addressing at ourselves are: how it will come into being – by cataclysm, drift, more or less rational design – and whether it will be totalitarian, benignly elitist, or partici-patory (the probabilities being in that order).[132]

Seeking to deflect the charge of unrealism, Richard Falk described the belief that a straight line led from the 'present impasse to the future utopia' as 'sheer phantasy', as 'the dream of a rationalist'; yet it was the problem of 'transition' not the plausibility or worthiness of the goal of one world that vexed Falk. In *The Study of Future Worlds* (1975) he elaborated his 'preferred world' for the 1990s as one which included a 'central guidance framework' under the auspices of a World Assembly comprising an Assembly of Governments, an Assembly of Peoples and an Assembly of Organisations and Associations; he saw this coming about after a sustained period of consciousness raising and political consensus building concluding in political transformation.[133]

Anthony Dolman, writing in 1981 and reflecting on the previous decades of discussions of world order, identified Mendlovitz as a supranationalist for whom global governance meant much the same thing as world government; that is an institution, and here Dolman cited the Marxist Silviu Brucan, 'vested with the authority to plan, to make decisions, and to enforce them'. Yet Dolman thought approaches demanding radical transformation of the system, promoting one-worldism, would curry little favour with the public and the 'policy-making mainstream, both of which are inherently conservative, overwhelmingly gradualist and intolerant and fearful of things which smack of "extremism"'. The persuasiveness of such proposals relied very much on a sense of ongoing and deepening sense of crisis. Dolman noted Geoffrey Barraclough's observation that the 1970s had witnessed a 'growing awareness of the fragility and precariousness of civilization', adding that 'words like "catastrophe", "collapse", "chaos", "disaster" and "despair"' had become *de rigueur*.[134] As we have seen almost exactly the same observation was made in the 1920s and 1930s. But the rhetoric of crisis had less purchase in 1981 than it had in the interwar period in Western countries, an issue taken up in Chapter 6. After decades of warnings of imminent collapse, audiences might have become somewhat jaded. At least in the interwar years talk of decline and collapse meshed with clear and apparent signs of social decay and conflict. One is not denying the seriousness with which nuclear weapons and environmental issues came to be regarded and the importance of the social movements that concern about these matters unleashed. Yet this was not enough to see the emergence of broadbased support for global integration. It might be salutary that 20 years on it still has yet to materialise.

6 COMMON SECURITY AND GLOBAL DIVERSITY

GLOBALISATION AND GLOBAL GOVERNMENT

We have seen that the term internationalisation, along with rationalisation, was used in the interwar period to refer to private processes of worldwide integration as well as either world or international government. The convenors of the Amsterdam Conference on World Social Economic Planning in 1931 had chosen the word world rather than international to be included in the conference's title in order to highlight the appearance of greater relations of intimacy among the world's governments and people. There was an awareness that the term international had a weaker significance. References to the globe, as well as to the planet, as our common home also appeared in arguments for world order prior to and after the Great War. Yet it was not until the 1960s that the term globalisation, referring to a process of worldwide integration, began to come into vogue. What is interesting is that at the outset the term was used to refer to long-term historical developments as well as a wide range of phenomena.

In his *Principles of World Politics* (1972) George Modelski included a discussion of the 'process of globalization', a term which he used to signify global interaction, awareness and 'some degree of world wide value commonality'. It was a process he dated back to 1000 CE, and saw speeding up during the age of exploration in the fifteenth and sixteenth centuries and then, fuelled by European 'arrogance and violence', accelerating exponentially in the nineteenth century. Yet if globalisation was in a sense very old it was also a bearer of the new. Globalisation, he stated, gives birth to modernity. For a long time, modernity had largely been confined to European states and indeed he stated that globalisation had served to prop up the state in that region. Yet in the present era it escaped state control and in connection with this he argued, and here the normative point to his discussion becomes apparent, it was necessary wisely to direct globalisation towards the goal of establishing a 'governmental structure that would give equal, not to speak of higher priority to a rounded concern for all aspects of the welfare of the human race'.[1]

Noting the connecting between early pluralist and functionalist thought, such as that of Duguit and Laski, and the thinking on world politics of Leonard

Woolf, H.G. Wells and David Mitrany, Modelski called for measures to control world growth, wealth and welfare and to facilitate a 'general loosening up of world society' not only in the sense of a loosening of borders but also in the sense of unleashing new independencies and differences. He wrote:

> There is promise in the conception of a complex, pluralistic world that can move toward a more just society...This emergent type of world structure could be described as a system of multiple autonomy; being open-ended, it allows for a multiplicity of possible successful outcomes in complexity.

There are two points to make here. First, the plurality of which he spoke would be centred not on states alone but on both state and non-state actors. He suggested that the state, once a container of modernity, is from a world society perspective a backward-looking formation because of its 'continued institutionalisation of war' and the obstacle it posed to the 'long-overdue modernization of world politics' which is precisely the globalisation of policy and government. The second point is one I have made in relation to Wells's and Laski's portrayals of world order, that the differences he would like to see blossom and thrive are imagined to be benign.[2]

In 1979 in an essay called *The Positive Role of the State* Hedley Bull expressed irritation with the rising chorus of voices urging that the 'state-centric paradigm' was 'an obstacle to the achievement of a viable world order'. He noted the constant reiteration of the theme that there was

> some basic contradiction between on, on the one hand, the unity of interconnected-ness of the global economy, the global society, the global polity, and, on the other, the system under which each state claims exclusive jurisdiction over particular area of the earth's surface.[3]

Bull could see no contradiction between the legal status of states and their involvement in all manner of relations of interdependence; indeed, the sovereign state was an efficient instrument for managing such relations. He stated: 'So far from it being the case that the sovereignty of the state is something antithetical to international order, it is the foundation of the whole edifice.'[4] That is, the theory of sovereignty does not imagine the world to be composed of irreducibly isolated and autonomous units. Sovereignty is rather a means of negotiating relations among diverse entities who are bound to both need and collide with each other. Further, he added that states had done much in the way of cooperating together on matters to do with the world economy, standards of living, literacy, human rights and so on. He doubted whether a world government would better deal with violence, economic oppression and the exploitation of nature, all of which, he emphasised, predate and have far deeper causes than the state system.[5] Yet the most crucial leg of his argument was that in Socialist countries and those of the South there was little trace of globalist views among state elites and he thought no amount of invoking spaceship earth or the global village would rapidly alter this situation. He wrote: 'From the perspective of the two weaker sections of the world political system, the globalist doctrine is the ideology of the dominant western powers'; in particular for former colonies' sovereignty was a defence against the neo-imperialism implicit in expressions such as '"basic human needs," "the international protection of human rights," or (more sinister still) "humanitarian intervention"'. Bull thought such suspicions were correctly founded as he added that the:

> ... Western globalist does indeed express, among other things, an exuberant desire to reshape the world that is born of confidence that the economic and technological power to accomplish it lies at hand. One senses in it a feeling of impatience that the political and legal obstacles ('ethnocentric nationalism', 'the absurd political architecture of the world', 'the obsolete doctrine of state sovereignty') cannot be brushed aside. It is also notable that the prescriptions they put forward for restructuring the world, high-minded though they are, derive wholly from the liberal, social-democratic, and internationalist traditions of the West, and take no account of the values entertained in other parts of the world, with which compromises may have to be reached.[6]

Bull was not merely being sensitive to the feelings of those outside the Western orbit. Here he is expressing an intellectual or temperamental dislike of political rationalism. The rationalist is one who disregards the real and resistant quality of tradition and sentiment and instead treats social forces, once stripped of emotion, superstition and prejudice, as readily amenable to reconfiguration. Bull observed the tendency on the part of those whom he dubbed western 'solidarists', 'one-worlders' and 'global centralists', to elaborate '"goals" or "relevant Utopias"' and set down 'plans for reaching them'; he criticised this on the grounds that while this might be how the 'policy-scientist's mind works' it was not 'what happens in world politics'. Bull was by no means denying, in the manner of the fatalist, that experience was open to injections of human will, it was just that it was not as easily remoulded as the rationalist thought. He thus counselled a pragmatic course arguing that world order was best served, not by trying to remove state borders and attempting to push on the rest of the world 'our own preferred values and institutions', but rather by accepting and finding a means of negotiating among the 'very different values and institutions' existing in various parts of the world while at the same time attempting to build on these 'elements of world order' already in existence.[7]

   In this chapter I develop some of the lines of argument Bull offers in his critique of 1970s globalism. It hardly needs saying that in the post-Cold War era the rhetoric of globalism has, if anything, intensified, although I would suggest that most of it runs down the same argumentative grooves traced by Modelski and before him by the supporters of rationalisation. I will be arguing that Bull's position still holds to the extent that it remains evident that the institution or idea of the state still commands the allegiance of large sections of public opinion, regardless of economic and other forms of globalisation. In addition, I want to defend the view that there still exists in this world differences that go a long way down and that these are not otherwise capable of being harmonised into some putative good. Further, I will be arguing that if one is genuinely committed to the idea of an open-ended universe then one must accept the possibility of irreconcilable differences arising, as shocking as these might be. Social theorists who, as part of their assault on the state toy with a metaphysics of flux and fluidity, have yet to face this issue squarely often end up reaching for that disingenuous formula of many inside the one.

On 12 June 1950 the Danish physicist Niels Bohr issued an 'Open Letter to the United Nations' in which he pressed for an urgent and coordinated response to atomic weapons, For Bohr the nuclear age demanded a 'radical' overhaul of 'international relationships' and 'a proper appreciation of the duties and responsibilities implied in world citizenship'; he further insisted that 'full mutual openness, only, can effectively promote confidence and guarantee *common security* [my emphasis]'.[8] From the 1960s depictions of the essential oneness of the planet along with forecasts of ecological breakdown were harnessed to programmes aimed at reorganising world politics, just as nuclear weapons had been since their advent. One of the key concepts that was elaborated in this context was that of common security, a concept, as Bohr's letter to the UN intimates, predicated on an understanding of the world as an integral and shared space. In 1977 Lester Brown insisted on the need to look beyond military-territorial definitions of security and seek international cooperation in order to secure those environmental systems, such as the climate and the oceans, on which all people depended, adding that 'political leaders have yet to realize that national security is meaningless without global security'.[9] As the period of detente faded with renewed Cold War hostilities, albeit acted out in pantomime fashion, the spectre of thermo-nuclear war once again prompted thoughts about the need to move beyond a fragmented state system. In 1982 the UN's Independent Commission on Disarmament and Security Issues, chaired by Olof Palme and including prominent international figures such as Gro Harlem Brundtland and Shridath Ramphal among its members, produced *Common Security: A Blueprint for Survival*. Noting mounting public anxiety about the game of nuclear bluff and counter-bluff being played by the two superpowers and seeking to reduce tensions especially in Europe, it proclaimed that in a nuclear age, given the scope and impact of nuclear weapons, war was no longer an instrument of policy and denounced the doctrine of national security. The Commission declared:

States can no longer seek security at each other's expense; it can be attained only through cooperative undertakings. Security in the nuclear age means common security...*International peace must rest on a commitment to joint survival rather than a threat of mutual destruction.*

The Commission upheld the goal of general and complete disarmament although it conceded that this would not be achieved in the short or medium term. In the meantime the Commission urged 'all states to adhere' to the Non-Proliferation Treaty (1970) so as to forestall the horizonal proliferation, stressing at the same time that: 'Failure to stop vertical proliferation will compromise the integrity' of the treaty.[10] Beyond this, the Commission sought to emphasise the UN's 'primacy international peace and security and to enhance the role of the Security Council'. Unsurprisingly, given the geo-political realities of the day and the make-up of the Commission itself, it recommended only a limited implementation of the UN Charter's collective security provisions, limited in the sense that intervention by the Security Council would be confined to 'Third World conflicts arising out of border disputes or threats to territorial integrity caused by other factors'. Despite these qualifications and the assurance that this modified form of collective security would be based on some sort of concordat between permanent members of the Security Council and Third World countries, there are traces in *Common Security* of the military-hierarchical thinking that would come to the fore in discussions of world order at the end of the Cold War.[11]

While the Commission treated economic security as a key aspect of common security which 'requires that people live in dignity and peace, that they have enough to eat and are able to find work and live in a world without poverty and destitution' it did not discuss its environmental implications, perhaps reflecting the weakeness of global spatial imagery in the early 1980s.[12] This was left to the World Commission on Environment and Development (WCED) which was chaired by Brundtland and which issued a report in 1987 called *Our Common Future*. The type of commonality suggested by environmental problems resulted in a report softer in tone than that of *Common Security* which conveyed a sense of impending destruction. Reminding audiences of the interrelated nature of ecosystems the WCED declared that: 'The Earth is one but the world is not.'[13] Repeated in tones that suggest it is a kind of spiritual revelation, it is an incantation which is seen as trumping any defence of the system of sovereign states. The report went on to state that the environment: 'locks countries together as the effects of national policies and actions spill over national borders. Separate policies interlocked issues...[t]he real world of interlocked economic and ecological systems will not change; the policies and institutions must.'[14] In literature on environmental issues we often find the organic analogy being brought into play. A specific image of nature is appealed to in order to justify certain political forms. Nature is typically presented in the literature on politics and the environment as a place of 'grace' rather than 'rude will'; it should be clear that proposals to standardise environmental and economic policies will be all the more inviting when they come bathed in a beneficent fluid. Yet it is crucial to note that nature is also suggested to be somewhat unbending. Hence the argument that the political manyness of the state system must yield, for the sake of our well-being, to the principle of harmonious integration. It is not to discount the gravity of environmental problems to note that this is a move no less dubious than nineteenth-century depictions of nature as a place of sharp differentiation and self-regarding competition so as to naturalise policies of social exclusion.[15]

In one example of this genre of argument Patricia Mische argued that we needed to 'reconceptualize sovereignty' because: '...The Earth does not recognize sovereignty as we now know it. Existing concepts and systems of state sovereignty are incongruent, even antithetical, to the prerequisites for global ecological security...*the sovereignty of the Earth is indivisible.*' Again, a particular conception of nature is selected and then reified in the form of the biosphere. Mische goes further and endows the biosphere with human capacities such as knowing and feeling, albeit under the guise of that epistemologically impossible stance of non-anthropocentrism. In this way, the earth and the term planet is frequently discussed in the same manner, comes to be seen itself as a subject worthy of consideration, or indeed, of elevation. We might be able to see how this line of thinking might encourage support for the authoritarian type of world government proposed by Ophuls. Mische's organicism, however, is cast in terms of friendly, horizontal relations among localised units. The political harmony which nature recommends does not have to be induced but is ensured by, and here Mische's argument resonates with a key feature of Bergsonian metaphysics, a life force which pulses through the whole world and empowers each individual living thing. Thus she writes: 'Our national boundaries are more like the skin on our bodies than solid walls. They are permeable membranes through which there is flow of life between our own existence and that of the rest of the world.'[16]

THE DEATH OF CRISIS

Proponents of world integration frequently build their case on the twin pillars of crisis and spiritual oneness. Yet in the latter part of the twentieth century the potency of the sign of crisis diminished. A matter that concerned Marcuse was that people in general were blinded by the distorting mirror of instrumental reason to the reality of crisis. Rosen's chief concern was that the response of many to crisis was to become comatose or rejoice in absurdity. In the mid-1980s the American sociologist Christopher Lasch argued that it was not the absence of any sense of crisis that was the problem rather it was the term's very proliferation. Lasch perceived in the middle of the 1980s a widespread sense of social anxiety which quickly transmuted into apathy and indolence. The mystification of existence, mass torpidity or a descent into the comic consciousness which were seen as key features of late modern society were effects of the normalisation of crisis. Further, because the word crisis is now applied to every domestic detail we can no longer identify the real crises that we face.

The infiltration of every day life by the rhetoric of crisis and survival emasculates the idea of crisis and leaves us indifferent to appeals founded on the claim that some sort of emergency commands our attention. Nothing makes our attention wander so quickly as talk of another crisis. When public crises pile up unresolved, we lose interest in the possibility that anything can be done about them.[17]

Thus the rhetoric of crisis, when it is tamed by social analysis and reduced in impact by constant reiteration in the media, is also a weapon of repression. Crises are constructed and manipulated by authorities in order to shift the focus away from the real dangers. For Lasch the contemporary crisis was real and was the result of the escalating arms race, crime and terrorism, environmental deterioration, and the prospect of prolonged economic decline. These developments had resulted in a loss of 'confidence in the future' and a preparedness for 'the worst'. While also seeing crisis as a twentieth-century phenomenon, it being a century of mass murder and destruction, he thought the situation had become much graver in the previous 20 years. This was due, he said, to the increased instability of social and economic conditions and to the decline in faith in remedial political action. This loss of faith, he thought, was no little due to the writings of Marcuse and his ilk according the modern political system such an overwhelming capacity to incorporate or repulse alternatives that seemed almost to deny any hope or possibility of transcendence. Marcuse, Lasch wrote, had contributed to the 'general air of crisis'.[18]

Lasch also complained that the apocalyptic rhetoric of the closely related peace and environmental movements, the calls for, as Richard Falk put it in *This Endangered Planet* (1971), a 'moral commitment to survival' might have, as Falk acknowledged, an equally immobilising effect. Lasch thought people would probably regard as scary the 'new system of world order', the 'unified "city of man"' corresponding with Falk's 'vision of the earth's wholeness'. For Lasch the peace and environmental movements when seeking to persuade audiences relied too much on appeals to abstract ideals whereas instead they should be speaking to the concrete, emotional attachments of people.[19] He wrote:

...emphasis on the global dimensions of the survival issue – on the need for global controls and for the development of a 'global mind' – probably helps to undermine attachments to a particular place and thus to weaken still further the emotional basis on which any real interest in the future has to rest. Rootless men and women take no more interest in the future than they take in the past; but instead of reminding us of the need for roots, many advocates of disarmament and environmental conservation, understandably eager to associate their case with the survival of the planet as a whole, deplore the local associations and attachments that impede the development of a 'planetary consciousness' but also make it possible for people to think constructively about the future instead of lapsing into cosmic panic and futuristic desperation.[20]

Lasch objected to the dictatorial and totalising implications of proposals for world government grounded in fears of environmental or nuclear catastrophe. While he exaggerated the prominence of such proposals, at least in the context of the 1980s, he queried the equation of the global with goodness. The idea that the world is moving towards political unity, whether reinforced by naturalistic or technological imagery, has been generally been cast in a golden light throughout the twentieth century. Those denying this shift have been portrayed, often justifiably, as atavistic or self-regarding. Yet critiques of one worldism did not solely emanate from those bent on domination at home and aggression abroad. Philosophical and political pluralism celebrated in the vitality of the small and the local, informed criticism of one worldism as much as it did of statism in the early part of the century. It is true that this was not as powerful a current of thought as was social monism after the First World War, yet as I have shown, nearly all advocates of globalism have felt the need to find a place within their scheme for diversity and even to portray the social pattern being elaborated as a case of many inside the one. By the 1980s, following a revival and radicalisation of pluralist theory, this need was felt more keenly. Related to this was a sharpened concern that the emergence of a '"superculture" of airports, automobiles, fast food establishments, blue jeans' and so on would see the obliteration of 'cultural variety'. Kenneth Boulding in *The World as a Total System* (1985) wrote that given the astonishing rapidity with which the world was advancing towards unity perhaps the most significant question facing humanity in the twenty-first century, a question of more relevance than the choice between 'one world or none', would be that of how to preserve variety.[21]

What is notable about the twentieth century is not simply the intensity of the crises that it experienced. Spengler long ago pointed to the ethnocentrism lying behind the belief that the modern epoch was more greatly characterised by transition and disturbance than earlier eras. Just as he had in *The End of Ideology* (1960) Daniel Bell in 1987, rejecting the notion that the twentieth century was the century of despair, cited a 4,000-year-old Egyptian papyrus which described a time in which 'Great men and small agree in saying: "Would that I had never been born."'[22] What we might say, however, is that what characterised the twentieth century in the West was the ubiquity of a self-conscious rhetoric of crisis. In the realm of both intellectual and political discussion the twentieth century was indeed the century of crisis. To pose the question as to the meaning of the twentieth century, as Kenneth Boulding did, is to invite an ironic answer. For the meaning of the twentieth century does not lie in any one thing external to the word crisis, despite the grappling and analyses of so many thinkers and specialists, but precisely in the central place the term occupied in the Western political vocabulary.

Yet the linguistic continuity of the rhetoric of crisis, both over time and across various discursive contexts, masked much conceptual discontinuity. The sources of and solutions to crisis are manifold. Umberto Eco pointed out in 1986 that there was no such thing as 'the crisis', rather there are crises and one must distinguish between them. He added that if we refuse to view crisis as a 'massive object' then we must also refuse requests to find a 'global answer' to the difficulties we face. Neither 'the crisis' nor 'the answer' are real things; but are the effects of linguistic strategies. Eco pointed out that crisis is simply a way of viewing change and he argued that given the ferocious speed at which change now takes place, which is part of the experience of modernity, we are indeed compelled to live under the sign of crisis. There is no transcendence or resolution of crisis in this sense. Yet just as we may choose to view change as crisis, we are also able to choose whether to view crisis as either a sinister or liberating phenomenon.

That the term crisis had lost much of its allure is evident in a December 1987 issue of *Encounter*. The magazine's editors, concerned about the 'modern malaise', sent out a questionnaire to a number of eminent writers and scholars which asked whether there was a 'crisis of "confidence in western civilisation"'. The result was a symposium entitled 'The Climate of Fear' and it was argued by the editors that: 'The Western World appears to be undergoing one of its periodical losses of confidence.' This lack of confidence, they claimed, had been present throughout the century as shown by 'Thomas Hardy's "time of the breaking of nations", Spenglerian 'gloom and doom'...Sidney Hook's "failure of nerve"... with Orwell's "1984"...with the Club of Rome's "year zero".' All of the difficulties these expressions referred to, the editors said, could be subsumed under the heading of W.H. Auden's 'age of anxiety'.[23] Yet what was interesting was that the editors wrapped quotation marks around expressions like crisis in civilisation as though they felt the need to establish a degree of distance between themselves and what was by then a somewhat hackneyed idea. Sensing this, one respondent replied: 'Yes, There's a "crisis of confidence in civilisation", even without quotation marks.'[24] The editors felt the cause of crisis lay with known dangers such as drugs, depletion of the earth's resources, population explosion, Aids and 'other sex-related disasters', terrorism and urban violence, whereas some respondents viewed the supposed erosion of intellectual and moral foundations throughout the century, the ever-widening fashion for ontologies of nothing, as a source of worldly difficulties.[25] Yet others questioned the Western conceit that crisis and an attendant profound sense of anxiety were peculiarly twentieth-century conditions. The historian Ian McNeil, the author of *Plagues and Peoples* (1976) among other works, wrote:

For nearly two millennia, most of our ancestors lived in expectation of an early end of the world by divine intervention. Secular visions of atomic or some other apocalypse are remarkably similar to the prophecies of the *Book of Revelations*. If our predecessors could live with that hanging over their heads, believers and unbelievers of the twentieth century can surely do the same.[26]

Indiscriminate use, awareness of the egocentric presumptions which frequently underlay its deployment, as well as an expanding ironist culture all worked to undermine the rhetoric of crisis. There is a greater awareness that the term is used less to reach out and capture experience than as a technique of persuasion. In the Western world at least, the rhetoric of crisis does not appear to mesh with obvious signs of decline or collapse. As we have seen, a global environmental crisis has been described since the 1970s in a manner that seems to recommend one-world solutions. Andrew Hurrell argues that the notion of environmental crisis is unlikely to have the political effect many of its advocates would like, not least because the effects of environmental problems are often long-term, diffuse and unclear.[27] More importantly Hurrell goes on to elaborate in reference to the United Nations Conference on Environment and Development which took place at Rio in 1992, that the 'one-worldism' which characterises much environmental discussion ignores the presence of genuine conflicts of interest and value, as well as differing perceptions of danger:

> ... [the] image of the Global Forum in Rio as a 'world community in waiting', although a seductive one, is deeply misleading. The state system may well be part of the problem but it is also an essential part of the solution. The lack of global solidarity about resources and environmental issues is not primarily rooted in the state system but in the inability of human beings to agree on the nature and seriousness of the environmental threats, on the meaning of sustainability, and on the principles of global environmental management. Unless the present international system breaks up in some dramatic and unexpected way, these tensions need to be managed on a global basis...The political and moral tensions that have long been central to international society – above all between the respect for difference and pluralism on the one hand and the cultivation of an overlapping consensus on the nature of a common world good on the other – would not go away, but would merely reappear in a different form. There is no obvious reason for believing that an alternative to the state system would prove a better means of achieving this (already extremely difficult) end.[28]

The Rio 'Earth Summit' was believed to signal the embrace of the 'world environment ...[as] the "central, organising principle" of international relations'.[29] Yet an examination of the debates which took place at the UNCED reveals a strong determination on the part of signatories that the 'sovereign right' of states to 'exploit their own resources', as articulated under Principle 2 of the 1972 Rio Declaration and before that under Principle 21 of the Stockholm Declaration (albeit with the qualification that states are responsible for the external consequences of activities taking place within their jurisdiction) should not be undermined in either a moral or legal sense.[30] We should also note that the tendency to reify nature and turn it into a sacred category proved to be a source of tension between some Western delegates and non-government organisations and representatives of the G-77 and China at the Rio Conference, manifest in the dispute over the attempt to name the Rio Declaration the 'Earth Charter' and announce a radical change from the human-centred thinking of past UN statements on the environment. These moves were opposed by leaders of developing countries who viewed them as reflecting a fixation with the 'inanimate workings of nature' on the part of Western countries to the detriment of the world's poor. This was why Principle 1 of the Declaration insists that: 'Human beings are at the centre of concerns for sustainable development.'[31]

The lack of commonality on and resistance to cooperation on environmental matters led Elizabeth Dowdeswell, as director of the UN's Environmental Programme in 1996, to contrast the developing 'sovereignty of the marketplace' with the 'shrinking power of the nation state' insisting that as

we are losing the ability to control forces that are impoverishing both people and planet, we must answer with governance that is coextensive with the market, in other words, global...the multilateral process and international agreements must be given teeth.[32]

The full implications of this statement are made clear in the following statement on the need for:

Enforcement by the Security Council of World Court decisions...One could imagine the creation of an international criminal court...Another proposal is to replace ECOSOC [the UN's Economic and Social Council] with an Economic Security Council that would assess the state of the world economy, provide a long-term strategic policy framework for sustainable development, and secure consistency between the policy goals of the Bretton Woods institutions [the World Bank and the International Monetary Fund] and the WTO [the World Trade Organisation].[33]

Such statements are anathema to many in the North and are a cause of great anxiety in the South. Moves towards global enforcement of sustainable development, as is implied by proposals for world environmental courts or more generally for the UN's authority to be buttressed so that it can 'assist in the emergence of a new regime of planetary management' might not only see a breakdown of environmental negotiations but quite likely an exodus from the UN system.[34]

ANOTHER NEW WORLD ORDER

President George Bush's 1990 Congressional address *Toward a New World Order* heralded the dawn of a new era in which 'the rule of law supplants the rule of the jungle, a world in which nations recognise the shared responsibility for freedom and justice'. Continuing in this vein, both he and his successor President Bill Clinton, told the United Nations General Assembly that promoting liberal democracy and free markets would be the overriding aims of United States foreign policy in the post-Cold War era.[35] The post-Cold War New World Order (NWO) was attacked from a number of different directions. It was quickly challenged by bleaker projections; neo-Spenglerian themes like the clash of civilisations and a return to 'tribalism' were proffered in the closing years of the century.[36] Danilo Zolo, portraying the Gulf War as the first war of the new world order, claimed the promotion of the NWO was an attempt to establish a 'hierarchical-military utopia' by powerful states and their allies to uphold their interests and preferred norms of conduct. He sees well-intentioned proponents of global governance as complicit in this process.[37] But some advocates of one-worldism found Bush's new world order too thin a concoction. Bush's NWO was sometimes contrasted unfavourably with that of Woodrow Wilson. Bush was criticised for not projecting democracy as a central tenet of any NWO and for coupling his call to 'defend the Charter's emphasis on inalienable human rights' with the assertion that 'no nation must surrender one iota of its own sovereignty'.[38] It was the years between 1993 and 1995 under the Clinton presidency that marked the high-tide of American attempts to operationalise the new world order in respect to human rights through its military interventions in Bosnia, Somalia and Haiti. Michael Mandelbaum saw these fraught exercises as pointing to the futility of treating foreign policy as 'a branch of social work' and others have noted the marked reluctance of the Clinton administration, despite its rhetoric, to expend American lives and resources in carrying out such operations during the rest of the decade.[39] Whether the promises made in the name of an NWO in the early 1990s will continue to be backed by a significant degree of political will is doubtful, although the NATO intervention in Kosovo certainly revived hopes that the post-Cold War era had seen the acceptance of war in the name of humanity.

The advocacy of an NWO was not just the preserve of American presidents. This rhetoric was also espoused by international bureaucrats, academic lawyers and independent scholars who, invoking the 'new spirit of commonality' abroad in the world, offered a range of plans for global peace and welfare throughout the 1990s. Ingvar Carlsson, a member of the UN Commission for Global Goverance, in a speech given in Chicago in 1996, called for a 'new order in world affairs, a new style of managing our relations on this planet, and a new way of relating to the planet itself'.[40] In the preceding year the Commission had issued a report entitled *Our Global Neighbourhood in* which it asserted that while states 'retain sovereignty... governments have suffered an erosion of their authority' due to the 'pressures of globalization', (for example, they are 'less able...to control the transborder movement of money or information') as well as to internal social and cultural fissures. The deference paid to sovereignty was seen as superficial. In *Our Global Neighbourhood* references to the reduced capacity of states, as well as to their propensity to abuse the freedoms that sovereignty accords, reflected a desire to transcend the current system.[41] Michael Barnett correctly observed that, unlike Boutros Boutros-Ghali in his 1992 *Agenda for Peace*, the authors of this report were 'less constrained by or committed to the idea of state sovereignty'; they went further than the former UN Secretary General in placing the state 'alongside' international organisations and 'transnational actors' and in 'seeing the UN as the most likely candidate to guide the ongoing global transformation'.[42]

In its advocacy of tighter relations of interdependence and the strengthening of institutions of governance in such fields as human rights and the environment, the Commission's version of a NWO can be seen to differ from that envisaged by Washington policy-makers at the end of the Cold War, which was centred on police action under the auspices of the Security

Council. The latter certainly had the somewhat autocratic, martial cast that Danilo Zolo has attributed to it. Yet as fraternal as the Commission's vision might seem, perhaps it is something even more to be feared by states jealous of their prerogatives. The great powers' NWO seeks only to restrain states when it comes to interstate aggression or gross human rights abuses, and this is likely to be only on a selective and haphazard basis. It would seems more hospitable to liberty of state action than a system of global governance of wide scope and intensity. Robert Latham argues in *Liberal Moment: Modernity, Security, and the Making of Postwar International Order* (1997) that there is a 'unique relationship' between what he calls liberal order-building and military force. The former provides order while avoiding the need for 'more thickly institutionalized political relations of governance'; in this way the relative autonomy or liberty of 'actors in the international system can be preserved'.[43] The correlation between the thinness of international society and military relations is perfectly clear. What might be questioned is the nexus between liberalism and the state system. Liberalism can be pulled in either particularist or collectivist directions in respect to both domestic and international arrangements. Justifications of conscious social control from the 1920s to the 1940s were often couched in liberal terms. Harold Laski and Karl Mannheim argued throughout this period that economic planning was necessary for freedom. Many of those involved in the elaboration of the 1940s NWO echoed this sentiment representing it as a new deal for the world. The adaptability of liberal arguments is further underlined by Friedrich von Hayek who dismissed international planning in order to equalise standards of living as a danger to the independence of states and societies, yet argued in favour of a super-national authority with the power to prevent both international and national authorities from behaving in a tyrannical fashion. In the contemporary period liberal values are invoked in order to justify both sovereign statehood and a cosmopolitical state. Liberal arguments thus may or many not follow a statist logic. Further, a global order based on the ideals of human freedom and flourishing could well be a militarised one insofar as the use of force might be necessary to defend these goals. This possiblity tends to be obscured by the use of the expression global governance when discussing political arrangements beyond the state system; it is a notion which is strongly distinguished from the now dowdy and autocratic-seeming idea of world government. While the latter is taken as implying a superstate in the juridical sense the former stands for a much more constitutionally ambiguous state of affairs.[44]

In Jan Aart Scholte's view global governance means the state is immersed in a network of substate and superstate relations of a governmental and non-governmental kind in which it is not possible to locate supreme authority or even to imagine it exists. Certainly, he suggested that '...as part of our shift from national conceptions of society to a world society idea, we ought to replace the conventional notion of the state with the concept of a world state' yet his world state is not obviously the sovereign state enlarged. It is a 'world-scale phenomenon with interlocking global, regional, national and local branches' making up a 'complex of regulation'. Such a political structure is flatter, looser and more particularistic than is implied by the sovereignty model; it thus circumvents the problems of tyranny and social monism while achieving the globalisation of policy. Construed in this way, global governance has much in common with the theories of organic or functional solidarity popular among pluralists in the interwar years and discussed in relation to both the state and the world. However, such theories, while explicitly repudiating the principle of state sovereignty and putting in its place a *droit objectif*, implicitly endorsed the need for mechanisms of law enforcement.[45] Global governance can be conceived along more or less anarchistic lines. Scholte seems to tend in the former direction although why one should assume that all the various relations of governance will operate relatively smoothly in the absence of supreme authority is not clear. That aside, it should be noted that sometimes the distinction between global governance and world government disappears. The Commission on Global Governance must have been wary of the charge that it was proposing of top-heavy global administration. Its assertion of the 'need for integrated global approaches to their management and world-wide embrace of the discipline of sustainable development' might have given rise to such concern. It pointedly emphasised that it conceived of global governance along democratic and pluralistic lines.[46] Yet one of its most prominent members, Sir Shridath Ramphal, insisted that what the expression common future really meant was that our ultimate 'oneness' which must and will triumph over the 'instinct of "otherness"'.[47] This assumption of essential oneness, along with the appearance of ominous transborder pressures, led another Commission member Brian Urquhart to conclude that the UN would eventually 'cross the line from being a purely intergovernmental association to having at least some elements of a world community organization'; the use of the word community, so rich in grass-roots meaning, cannot disguise the fact that Urquhart has in mind a cosmopolitical state.[48]

RHETORIC OF GLOBALISATION

Those declaring the decline of the state often confuse the politico-legal condition of sovereignty with empirical power. An example would be Scholte's assertion that 'globalization has brought an end to sovereignty'.[49] One does not deny that actual capacity is crucial to the exercise of juridical sovereignty. Yet weak states remain sovereign, or as Alan James puts it 'con-stitutionally independent', even though they are limited in their ability to enjoy their independence fully. And, as Robert Jackson has argued, the rights that go with sovereignty, even in the case of weak states, are not trivial as their vigorous defence would indicate. That states may come and go, they may be absorbed through conquest or internal collapse, does not mean an end to the state system as such.[50] To show that the state system is in decline much fine-grained analysis of the condition of states would have to be done. Yet claims about borders melting away are often not seriously empirical in their thrust. Rather, in being told that sovereignty is eroding we are being called upon to relinquish a way of thinking about legal and political relations both within and among states, a way of thinking which many regard not merely as no longer relevant, but as intrinsically troublesome and vicious. Pierre van den Berghe wrote in his contribution to a symposium on state behaviour and the deepening global crisis several years ago that:

...the state is the ultimate protection racket, the consummate social parasite. I like to define it as a killing machine controlled by the few to steal for the many...It cannot even be said that they have outlived their utility, because they never had any except to those who run them. Either they must wither away, or we must as a species.

Another contributor, Yuwa Wong, expressed much the same attitude while also revealing the core concern behind much of global rhetoric in stating that: 'Without exaggeration, sovereign states today are the most serious roadblocks to realizing visions of a common humanity with a viable common future.'[51]

The rejection of the sovereignty of the state and the acceptance of the global governance project very much pivots on the belief that globalisation is like a juggernaut: almost unstoppable and sweeping all before it. We have to be convinced that the state is floundering, becoming impotent and irrelevant, in the midst of this process. What might be particularly emphasised in this regard is globalisation's more unsettling manifestations such as the drugs trade, transnational pollution and currency instability. At the same time, we have to be convinced that global governance is possible, that there is coming into existence a world society based on which systems of governance can be elaborated or constructed, hence the frequent emphasis on the common consciousness being forged by global communications and transport networks.

Yet here a paradox arises. On the one hand, we are presented with a scene in which states are fast becoming moribund institutions and where there is a wide constituency for global solutions. On the other hand however, we are told that the move towards global governance is being inhibited by the legal principle of sovereignty which permits states to misbehave with impunity and refuse to participate in cooperative regimes. The sovereign state is thus empirically incapable but legally strong. That we are constantly being told that sovereignty is in decline is precisely because, in the legal sense, it is not. Arguments which purport to show that sovereignty, as a matter of fact, is under challenge too easily merge with exhortations to throw off its burdensome yoke. One is reminded here of Laski's assertion that the concept of sovereignty should be expunged from political thought as it was of dubious validity in fact as well as being morally pernicious. In discussions of global-isation and the state, there is much slipping and sliding between empirical and normative points. Globalisation, understood in its expansive sense, is less a clearly discernible feature of experience than a rhetorical effect. Stemming from a desire to reconfigure the political and social contours of the planet, narratives of globalisation have crystallised into myth.

An array of articles and phenomena, many of which bear no close or even discernible relation to one another, have been placed under this rubric. Laden with significance, globalisation has been rendered as a motive power. In some accounts it is as if all the various manifestations of globalisation, such as intercontinental ballistic missiles, international drug cartels, pollution and capital flows, arise from an original impulsion, one which incites them to rupture established political arrangements and conceptual taxonomies. In other accounts globalisation is represented as the outgrowth of a fundamental biological drive, that is the 'tendency of the human species to grow, develop and expand'; developments in global communications, for example, are thus seen as superficial and more recent expressions of what can now be seen as a primitive rather than modern phenomenon, one which would seem to take in almost all of humanity's interactions with or impacts on planetary processes. [52] Defined in this way, it could be said that globalisation finds articulation in the sharpening of flint into crude tools and weapons no less than in the 'drifting clouds of radioactive gas' emanating from the nuclear power plant accidents such as Chernobyl in 1986. The term becomes coextensive with the history of technological development. Yet the Chernobyl incident is cited as a stark example of globalisation for a more intuitively satisfying reason. Joseph Camilleri and Jim Falk wrote in 1992 of how the radioactive gas utterly bypassed the 'fixed boundaries of the national domain and the supposedly supreme authority of the sovereign state'; the glib response to this sort of claim is to point out that the weather similarly escapes state control but then no one ever suggested that the assertion of constitutional independence was an affirmation of mastery over geophysical phenomena. Yet the point of the rhetoric is not so much to define sovereignty accurately but rather to convince audiences to stop thinking of states as discrete units and instead to imagine themselves as part of a larger society and system. Citing destructive forms of globalisation such as transnational pollution is one means of achieving this end; the hope is that it will awaken in us a renewed planetary awareness, that it will revive that 'long-standing perspective of a living planet as an integrated whole', 'ultimately governed by natural law'. In relation to Camilleri's and Falk's narrative it should be noted that it is not simply that contemporary problems have becomes so intractable that we need to modify existing arrangements. They see the construction of the sovereign state and multiplication of this form as involving the 'partitioning of the biosphere', which was always an act of disfigurement; to conceptualise the world in terms of the state system was an act of bad faith which involved a denial of the reality of planetary wholeness, a reality now perhaps beginning to burst forth again. [53]

We encounter here the temporal ambiguity that was present in early twentieth-century discussions of modernity. As we saw, the futuristic element in narratives of new eras is often softened by appeals to older cosmopolitan ideals. Throughout the interwar period electric machine power, especially in the form of the radio and aeroplane, was often thought to be propelling humanity towards its shared and finer destiny. Yet this same forward movement was also seen as marking a return to the medieval notion of an ever-widening ethical commonwealth. In the contemporary context, globalisation is often illuminated by the white light of technology. Whereas it was once the radio-machine it is now cyber-space that supposedly defies and challenges the territorial integrity of the state. Today, in a way this is similar to Wellsian paeans to the promise of liberation held out by the age of flight, contrasts are drawn between a weightless, flowing 'dematerialised' realm of 'electronic space' and the dead weight of the state, of traditional loyalties and geographical determinations. Globalisation as electronic flows acquires a dreamy, ethereal glow with flashes of science fiction. The normative implication of this image should be apparent: to enter the cool and fluid electronic realm is to free ourselves from the aggression inducing 'grip of blood and soil' and enter a domain of peace.[54]

Just as in the interwar period, medieval patterns are today embroidered onto glittering scenes of technological futures. The medieval scenario has different significations for different authors. For some it is suggestive of a vast and generous cosmopolis with differences flowering happily alongside each other under the sway of natural law. While there is compenetration among jurisdictions this does not result in disharmony. Yet others might emphasise the uncertain and arbitrary nature of boundaries in the medieval era, a tendency paralleled in the use of the term globalisation to signify less the ethically charged notion of natural interconnectedness, than the idea of unbounded movement. In this way globalisation becomes associated not only with science fiction fantasies but romantic tales of past adventures, hence the references to desert nomads, the caravan trade, the Roman Empire, the crusades and the exploration of unknown lands and seas as early forms of globalisation. The neo-medieval scenario can be pulled in more or less anarchical directions depending on one's temperament and desires. It should also be mentioned that where it is seen to be suggestive of disorder and the arbitrary exercise of power, a more formal, less loose-ended model of governance might be preferred. As Pierre Hassner wrote, while for some the neo-medieval model 'holds the promise of more flexibility and tolerance' to others it 'evokes memories of the Inquisition and of witch hunts, of bands of beggars and robbers, or wandering knights and pirates'.[55]

THE ONE AND THE MANY

Narratives of globalisation seduce through emotional and aesthetic appeals and the play of metaphors. Quite striking is the use of organic and technological imagery. The former naturalises and imbues with a sweet air the idea of a globalised world while latter makes this prospect seem dynamic and thrilling. Nature is painted in some discussions as a complex and lively network of interrelations and in this regard it is fused with the image of a technologically wired planet. Biological and mechanical metaphors have a long history of interplay and we might recall here the vitalistic implications of depictions of a world awash with electricity in the interwar period. A number of commentators on environmental issues have compared nature's dynamic, interactive processes with the rapid flows of information around the globe. Gwyn Prins, for example, tells us that information technology 'gives us the ability to manage large, multivariate analyses which can begin to model the circular, interactive reality of the planet', to think in a 'new way' that mirrors 'the natural circularity of environmental processes'.[56] Organic and technological imagery are entwined so as to represent the coming postmodern world as a vibrant scene of multiplicity in unity. Yet these two sets of images can be contrasted with each other, with the first implying holism and the second a rupturing dynamism. Holistic imagery features strongly in writings urging that forms of global governance supplant the artificial divisions of the state system. Governance of this kind is also seen as the best way of coping with globalisation's more dangerous and unpredictable manifestations. Notions associated with technology throughout the century, such as temporal acceleration, speed and velocity, are more typically deployed by dedicated pluralists who are uncomfortable with all-encompassing frameworks, however loose and pliable their internal structures.

Richard Falk has long been an influential and powerful voice among those academicians pushing for a just and environmentally secure existence beyond the sovereign state. He was one of the targets of Hedley Bull's critique of the fashion for one-worldism in the 1970s.[57] Falk continued to prosecute his case against the state into the 1990s in studies such as *Humane Governance: Toward a New Global Politics* (1995). Falk sharply distinguished between the corporate globalism characteristic of the new world order designs of great powers, which he called 'globalization-from-above' and 'globalization-from-below' which

...consists of an array of transnational social forces animated by environmental concerns, human rights, hostility to patriarchy, and a vision of human community based on the unity of diverse cultures seeking an end to poverty, oppression, humiliation and collective violence.[58]

Arguments about the decline of the state in an era of globalisation are often deficient in that there is a tendency to pass over the legal significance of the term sovereignty and to equate it with near-absolute autonomy in the economic, cultural, environmental and military fields. Its meaning stretched in this way, its moral and factual resonances becomes easy to dispute. Falk stands out in that he addresses the question of how sovereignty is to be legally transcended. For Falk the transnational movement with which he identifies is at present carrying on the 'evolving normative project' which began with The Hague Peace Conferences of 1899 and 1907. This is a project which he describes as a 'global constitutional process culminating in a progressive form of geogovernance' or 'humane governance' suggesting that the accumulation and thickening of legal and diplomatic relations among states throughout the century amounts to a gradual willing away of their sovereign legal status. The legal and political contours of humane governance are not sharply delineated, partly because he wants them to be viewed in fluid rather than static terms. Yet it is clear that humane governmance grants little space to the principle of sovereignty as that term is understood in the diurnal world of political discourse. He writes of it:

Humane governance emphasizes the achievement of comprehensive rights for all peoples on earth. It accords priority to those most vulnerable and abused, providing an alternative source of security...seeking to resolve conflict and establish order with a minimum reliance on violence and through dismantling by stages the mental and material components of the war system.

Humane governance involves 'as much decentralism as possible, with as much centralism as necessary'; he distinguishes it from world government, which he says is not likely to be feasible under current conditions.[59] Wary of the global agendas of powerful interests and sensitive to the vulnerability of communities in the South Falk does allow the sovereign state a role for some time to come. He recognises that it can serve as a protective shell in the face of the predations of economic and political hegemons. Yet he ultimately argues, similarly to the Commission on Global Governance, that socially regressive forms of globalisation, for example, 'cultural homogenization' and 'franchise capitalism', can only be answered by globalisation of a constructive and inclusive kind.[60]

Yet humane governance might be regarded with some ambivalence by those who valorise difference. Humane governance, which is the culminating point of a 'continuous unfolding', might be seen as suggestive of an essential oneness to which ultimately we can be all reconciled. Falk has specified the source and nature of our commonality. He has written that: 'In effect, an emergent global ethos suggests the reality of a shared destiny for the human species and a fundamental unity across space and through time, built around the bioethical impulse of all human groups to *survive* and *flourish*.'[61] His use of the expression 'benevolent global civil society' and his appeals to the notion of diversity in unity in *Humane Governance* further underline this point. Falk employs at points a postmodern idiom and acknowledges social manyness. He writes that the emerging world civil society must be 'respectful and celebratory toward cultural diversity' while also fostering 'human solidarity and planetary unity in the struggles against cruelty, violence, exploitation, and environmental decay'.[62] Yet his world civil society from the perspective of the radical pluralist may be too rounded and complete.

Humane governance is evocative of the idea of *manyness in oneness* and, to transpose this into political terms, this seems to imply a world in which differences bloom and grow, albeit in the midst of a larger whole. We can contrast this picture with the more restive and unruly universe disclosed by postmodern theory.

I noted earlier that the world orders proposed in the early decades of the century similarly only gave space to congenial or wise diversities. In the literature on rationalisation exultations in the tempo and multiformity of modern life obscured what was really a programme of social simplification and standardisation. Harold Laski constantly affirmed his preference for political arrangements which were experimental and untidy. He recognised that the genuine pluralist, by which he meant one who denied that experience came with any guarantees, or even offered the possibility of final harmony, must permit the universe a real and irreducible element of wildness. Following James, he preferred the expression multiverse to that of universe and the former representation of the cosmos was one of the constituent elements of his political pluralism. Nonetheless, his concern for economic justice ultimately led him to favour collective organisation over polyarchy in both the domestic and international arenas. His social sympathies triumphed over his pluralistic partisanship.

Laski was arguing in an intellectual and political context in which it was not necessary to make great efforts to deflect the criticism that rational control of social forces meant conformity. As one would expect, enlightened opinion in the interwar period tended to view national and cultural divisions as backward and threatening. Further, a progressive air and icy scientific glamour surrounded the idea of conscious control of social forces in the interests of solidarity. In the contemporary intellectual context science cannot be used convincingly to authorise monistic social theories. Philosophical and political pluralism have been theorised in an increasingly sophisticated and nuanced fashion over the last quarter of a century. Individuals are more than ever seen as, to use Laski's description, 'bundles of hyphens' in their loyalties.[63] What follows from this is that universalism, even if crowned with the best of ideals, does not command allegiance or elicit verbal obeisance in the way it once did. On the contrary, social monists now find themselves in an intellectual environment in which it is necessary to pay homage to the notion of difference.

THE STATE SYSTEM AND THE METAPHYSICS OF FLUX

We might usefully contrast the metaphysical pattern of diversity in unity celebrated in contemporary international relations as the destiny of the human race with the much more jagged and explosive depictions of experience given by Gilles Deleuze and Félix Guattari in their *A Thousand Plateaus* (1980). In that work they counterpose to the defined and organised space of the state model Bergsonian representations of experience as 'becoming' and 'undivided flux'.[64] As we saw, Bergson thought these descriptions were supported by the study of evolutionary biology and he contrasted them with a scientific outlook which spatially disperses and freezes the indeterminate rush of life. In a similar fashion, Deleuze and Guattari invoke what they call 'nomad' or 'vagabond' science, which is centred on the idea of vague essences and which they contrast with a 'Royal' or 'State science' which promotes the segmentation of space.[65]

A Thousand Plateaus is rich in metaphysical allusion. It is as though the political actors and institutions which the authors place on stage are but individual articulations of larger conceptual systems and cosmologies. The forces which collide with the state are presented as individuations of an underlying vital current while the state itself can be seen as the deduction from a posited geometrical order. We should recall here that Bergson depicted particulars as congealed expressions of an energy flow and rigid social systems as the by-product of the mechanistic thought.[66] One of the key concepts wielded by Deleuze and Guattari is that of the war machine, a metaphysic which is akin to Bergson's idea of the *élan vital* in that it is a 'diffuse and polymorphous energy', it is like perpetual motion.[67] As with Bergson's life force, whatever happens to its specific manifestations the war-machine itself presses on throwing up new forms. The war machine is ever outside the state. To put it in Bergsonian terms, it is 'unseizable multiplicity' or as Deleuze and Guatarri describe it in a section of *A Thousand Plateaus* called 'Treatise on Nomadology: The War Machine' it is 'a pure form of exteriority'; it cannot be wholly captured by or thought through the categories of the state.[68] It would seem that the war machine can only be reached through immediate perception just as Bergson thought that the *élan vital* could only be fully understood, as Sorel also observed of socialism, through an act of intuition. Arguably it is Sorel, in his adaptation of Bergson, who is closer in political spirit to Deleuze and Guattari, for he too invested a creative will in movements or circles which ran counter to the bourgeois state; importantly, it was not the idea of seizing the state after the moment of rupture which enthused him but rather it was the sheer energy of the act.

The war machine is not, in a crucial sense, opposed to the state; it is more like a blind impulse which in pressing on comes up against states. It is meant to be in a dichotomous relation with the state, dichotomies belonging to that 'form of interiority' which is the state model. It is thus a third force, so radically and unassimilably distinct that it cannot be fully incorporated into the official bifucations of state thought.[69] In elaborating his metaphysics Bergson had constructed two opposing chains of concepts privileging the chain comprising terms suggestive of the stream of life. Deleuze and Guattari attempt to avoid this pitfall and think outside dichotomies, nonetheless there are implied oppositions at work in *A Thousand Plateaus*, most notably between the notions of flowing and divided space. It might be telling that in their account the state is ascribed a heavy, dull presence while the manifestations of the war machine are endowed with all the fluency of quicksilver. Further to this, and despite attempts ethically and politically to neutralise the war machine and to render it random in its operations, the state is largely the target of its issue. Vast, piratical commercial complexes and 'local mechanisms of bands, margins, minorities' are particular instances of the war machine and while they may stand against each other typically these stand 'against States'. Yet the war machine is more than a simple if somewhat curious counterpoint to the state.[70] Its expressions may flit past the state or be suppressed by it; the war machine may unravel the state from within or without or the state may appropriate and absorb some of the fluid which animates it turning it to its own account. Fittingly, the state can never wholly capture the war machine. Nor can the state wholly govern its own military apparatus precisely because that apparatus is partly fuelled by the energy of the war machine. In the 'Treatise on Nomadology: The War Machine', the authors write:

> As for the war machine in itself, it seems to be irreducible to the State apparatus, to be outside its sovereignty and prior to its law: it comes from elsewhere...*The State has no war machine of its own*; it can only appropriate one in the form of a military institution, one that will always cause it problems.[71]

As Daniel Pick points out, the energy of the war machine has the 'wandering, excessive quality' of the nomads, the desert tribes from whose world it first issued and to which it most properly belongs. Deleuze and Guattari write that: '...each time there is an operation against the State – subordination, rioting, guerrilla warfare or revolution as act – it can be said that a war machine has revived, that a new nomadic potential has appeared'.[72] Thus the state's military apparatus must also contain some of the same disorderly impetus or rebel's impulse. It is relevant that Deleuze and Guattari were writing on the war machine in that surreal period between the unravelling of detente and the formal cessation of the bipolar conflict. It has been argued, although largely in retrospect, that by the 1980s the Cold War was over. Yet it continued to be acted out in cartoon-like fashion at the level of gesture, image and spectacle. Jean Baudrillard was asked at a public lecture in 1983 when the nuclear war would begin. His response that the nuclear war had already begun drew the ire of a few in the audience who misunderstood his point. The nuclear war was precisely the vast and elaborate deterrence system, a system designed to preclude war. It was a virtual war which denied actual war a platform. In an essay of the same year he wrote:

> There is no longer any practical correlation between the potential for destruction and its purpose, and referring to it becomes ridiculous. The warfare system dissuades itself, and is the paradoxically beneficial aspect of deterrence (*dissuasion*): there is no longer any space for warfare. Hence we must hope that nuclear escalation and the arms race will persist. This is the cost of pure warfare; that is, of the pure and empty form, of the hyperreal and eternally dissuasive form of warfare.[73]

In a certain respect Baudrillard's argument was a restatement of the Clause-
witzian orthodoxy. Nuclear war cannot take place because strategic and
political capital can be extracted from a war of annihilation. There are no
stakes to be had.[74] But Baudrillard mounted the more curious argument that
what dissuades us from war is less the fear of physical annihilation for
humanity would accept this, but the fact that real war would deny us the
secret pleasure of living under the threat of catastrophe. It is its 'distillation
in the simulated panic of our daily life, in the spectacular obsessions and
thrills that feed our fear' rather than nuclear war's strategic futility coupled
with our fear of death which restrains us.[75] Baudrillard further elaborated on
the evolution of the balance of terror, a balance which he sees as but the
'spectacular' manifestation and guarantee of a 'system of deterrence that
has crept from the inside into all the *cracks* of daily life'.[76] In a way similar to
the space race of the 1960s, the nuclear arms race served as a warrant for
establishing global systems of control, for the displacement of the order of
law and violence and the 'progressive satellisation of the whole planet by
that hypermodel of security'. Planet earth and its surrounding galaxy are
increasingly subdued and pacified: they come to comprise a 'programmed'
macrocosmos, 'where *nothing can be left to chance*'; there is more than a faint
echo of Spengler in Baudrillard's portrayal of a universe ever more perfect,
'purged of every threat to the senses, in a state of asepsis and weightless-
ness'.[77] No single agency escapes the mechanisms of planetary control. The
superpowers are tightly locked into a system of peaceful coexistence,
meanwhile the rest of world is neutralised, homogenised.[78] Some aspects of
Baudrillard's arguments parallel points made by William James in his 1910
essay *Moral Equivalent of War*. James argued that the state of passive war
among nations, during which armies were massed and poised for attack, was
the *real war*, albeit war with a dissuasive function. James also evoked the
potent brew of fascination, terror and yearning for certainty that sucks us
into the fear-regime. I am not implying a sharp distinction between simulated
and real war. Real war, in the sense of the physical clash of bodies and arms,
is threaded through with powerful symbolism. Saturation bombing and
spilling blood have the dual function of disabling the enemy and breaking
its will. The morale of one's own forces and population must also be
nourished. War is thus always a case of psycho-physics. Equally, wars which
take place at the level of images may at some moment in their construction
or play cause damage to both bodies and the earth. One cannot thus draw a
clear distinction between light wars of the mind and wars of flesh and iron.
Further, we might say that the former exists for the sake of the latter in two
crucial respects. First, it acts as a surrogate. War played out at the level of
psychology, by silent contract between the parties, may be preferable to
physical combat. Second, however, while a war of images is not always born
of a genuine will to fight, and may be no more in fact than a game of bluff
and counter-bluff, its utility as a political tool, its disciplinary power, depends
on the perception that behind the military posturing, manoeuvring and

positioning there is a will to fight. This holds no less for nuclear deterrence. The atypical situation of mutual assured destruction, as Baudrillard observes, sought to deny the fighting will a space in which it could operate. Yet accompanying this was research into various ways of opening up that space, hence the weapons and strategies developed for fighting a limited nuclear war. Baudrillard's claim in the context of the 1991 Gulf War that with deterrence: 'we are no longer in a logic of the passage from virtual to actual but in a hyperrealist logic of the deterrence of the real by the virtual' obscures the point that the real is deterred not by the virtual in itself but because the passage to the real is never entirely foreclosed.[79] These qualifications aside, Baudrillard can be seen as updating James's insight; it is the unceasing rehearsal of war, the preparations for wars too monstrous in their consequences to actually undertake, that is a kind of war. For James the military side-show was a product of states vying to assert their national interest. For Baudrillard and for Deleuze and Guattari the state ceases to be the prime centre of active willing. The bipolar conflict and consequent quest for military-territorial security had generated a military-industrial complex of global proportions. A not unrelated phenomenon is the formation of massive transnational conglomerates in the midst of market conditions designed and authorised by states. These entities have gained their own momentum and become relatively autonomous. Deleuze and Guattari write of a '...new nomadism' accompanying a 'worldwide war machine the organization of which exceeds the State apparatuses, and passes into energy, military-industrial and multinational complexes'.[80] Rather than remaining the tool of the state the war machine has seized the state as its own instrument. Clausewitz has thus been turned on his head. Politics is the continuation of war with a mixture of other means. The state has become sentinel and servant of the war machine. '...the States, having appropriated a war machine, and having adapted it to their aims, reissues a war machine that takes charge of the aim, appropriates the States and assumes increasingly wider political functions'.[81] The state polices dissidence, nomadic eruptions on behalf of the worldwide war machine while perpetuating those public enmities which help keep it in business. We might recall here the fact that the doctrine of the offensive, elaborated in the years before the Great War, which encompassed the idea of military force imbued with a fierce sense of pride and *esprit de corps* was informed by the Bergsonian notion of the *élan vital*. I said that here was an example of the life force being harnessed by the state. Yet we might also discern in the unfolding of the Great War that same excessive quality as it erupted into a war of escalation which was, to draw on Clausewitz's words, 'something pointless and devoid of sense'.[82] Clausewitz was aware that the two key terms of the formula he devised and called real war could be transposed, at least in particular instances as revealed by his warning against extended and escalating duels or what he calls absolute war, duels little disciplined by policy goals. Yet the instruments which now escape state control, which have seized the state as their own, are not simply ungoverned energies driven by nought but the restless desire to range freely across space, although the the worldwide war machine contains some of this impulse. For there is no less a logic of domination discernible in the operations of the worldwide war machine than there is in the activities of the state. Deleuze and Guattari's account of it is no naive nor lunatic rejoicing in a dynamic capitalism's seduction and seizure of the state.

The conceptual motifs, imagery and vocabulary used by Deleuze and Guattari infuse many writings on the state and theories of global transformation. Discussions of the state in an era of globalisation echo their playful celebration of fluency and fleeting being and the various manifestations of globalisation are frequently described in a way that suggests they are the terminal expressions of a deeper flow. Bergsonian metaphysics dances across the pages of International Relations (IR) theorists whether authors are conscious of it or not. We might also note the contemporary employment of many of the same linguistic terms that appeared in early twentieth-century discussions of modernity and international relations. Expressions such as speed, space, multiplicity and temporal acceleration litter recent narratives on world politics. Robert Walker is unusual in the field of IR theory in that he is conscious of the Bergsonian inheritance reflected in contemporary depictions of a world of flux and fluidity. He cites Deleuze's study *Bergsonism* (1966) and suggests that a reinvestigation of late nineteenth-century philosophies such as that of Bergson reveals that modernity is a more multi-faceted and complex phenomenon than has perhaps been thought. He observes in passing that:

The theme of modernity as an era not only of rapid socio-political, economic and technological transformations but also of a new consciousness of temporality and the contingency of specifically modern experience, has been especially familiar since the late nineteenth century. In fact, much of the recent literatures on dynamics of late or postmodernity, as on late capitalism, may be read as a recovery and extension of ideas once associated with, say, Baudelaire, Bergson and Nietzsche as well as Marx.[83]

Walker also hardens the binary opposition which has only an incipient presence in *A Thousand Plateaus* for he draws a sharp contrast between a politics of becoming and flux, on the one hand, and the sovereign state on the other with the latter involving a 'fixing of temporality within spatial categories'. He follows Deleuze and Guattari in presenting the theory of sovereignty as an extension of the 'spatial metaphysics' of geometricians and scientists, of whom Newton is presented as an archetypal representative, into the political realm; for Walker this helps explain why, in many accounts of international relations, the real is divided into structurally identical units called states which are placed under the sway of 'unchanging rules' such as the balance of power. In such a world nothing new can occur; all that can happen are periodic redistributions of power, just as in the universe of the classical physicist change is confined to redistributions of particles in space. Walker wonders how long this 'spatial order' can be maintained in a 'world of profound temporal accelerations', a description he prefers to that of globalisation, 'and spatial dislocations'; he thinks that already this frame is cracking, its 'profound' metaphysical roots laid bare.[84]

Where the sovereign state system is treated as a microcosm of the cosmology of Newton, destabilising the former involves challenging the scientific authority of the latter. Concepts thought to spring from the fields of astrophysics, chaos and quantum theory have been called upon in order to underscore the image of the world characterised by indeterminacy and speed. Like their interwar counterparts, contemporary social theorists discern in modern physics the supposition that ultimacy is to be found in flux. To authenticate a metaphysics of flux in this way is to bring further into question the carving of the world into discrete and sharply defined units.[85]

Thom Kuehls, who asserts that Deleuze and Guattari have developed a 'chaos theory' of political philosophy, draws on their notion that global flows are generating expanding zones of 'smooth space' and like them puts these flows in dynamic interaction with the 'striated space' of the state.[86] Of most significance in the context of this discussion is the way he unites the representation of space as becoming and the ecological paradigm that is often invoked against the state system. Ecological analogies are suggestive of holism; those who employ them tend to privilege unity over complexity. For this reason Jean Chesneaux has cautioned against an 'eco-globalist levelling of the *New Age* variety' which might submerge older forms of solidarity.[87] It is because of this concern that the organic analogy is adapted in some writings, Chesneaux's included, so that it appears to accommodate difference while allowing for an underlying interconnectedness.

Yet the problem confronted by James and Laski remains: can a universe in which differences merge into each other at some deep level be described as authentically pluralist. Must there not be, from the radical pluralist point of view, the possibility of differences which, 'go all the way down'?[88] In respect to the ecological paradigm, Kuehls goes some way to overcoming this problem. He renders the natural world in kaleidoscopic terms, emphasising its dynamic, 'complex, contingent, chaotic' side. While this more open-ended picture is intended to undermine the bounded space of the sovereign state it is also intended as a rejection of all-encompassing global institutions. In Laski's terms, Kuehl's model does not include a plane on which all differences melt into unity.[89]

If the metaphysical complement to the state system can be described as homogeneous discontinuity – that is, a world comprising distinct entities which are each of them modelled along similar lines – the pattern traced by those working in the Bergsonian or Jamesian traditions of thought is one of heterogeneous continuity. This last notion can be distinguished from the idea of diversity in unity. Heterogeneous continuity allows us to think of reality as a moving and endless stream comprising diverse elements and relations which are of varying degrees of intimacy and proximity. Unities can be built out of this stream but, in so far as the novel and alien keep appearing, nothing can absorb everything.[90] To translate this politically, a universe thought of in terms of diversity in unity might be seen as recommending a federal republican model of governance. Such a model is not ruled out by an understanding of experience in terms of heterogeneous continuity. However, such an understanding would dictate, at the minimum, that any organisational structures we establish must be surrounded by what Harold Laski called a 'penumbra of anarchy'; the loose threads of institutions hold out the prospect of their future unravelling and these should not be obscured.[91]

Laski claimed he always had a 'sneaking sympathy' for James's definition of the good as that which 'satisfies demand' although he reformulated this prescription so that it read as 'maximum demand'. (As with James he employed this criterion in a flexible manner taking it to mean the satisfaction of the yearning for self-expression as well as economic needs.) This social utilitarian criterion served as a point of departure for his movement towards reconciliation with the sovereign state. Laski could endorse the sovereign state as long as its contingency was laid bare and its purely instrumental value was recognised. Much of the contemporary controversy surrounding the sovereign state similarly boils down to the pragmatic question as to whether it can serve as an instrument of happiness.[92] Many argue for significant numbers of people, if not most, it cannot; hence, the call for effective world institutions or forms of global governance. However, there are compelling reasons why Laski's approach needs to be looked at seriously. First of all, we might consider Robert Jackson's prediction that the world in 100 years will still be organised along the lines of the sovereign state system – even thought some states may disappear and statuses other than sovereign statehood may be reintroduced.[93] Certainly, state practice suggests that membership of the UN and participation in international regimes are not regarded as indicia respecting the formation of a wider constitutional arrangement. For good and ill, states vigorously defend what they regard as their rights and these are not seen as insignificant. Further political groups struggling to find their place in the sun invariably follow, as Hedley Bull once put it, a 'statist logic' and are not to be found calling for a borderless world. Typically, they want to establish for themselves a greater presence in the body politic, reconstitute their state altogether or establish a new, breakaway state.[94]

Acts of cruelty and the abuse or power were a feature of the world long before we began to conceptualise political and legal relations in terms of sovereignty and will persist should we cease to do so. Some would argue that arbitrary violence and ruthless interventions would be more prevalent in a world from which the concept had all but disappeared. Defenders of the principle point out that sovereignty was developed in opposition to the doctrine of might makes right. Yet while one can concede that legally speaking sovereignty means only constitutional independence, that a state is not part of a wider constitutional arrangement, and that this status was never intended as a license to kill, the very freedom this condition accords means that governments are well positioned to to do what they can. They can literally get away with murder.

The sovereign state form is historically contingent and it is unlikely that it will be with us forever. Yet since sovereignty will be with us for some time to come it is necessary to examinine constructive ways of thinking about this concept. In order to do this I am going borrow and rework the notion of the sovereignty discourse, a notion which crops up frequently in critiques of existing arrangements. To explain, the frequent response of critics of the principle to those who insist that sovereignty means simply constitutional independence is that it is more than a legal concept. Whatever it may be in a formal sense, in practice it drags along with it a whole discourse. In this way sovereignty becomes whatever is authorised and justified in its name. The construction of the sovereignty discourse, involving the conceptual inflation of the term, clearly expands the terrain on which the intellectual battle can be fought. It offers a means of identifying sovereignty with political absolutism, social monism, isolationationism and physical self-sufficiency – these being grounds for dismissing it as inherently pernicious and factually dubious. This discourse is also inscribed with cosmological meanings to the extent that a geometrical conception of space and a spatial understanding of time are seen as immanent in the sovereignty principle. I would argue that the sovereignty discourse as described here is less a coherent conceptual and historical presence than a warrant for building straw men.

We should define the sovereignty discourse less expansively: as that discursive realm in which intense controversies and negotiations take place over definitions of the rights and obligations of states. This is a realm in which semantic anarchy, reflecting a tendency towards what Hans Kelsen called state 'solipsism', is possible and ambiguity is necessitated in the course of navigating among a myriad of understandings and nuances.[95] Wilful silence may also be encountered. In these ways, sovereignty might be said to inhibit and distort communication. Yet it also facilitates it. To imagine international relations as a sovereign state system is to designate, in the midst of a potential confusion of tongues, a set of authoritative, legal voices. It is also to lay down a set of protocols governing discussion and, while distortion may be an effect of their observance they are necessary if it is to proceed. Alfred Zimmern offered a somewhat similar view in 1934 noting that international 'etiquette' dictated that while sovereignty is 'compatible' with various means 'for minimising friction and settling disputes these means can only be efficacious if the limits within which they are employed are clearly understood'.[96] Zimmern's notion of international etiquette necessarily addresses the comportment and not just the entitlements of states. And there have been greater expectations with regard to the former than critics of the sovereignty discourse have allowed, manifested in efforts, more or less vigorous, to redefine the duties of states in respect to their citizens. These have taken the form of legal and moral arguments, diplomatic remonstrances and expressions of outrage. It might be thought that the accumulation of these along with post-Cold War interventions have pushed back and diluted the limits which Zimmern found so rigid in 1934.[97]

Such a development might approximate the evolving constitutional process which Falk canvassed in *Humane Governance*. Others would insist that while this century has seen a significant expansion of state responsibilities the cumulative impact of declarations, conventions and the hardening of certain norms of conduct is not to lay the basis of a wider constitutional framework. Although I have indicated that state practice favours the latter option, the scholar's choice of outlook is likely to hinge on normative preferences. There is no theoretical reason why we cannot conceptualise the evolution of international society in the way Falk suggests. Yet it is perhaps in recognition of the fact that sovereignty remains entrenched in our thinking that we are being urged to adapt it rather than, as Laski once suggested, surrender it altogether.[98] Boutros Boutros-Ghali offered a reconceptualisation of sovereignty in claiming that it had acquired a

new meaning. Added to its dimension of rights is the dimension of responsibility, both internal and external. Violation of state sovereignty is and will remain an offense against the global order, but its misuse may also undermine human rights and jeopardize a peaceful global order.[99]

In *Human Rights Horizons: The Pursuit of Justice in a Globalizing World* (2000) Richard Falk moves towards reconciling himself with the principle of sovereignty the conceptual bridge being precisely the theme of responsibility. Falk calls for a 'more balanced, complex view' of an idea which remains central to the way we think about international legal and political relations. While sovereignty is often interpreted, by both its champions and critics, as a state's 'right to say no' to outside challenges and interference, like Boutros-Ghali Falk maintains that the meaning of the word has evolved; he writes that there is a

clear trend away from the idea of unconditional sovereignty, namely, that governmental legitimacy depends upon adherence to minimum humanitarian norms and on a capacity to act effectively to protect citizens from acute threats to their security and well-being that derive from adverse territorial conditions.[100]

Falk's analysis is a timely and constructive addition to the debate about sovereignty yet it is worth noting that as sovereignty was developed in a conceptual environmental of which natural law was very much a part the idea that it entails, in principle, obligations to keep the peace domestically as well as internationally is not new. Many past theorists, jurists and diplomatists have acknowledged that certain actions fall outside, in words penned by the American jurist Ellery Stowell 1921, the 'limits of that authority within which the sovereign is presumed to act with reason and justice'.[101] A reinvestigation and elaboration of traditions of thinking about sovereignty might provide moral and legal ballast for efforts to challenge jurisdictional claims of the more abusive states. Such an exercise could also yield compelling arguments for enlarging the normative basis of statehood in general and one should consider here the way in which the customary principle of state responsibility has provided grounds for urging on states more extensive obligations in respect to the environment. Certainly some governments claim that 'traditional' understandings of sovereignty support the conclusion that the 'global environment, democracy and human rights' remain '"essentially within the domestic jurisdiction" of a sovereign state'.[102] Yet tradition might prove subversive of this line of argument where it is used as an alibi for malpractice. I realise my suggestions with regard to strategies of persuasion is a modest and incomplete response to the problem which is the abuse of sovereign power. Conceptually there is no obstacle to reconciling sovereignty and human rights and, as Falk underlines, recent international war crimes tribunals have '*legally* interpreted [sovereignty] in a manner that accommodates claims of responsibility and accountability'. Yet political commitment to this formula remains soft where it is not negligible. My assumption has been that the sort of punitive cosmopolitanism critiqued by Danilo Zolo is widely regarded as intolerable, although my analysis does not entirely rule it out.[103]

I have attempted to tease out the metaphysics which underlie some of the arguments advanced in the course of such discussions. This is because some current theorists see the sovereign state system as an effect of certain metaphysical presuppositions and thus think destabilising this system involves winning acceptance for alternative descriptions of reality. For this reason, in many studies concerning the destiny of world politics contesting metaphors and models features strongly in the narrative. However, I have suggested that the sovereignty principle retains a sufficient grip on the imagination of politicians and the public to withstand the metaphorical assaults of its antagonists.

Concerning the intellectual divide between those who picture experience as a multiverse and those who see it in more holistic terms I would make a number of related points. To start with, I think the preference for the former may often be aesthetically rather than politically motivated. Those who mobilise a metaphysics of multiplicity against the sovereign state system would concede with Bergson the need to construct unities and draw lines around spaces within which we all can act and live. At the same time, a multiversalist would deny whatever unities and bounded spaces that we will into being either finality or any assurance of success. There is a moral reason for declining to see history as an evolution towards a harmony of interests, that is, if we want the struggle against evil to be a genuine struggle rather than one in which the ultimate outcome is preordained.[104] Further, those who are inclined towards social holism do in fact accept that irreducible differences exist and will continue to erupt; talk of a global civil society is often accompanied by the demand that institutions of global governance be given teeth. To argue this is to concede that a harmony of interests may need, in some measure, to be deliberately produced and policed.

The spatial arrangement which is the sovereign state system equally presumes the possibility of differences which go a long way down. Coexistence is seen as preferable, for prudential and ethical reasons, to campaigns to convert by the sword. The effect is a thinly based international society which is often indifferent to suffering behind state lines. Voices that demand a hearing are excluded or ignored. Concern about these matters often lies behind pictures of borders melting into flux. As was the case with Laski's attacks upon the state, descriptive argument veils an attempt to impress on us the morally contingent nature of sovereignty. Yet historically sovereignty has been considered provisional for human purposes. Revivifying past patterns of thought would not only amplify this point but might provide compelling arguments for sharpening, deepening and expanding upon the responsibilities that *must*, for both moral and pragmatic reasons, accompany this status.

7   CONCLUSION

The term globalisation denotes a set of inducing arguments and seductive images rather than a stark and incontestable fact of life. It is telling of this that in many accounts we meet assertions, tactics and imagery so very similar to those which were invoked against state monism and particularism that were mounted in the interwar period. Globalisation, understood in an expansive fashion, is in many ways a rhetorical effect, as was international rationalisation before it. Claims about sovereignty in an era of temporal acceleration may say less about the trajectory of future events than about early twentieth-century dreams of modernity. The historical parallels I have highlighted might also remind us that convictions about the future can vanish quickly amidst the push and pull of experience.

We might also want to consider whether proposals for world order premised on a belief in universal rationality and harmony have lost their aura of scientific glamour and moral force. Heretical, dissident philosophies and a questioning of social monism featured prominently in intellectual life from the late nineteenth century onwards. Yet doctrines such as rationalisation, grounded in a hard, scientism, were on the ascendant. This is explained by the psychological shock and social convulsions attendant upon the Great War. The economic and political turmoil of the 1930s, culminating in the Second World War, only reinforced the fashion for rationalist social philosophies. It is their conceptual grounding in the interrelated themes of social crisis and scientific organisation that marks the first two New World Orders (NWOs) as progeny of twentieth-century modernity. This background is also what sets them apart from earlier peace projects and from the 1990s NWO. This last was not intended as a corrective to widespread fears of social decline and collapse. It was conceived amidst a sense of triumph rather than anxiety and has been greeted in political and intellectual circles worldwide with a greater measure of scepticism and hostility. To some the expression seemed like a political slogan rather than the title of a vast and ambitious scheme of social engineering – others feared it as such. Further, there is a tensile relation between NWO proposals, whether emanating from the camps of the hierarchs or humanitarians, and those who see globalisation as the futurists saw modernity: intense mobility in unbounded space. While globalisation is believed to be deepening world society it is also, because of the turbulence it is thought to generate, cited as grounds for strengthening and empowering global institutions. Others, however, are drawn to the scenes of motion and commotion associated with globalisation and welcome the idea of a world freed from institutional control. The NWO is the intellectual offspring of the rationalist faith in glittering formulas for salvation, a faith which pervaded early to mid-twentieth-century political and intellectual discussions. In an environment in which multiplicity is celebrated and which questions the quest for foundations and warnings of impending ruin it is doubtful whether NWOs can elicit the reverence and enthusiasm they once enjoyed.

The concern that there might be renewed attempts to translate NWO thinking in practice has, however, inspired a number of polemics. Proponents of humane global governance are at great pains not only to distinguish this from the globalism of the elites and more generally world government. Falk has stressed that human governance 'can be achieved *without* world government, and that this is both the more likely and desirable course of action'.[1] While Danilo Zolo concedes that Falk's 'complex "global constitutionalism" admits of subtler distinctions' than do many current plans for a world Leviathan, for example that of Norbeto Bobbio, he is doubtful whether these distinctions can be sustained in practice.[2] For him the distinction between global governance and a world state is very much a distinction without a difference. He claims that what is being advocated by both Bobbio and Falk is a 'form of modern Cosmopolis...in which relations not only between one state and another but between a state and its citizens would be subject to the control and inverventive direction of a "world government"'.[3] For Zolo efforts to institutionalise pacifism are *'political engineering'* on a grand scale. Potentially, cosmopolitan pacifism would be even more oppressive than the post-Cold War American NWO because it would be more totalising and intrusive with complex systems of surveillance and discipline spanning the globe searching out violations not only of peace but of human rights and ecological security. Zolo's nightmare scenario is a military hierarchy bestriding the world with unlimited discretion in its use of force and under no compulsion to exhaust all peaceful means before embarking on violence. He notes that Falk, unlike other cosmopolitan theorists, rejected the idea that the Gulf War was a just war because he thought it could not be defended in terms of the Charter. Yet Zolo believes that Falk places too much faith in the notion that international law can be applied impartially. Great powers will assuredly, as they have in the past, 'violate the rules of the very international institutions which they have set themselves in place'.[4] At the same time, Zolo believes that current efforts to establish a cosmopolitan will suffer the same inglorious fate as past attempts. Enormous disparities in wealth and power make sovereignty, as Falk recognises, a highly valuable commodity in the eyes of those who feel insecure. Zolo adds that despite creeping westernisation the world is becoming more differentiated, turbulent and fragmented and this means that any model of cosmopolitanism 'would of necessity be a despotic and Totalitarian Leviathan'. Cosmopolitan theorists fail to appreciate these points fully because they are:

...imprisoned in the eurocentric schema of the domestic analogy, cosmopolitan pacifism fails to perceive the dangers present in an institutional outlook which continues in traditional fashion to enshrine the hegemony of the western powers. Instead it remains stuck in the mould of a hierarchical and monocentric world order. And it deceives itself in believing that it can use the doctrine of human rights as a basis, or as the ideological flag, of an order which is universally just because it conforms to western values. It appears not to realize that the established set of international political and economic relations has been overtaken by a cataclysm and that the situation is now very far from being one of equilibrium.[5]

In his *Law of Nations* (1760) the lawyer and diplomat Emerich de Vattel accepted that states like individuals 'were subject to the Law of Nature...independent of their will'; yet he was wary of the notion put forward by Hugo Grotius that a proper authority could intervene in states guilty of violations of the moral law. Vattel argued that it opened the door to 'all the passions of zealots and fanatics' and afforded 'ambitious men' numerous 'pretexts' for conquest. The right to avenge an injury inflicted on subjects belonged to the subjects themselves. He did not rule out intervention altogether, allowing that an alliance of states could intervene to halt the persecution of religious minorities where the society concerned was 'unable to assert itself against the ruler'; such an attack could be further justified where there was a common interest in checking the rise of a fanatical, disruptive regime. Generally however, Vattel placed prudence on the side of non-intervention.[6] Zolo's resistance to NWO proposals derives partly from the same concerns about the misuse or abuse of power. Yet it is also his conviction that a genuine commitment to the principle of difference must lead one to embrace the state as the fundamental unit of political autonomy. He advances an argument that is discernible in Kant's *Perpetual Peace*, although he clearly thinks the latter is squarely in the cosmopolitan camp:

In opposition to the cosmopolitan attitude which looks with disfavour on multiplicity and diversity, tending to compress them within the bounds of a hierarchical macro-structure comprising only a very limited number of states, a culture of human diversity should aim towards the free self-assertion of political subjects, which should in effect also imply the free self-assertion of states.[7]

Zolo thinks that under global governance, even were it not to be a creature of Western communities interest or value, power would coagulate at some central point. A governing class would emerge which would seek to lay down the law severely circumscribing diversity in the process. He seems to regard as bad faith claims that with the globalisation of policy a thousand differences would bloom.

Zolo's interpretation of global governance plans is unduly suspicious. Certainly his forecasts of the possible breakdown of the current international system and its governing institutions seem premature. While there are certainly sharp tensions between the North and South over issues of development, environment and human rights, there is little evidence that the members of the latter are about to exit the system. China's much desired entry into the World Trade Organisation suggests it is not about to establish a political and economic orbit independent of the one dominated by the United States and its allies. It is no revelation that international regimes are biased towards the interests and values of the predominant powers. The question is whether weaker players view participation, or a commitment in principle to participation, in them as a source of benefit whatever their biases. Such a conservative challenge to Zolo would not satisfy Falk who might argue that Zolo glosses over the radical nature of the transformation which Falk wishes for the international system and his emphasis on open, multilayered governance. More persuasive is Zolo's argument that the sovereign state might be viewed constructively as a space which gives reign to and protects individual self-expression. He clearly regards it as a better guarantor of individual freedom than an unavoidably imperious global political and legal regime. He favours the state because he sees it as offering a protective shell in which communal or national differences can thrive. It should be recalled here that William James, whose ultimate commitment was to the sacredness of the individual, also accorded moral standing to national communities and resisted that type of humanism which regards national distinctiveness as an irrational excrescence. In protesting that in conquering the Philippines the American government had ruthlessly disregarded something holy, that being the unique national identity of the Filipinos, James was echoing sentiments of Kant who had defended in *Perpetual Peace* the right of the Chinese and Japanese governments to resist the attempts by the Europeans to make these countries open up to the world. Neither Kant's ethical individual nor his universalism prevented him from recognising the significance of communal ways of life. This is not to posit anything like a national ghost. To put it in Laski's terms, when we talk of a social will, we are talking of the lodgement in finite minds of shared thoughts and perceptions and no new level of personality is created. We might also usefully recall here Laski's insight, one which he derived from William James's pluralistic metaphysics, that whatever relations one enters into something of oneself is left out and omitted, the self is unreduced to unity.

For a time Laski appeared to believe that the sovereign state was by its nature oppressive. He interpreted sovereignty as a license to suppress and destroy individual or group manyness. During the years of the Great War he tended towards anarcho-sydnicalism as an alternative to the state. By the mid-1920s, however, was recommending that state behaviour be controlled by a supranational authority. The point is that Laski ultimately did not object to statist solutions. His supranational authority was nought but the sovereign state on a larger scale. This is further borne out by his simultaneous endorsement of the collectivist state and indeed, his concern that groups not impede the state provision of social services to the public. Laski had also come to accept the value of routine that the state imparted to peoples' lives and that groups could be as oppressive as any state. His friend Morris Cohen had stated in 1919, in response to the syndicalist assault on the state by Laski and others, that the 'evils of an absolute state are not cured by the multiplication of absolutes'.[8] Nor, Zolo would add, are they cured by its enlargement.

There is no theoretical answer to the question as to whether polyarchy, the state system or global governance best secures individual freedom and cultural diversity. One's choice will depend on the kinds of self-assertion and forms of difference that one values and the historical forces in play at a given juncture. It is a matter to be determined on the basis of temperamental preferences, circumstance and practical possibilities. Those who paint the state as the greatest threat to individual and group autonomy in the world today do so with much justice. Yet as I have argued, those who are unhappy within the state in which they live typically direct their efforts towards finding a stronger voice inside the body politic, reconstituting their state altogether or establishing a breakaway state.

This is not to disregard the ongoing significance and relative autonomy of international and transnational society, or more particularly, of constructing audiences and bodies of authoritative opinion across national lines in front of which individuals, states, associations and corporations feel they have to in some way justify themselves. It would be even more mistaken in the variegated world of the twenty-first century to speak of world public opinion as was done in the early days of the League. Yet there are nonetheless, to borrow James's description, 'little hangings-together of the world's parts within the larger hangings-together' so as to form worlds of discourse as well as operation. The existence of such worlds of discourse and the fact that they count is shown by the fact that when crimes or breaches are committed, actors justify their behaviour by appeal to accepted codes of conduct, albeit sometimes torturing the meaning of these in the process. Another way of putting this is to say that the rules and customs of a given society, as well as the various streams of opinion and sentiment that course through it, determine the outer limits of what can be said in defence of a particular action and mark off what cannot. The boundaries of an acceptable rhetoric of justification are likely to be blurred; even so, the awareness of them, however vague, that comes with moving through society may well condition action.

In finishing I want to draw attention to some points made by Robert Latham in *The Liberal Moment* in which he sees Cold War hostilities not simply arising from conflicting interests, misperceptions or mendacity, but as a function of the West's attempt to build a universal order in which the Soviet Union, a state with the will and capacity to challenge this order, could not be accommodated. The bipolar conflict was significantly a by-product or an effect of the attempt to construct a new world order. Latham rightly notes that behind the idea of world order planning lies a conjunction of modernist themes including 'rational administration, mass movements and scientific endeavour'; he further correctly points out that modernity has been experienced as not only an 'over-rationalized existence' but also as 'flux and volatility'.[9] He too suggests that it is the fear of chaos, both sensual and supersensual, that impels attempts to streamline experience. Given that Latham views the quest for a world order through the prism of American Cold War foreign policy it is not surprising that he regards as folly attempts by preponderant powers to build a model world community out of a genuine and resistant multiplicity. He is sharply aware of the existence of profound differences which cannot be merged happily within a larger framework. There is a superficial resemblance between Latham's argument and E.H. Carr's polemic on the 'political implications of the assertion of a common interest in peace' in the interwar period: that all-embracing schemes for world order result in conflict in so far as they entail the denial and suppression of radical otherness. Yet Latham goes further than Carr by tightly intertwining the activity of 'making an order' with that of 'making an other'.[10] He is acutely sensitive to the particularity of world order designs and to the fact that their vigorous prosecution will not only see one come up against others but also actually generate tension and opposition. In relation to the Cold War Latham's point is that if the United States had been less intent on pressing its definition of order on the Soviet Union, a determination which flowed from its fear of failing as a builder of a liberal world order, the Cold War might not have intensified to the degree it did in the late 1940s.[11]

Latham appears to reject the view that the last century has seen, despite set-backs such as the Cold War, a movement towards greater harmony in world affairs with globalisation being the most recent facilitator, albeit an ambiguous one, of such a process. Instead he depicts the contemporary period as a scene of intense complexity and multiplicity. Unlike many who criticise the state on pluralist grounds, Latham is consistent in his anti-monism and thus rejects all-encompassing global governance. For Latham the world is now even less hospitable to standardisation and more open to the possibility of multiple orders, although this by no means precludes cooperative action to improve the welfare of communities. Most importantly, he argues that in the face of a manifold and restless reality policy makers should adopt a tolerant and flexible approach to 'order making'. He implicitly acknowledges that tolerance may not be reciprocated or that its limits will be tested sorely in calling for courage. He argues that an open and less punitive world order, one which aims at reducing threat perceptions, must overcome the fear of freedom and be ready to take risks. What is urged is that state actors accept insecurity as a condition of being without feeling the need to either construct fortresses or control of ever-widening domains of certainty. We must thus overcome our fear of liberation from the fear-regime, our fear of freedom as Fromm put it, while desisting from the search for global answer to the difficulties we face.[12]

Both Zolo and Latham would disagree with those who believe that it is the oneness of humanity that is of the essence although both leave room for the creation and addition of relations of various degrees of intimacy. Yet Latham condemns as 'foolish' the quest for universal world order. Better that we recognise that a 'variety of orders are operating in different domains, regions, or even locales' at any one time. Rather than grand and totalising projects he commends a 'foreign policy of the local' by which he means actions by states and NGOs aimed at improving levels of welfare.[13] Zolo condemns the quest for one world order for similar reasons but he also offers the speculation that such a quest is futile given human disposition towards aggression, an impulse which is as real and necessary a part of our make-up as the feeling of comity. He writes that 'aggression and reconciliation (together with conflict and pacification) are evolutionary constants of the human species that rule out the cosmopolitan project for a stable and universal peace'.[14] Zolo believes in the depth and resilience of our aggressive impulses although he also thinks that these can be culturally modified over time. What he refers to as a 'modern realist standpoint' does not rest on the idea of an eternal human nature according to which we are forever condemned to a life of ego-driven conflict. It does not uphold that war is the destiny of the human race. Yet for a long time still war is likely to be with us. In what might be viewed as an inversion of Deleuze and Guattari's line of argument he wants to see politics seize control of war. Yet we are not talking here of Clausewitz's caution that war, due to the logic of escalation intrinsic to it, must be disciplined by a political brain. Rather, Zolo is arguing in a Jamesian fashion that politics should harness our war energies and canalise them. We must find a way of 'integrating war' into international politics instead of taking the naive and morally excessive path of seeking to stamp out warfare and aggression by force. This would perhaps be the beginnings of the cultural modification of which Zolo speaks. Yet the impulse towards aggression is not enough to explain war for it is also a question of the circumstances in which we find ourselves. Zolo would concur with Latham that we have to defuse the atmosphere of fear and paranoia. This means more than making the conscious choice to unburden ourselves of many of our trepidations and accept uncertainty as a way of life. Such a psychological leap must be accompanied by steps, albeit halting steps and very much at the local level, in the direction of social amelioration. This could of course be but a staging post on the way to Falk's humane governance, and Zolo's analysis does not, in principle, discount this possibility. If it is not nothing has been lost.[15]

Exultant predictions of an NWO made at the beginning of the 1990s were looking rather threadbare by the decade's end. Yet counsels of prudence as regards attempts to regiment the flux of social experience into a single world order bear repeating. This is not only because hegemons cannot be relied on to act with restraint and modesty. It is high-minded, not to mention tediously unoriginal, to argue that if only people the world over consulted right reason and came to know their true interests they would give up their sovereignty as well as their primitive senses of kinship, national identity and state loyalty and submit to global regimes. There is a hint of moral vanity in the belief the world will become a better place when shaped in accordance with this or that group's pet ideals. This is not to dismiss the utility of healthy, regulatory ideals, ideals which while never wholly realisable may shape experience even if only remotely entertained. Yet to press them too hard on a wary public may induce panic. There are xenophobic groups in some Western countries who bizarrely believe that globalisation is part of a strategy to create a world empire run by UN officials in conspiracy with a phalanx of international élites. The glittering world technopolis of Wells' imaginings is transmogrified into a frightening dystopia. To talk up global governance and talk down the state feeds such fevered imaginings. There are those who, because their oxygen is hate or because they thrive on a diet of struggle and strife, have no desire to breathe the fresh air of peace. Yet it hardly needs to be added that there are countless communities around the world who simply see and feel things differently. If multiplicity could so easily be submerged or smoothed over, then it would not be necessary to invent myths such as globalisation which, some promise, is transporting us like a magic carpet to a higher plane.

NOTES

INTRODUCTION

1. Zweig, S., *Conqueror of the Seas: The Story of Magellan* (Viking Press, 1938), pp. 235, 294–5.
2. Conrad, P., *Modern Times, Modern Places: Life & Art in the 20th Century* (Thames & Hudson, 1998), p. 8.
3. Brady, R.A., 'The Meaning of Rationalization: an analysis of the literature', *Quarterly Journal of Economics* (1930), 44: pp. 526–40, esp. p. 533n.
4. Gay, P., *Education of the Senses: The Bourgeois Experience: Victoria to Freud* (W.W. Norton, 1984), See Ch.2, 'Architects and Martyrs of Change'.
5. Barraclough, G., *An Introduction to Contemporary History* (Penguin, 1967), pp. 10, 23. Barraclough echoes the American sociologist C. Wright Mills. In 1959 Mills had declared that 'we are at the ending of the Modern Age' and the beginning of 'a post-modern period'. Quoted in Conrad *Modern Times*, p. 559.
6. Barraclough *Contemporary History*, p. 235.
7. Ibid., p. 25.
8. Ibid., pp. 237–8, 241–2.
9. Fülöp-Miller, R., *The Mind and Face of Bolshevism: An Examination of Cultural Life in Soviet Russia*, trans. F.S. Flint and D.F. Tait (G.P. Putnam's Sons, 1927), p. 45.
10. Ibid., pp. 49, 206–8.
11. Ibid., p. 47.
12. Ibid., pp. 94, 98, 99.
13. Ibid., pp. 98, 101. Conrad *Modern Times*, pp. 246, 284. Conrad writes that Tatlin even dreamed of 'mobilizing his monument to dramatize the will of history'.
14. Marinetti, F.T., 'War, the World's Only Hygiene: 1911–1915', reproduced in R.W. Flint (ed.) *Selected Writings*, trans R.W. Flint and A.A. Coppotelli (Farrar, Straus and Giroux, 1971), pp. 81–2. Starr, S.F., 'Visionary Town Planning during the Cultural Revolution', in *Cultural Revolution in Russia: 1928–1931*, Sheila Fitzpatrick (ed.) (Bloomington, Indiana University Press, 1978), p. 211.
15. Starr *Cultural Revolution*, pp. 214–16.
16. Ibid., pp. 208–10.
17. Gasset, J.O.Y., *The Revolt of the Masses* (Unwin Books, 1930), pp. 29–33.
18. Ibid., pp. 55–7.
19. Karl Mannheim, *Ideology and Utopia: An Introduction to the Sociology of Knowledge* (Routledge & Kegan Paul, 1936), p.xiii.
20. Hayek, F.A., *The Road To Serfdom* (Dymock's, 1944), p. 27.
21. Mannheim *Ideology and Utopia*, pp. 169–70, and Karl Mannheim, *Man and Society in an Age of Reconstruction* (Routledge & Kegan Paul, 1940), pp. 360–3.
22. Mannheim *Man and Society*, p. 363.
23. Ibid., pp. 365–6.
24. Mannheim, K., *Freedom, Power & Democratic Planning* (Routledge & Kegan Paul, 1951), pp. 213, 241, 302. In the foreword to this study Adolf Lowe notes that it was compiled after Mannheim's death in 1947 from a number of unpublished

manuscripts. Louis Wirth writes in the introduction to *Ideology and Utopia* that Mannheim's work would not seem completely foreign to those familiar with the pragmatist philosophy of William James, Charles Sanders Pierce, George Herbert Mead and John Dewey, p. xx.

25. Mannheim *Freedom*, p. 127. See Charles Frankel, *The Case For Modern Man* (Harper, 1955), pp. 119, 127–8, 140.
26. Barraclough *Contemporary History*, pp. 234, 245, 248.
27. Ibid., pp. 248–9.
28. Ibid., pp. 42, 228.
29. For expressions of this sentiment see P. Parkinson, 'Review of Julian Huxley, Scientific Research and Social Needs', *Australian Quarterly* (1934a), 6, pp. 111–15; and P. Parkinson, 'Capitalism: a Stage in Civilisation', *Australian Quarterly* (1934b), 22, pp. 96–8.

CHAPTER 1

1. Wells, H.G., *The World of William Clissold*, Vol. III, p. 164, cited in N. Skene Smith, *Economic Control: Australian Experiments in Rationalisation and Safeguarding*, with an Introduction by H. Dalton (P.S. King & Son Ltd, 1929), p. 5.
2. Balfour, A. cited in L.F. Urwick, *Management of Tomorrow* (Nisbet, 1933), p. 33.
3. Fülöp-Miller, R., *The Mind and Face of Bolshevism: An Examination of Cultural Life in Soviet Russia*, trans. F.S. Flint and D.F. Tait (G.P. Putnam's Sons, 1927), p. 109.
4. Rorty, R., 'Religious faith, intellectual responsibility, and romance', in Ruth Ann Putnam (ed.), *The Cambridge Companion to William James* (Cambridge University Press, 1997), p. 87.
5. Perry, R.B., *The Present Conflict of Ideals: A Study of the Philosophical Background of the World War* (Longmans, Green and Co., 1918), p. 45.
6. Ibid.
7. Poincaré, H., *The Value of Science*, trans. G.B. Halstead (Dover, 1958), p. 85. First published in 1902.
8. Comte, A., *Catéchisme positiviste* (Paris, 1852), pp. 42–3, quoted by M. Harris, 'Comte and James', *Philosophical Review* (1925), 34, pp. 154–64, esp. p. 158.
9. Kolakowski, L., *Positivist Philosophy: From Hume to the Vienna Circle*, trans. N. Guterman (Penguin: 1972), p. 125.
10. Mach, E., 'The Analysis of Sensations: Anti-Metaphysical', *Monist* (1890), 1, pp. 52–6, 64.
11. Kolakowski *Positivist Philosophy*, p. 143.
12. Pearson, K., *The Grammar of Science* (Walter Scott, 1892) pp. 76–7, 130.
13. Ibid., pp. 63, 80–1.
14. Ibid., pp. 57, 103, 122.
15. Ibid., pp. 134, 159, 285–8.
16. Ibid., pp. 51, 81, 103, 122, 124. See also Perry, R.B., *Present Philosophical Tendencies: a critical survey of naturalism, idealism, pragmatism and realism, together with a synopsis of the philosophy of William James* (Braziller, 1955) p. 78. First published in 1912.
17. Ibid., pp. 63, 80–8.
18. Ibid., pp. 20–1, 42, 81, 88.
19. Webb, S. and B., 'Labor', in C. A. Beard (ed.), *Whither Mankind: A Panorama of Modern Civilization* (Longmans, Green & Co., 1928), pp. 118, 134.
20. Poincaré *Value of Science*, pp. 13, 91, 96, 142.
21. Poincaré, H., *Science and Hypothesis* (Dover, 1952), p. 50. First published in 1905.
22. Le Roy, E., *The New Philosophy of Henri Bergson* (Henry Holt and Co., 1913), p. 130.

23. Perry *Present Philosophical Tendencies*, p. 80. See also E. LeRoy, 'Science et Philosophie', *Revue de Métaphysique et de Morale* (1899), 7, pp. 375ff and Poincaré *Value of Science*, pp. 112–14.

24. Poincaré *Value of Science*, pp. 112–13.

25. Ibid., pp. 14, 122, 136–7.

26. Ibid., pp. 4–5, 114–15.

27. Ibid., pp. 6–9 and Poincaré *Science and Hypothesis*, p. 50.

28. Mach 'Analysis of Sensations: Anti-Metaphysical', p. 56; Mach, E., *The Analysis of Sensations and the Relation of the Physical to the Psychical*, trans. C.M. Williams (Dover, 1959) pp. 10, 13–14, 17–18, 21–2. First edition published in 1885.

29. Perry *Present Philosophical Tendencies*, p. 79.

30. Mach *Analysis of Sensations and the Relation of the Physical*, p. 22.

31. Kolakowski *Positivist Philosophy*, p. 125.

32. Mach *Analysis of Sensations and the Relation of the Physical*, p. 22. See also Perry *Present Philosophical Tendencies*, p. 79.

33. Lenin, V.I., *Materialism and Empirio-Criticism* (Foreign Languages Press, 1972), pp. 15, 99–103, 301–2.

34. Ibid, p. 35. See also Fülöp-Miller *Bolshevism*, pp. 54–6. He quotes Lenin as stating that positivism was a 'Middle Party' philosophy which 'confuses materialistic and idealistic views'. No date is given for this quotation but it is clear that the battle against positivism continued into the 1920s. Mach's works, along with those of numerous others, were removed from public libraries by a committee chaired by Lenin's widow Nadezhda Krupskaya. Perry wrote that: 'Lenin was instinctively, and perhaps strategically, opposed to modernist interpretations of Marx; preferring the premise of materialistic determinism to more flexible philosophical doctrines having no fixed economic and political implications.' See R.B. Perry, *The Thought and Character of William James*, 2 vols (Little Brown and Co., 1935), II, p. 576.

35. Lenin *Materialism and Empirio-Criticism*, pp. 298–301, 308.

36. Ibid., pp. 298–301, 308.

37. Ibid., pp. 307, 321–8; Mach 'Analysis of Sensations: Anti-Metaphysical', pp. 52–6, 64. He saw it as opening a 'fideistic way to "the God-markers" and having a 'general spirit of "conciliatory quackery"'. Note that Mach had read and been powerfully 'gripped' by W. James, *The Varieties of Religious Experience: A Study in Human Nature* (Longmans, Green & Co.,1902). Lenin and Mach quoted in Perry *William James*, pp. 341, 576.

38. Adams, H., *The Education of Henry Adams* (Modern Library, 1918), p. 457.

39. Ibid., pp. 453, 460–1.

40. James, W., *Principles of Psychology*, 2 vols (Encyclopaedia Britannica, 1952), I, pp. 237–9, 245.

41. Ibid., pp. 239, 285–9.

42. James, W., *Pragmatism* (Longmans, Green & Co., 1907), pp. 51, 57, 261.

43. Ibid., pp. 53, 81, 186, 199, 207, 209, 244–8, 218, 260.

44. James, W., *Essays in Radical Empiricism and A Pluralistic Universe*, R.B. Perry (ed.) (Dutton, 1971), pp. 17–18, 53.

45. On this point see James *Essays*, pp. 25, 26, 46, 50 and *A Pluralistic Universe*, p. 276.

46. James *Pragmatism*, pp. 80, 190–1, 218, 222, 299.

47. Ibid., pp. 51, 136, 158–9, 186, 260.

48. Ibid., p. 160.

49. Morris, C., *The Pragmatic Movement in American Philosophy* (Doubleday, 1970), pp. 112–13.

50. James *A Pluralistic Universe*, pp. 247, 258–64, 269, 274–7. The description of mental states is cited in Perry *Thought and Character*, p. 589. See also James *Pragmatism*, p. 156, where he wrote that the '...world is One just so far as its parts

hang together by any definite connexion. It is many just so far as any definite connexion fails to obtain.' On the finitude of James's higher being see *Essays*, p. 102.

51. James, W., *Will to Believe and other Essays in Popular Philosophy* (Longmans, Green & Co., 1897), p. 61. See also *Pragmatism*, pp. 282, 286.
52. James, W., Letter to Henri Bergson, 13 June 1907 in Perry *William James*, p. 618. James *A Pluralistic Universe*, pp. 241–2.
53. Gunn, J.A., 'Great Thinkers II – Henri Bergson', *Australasian Journal of Psychology and Philosophy* (1925a), 3, pp. 277–86, esp. pp. 279, 283.
54. Gunter, P.A.Y., Introduction to H. Bergson *Creative Evolution*, trans. A. Mitchell (University Press of America, 1983), p. xvii. First published in 1911 by Henry Holt & Co. Geraldine, J., *The Sane Positivist: A Biography of Edward L. Thorndike* (Wesleyan University Press, 1968), p. 334. See also Gunn 'Great Thinkers', p. 277.
55. Carr, H.W., *Henri Bergson: The Philosopher of Change* (T.C. & E.C. Jack, 1919), p. 30.
56. Bergson *Creative Evolution*, p. 208, 248–9, 307, 314, 342–3.
57. Gibson, A.B., 'Mystic or Pragmatist?', *Australasian Journal of Psychology and Philosophy* (1947), 25, pp. 80–103, esp. p. 100.
58. P. Valéry's reply to 'Inquiry on 1900', *Les Marges*, 10 June 1932 cited in J. Mathews (ed.), *The Collected Works of Paul Valéry*, 10, trans. D. Folliot and J. Mathews (Routledge & Kegan Paul, 1963), p. 586. Schneider, H.W., 'Political Implications of Recent Philosophical Movements', in C.E. Merriam (ed.), *A History of Political Theories: Recent Times* (Macmillan, 1924), p. 324. See also, Le Roy, *New Philosophy of Henri Bergson*, p. 135.
59. Gibson 'Mystic', pp. 93, 98. On the notion of duration see also J.A. Gunn, 'Time and Modern Metaphysics – 1', *Australasian Journal of Psychology and Philosophy* (1925b), 3, pp. 258–67, esp. p. 260.
60. Gibson 'Mystic', p. 85.
61. Bergson quoted in Gibson 'Mystic', p. 91.
62. Bergson quoted in Le Roy *New Philosophy of Henri Bergson*, p. 111. This quotation is translated with slight variations in Bergson *Creative Evolution*.
63. Gunn 'Great Thinkers', p. 284.
64. Bergson, *Creative Evolution*, p. 54.
65. Gunn, 'Great Thinkers', p. 285.
66. Bergson *Creative Evolution*, pp. 44, 182, 299.
67. Bergson, H., *Mind Energy: Lectures & Essays*, trans. H.W. Carr (Macmillan, 1918) quoted in Schneider *Political Implications*, p. 325 and Bergson *Creative Evolution*, p. 270.
68. Poincaré *Value of Science*, pp. 6, 9.
69. Pearson *Grammar of Science*, pp. 4–11, 20.
70. Ibid., pp. 433–8.
71. Ibid., p. 438.
72. This definition of cosmopolitanism comes from Perry *Present Conflict*, p. 106. For his comments on Pearson see p. 139.
73. Mach 'Analysis of Sensations: Anti-Metaphysical', pp. 53, 68 and Mach *Analysis of Sensations and the Relation of the Physical*, p. 25.

> Mach and his adherents deny that the reduction of human personality or the self to a symbolic abstraction created solely for practical purposes entails dangerous moral consequences ('There is no saving the "I",' Mach wrote) by ignoring the ethical value of individual life. On the contrary, they argued, this doctrine prevents us from over-estimating our own 'self' and despising others, [and] furthers a conception of mankind as one cooperating, interdependent whole.

> Kolakowski *Positivist Philosophy*, p. 148.

74. James, W., *Talks to Teachers on Psychology: and to students on some of life's ideals* (Longmans, Green & Co, 1932), p. v. First published in 1899.

75. James, H. (ed.), *The Letters of William James*, 2 vols (Atlantic Monthly Press, 1920), II, p. 90 [7 June 1899].

76. The first quotation is from Perry *William James*. The second is James quoted in Perry *William James*, p. 315.

77. James in Perry *William James*, pp. 308–11.

78. Ibid., pp. 315–16.

79. James, W., *The Moral Equivalent of War and Other Essays*, J.K. Roth (ed.) (Harper & Row, 1971), pp. 4, 6, 11, 12.

80. Ibid., p. 7.

81. Ibid., pp. 10, 12, 13–15. James is drawing on H.G. Wells's *First and Past Things: A Confession of Faith and Rule of Life* (Constable, 1908), p. 169.

82. Ibid., p. 11 and Canby, H.S., *Education by Violence: Essays on the War and the Future* (Macmillan, 1919), p. 176.

83. Smith, J., 'The Committee for Intellectual Co-operation in Gilbert Murray's Papers', in J. Smith (ed.), *Gilbert Murray: An Unfinished Autobiography* (George Allen and Unwin, 1960), p. 198; Gunn, J.A., *Bergson and His Philosophy* (Methuen, 1920), p. 116; Gunn 'Great Thinkers', p. 279; Schneider *Political Implications*, pp. 325–7 and Bergson, *Mind-Energy*, pp. 26–7.

84. Carr *Henri Bergson*, pp. ix–x; Gunn 'Great Thinkers', p. 279. Gunn noted a small work Bergson published during the war called the *Signification de la Guerre* in which he 'patriotically conceived the conflict as one of the esprit of the French against the mechanism of the Germans'.

85. Bergson, H., 'Life and Matter at War', *Hibbert Journal* (1915), pp. 466, 475.

86. From a speech delivered in 1915, quoted by A. Lalande, 'Philosophy in France in 1915', *Philosophical Review* (1916), 25, pp. 523–45, esp. p. 535. Bergson to J. Chastenet. Bergson wrote to the editor in Chief of *Le Temps* in December 1939 that his article of 1914 applied exactly to the contemporary situation.

> It demonstrated that Hitlerism was no accident as was generally thought. In reality the Germany of 1939 was the same in its essence as the one of 1914. It is the Germany of Bismarck. Bismarck had converted Germany since 1871 to a brutal and unscrupulous materialism.

Reproduced in H. Bergson, *Mélanges* (Presses Universitaires de Paris, 1972), p. 1591.

87. Bergson *Mind Energy*, p. 25. See also Perry *Present Conflict*, p. 353, '...there is in Bergson...a sense of solidarity of all lives, as parts of one great forward movement, springing from a common source and serving a common cause'. For comments on his diplomatic activity and interest in sociology see Gunn 'Great Thinkers', pp. 279–80.

88. Bergson *Mind Energy*, pp. 26–7.

89. Ibid., p. 25 and Bergson *Creative Evolution*, p. 39. See Bergson's Columbia University Lectures of February 1913. Bergson *Mélanges*, p. 988. On Bergson's concept of God see A.B. Gibson, 'Review of Henri Bergson's "The Two Sources of Morality and Religion"', *Australasian Journal of Psychology and Philosophy* (1937), 15, pp. 65–75, esp. p. 69.

90. Kolakowski *Positivist Philosophy*, p. 127.

91. Urban, W.M., 'Origin and Value: The Unintelligibility of Philosophic Modernism', *Philosophical Review* (1923), 32, pp. 451–69.

CHAPTER 2

1. Dimnet, E., 'Syndicalism and its Philosophy', *Atlantic Monthly* (1913), 3, pp. 17–30, esp. pp. 24, 26. Sorel, G., *Reflections on Violence*, trans. T.E. Hulme and J. Roth with an introduction by E. A. Shils (Collier Books, 1950), pp. 84–8, 194, 270; Mott, R.,

'The Political Theory of Syndicalism', *Political Science Quarterly* (1922), 37, pp. 25–40, esp. p. 30; Fairchild, E.C., 'Socialism and the Syndicalists', *English Review* (October 1919), pp. 341–51, esp. p. 348; Harley, J.H., *Syndicalism* (T.C. and E.C. Jack, 1912), p. 72.

2. Dimnet 'Syndicalism', p. 24; Fairchild 'Socialism', pp. 349–50.

3. Laski, H., 'A Note on M. Duguit', *Harvard Law Review* (1917), 21, pp. 186–92, esp. p. 188; Laski's introduction to his and F. Laski's translation of L. Duguit's *Law in the Modern State* (Howard Fertig, 1970), p. xiii. First published in 1919. On the grouping process see Dimnet 'Syndicalism', p. 23. See also B. Russell, *Roads to Freedom: Socialism, Anarchism, and Syndicalism* (George Allen & Unwin, 1919), p. 81. 'Syndicalist aims are somewhat less definite than Syndicalist methods.'

4. Sorel quoted by W.K. Stewart, 'The Mentors of Mussolini', *American Political Science Review* (1928), 32, pp. 854–5; Sorel *Reflections*, pp. 230–1; Fairchild 'Socialism', p. 349; Douglas, P.H., 'Proletarian Political Theory', in C.E. Merriam (ed.), *A History of Political Theories: Recent Times* (Macmillan, 1924), p. 219–20; Dimnet 'Syndicalism', p. 24. Harley claimed that Sorel detested the syndicalist use of sabotage. The dawn of the syndicalist millennium demanded craftsmen dedicated to turning out the 'very best work' of which they were 'capable'. Harley *Syndicalism*, p. 58. See also Perry, R.B., *The Present Conflict of Ideals: A Study of the Philosophical Background of the World War* (Longmans, Green & Co., 1918), p. 341.

5. Dimnet 'Syndicalism', p. 24. Sorel, G., *The Illusions of Progress*, trans. J. and C. Stanley (Doubleday, 1906), pp. 58–9, 153.

6. Sorel *Reflections*, pp. 124–5. See also Russell *Roads to Freedom*, p. 81. 'The intellectuals who endeavour to interpret them [the syndicalists] – not always very faithfully – represent them as a part of movement and change following a Bergsonian *élan vital*, without needing any very clear prevision of the goal to which it is to take them.'

7. Sorel quoted in Stewart *Mentors of Mussolini*, p. 855. The last quotation is from Stewart himself. See also Sorel *Syndicalism*, p. 126.

8. Lagardelle, H. et al., *Syndicalisme et Socialisme* (Mi Rivière, 1908), p. 8. Quoted by Perry *Present Conflict*, p. 296. See also G. Wallas, *The Great Society* (Macmillan, 1920), p. 306, first published in 1914; and B. Bosanquet, *Social and International Ideals: being studies in patriotism* (Macmillan, 1917), p. 192. See also Harley *Syndicalism*, p. 56.

9. Sorel *Syndicalism*, pp. 127–8, 131. See also Harley *Syndicalism*, p. 57 and A. Gunn, 'Great Thinkers II – Henri Bergson', *Australasian Journal of Psychology and Philosophy* (1925a), 3, p. 277–86.

10. Sorel *Illusions of Progress*, pp. 180f. See also Perry, R.B., *The Thought and Character of William James*, 2 vols (Little Brown and Co., 1935), II, p. 576.

11. Sorel, G., *De l'Utilité du Pragmatisme* (Librairie des sciences sociales et politiques, 2nd Edition, 1928), pp. 1–2. First published in 1920. Quoted in W.Y. Elliott, *The Pragmatic Revolt in Politics: Syndicalism, Fascism and the Constitutional State* (Macmillan, 1928), p. 116. See also Perry *William James*, p. 577.

12. Elliott *Pragmatic Revolt*, pp. 116, 119–21, 130, and Sorel *Pragmatisme*, pp. 20n, 46, 85, 85n.

13. See 'Une heure chez Henri Bergson', Geores Aimel, *Paris-Journal*, 11 décembre 1910; 'Une heure chez M. Bergson', par Jacques Morland, *L'Opinion, Journal de la Semaine*, 19 août, 1911 and Bergson à G. Maire, mars–avril, 1912, reproduced in H. Bergson, *Mélanges* (Presses Universitaires de Paris, 1972), pp. 844, 941, 971. Rader quoted in A.B. Gibson, 'Mystic or Pragmatist?', *Australasian Journal of Psychology and Philosophy* (1947), 25, p. 102. On the relation between Sorel and Bergson see also Gunn, J.A., *Bergson and his Philosophy* (Methuen, 1920) pp. 110–17. On the marriage of the philosophies of James and Bergson and feminism see Walter Lippmann's 1909 defence of the suffragettes in *The Essential Lippmann: A Political*

Philosophy for Liberal Democracy, C. Rossiter and J. Lare (eds) (Vintage Books, 1965), p. 441 and Gunn *Bergson and his Philosophy*, pp. 119–20.

14. Bosanquet, B., *The Philosophical Theory of the State* (Macmillan, 1920), p. liiin and Douglas *Proletarian Political Theory*, p. 226.

15. Howard, M., 'Men Against Fire: The Doctrine of the Offensive', in M. Howard (ed.), *Theory and Practice of War* (Praeger, 1966), p. 521.

16. 'Fascism and the Worker: Signor Mussolini on Syndicalism', *The Times*, 1 June 1928.

17. Perry *William James*, pp. 570–71; Stewart *Mentors of Mussolini*, p. 862; Gentile, G., 'The Philosophic Basis of Fascism', *Foreign Affairs* (1928),6, pp. 290–304, esp. p. 296; Sternhell, Z., 'Fascism', in R. Griffen (ed.), *International Fascism: Theories, Causes and the New Consensus* (Arnold, 1998), p. 32. On the influence of Bergson, Sorel and Vilfredo Pareto see also K. Mannheim, *Ideology and Utopia: An Introduction to the Sociology of Knowledge* (Routledge & Kegan Paul, 1936), pp. 119, 120–3. Mannheim, citing Gaëtan Pirou and Ernst Posse, mentions that Sorel knew Mussolini before 1914 and that the theoretician had predicted:

> Mussolini is no ordinary Socialist. Take my word, some day you will see him at the head of a sacred battalion, saluting the Italian flag. He is an Italian in the style of the fifteenth century – a veritable condottiere. One does not know him yet, but he is the only man active enough to be capable of curing the weakness of the government.

18. James, W., *Pragmatism* (Longmans, Green & Co., 1907), pp. 54, 79, 159, 257.

19. Papini, G., 'What Pragmatism is Like', trans. K. Royce, *Popular Science Monthly* (1907–08), 71, p. 51–358.

20. Perry *William James*, pp. 571, 577; Griffen *International Fascism*, p. 57; Sarfatti, M.G., *Life of Benito Mussolini*, trans. F. Whyte (Butterworths, 1934), pp. 155–6; Mowrer, E.A., *Immortal Italy* (D. Appleton and Company, 1922), pp. 157–8.

21. Griffen *International Fascism*, pp. 57, 58; Papini, G., *Dante Vivo*, trans. E. Hammond Broadus (Lovat Dickson, 1934), p. vi.

22. Perry *William James*, pp. 573–4. See also Fouillée, A., Charmont, J., Duguit, L.and R. Demogue, *Modern French Legal Philosophy*, trans. Mrs F.W. Scott and J.P. Chamberlain (Augustus M. Kelley, 1916), p. 102. Papini and Prezzolini were both charged with changing significantly the 'aspect of Pragmatism by an admixture of fancy and dilettantism'.

23. Papini 'What Pragmatism is Like', p. 358.

24. Marinetti, F.T., 'Manifesto of Futurism', reproduced in R.W. Flint (ed.) *Selected Writings*, trans. R.W. Flint and A.A. Coppotelli (Farrar, Straus and Giroux, 1971), p. 41.

25. Lee, G.S., *The Voice of the Machines: An Introduction to the Twentieth Century* (Mount Tom Press, 1906), pp. 58–9, 153. Quoted in D. Pick, *War Machine: The Rationalisation of Slaughter in the Modern Age* (Yale University Press, 1993), p. 175.

26. Marinetti, F.T., 'War, the World's Only Hygiene: 1911–1915', reproduced in R.W. Flint (ed.), *Selected Writings*, trans. R.W. Flint and A.A. Coppotelli (Farrar, Straus and Giroux, 1971) and 'Beyond Communism', 1920 also in *Selected Writings*, pp. 80–1, 148. See also F.T. Marinetti, 'The Futurists are the "mystics of action" (1909)', reproduced in H.W. Schneider, *Making the Fascist State* (Oxford, 1928), pp. 260–2.

27. Marinetti 'War, the World's Only Hygiene', in *Selected Writings*, p. 107 and Marinetti, '*Futurismo e fascismo*', 1914, pp. 96–7 quoted in Schneider *Making the Fascist State*, p. 8.

28. Marinetti, cited in C. Tisdall and A. Bozzolla, *Futurism* (Thames and Hudson, 1977), pp. 19–20.

29. Marinetti, 'War, the World's Only Hygiene', and 'Beyond Communism', in *Selected Writings*, pp. 105, 149; '*Futurismo e fascismo*', 'The Futurists are the "mystics of action" (1909)' and other selected writings in Schneider *Making the Fascist State*,

pp. 261, 267–9. Conrad, P., *Modern Times, Modern Places: Life & Art in the 20th Century* (Thames & Hudson, 1998), p. 74, 248.

30. Marinetti, 'The Futurists are the "mystics of action" (1909)', in Schneider *Making the Fascist State*, pp. 261–2.

31. Marinetti, 'War, the World's Only Hygiene', in *Selected Writings*, p. 107; 'The Futurists are the "mystics of action" (1909)', Schneider *Making the Fascist State*, pp. 260–2.

32. Prezzolini, G., 'World Coöperation', *La Voce*, 28 April 1914 quoted in Schneider *Making the Fascist State*, p. 7n.

33. On the significance of X-rays see Conrad *Modern Times*, p. 71. On Marinetti's experience of mature fascism see Tidsall and Bozzolla *Futurism*, pp. 201–4, 205–9. See also Marinetti, 'The Futurists are the "mystics of action" (1909)', in Schneider *Making the Fascist State*, pp. 261 and Marinetti, 'Beyond Communism', in Flint *Selected Writings*, p. 148.

34. These quotes appear in Elliott *The Pragmatic Revolt*, p. 118n and Stewart 'The Mentors of Mussolini', p. 862. Mussolini also adopted Sorel's theory of the myth.

> We have created a myth. This myth is a faith, a noble enthusiasm. It does not have to be a reality [!], it is an impulse and a hope, belief, and courage. Our myth is the nation the great nation which we wish to make into a concrete reality.

Mannheim *Ideology and Utopia*, p. 123n. The quote is sourced to C. Schmitt, *Die geistesgechichtliche Lage des heutigen Parlamentarismus*, (Duncker and Humblot, 1926), p. 89.

35. Interview with Dr André Révesz, foreign editor of Madrid newspaper *A.B.C.*, *Sunday Times*, 11 April 1926 p. 15.

36. Mussolini quoted in Stewart 'The Mentors of Mussolini', p. 863.

37. Smith, T.V., 'The Ethics of Fascism', *International Journal of Ethics* (1936), XLVI, pp. 127–77, esp. p. 152. See also B. Mussolini, *Fascism: Doctrine and Institutions* (Ardita, 1935); (first published in Italian in 1932), pp. 7–22. Reproduced in Griffen *International Fascism*, p. 254. 'A doctrine must therefore be a vital act and not a verbal display. Hence the pragmatic strain in Fascism, its will to power, its will to life, its attitude toward violence, and its value.'

38. Perry *William James*, p. 578; Gentile 'Philosophic Basis of Fascism', pp. 292, 296. Fite, W., 'Review of Giovanni Gentile's *Theory of Mind as Pure Act*', *Philosophical Review* (1923), 32, pp. 548–9; Gentile, G., *The Theory of Mind as Pure Act*, trans. H.W. Carr (Macmillan, 1922), pp. 81–2.

39. Michels, R., 'The Sociological Character of Political Parties', *American Political Science Review* (1927), 21, pp. 753–72, esp. pp. 770–1. Mussolini stated: 'You know that I am no worshipper of the new god, the masses. At any rate, history proves that social changes have always been first brought about by minorities, by a mere handful of men.' Mussolini, B., *Reden: eine Auswahl aus den Jahren 1914 bis Ende August 1924 von Fred C. Willis*, H. Meyer (ed.) (K.F. Koehler, 1925), p. 13, quoted in Mannheim *Ideology and Utopia*, p. 119n.

40. Perry *William James*, p. 579. Mussolini himself noted: 'It is incredible how a roving, free-lance soldier can change when he becomes a deputy or a town official. He acquires another face. He begins to appreciate that municipal budgets must be studied, and cannot be stormed.' Quoted in Mannheim *Ideology and Utopia*, p. 126n.

41. See also W.K. Wallace, *The Passing of Politics* (George Allen & Unwin, 1924), p. 71. See also K.C. Hsiao, *Political Pluralism: A Study in Contemporary Thought* (Kegan Paul, Trench, Trubner, 1927), p. 207.

42. Perry, R.B., *In the Spirit of William James* (Yale University Press, 1938), pp. 143–6.

43. Olivetti, A.O., *Il sindacalismo come filosofia e come politica: lineamenti di sintesi universale* (Alpes, 1924), pp. 15, 16, 21, 38, quoted in Schneider *Making the Fascist State*, pp. 151–2.

44. Smith 'The Ethics of Fascism', p. 154; Mussolini, B., 'Dottrina', *Enciclopedia Italiana, Ristampa Fotolitica Del* (1932), Vol. VIV, pp. 850–1 and Gentile 'Philosophic Basis of Fascism', p. 300. Sarfatti *The Life of Mussolini*, p. 101.

45. Mannheim, K., *Freedom, Power & Democratic Planning* (Routledge & Kegan Paul, 1951), p. 25.

46. Gini, C., 'The Scientific Basis of Fascism, *Political Science Quarterly* (1927), 42, pp. 99–115, esp. p. 104; Gentile 'Philosophic Basis of Fascism', p. 298.

47. 'Strife is the Origin of All Things'; excerpts from Mussolini's speech at Trieste, 20 September in Schneider *Making the Fascist State*, p. 276. See also Sarfatti *The Life of Benito Mussolini*, p. 182 and Mussolini *Fascism: Doctrine and Institutions* in Griffen *International Fascism*, p. 250. Mussolini stated that fascism rejects the 'possibility or utility of perpetual peace. War alone keys up all human energies to their maximum tension and sets the seal of nobility on those who have the courage to face it.'

48. Mussolini quoted in Schneider *Making the Fascist State*, pp. 28–9. See also Gini 'Scientific Basis of Fascism', pp. 104–5. See also Mowrer *Immortal Italy*, p. 158.

49. Quotation appears in Smith 'The Ethics of Fascism', p. 155.

50. Discussion of Rationalisation, Report and Proceedings of the World Economic Conference, 4–23 May 1927, p. 141. LON C356.M.129.1927.II[C.E.1.4.6.]. The quotation is from Elliott *Pragmatic Revolt*, p. 139. See also Schneider *Making the Fascist State*, p. 8. See also Mussolini *Fascism: Doctrine and Institutions* in Griffen *International Fascism*, p. 250. Mussolini stated that:

> Equally foreign to the spirit of Fascism, even if accepted as useful in meeting special political situations – are all internationalistic or League superstructures which, as history shows, crumble to the ground whenever the heart of nations is deeply stirred by sentimental, idealistic or practical considerations.

51. Elliott *Pragmatic Revolt*, p. 14.

52. Forges-Davanzati, R., 'American Imperialism', *La Tribuna*, 2 January 1927 cited in Schneider *Making the Fascist State*, pp. 278–9. Mussolini stated that Italy needed to disentangle itself from the 'Holy Alliance of Western plutocratic nations' (p. 29).

53. See Duguit *Law in the Modern State*, p. xii. First appeared as *Les Transformations du droit public* (A. Colin, 1913). See also F.W. Coker, 'The Technique of the Pluralistic State', *American Political Science Review* (1921), 15, p. 198 and M. Cohen, 'Communal Ghosts and other Perils in Social Philosophy', *Journal of Philosophy* (1919), 16, p. 201.

54. Modelski, G., *Principles of World Politics* (Free Press, 1972), p. 320.

55. Duguit, L., 'Law and the State', *Harvard Law Review* (1917), XXXI, pp. 1–185, esp. pp. 182–5. Duguit was quoting from his *Les transformations*. See also W.Y. Elliott, 'The Metaphysics of Duguit's Pragmatic Conception of Law', *Political Science Quarterly* (1922), 37, pp. 641–54.

56. Duguit *Law in the Modern State*, pp. 39–44, 49–51, 73. See also W.J. Brown, 'The Jurisprudence of M. Duguit', *Law Quarterly Review* (1916), 136, pp. 168–83, esp. p. 179. See also Fouillée et al. *Modern French Legal Philosophy*, p. xvi. Arthur W. Spencer writes in the preface that Duguit revived 'natural law dogma in a new form'.

57. Duguit *Law in the Modern State*, pp. 49–50.

58. Panunzio, S., in *Popolo d'Italia*, 12 May 1923 quoted in Schneider *Making the Fascist State*, p. 149.

59. Programme of Fascist Party quoted in A.B. Gibson, 'The State as an Organism', *Australasian Journal of Psychology and Philosophy* (1934), 12, pp. 119–37, esp. p. 123. See also Stewart 'The Mentors of Mussolini', p. 857 and B. Mussolini, *Fascism: Doctrine and Institutions* (Ardita, 1935), pp. 17, 38–42, 60.

60. Hsiao *Political Pluralism*, pp. 55, 193, 204–7.

61. Follett, M.P., *The New State: Group Organisation in the Solution of Popular Government* (Longmans, 1918), pp. 9, 23, 30, 87; Le Bon, G., *The Psychology of the Great War: The*

First World War & Its Origins (Transaction, 1999), p. 30. Originally published in 1916.

62. Follett *The New State*, pp. 97–8. See also L. Woolf, *International Government* (George Allen & Unwin, 1916), p. 92.

63. Follett *The New State*, pp. 11, 84. See also Follett, M.P., 'Community is a Process', *Philosophical Review* (1919), 28, pp. 576–88, esp. pp. 577, 583.

64. Follett *The New State*, pp. 10, 263–7.

65. James, W., *Essays in Radical Empiricism and a Pluralistic Universe*, R.B. Perry (ed.) (Dutton, 1971), pp. 275–6.

66. Follett *The New State*, p. 266.

67. James *Radical Empiricism*, p. 274.

68. Follett *The New State*, p. 302.

69. Ibid., p. 40.

70. Follett 'Community is a Process', pp. 582–3 and Follett *The New State*, p. 99.

71. Follett *The New State*, pp. 67, 74 and Follett 'Community is a Process', p. 581.

72. Follett *The New State*, p. 39.

73. Follett 'Community is a Process', pp. 577, 583 and Follett *The New State*, pp. 11, 344, 353.

74. Follett *The New State*, pp. 161, 202, 352.

75. Follett 'Community is a Process', pp. 577, 583.

76. Follett *The New State*, p. 354.

77. Ibid., pp. 355, 360.

78. Follett 'Community is a Process', pp. 576–7.

79. Bosanquet, B., *The Philosophical Theory of the State* (Macmillan, 1920), pp. xiii, xli, liv, lxi, lxii.

80. Follett *The New State*, p. 267.

81. James *Radical Empiricism*, pp. 222–4.

82. Follett *The New State*, pp. 266–7; Follett 'Community is a Process', p. 583. See also H.M. Kallen, *William James and Henri Bergson* (University of Chicago Press, 1915), pp. 10f, 105.

83. Laski, H., 'The Pluralistic State', *Philosophical Review* (1916), 28, pp. 562–75, esp. p. 563.

84. Laski, H., 'The Apotheosis of the State', *New Republic* (22 July 1916), pp. 302–4; Laski, H., 'The Personality of the State', *The Nation* (22 July 1915), pp. 115–17; Hobhouse, L.T., *The Metaphysical Theory of the State* (Allen and Unwin, 1918), pp. 134–6. On Laski's usage of the word pluralism see Hsiao *Political Pluralism*, p. 126.

85. Sollors, W., 'A Critique of Pure Pluralism', in Bercovitch, S. (ed.), *Reconstructing American Literary History* (Harvard University Press, 1986), pp. 258, 265, 269; H.M. Kallen, 'Culture and the Ku Klux Klan' and 'Democracy Versus the Melting Pot', in *Culture and Democracy in the United States* (Arno Press, 1970), pp. 43, 124–5. First published in 1924.

86. Posnock, R., 'The Influence of William James on American Culture', in Putnam, R.A. (ed.), *The Cambridge Companion to William James* (Cambridge University Press, 1997) pp. 335–6.

87. De Wolf Howe, M. (ed.), *Holmes–Laski Letters: The Correspondence of Mr. Justice Holmes and Harold J. Laski 1916–1935*, 2 vols (Oxford University Press, 1953), foreword by Felix Frankfurter, I, p. 22 [16 September 1916].

88. Laski, H., 'The Personality of Associations', *Harvard Law Review* (1916), 29, p. 425.

89. Laski, H., *The Foundations of Sovereignty and other Essays* (Books for Libraries Press, 1938), p. 261. First published in 1921.

90. Laski 'Personality of Associations', p. 426.

91. Laski, H., *Studies in the Problem of Sovereignty* (Allen and Unwin, 1968), p. 18; Laski, H., *A Grammar of Politics* (Allen and Unwin, 1925), p. 35. For Laski's comments on the value of the state see *Holmes–Laski Letters*, I, pp. 246–7 [28 February 1920].

92. Laski *Studies*, pp. 304n, 315.
93. See Laski, *Studies* pp. 23–4; Laski *Grammar*, pp. 276, 287 and M.P. Follett, *Creative Experience* (Peter Smith, 1924), p. 264.
94. Laski *Grammar*, pp. 262–3.
95. Ibid., pp. 261–2, esp. p. 37 and p. 282. See also Follett 'Community is a Process', pp. 587–8.
96. Laski *Grammar*, pp. 260, 263–5.
97. Ibid., pp. 260, 262.
98. Ibid., pp. 26, 29–34, 68.
99. Hsiao *Political Pluralism*, pp. 165–6, 207.
100. Laski, *Grammar*, p. 261.
101. *Holmes–Laski Letters*, I, p. 633 [15 July 1924]. See also Laski *Grammar*, p. 260.
102. Laski reaffirmed his liking for a messy universe in an appreciative review of Hsiao's book, see *New Republic* (28 March 1928), pp. 197–8. The comments on world unity are from Laski *Grammar*, pp. 250, 263, 664–5.
103. Laski *Grammar*, pp. 229, 233, 238, 287.
104. Ibid., pp. 226, 263, 664–5.
105. Wilde, N., 'The Attack on the State', *International Journal of Ethics* (1920), 30, pp. 349–71, esp. p. 354. See also Laski 'A Note on M. Duguit', p. 192. William James's pragmatism influenced early twentieth-century French legal philosophy. See Chapter 8 'Pragmatism' in Fouillée et al. *Modern French Legal Philosophy*, pp. 99–105.
106. Laski *Grammar*, pp. 229, 233, 261, 588, 662, 666.
107. Ibid., pp. 64, 538–9.
108. Kallen, H.M., *The Structure of Lasting Peace: An Inquiry into the Motives of War and Peace* (Marshall Jones, 1918), pp. vii, 159, 162–71, 181–7.
109. Laski *Grammar*, pp. 226–7, 588–9. See H.M. Kallen, *The League of Nations Today and Tomorrow* (Marshall Jones, 1919), p. 40 and L. Woolf, *International Government: Two Reports by L.S. Woolf prepared for the Fabian Research Department: Together with a project prepared by a Fabian Committee, for a supranational authority that will prevent war* (Fabian Society, Westminster, 1916), p. 69.
110. Laski *Grammar*, pp. 19, 261, 588, 618, 640.
111. Ibid., pp. 20, 227, 239–40.
112. Coker, F.W., 'Pluralistic Theories and the Attack Upon State Sovereignty', in Merriam *History of Political Theories*, pp. 98–9 and Hsiao *Political Pluralism*, pp. 52, 53–4, 56–7. Hsiao wrote:

    ...while the state loses its sovereign self-sufficiency in becoming a humble subject of international (or supernational) law...it ceases...to be a pluralistic entity...the national legal community undergoes metamorphosis and is merged into world-empire, 'the One State uniting the whole of mankind'...the universal empire of Dante comes back with a vengeance – a far cry from pluralism.

    Hsiao is writing of Hugo Krabbe. He thought Laski's tendency as regards the shape of the prospective world community was to favour a 'relationship of negotiation' among its constituents rather than a world state, although Hsiao thought this would likely descend into class struggle on a global scale.

CHAPTER 3

1. Adams, H., *The Education of Henry Adams* (Modern Library, 1918), p. 380.
2. Schumate, R.V., 'The Philosophy of Henry Adams', *American Political Science Review*, (1934), 28, pp. 600–3; Adams *Education*, p. 501 and H. Adams, 'A Law of Acceleration', in E. Stevenson (ed.), *A Henry Adams Reader* (Doubleday, 1959), pp. 327–30.

3. On Wells see J. Carey, *The Intellectuals and Masses: Pride and Prejudice among the Literary Intelligentsia, 1880–1939* (Faber & Faber, 1992), pp. 119–23.

4. Carey *Intellectuals and Masses*, pp. 135–6.

5. Wells, H.G., *A Modern Utopia* (Thomas Nelson and Sons, 1905), pp. 16, 21, 30, 32, 41–2, 48, 251, 265, 330, 377; see also Carey *Intellectuals and Masses*, p. 148. A revised version of 'Scepticism of the Instrument' is included as an appendix to *A Modern Utopia*. It was first published in *Mind* (1904), 13, pp. 377–93.

6. Wells *Modern Utopia*, pp. 16, 21, 30, 32, 41–2, 48, 251, 265, 330, 377. On the nature of God and James's influence, see H.G. Wells, *God The Invisible King* (Cassell and Co. Ltd, 1917), pp. viii, xvi, 25. Perry claimed that Wells's God was modelled upon the God described by James in the *Will to Believe*. Perry, R.B., *The Present Conflict of Ideals: A Study of the Philosophical Background of the World War* (Longmans, Green and Co., 1918), p. 329.

7. Wells, H.G., *The War in the Air: And particularly how Mr. Bert Smallways fared while it lasted* (Collins Press, 1925), pp. 2, 5, 177, 181–3, 251.

8. Archer, W., *The Great Analysis: A Plea for a Rational World-Order*, with an Introduction by G. Murray (Methuen, 1912), pp. 23, 69–70. It is testimony to the continuity between pre and postwar thinking on world government that Archer's views were cited in the introduction to the published proceedings of the Social Economic Congress which took place in Amsterdam in 1931. See *World Social Economic Planning: The Necessity for Planned Adjustment of Productive Capacity and Standards of Living* (The Hague, International Industrial Relations Institute, 1931) p. xx.

9. Archer *Great Analysis*, pp. 103, 121–2.

10. Gisborne, F.A.W., 'The Foundations of Peace', *Australasian Journal of Psychology and Philosophy* (1925), 3, pp. 77–90, esp. p. 77.

11. Spengler, O., *The Decline of the West*, 2 vols, trans. with notes by C.F. Atkinson (Knopf, 1926), I, pp. xiii, xv. Revised edition first published in 1922.

12. On Spengler's influence see A. Liebert, 'Contemporary German Philosophy', *Philosophical Review* (1933), 42, pp. 31–48, esp. p. 34.

13. Spengler *Decline of the West*, I, pp. xiii–xiv, 46; Sorokin, P., *The Crisis of Our Age* (E.P. Dutton & Co., 1957), p. 16. First published in 1941.

14. Spengler *Decline of the West*, I, pp. xiv, 17, 21.

15. Ibid., pp. 3, 17.

16. Ibid., pp. 15, 17.

17. Spengler, O., *Man and Technics: a contribution to a philosophy of life* (Allen & Unwin, 1932), p. 14; Spengler *Decline of the West*, I, pp. 21, 31.

18. Spengler *Decline of the West*, I, p. 3.

19. Ibid., pp. 502–3.

20. Ibid., pp. 503–4.

21. Ibid., p. 463.

22. Ibid., pp. 463–65. See also P. Conrad, *Modern Times, Modern Places: Life & Art in the 20th Century* (Thames & Hudson, 1998), pp. 323, 326.

23. P. Valéry, 'Foreword (1931)' and 'The Crisis of the Mind (1919)', in J. Matthews (ed.), *The Collected Works of Paul Valéry*, 10, 'History and Politics', trans. D. Folliot and J. Matthews (Routledge & Kegan Paul, 1963), pp. 19, 25.

24. Valéry 'Crisis of the Mind', pp. 25–8.

25. Ibid., pp. 28–30.

26. Ibid., pp. 34–6. See also Valéry 'Foreword', pp. 4, 18.

27. Valéry 'Crisis of the Mind', p. 31.

28. Valéry, 'The European (1922)' and 'The Persian Letters (1926)' in Matthews *Collected Works*, pp. 307, 218–19.

29. Valéry, 'Remarks on Progress (1929)', in Matthews *Collected Works*, p. 165.

30. Valéry, 'The European', p. 314 and 'Persian Letters', p. 219.

31. Valéry, 'League of Nations: League of Minds', in Matthews *Collected Works*, p. 345.

32. Schiller, F.C.S., 'Review of William Mackintire Salter, Nietzsche, the Thinker', *Mind* (1919), 28, pp. 107–8. On post-reception of Bergson see J.A. Gunn, *Bergson and his Philosophy* (Methuen, 1920), p.vii.

33. Radhakrishnan, S., 'Bergson and Absolute Idealism III: Mechanism and Teleology', *Mind* (1919), 28, pp. 275–96, esp. p. 276.

34. For this line of argument see N. Berdyaev, *The Meaning of History*, trans. G. Reavey (Geoffrey Bles, 1923). This book is based on lectures delivered in Moscow by Berdyaev before his expulsion from Russia by the Soviets in 1922.

35. The first quotation is from E.L. Hinman, 'Review of H. Wildon Carr, The Scientific Approach to Philosophy', *Philosophical Review* (1926), 35, pp. 477–81, esp. p. 478. The second is from H.W. Carr, 'Review of John Dewey, Experience and Nature', *Philosophical Review* (1926), 35, pp. 64–9, esp. p. 65. See also J.A. Leighton, 'Review of H. Wildon Carr, A Theory of Monads: Outlines of the Philosophy of the Principle of Relativity', *Philosophical Review* (1923), 32, pp. 544–8; Carr, H.W., *A Theory of Monads: Outlines of the Philosophy of the Principle of Relativity* (Macmillan, 1922), pp. 3–5, 89, 176, 339; Carr, H.W., *The Scientific Approach to Philosophy* (Macmillan, 1924), p. 118.

36. Curtis, M., 'Review of C. E. Merrian's and H.E. Barnes's "A History of Political Theories in Recent Times"', *Philosophical Review* (1925), 34, pp. 491–500, esp. pp. 491, 495.

37. Gunn, J.A., 'Bergson and Einstein', *Australasian Journal of Psychology and Philosophy* (1925c), 3, pp. 215–18, esp. p. 215. 'Nothing is more striking in modern thought than the rapprochement between physics and metaphysics.' W.K. Wallace, *The Passing of Politics* (George Allen & Unwin, 1924), p. 296. Sarfatti, M.G., *The Life of Benito Mussolini* (Butterworths, 1934), p. 101. First published in 1925.

38. Bergson quoted in J.A. Gunn, 'Time and Modern Metaphysics – 1', *Australasian Journal of Psychology and Philosophy*, (1925b), 3. See also Gunn *Bergson and Einstein*, p. 216 and G. Deleuze, *Bergsonism*, trans. H. Tomlinson and B. Habberjam (Zone Books, 1988), p. 82.

39. Bergson , H., *Mélanges* (Presses Universitaires de Paris, 1972), pp. 1340–7.

40. Frank,W., *The Rediscovery of America* (Charles Scribner, 1929), pp. 36–43. See also T. Greenwood, 'Einstein and Idealism', *Mind* (1922), 31, pp. 205–7 and R.W. Clark, *Einstein: The Life and Times* (Hodder and Stoughton, 1973), p. 327.

41. Frank *Our America*, pp. 36–43.

42. Ibid., pp. 129–30.

43. Ibid., pp. 36–43.

44. Ibid., pp. 90ff, 108–9, 271–2.

45. Lewis, W., *Time and Modern Man* (Harcourt, Brace & Co., 1928), pp. xiv, 208, 400.

46. Ibid., pp. 35, 195, 207–9.

47. Ibid., pp. 20–1, 357–8.

48. Ibid., pp. 20–1, 346, 351–2, 359.

49. Ibid., pp. vii, xiii, 80–2.

50. Ibid., p. 85.

51. Ibid., pp. 437, 442.

52. Fülöp-Miller, R., *The Mind and Face of Bolshevism: An Examination of Cultural Life in Soviet Russia*, trans. F.S. Flint and D.F. Tait (G.P. Putnam's and Sons, 1927), pp. 2–5, 12–14. See also Lewis *Time*, p. 251.

53. Carey *The Intellectuals and Masses*, pp. 193–7.

54. Keyserling, Count H., *The World in the Making*, trans. M. Samuel (Harcourt, Brace and Company, 1927), pp. 119, 127–9, 135, 166. See also Keyserling, Count H., *The Travel Diary of a Philosopher*, trans. J. Holroyd-Reece (Jonathan Cape, 1925), pp. 5–7. On Keyserling's reputation see C.A. Beard (ed.), *Whither Mankind: A Panorama of Modern Civilization* (Longmans, Green and Co., 1928), p. 1 and J. Dewey, *Individualism Old and New* (Capricorn, 1929), p. 27.

55. Keyserling *World in the Making*, pp. 182–3.
56. Ibid., pp. 171, 182.
57. Ibid., pp. 192, 194.
58. Ibid., pp. 194.
59. Ibid., pp. 188, 190.
60. Loewenberg, J., 'Metaphysics of Modern Scepticism', *Philosophical Review* (1923), 32, pp. 278–88, esp. p. 280. Perry noted the canonisation of Mach as the father of

> a new school of philosophy in Vienna. But this Mach redivivus is the positivistic and not the pragmatistic Mach. The substitute of logistics for ethics and metaphysics, as proposed by Mach's latest disciples, is profoundly alien to James in temperament as well as in doctrine.

Perry, R.B., *The Thought and Character of William James*, 2 vols (Little Brown and Co., 1935), p. 580.
61. Schlick, M., *Space and Time in Contemporary Physics: an introduction to the theory of relativity and gravitation*, trans. H. Brose (Clarendon, 1920), quoted in C.O. Weber, 'The Reality of Time and the Autonomy of History', *Monist*, 37, 1927, p. 251.
62. The first quote is from A.E. Blumberg, 'Logical Positivism: A New Movement in European Philosophy', *Journal of Philosophy* (1931), 28, pp. 281–96 and the second is from Loewenberg 'Metaphysics', p. 281.
63. Carnap and Schlick quoted in J. Passmore, 'Logical Positivism (1)', *Australasian Journal of Psychology and Philosophy* (1943), 21, pp. 65–6.
64. Russell, B., 'Science', in Beard *Whither Mankind*, pp. 65, 77; Wright, W.K., 'Review of Emmanuel Lerroux, Le Pragmatisme Americain et Anglais', *Philosophical Review* (1924), 33, pp. 107–12. See also O.L. Reiser, 'The Problem of Time in Science and Philosophy', *Philosophical Review* (1926), 35, pp. 236–52, esp. p. 237.
65. Gunter, P.A.Y., Introduction to H. Bergson *Creative Evolution*, trans. A. Mitchell (University Press of America, 1983), p. xvi. First published in 1911.
66. Wallace *Passing of Politics*, p. 277.
67. Ibid., pp. 5, 7, 95, 102–3, 120n, 276–7, 302.
68. Ibid., 277, 282–5, 297, 303, 306.
69. Ibid., pp. 24–5, 73n.
70. Tait, W.D., 'Psychology, Leadership and Democracy', *Australasian Journal of Psychology and Philosophy* (1928), 6, pp. 28–34, esp. p. 29.
71. Lippmann, W., *A Preface to Politics* (Ann Arbor, 1962), pp. 63, 93, 137–8, 157–8, 176. He wrote in 1915 that: 'H.G. Wells and William James...write in terms which convey some of the curiosity and formlessness of modern life...But the political writer who gave me the nightmare...aimed at impersonal truth which is like the inscription on monuments.' In W. Lippmann, *The Essential Lippmann: A Political Philosophy for Liberal Democracy*, C. Rossiter and J. Lare (eds) (Vintage Books, 1965), p. 531.
72. Lippmann *Preface to Politics*, pp. 62–3, 163, 171–6, 238; Wallas, G., *Nature in Politics* (Constable, 1948).
73. Lippmann, W., *Drift and Mastery* (Prentice-Hall, 1961), pp. 13–15.
74. Ibid., pp. 18, 115.
75. Leuchtenburg, W.E., 'Walter Lippmann's Drift and Mastery', in Lippmann *Drift and Mastery*, pp. 1–2.
76. Lippmann *Drift and Mastery*, p. 118.
77. Ibid., pp. 16–17.
78. Ibid., p. 111; Posnock, R.,'The Influence of William James on American Culture', in Putnam, R.A. (ed.), *The Cambridge Companion to William James* (Cambridge University Press, 1997) p. 325.
79. Lippmann *Drift and Mastery*, pp. 155–6.
80. Ibid., pp. 159, 174.
81. Ibid., p. 62.

82. Ibid., pp. 4, 150–1.

83. Posnock 'Influence of William James', p. 330 and Lippmann *Drift and Mastery*, pp. 42–3, 67.

84. See Lippmann, *The Essential Lippmann*, pp. 20–2, 95, 156–8. See also excerpts from W. Lippmann, *The Phantom Public* (Harcourt, Brace, 1925), pp. 106–14.

85. The quotations are from H.E. Barnes, 'Dynamic Politics and the New History', *Monist* (1925), 35, pp. 110–60, esp. p. 148.

86. Wallas, G., *The Great Society* (Macmillan, 1920), pp. 3, 14. First published in 1914.

87. Ibid., pp. 132–7.

88. Ibid., pp. 20.

89. Ibid., p. v.

90. Ibid., pp. 10–11, 218–24, 306.

91. Ibid., pp. 43–4.

92. Ibid., pp. 289, 306–9, 318–19.

93. Wells, H.G., *The World Set Free* (Ernest Benn, 1927), pp. 5, 34, 41, 59, 157–60, 168, 177. Wells, H.G., *The World of William Clissold* quoted in Carey *Intellectuals and Masses*, p. 148.

94. Wells *The World Set Free*, pp. 193, 195.

95. Rivett, Sir D., 'The Scientific Estate', *Australasian and New Zealand Association for the Advancement of Science*, 23rd Meeting, Auckland, January 1937, pp. 1–13.

96. Mumford, L., 'Wardom and the State', *The Dial* (4 October 1919), pp. 303–5.

97. J. Dewey in his introduction to Sidney Hook's, *The Metaphysics of Pragmatism* (AMS Press, 1927), p. 4.

98. Dewey, J., *Reconstruction in Philosophy* (Beacon Press, 1957), pp. 43, 71. First published in 1920.

99. Dewey *Individualism*, pp. 64, 96 and Dewey *Reconstruction*, p. 96.

100. Bourne, R., 'Twilight of Idols', *The Seven Arts*, 1917, 2, pp. 688, 692, 695, 700. See also R.B. Perry, 'What is worth fighting for?' reproduced in Charles Chatfield (ed.), *The Ethics of War: Bertrand Russell and Ralph Barton Perry* on World War I (Garland, 1972), pp. 822–31. Perry's piece first appeared in the *Atlantic Monthly*, 116 (December 1915), pp. 822–31.

101. Dewey, J., 'Social Absolutism', *The New Republic* (9 February 1921), pp. 316–17.

102. Ibid., pp. 317–18. On Dewey's internationalism see: *The Public and its Problems* (George Allen & Unwin, 1936), pp. 129–31, 142, 212–17. This work is the result of lectures Dewey delivered in January 1926. See also *Reconstruction*, pp. 204–5 where Dewey calls for a 'modification of hierarchical and monistic' theories of the state, champions pluralism and presents the dogma of 'exclusive national sovereignty' as the greatest hindrance to the 'effective formation of an international mind which alone agrees with the moving forces of present-day labor, commerce, science, art and religion'.

CHAPTER 4

1. On this matter see L. Woolf, *International Government: Two Reports by L.S. Woolf prepared for the Fabian Research Department: Together with a project prepared by a Fabian Committee, for a supranational authority that will prevent war* (Fabian Society, Westminster, 1916), p. 96–7.

2. Roosevelt and Wilson quoted in F. Morely, *The Society of Nations: Its Organization and Constitutional Development* (Brookings Institution, 1932), pp. 5–7.

3. Ibid., pp. 14, 34–5, 110.

4. Rappard, W., 'The League of Nations as an Historical Fact', in Geneva Institute of International Relations, *The Problem of Peace* (Oxford, 1927), p. 23.

5. On the preference for the French description see A. Zimmern, *The League of Nations and the Rule of Law: 1918–1935* (Macmillan, 1939), pp. 3–5 and S. de Madariaga, 'Gilbert Murray and the League', in J. Smith (ed.), *Gilbert Murray: An Unfinished Autobiography* (George Allen and Unwin, 1960), p. 184. The first statement by Wilson is quoted in E.H. Carr, *The Twenty Years' Crisis 1919–1939: An Introduction to the Study of International Relations* (Macmillan, 1952), p. 8. The second is from Wilson's Address to Congress of 11 February 1918, cited by Rappard 'League of Nations', p. 22.

6. Gathorne-Hardy, G.M., *A Short History of International Affairs 1920–1939*, Fourth Edition (Oxford, 1950), p. 148.

7. On Cecil and Smuts see Rappard *League of Nations*, pp. 26–8.

8. The quotation concerning Wilson's conception of the League is from A. Nussbaum, *Concise History of the Law of Nations* (Macmillan, 1954), p. 251. Kissinger, H., *Diplomacy* (Simon and Schuster, 1994), p. 51; Carr *The Twenty Years' Crisis*, p. 234.

9. Wilson, W., *The New Freedom: A Call for the Emancipation of the Generous Energies of a People* (Doubleday, Page & Company, 1913), p. 7.

10. Wallas, G., *The Great Society* (Macmillan, 1920), p. 3.

11. Wells, H.G., *In the Fourth Year: Anticipations of a World Peace* (Chatto & Windus, 1918), pp. v–ix. Wells, H.G., *The World of William Clissold*, Book 3 (Ernest Benn, 1926), pp. 285, 326, 336. On the shift in the League's character see Morely *Society of Nations*, pp. 606–7 and Laski, H., *A Grammar of Politics* (Allen and Unwin, 1925), p. 619.

12. *The Song of the League of Nations and International Brotherhood*, Words and Music by J.M. Dembleby (Geneva: Archives of the League of Nations, United Nations Library). Box R 5702, file 3184.

13. Greaves, H.R.G., *The League Committees and World Order: A study of the Permanent Expert Committees of the League of Nations as an Instrument of International Government* (Oxford, 1931), p. 1.

14. 'A Letter to Paul Valéry by Salvador de Madariaga', Madrid, 1933, in J. Matthews, *The Collected Works of Paul Valéry*, 10, 'History and Politics', trans. D. Folliot and J. Matthews (Routledge and Kegan Paul, 1963), p. 561. On the religious basis of Toynbee's politics see Madariaga in Smith, *Gilbert Murray*, p. 181.

15. Rappard 'League of Nations', pp. 18–19 and A. Zimmern, 'The Development of the International Mind', in *The Problem of Peace*, p. 10.

16. Rappard was responding to Laski's speech at the 1927 Geneva conference published as 'International Government and National Sovereignty' in *The Problem of Peace*, pp. 310–11. On Robert Cecil see Rappard 'League of Nations', p. 25 also published in *The Problem of Peace*. On the question of world government see Salter and Wells in 'Microphone Dictators: New Ideas on How to Run the World', *Headway*, December (1931), p. 229 and A. Zimmern, 'International Law and Social Consciousness', *Transactions of the Grotius Society* (1934), 20, pp. 37–8; Zimmern, A., *The League of Nations and the Rule of Law: 1918–1935* (Macmillan, 1939), pp. 3–5. See also Laski *Grammar*, pp. 588ff. and Greaves *League Committees*, pp. viii, 60. Madariaga in Smith *Gilbert Murray*, p. 178.

17. See Zimmern's and Toynbee's discussion of the teaching of international relations held at Chatham House 11–14 March 1929 organised by the ICIC, the Royal Institute of International Affairs and the London School of Economics. See 'The Conference of Institutions for the Scientific Study of International Relations', *International Affairs* (1929), 8, pp. 190–1, 200–1. See Zimmern 'The Development of the International Mind', 'The League and International Intellectual Co-operation' and J.C. Maxwell Garnett, 'The Psychology of Patriotism and the Aims of the League of Nations Associations', in Rappard 'League of Nations', pp. 1, 149, 333–4.

18. Bourgeois, cited in Greaves *League Committees*, p. 112.

19. For Bergson's speech on the ICIC's role see: Discours de cloture du Président, 5 August, 1922 reproduced in Bergson , H., *Mélanges* (Presses Universitaires de Paris, 1972), pp. 1349–52. See also Bergson speaking at a meeting of the ICIC November 4, 1922, pp. 1363–6. Gilbert Murray told the Third Assembly that the ICIC would seek to ensure 'that the great intellectual currents of the world shall at some time once again flow in harmony'. H. Wilson Harris, *Geneva 1922: Being an Account of the Third Assembly of the League of Nations* (League of Nations Union, 1922), p. 52.

20. Discours d'Ouverture de M. Bergson, Président, tenue le 26 juillet 1923. Committion Internationale de Coopération Intellectuelle. Archives de l'Unesco, C570.M.224.1923. XII, p. 7; Seconde session, Première séance; EP, III, pp. 540–1. Reproduced in *Mélanges*, pp. 1397–8. For Bergson's letter of resignation see Smith *Gilbert Murray*, p. 201n.

21. Bergson, H., *The Two Sources of Morality and Religion*, trans. R.A. Audra and C. Brereton (Doubleday Anchor, 1956), pp. 30–1, 281–2, 287–91, 310–11, 317.

22. Gibson, A.B., 'Review of Henri Bergson's "The Two Sources of Morality and Religion"', *Australasian Journal of Psychology and Philosophy* (1937), pp. 65–75, esp. p. 68.

23. Toynbee, A.J., *A Study of History*, 3 Vols (Oxford, 1934), 3, pp. 388–90.

24. Ibid., 1, pp. 8–9.

25. Ibid., 3, pp. 118, 231–7.

26. Ibid., 3, 106, 243–7 and 1, pp. 14–15.

27. Valéry, 'The Future of Culture' (1933), p. 539. See also Valéry, 'Toward a Correspondence', 1933, p. 349. This last piece was written in collaboration with another ICIC member, Henry Focillon.

28. Valéry, 'League of Nations: League of Minds' (1930) and 'Politics of the Minds' (1932), pp. 91–3, 345–7.

29. Madariaga writing in the introduction to Matthews *Collected Works*, p. xxxv.

30. See the Forenote to Appendix III, Valéry's 'Role in the League of Nations' and Salvador de Madariaga, 'A Letter to Paul Valéry' (1933), in Matthews *Collected Works*, pp. 531–2, 555.

31. Valéry, 'Towards a Correspondence', p. xxxv, 345, 349.

32. Ibid., p. 349.

33. Ibid., p. 348.

34. Madariaga, 'A Letter to Paul Valéry', pp. 559–65.

35. Ibid., pp. 561–3.

36. Ibid., p. 564.

37. Wallace, W.K., *The Scientific World View* (Simpkin Marshall, 1931), pp. 306–7. On the universality of scientific meanings see Greaves *League Committees*, pp. 108, 138. For science's blindness to group allegiances see R.A. Brady, *The Rationalisation Movement in German Industry: A Study in the Evolution of Economic Planning* (University of California Press, 1933), pp. 10–11 and 'General Reports: News Reports of International Movements', *Bulletin of the International Management Institute* (December 1927), No. 5, p. 3.

38. On the importance of disinterested service see: Greaves *League Committees*, pp. 108, 138. On the League as a centre for intellectual cooperation and scientific research see Zimmern, 'The Development of the International Mind', in *The Problem of Peace*, p. 6 and R.G. Watt, 'The League of Nations: Some Current Tendencies', *Morpeth Review* (1931), 2, pp. 30–7.

39. For such descriptions of economic activities of the League see W. Stucki and Sir H. Samuel in *World Prosperity and Peace: Being the Report of a Conference held by the League of Nations Union at the Guildhall on the work of the International Economic Conference: December 13–15, 1927* (P.S. King & Son, 1928), pp. 69, 162. Salter, A., *Economic Conference of the International Federation of League of Nations Societies*, Prague, 4 October 1928, pp. 1–2. LON 10A/39827/2697.

40. Sir Robert Cecil expressed concern about a pervasive sense of 'demoralization'. See
    P. Raffo, 'The League of Nations Philosophy of Lord Robert Cecil', *Australian Journal
    of Politics and History* (1974), 20, p. 188. See also Lord Cecil's comments which
    appeared in 'The Tenth Assembly of the League of Nations: Papers Read on October
    22n, 1929', *International Affairs* (1929), 8, pp. 541–6.

41. Sir A. Salter, 'The Progress in Europe of Economic Reconstruction', in *The Problem
    of Peace*, p. 111.

42. Report of the Economic Committee 'Economic Crisis' Sub-Committee, 22 February
    1924. 'The psychological element in trade cycles'. LON E/C.E.4. Economic
    Committee Sub-Committee On Crises 'Economic Barometers Memorandum' by the
    International Labour Organisation (ILO). 19 April 1924, pp. 1–2. LON E/C.E.8. See
    also Economic Committee Crises Sub-Committee, Memorandum by Mr Loveday, 3
    February 1926. LON E.257. E/C.E./19 1 and Monetary and Economic Conference,
    17 January 1933. LON 1070/735 R C.P./Conf.M.E./R.12 (R)4637 p. 18. Speech of
    Gustav Ador, the President of the Economic Committee, at the Opening of the First
    Session, 26 April 1926. LON Annex to C.E.C.P./1st Session/P.V.1.

43. Economic Consultative Committee Report on Recent Developments in the *Rational-
    isation Movement*. Submitted to the Consultative Committee by the International
    Management Institute. This Report covers the period from the World Economic
    Conference, May 1927, to the second meeting of the Economic Consultative
    Committee of the League of Nations, May 1929. 2 April 1929, p. 1. LON C.C.E.62.
    On the liberal character of League schemes see: A. Nussbaum, *Concise History of the
    Law of Nations* (Macmillan, 1954), p. 256.

44. On the WEC and other 1927 international conferences see T.P. Conwell-Evans, *The
    League Council in Action: A Study of the Methods Employed by the Council of the League
    of Nations to Prevent War and to Settle International Disputes* (H. Milford, 1929), p. 425.
    On the issues addressed by the Transit and Communications Conference and Inter-
    national Press Conference see: Greaves *League Committees*, pp. 152, 154.

45. Harris, C.R.S., 'International Conferences on Economic Co-operation', in A.J.
    Toynbee and V.M. Boulter (eds), *Survey of International Affairs 1929* (Oxford, 1930),
    p. 84. On the denunciation of economic nationalism at the WEC see: 'Caracteristic
    [sic] Features of the Geneva International Economic Conference From the Point of
    View of the ILO', p. 1. Summary of speech delivered by M. F. Maurette, Chief of the
    Research Division of the ILO. *Economic Conference of the International Federation of
    League of Nations Societies*, Prague, 4 October 1928, pp. 1–2. LON 10A/39827/2697.

46. On the need for tariff stability rather than free trade and regulation of customs
    nomenclature see: M. Mauro. Discussion of Rationalisation, Report and Proceedings
    of the World Economic Conference, 4–23 May 1927, II, p. 141. LON
    C.356.M.129.1927. II [C.E.1.4.6]. See also Fifth Meeting, 10 a.m. Friday 6 May
    1927, 'Report and Proceedings of the World Economic Conference', 4–23 May
    1927, 1, p. 96. LON C.356.M.129.1927.1 [C.E.1.4.6]; Sir A. Salter, 'The Economic
    Conference: Prospects of Practical Result', *International Affairs*, (1927), 6, p. 352.
    On 'future needs' see: Maurette, *Economic Conference of the International Federation
    of League of Nations Societies*, pp. 1–2.

47. On the role of experts in preparing and participating at the WEC see: Harris, 'Inter-
    national Conferences on Economic Co-operation', pp. 91–3; Salter, *Economic
    Conference of the International Federation of League of Nations Societies*, p. 10. On the
    need for a united viewpoint see Ador, LON Annex to C.E.C.P./1st Session/P.V.1 and
    Sir A. Salter discussing W.T. Layton's, 'The Forthcoming Economic Conference of the
    League of Nations and its Possibilities', *International Affairs*, (1927), 6, p. 83.

48. The quotation is from Ador, LON Annex to C.E.C.P./1st Session/P.V.1 Annex to
    C.E.C.P./1st Session/P.V.1. On the idea of rationalisation in relation to industrial
    disorder and waste see. LON C.356.M.129.1927.1 [C.E.1.4.6]. On the importance
    of rationalisation see 'Report of the Economic Consultative Committee on its Second

Session', 16th May 1929, p. 16. Economic Organisation. LON C.192.M.73.1929.II [C.C.E.87] (I).

49. The Russian sources are quoted in Fülöp-Miller *Mind and Face of Bolshevism*, pp. 20–3, 211. On the WEC's view of the United States see: 'Report of the Liberal Industrial Inquiry', *Britain's Industrial Future* (Ernest Benn, 1928), p. 50. On the identification of rationalisation with America see International Labour Office, Preparatory Committee for the International Economic Conference. 'Documentation for the 2nd Session', November 1926, 6 October 1926, pp. 1–5. B: 'Problems Concerning Industrial Production'. Provisional Minutes. LON C.E.C.P.31. On proposals for a United States of Europe see F.P. Walters, *A History of the League of Nations* (Oxford, 1952), pp. 430–1; Grossmann, E., 'Methods of Economic Rapprochement', p. 15. Submitted to the Preparatory Committee for the International Economic Conference LON II. Economic and Financial Committee 1926.II.69.

50. Economic Consultative Committee: Information Supplied by the International Labour Organisation: 'Preliminary Notes on Rationalisation and Labour Conditions', 9 May 1929, p. 4. LON C.C.E. 65 and Economic Consultative Committee. Information Supplied by the ILO. 'Preliminary Notes on Rationalisation and Labour Conditions'. 3 May 1929, p. 22. LON C.C.E. 65; International Labour Office, Preparatory Committee for the International Economic Conference. 'Documentation for the 2nd Session', November 1926, 6 October 1926, p. 9. B: 'Problems Concerning Industrial Production'. Provisional Minutes. LON C.E.C.P.31.

51. Bruck, W.F., *The Road to Planned Economy: Capitalism and Socialism in Germany's Development* (Cardiff University Press, 1934), p. 62.

52. Macgregor, D.H., 'Review of *The Rationalisation in German Industry* by Robert A. Brady', *Economic Journal* (1934), 44, p. 714. See also Brady *The Rationalisation Movement in German Industry*, pp. 6–7 and R.A. Brady, 'The Meaning of Rationalization: an analysis of the literature', *Quarterly Journal of Economics* (1930), 44, pp. 526–40. On its early meanings see also D.H. Macgregor in *World Prosperity and Peace*, pp. 122–3; Urwick, L., *Management of Tomorrow* (Nisbet, 1933), p. xiii; Mond, A., 'International Cartels', *International Affairs* (1927), 6, p.272.

53. On the definition given to rationalisation at the WEC see 'Economic Consultative Committee Report on Recent Development' in the *Rationalisation Movement*, pp. 1–2. LON C.C.E.62. On the more limited meaning of Taylorism see: LON International Labour Office Preparatory Committee for the International Economic Conference 'Documentation for the 2nd session' November 1926 B. 'Problems Concerning Industrial Production'. Provisional Minutes, 6 October 1926, pp. 1–3. LON C.E.C.P.31. 17. For Balfour's comments see 'Report and Proceedings of the World Economic Conference', 4–23 May 1927, I, pp. 153–5. LON C.356.M.129.1927.I [C.E.1.4–150.6]. See also League of Nations, *Final Report of the World Economic Conference*, Geneva, May (1927), pp. 38–9. LON C.E.I. 44 (1).

54. On international rationalisation see W. Ouaild, 'The Social Effects of International Industrial Agreements: The Protection of Workers and Consumers', Geneva, 1926, pp. 3–4. Submitted to the Preparatory Committee for the International Economic Conference. LON – ILO C.E.C.P.94. On the tariff issue see M. Battaglia of Poland: 'Discussion of Rationalisation, Report and Proceedings of the World Economic Conference', 4–23 May, 1927, II, p. 147. LON C.356.M.129.1927II [C.E.1.4.6].

55. On the 'fashion' for cartels see Mond, 'International Cartels', pp. 265–6 and Sir Hugo Mirst and D.H. Macgregor in *World Prosperity and Peace*, pp. 279–80, For the Conference resolutions and commentary on standardisation and harmonisation of nomenclature and research see: 'Report and Proceedings of the World Economic Conference, I. III Rationalisation'. LON C.356.M.129.1927 I [C.E.I.46], December, 1927, p. 14.

56. H. Bosanquet quoted in Grossmann *Methods of Economic Rapprochement*, pp. 27–9, 32, 38.

57. De Király, F., 'International Cartels and their Effects on the Progress of International Law', *Transactions of the Grotius Society* (1929), 15, pp. 17–33, esp. p. 19.

58. H.M. Robinson (US) Fifth Meeting, 10 a.m. Friday 6 May 1927, 'Report and Proceedings of the World Economic Conference', 4–23 May 1927, I p. 96. LON C.356.M.129.1927.1 [C.E.1.4.6] and M. Sokolnikoff (USSR), 'Draft Resolution on Industrial Ententes Submitted by the Drafting Committee: Examination of Draft Recommendation Submitted by the Drafting Committee on Rationalisation'. Twelfth Meeting Held on 20 May 1927, p. 162. LON C.356.M.129.1927.1 [C.E.1.4–150.6].

59. Harris noted that the 'fear of the dangers of monopolistic abuses also inspired the proposal for the creation of a separate economic organisation of the League which was strongly but unsuccessfully urged by the workers' representatives'. 'International Conferences on Economic Co-operation', p. 96. For examples of calls for international supervision in the name of social purposes see: M. Jouhaux (France): Eighth Meeting, 3.30 p.m. 12 May 1927, 'Report and Proceedings of the World Economic Conference', 4–23 May 1927, I, p. 151. LON C.356.M.129.1927.1 [C.E.1.4–150.6]. See also the Statement by the Representatives of the Christian Workers taking part in the International Economic Conference. Distributed at the request of Baron Tibbaut, Belgian Member of the Conference: LON S.C.E.14. International supervision of economic activity is treated as a prelude to the free movement of peoples.

60. Mme Freundlich (Austria): Third Meeting, Thursday 5 May 1927, 'Report and Proceedings of the World Economic Conference', 4–23 May 1927, I, pp. 74–5. LON C.356.M.129.1927.1 [C.E.1.4.6].

61. On the issue that cartels would not see tariffs reduced but that they might serve as a way of protecting home markets see: D.H. Macgregor, 'International Cartels', LON Economic and Financial Section, Prepared for the Preparatory Committee of the International Economic Conference. C.E.C.P.93. For an attempted distinction between safeguarding and *tarifs de combat* see 'Letter from E. Elliott from Board of British Trade to V.T. Stencek'. LON 10A/11376/4043 R2663. For warnings that rationalisation might be a source of jealousy and strife see: M. Trepka of Poland, M. da Cunha of Portugal, 'Discussion of Rationalisation, Report and Proceedings of the World Economic Conference', 4–23 May 1927, II, p. 143. LON C.356.M.129.1927. II [C.E.1.4.6] pp. 142–3, 148.

62. Harris, 'International Conferences on Economic Co-operation', p. 106. See also 'Report and Proceedings of the World Economic Conference', LON C.356.M.129.1927 II [C.E.I.46], (December, 1927), pp. 14–15. See also 'Report and Proceedings of the World Economic Conference', I. IIV Industrial Agreements' LON C.356.M.129.1927 I [C.E.I.46], December 1927, p. 14. On the Inter-Parliamentary Conference see *Bulletin of the International Management Institute*, Geneva, No.5 December 1927, p. 3. LON 10AS61333/60089 R483.

63. Major L. Aman responding to Salter 'The Economic Conference: Prospects of Practical Result', p. 363.

64. On the influence of the WEC in publicising rationalisation in Anglo-Saxon countries and Europe see: 'Report of the Liberal Industrial Inquiry', *Britain's Industrial Future* (London, 1928), pp. xx–xxiv, 47–50, 128–30, 320–1; Walker, E.R.R., 'Internationalism and Economics', *Morpeth Review* (1928), 2, pp. 14–15; Mauldon, F.R.E., 'The Doctrine of Rationalisation', *Economic Record* (1931), 7, pp. 249, 252; Urwick, *Management of Tomorrow*, p. xiv; Skene Smith, N., *Economic Control: Australian Experiments in Rationalisation and Safeguarding* (London, 1929), p. 63 and 'Economic Consultative Committee Report on Recent Developments' in the *Rationalisation Movement*. Submitted to the Consultative Committee by the International Management Institute, 2 April 1929. LON C.C.E.62.

65. On the WEC as a harbinger of world economic control see Skene Smith *Economic Control*, p. 11 and Wallace *Scientific World View*, p. 265. Samuel *World Prosperity*, pp. 162–3.

66. See also Greaves *League Committees*, pp. vii–viii. On the League's weakness as a peace enforcer see W.Y. Elliott, *The Pragmatic Revolt in Politics: Syndicalism, Fascism and the Constitutional State* (Macmillan, 1928), p. 14. Elliott could write by 1928 that: 'No one takes Article Ten seriously now, and the sanctions of force written into the covenant are useful only to police minor clashes.'

67. Russell, B., *Education and the Social Order* (Allen and Unwin, 1977), p. 152. First published in 1932.

68. *World Social Economic Planning: The Necessity for Planned Adjustment of Productive Capacity and Standards of Living* (The Hague: International Industrial Relations Institute, 1931), p.xvii.

69. The quotations come from Dr R. Broda of Antioch Collect League and the organisers of the Amsterdam Congress. See *World Social Economic Planning*, pp. 55, 68. In the same volume see similar comments by Dr H.S. Person, Director of the Taylor Society in the United States, p. 26; P.J.S. Serrarens, Secretary of the International Federation of Christian Trade Unions, and Senator in Holland, p. 50; H. von Haan of the International Management Institute Geneva in 'European Aspects of the Rationalization Movement – Its Significance for Social Economic Planning', p. 28.

70. L.L. Lorwin in *World Social Economic Planning*, pp. 34–6. Dr F. Meyer Scwabedissen, industrialist and conference organiser: 'A national economic plan, however, can never be more than a mere measure of necessity...to be justified only if it is to be a first step toward the coming planning of world economy', p. 39. On the failure to move towards international planning after the WEC of 1927 see F.M. Wibaut in *World Social Economic Planning*, p. 21. On the state as a bar to world planning see Brady *Rationalisation Movement in German Industry*, pp. 394–9.

71. Urwick, *Management of Tomorrow*, pp. xiii, 197. See also L. Urwick, *The Meaning of Rationalisation* (Nisbet, 1929), p. 27.

72. At the WEC Valery V. Obolensky-Ossinski pointed out that 'some sixty local Russian organisations were endeavouring to bring about scientific organisation, with a central committee at Moscow as a nucleus'. Discussion of Rationalisation, 'Report and Proceedings of the World Economic Conference', 4–23 May 1927. II, p. 141. LON C.356.M.129.1927. II [C.E.1.4.6]. See also the statements by Sokolnikoff at the Seventh Meeting, 10 a.m. Saturday 7 May 1927, 'Report and Proceedings of the World Economic Conference', 4–23 May, I, pp. 120, 122. LON C.356.M.129.1927.1 [C.E.1.4.6].

73. Einzig, P., *The Economic Foundations of Fascism* (Macmillan, 1933), p. 2. On the rationalist credentials of the Soviet economy and the international dimension of capitalist rationalisation see F.R.E Mauldon, 'The Doctrine of Rationalisation', *Economic Record* (1931), 7, pp. 250–2. On the power of the Moscow myth see E.H. Burgman, 'Geneva, Moscow, and Jerusalem', *Morpeth Review* (1934), 3, p. 10.

74. On rationalisation in the Soviet Union see the Economic Consultative Committee Information Supplied by the ILO. 'Preliminary Notes on Rationalisation and Labour Conditions. Rationalisation and Labour Conditions in the USSR', 29 April 1929, pp. 1–2. Urwick *Management of Tomorrow*, p. 199. For the rationalisation schemes cited see: Economic and Financial Section International Economic Conference, May 1927. 'Documentation. Electrical Industry'. LON C.E.16. On the Advertising Research Institute and other examples see *Bulletin of International Management Institute*, no.5, December 1927, pp. 4–6. LON 10AS61333/60089 R483.

75. Young, A.P., *Forward From Chaos* (Nisbet, 1933), pp. 7–9, 10–13, 16.

76. For Smuts's comments, the analogy between the electron and the human and proposals for control see Young *Forward*, p. 37. See also pp. 33–4, 36, 40, 124.

77. Ibid., pp. xv–xvi, 28, 34, 39–40, 125, 128, 140.

78. Wittner, L.S., *One World or None: A History of the World Nuclear Disarmament Movement Through 1935* (Stanford University Press, 1993), p. 44; Wells, H.G., *Things to Come* (Gregg Press, 1975), pp. 60–1, 70. Note that here I have drawn from the 1953 film script which Wells wrote for the motion picture version of *The Shape of Things to Come* (Corgi Books, 1967). First published in 1933.

79. Ibid., p. 83.

80. Ibid., p. 88, 94, 106.

81. Ibid., p. 131, 141.

82. Ibid., pp. 71, 108.

83. Postbridge, W., 'How to Put the League Across: Calling Radio and Cinema into Service', *Headway* (May 1932), p. 92; Bell, O., 'Thinking Towards Peace: Intellectual Co-operation and Moral Disarmament', *Headway* (September 1932), p. 167; Howland, A., 'Control Broadcast Propaganda!' *Headway* (September 1934), p. 172.

84. 'The Aeroplane of Language', *Headway* (February 1933), p. 33. On the positive influence of aviation see: Brigadier General P.R.C. Groves, 'The Influence of Aviation of International Relations', *International Affairs* (1927), 6, pp. 133–52. On the internationalisation of air power see 'The Air Menace: Can Aviation be Internationalised', *Headway* (May 1932), p. 98. As an indication of the impact of the French Government's proposals to the 1933 Disarmament Conference in Geneva see the advertisement for Davies's *An International Police Force* (Ernest Benn, 1932), p. 93 of the same issue. See also D. Davies, 'An International Force: The League as Policemen of the World', *Headway* (April 1932), pp. 72–3. Note that the Annual Congress of the Federation of League of Nations Societies meeting in Madrid in 1929 passed a compromise resolution which requested that the 'suitability of air force as an instrument for the defence of international order' should be studied. See Vice Admiral S.R. Drury-Lowe, 'The Peoples Chamber: League of Nations Societies in Congress', *Headway* (July 1929), pp. 134–5. On Esperanto see Commission Internationale de Coopération Intellectuelle, Seconde Session, Dixième Séance, 13 juillet 1923, 'l'Enseignement de l'esperanto' in Bergson *Mélanges*, pp. 1414–16.

85. Brady *The Rationalisation Movement*, pp. 23, 401, 406–12, 414.

86. Ibid., pp. 7–9, 401.

87. Spengler, O., *Man and Technics: a contribution to a philosophy of life* (Allen & Unwin, 1932), pp. 93–4, 97, 102 and A. Raven, *Civilisation as Divine Superman: A Superorganic Philosophy of History* (Williams & Norgate, 1932) pp. 113–18.

88. Rathenau, W., *The New Society* (William & Norgate, 1921), p. 147. Rathenau quoted in Fülöp-Miller *Mind and Face of Bolshevism*, p. 20. The description of Rathenau's role in mechanising German industry comes from Fülöp-Miller. See also Brady *The Rationalisation Movement*, p. 314.

89. Brady *The Rationalisation Movement*, pp. 407, 411, 414, 415.

90. Ibid., pp. 410, 413.

91. Ibid., pp. 397, 402.

92. PEP 'Planning for Liberty', *Planning* (12 September 1933), no. 9, pp. 8–10. PEP, 'Cheap Electricity a National Want', *Planning* (31 December 1935), no. 65, pp. 1–3; 'Chaos Beneath the Grid' (20 June 1933), no. 5, *Planning*, pp. 3–4; 'Electricity and the Future' (4 June 1935), no. 52, *Planning*, pp. 1–3.

93. Mitrany, D., 'Economic Planning' in *Planned Society: Yesterday, Today, Tomorrow: A Symposium by Thirty-Five Economists, Sociologists, and Statesmen*, F. Mackenzie (ed.) (Prentice-Hall, 1937), pp. 641–2. On the imitation of Soviet planning rhetoric see: L. Ross, 'Planning in Australia II' and A.G.B. Fisher, 'An Impression of the Conference', in *National Economic Planning*, W.G.K. Duncan (ed.) (Angus & Robertson, 1934), pp. 140, 182; Burrows, R., *The Problems and Practice of Economic Planning* (P.S. King & Son, 1937), p. 226. Note W. MacMahon Ball's comment that: 'Planning means much more than the extension of the movement called rationalization. Both involve the re-organization of individual industries, but planning,

unlike rationalization, means that every single act of re-organization must be clearly related to an agreed social-economic goal.' 'The Political Implications of Planning', *National Economic Planning*, p. 83.

94. Zimmern, A., 'Reflections on the Crisis: Thoughts from Geneva', *Political Quarterly* (1931), 2, p. 474.

95. 'As to the relation of Russian planning to world planning, Mr. Ossinsky and Mr. Alexander Cohn...[stated that Russia]..."is actually planning nationally."' *World Social Economic Planning*, pp. 46, 57–8.

96. On the flimsiness of the idea of world planning at Amsterdam see *World Social Economic Planning*, p. 68.

97. Young *Forward From Chaos*, pp. 176–81.

98. Monetary and Economic Conference Preparatory Committee of Experts. Sir F. Leith-Ross, 'Monetary Situation Exposé', Geneva, 9 January 1933. LON C.P./Conference. M.E./34.

99. Schrecker, C., 'The Growth of Economic Nationalism and its international consequences', *International Affairs* (1934), 13, p. 210.

100. The quotations are from PEP, 'Planning begins at Home', *Planning* (1933), no. 3, pp. 1–3 and 'Planning is on the map' (12 September 1933), p. 1.

101. On the change in the League's orientation see A. Loveday, 'The Economic And Financial Activities of the League', *International Affairs* (1938), 17, pp. 795–9. The ILO vigorously pursued welfarist questions during the war. See E.J. Phelan, *The I.L.O. and Reconstruction*, Report by the Acting Director of the International Labour Office to the Conference of the International Labour Organisation, New York, October 1941. See Part II, 'Future Policy', pp. 39–40, 97. LON 10A/42300/J914. See also LON Economic and Financial Committees. 'Report to the Council on the Work of the Joint Session', London, April 27–1 May 1942. Princeton, 7–8 August 1942, pp. 9–10. LON 10A/41803/1778 R4384 C.52.M.52.1942.II.A, p. 15 and LON 10A/42227/1778 R4384.

102. Urwick *Management of Tomorrow*, p. 197. See also Young *Forward From Chaos*, pp. 16–17.

103. The quotation is from a respondent to Sir A. McFadyean's paper 'The State and Economic Life', *International Affairs* (1932), 9, in which McFadyean advocated international planning, p. 20.

CHAPTER 5

1. Wells, H.G., *In the Fourth Year: Anticipations of a World Peace* (Chatto & Windus, 1918), p. vii.

2. Carr, E.H., *The Twenty Years' Crisis* (Macmillan, 1946), pp. 224–5.

3. Avenol, J., 'The Future of the League of Nations', *International Affairs* (1934), 13, pp. 143–58, esp. pp. 144–5.

4. Ibid., pp. 146–8.

5. Valéry, P., 'Our Destiny and Literature' in J. Matthews, *The Collected Works of Paul Valéry*, 10, 'History and Politics', trans. D. Folliot and J. Matthews (Routledge & Kegan Paul, 1963), pp. 172–6.

6. Sorokin, P., *The Crisis of our Age: The Social and Cultural Outlook* (Dutton, 1941), pp. 14–16, 211–12, 217.

7. Ibid., pp. 116–17, 245.

8. Ibid., pp. 76–7.

9. Ibid., pp. 16, 226.

10. Ibid., pp. 307–9, 319.

11. De Madariaga, S. in J. Smith (ed.), *Gilbert Murray: An Unfinished Autobiography* (George Allen and Unwin, 1960), p. 182.

12. Williams, A., *Failed Imagination: New world orders of the twentieth century* (Manchester University Press, 1997), pp. 80, 86, 130, 134.

13. *Planning*, 'Plans for Physical Reconstruction' (19 January 1943), p. 13; *Planning*, No. 214 (16 November 1943), p. 1. 'Britain and Russia' and 'Soviet Planning in War-Time', *Planning*, No. 196 (17 November 1942) pp. 1–16.

14. Williams *Failed Imagination*, pp. 123–4.

15. Crossman, R., 'Nationalism and Democratic Socialism', *Where Stands Democracy: A Collection of Essays by Members of the Fabian Society* (Macmillan, 1940), pp. 87–92, 106.

16. Menzies, R., 'Post-War International Relations: The Nature and Importance of the Problem' in *Post-War Reconstruction in Australia*, D.A.S. Campbell (ed.) (Australasian Publishing Co., 1944), p. 13.

17. Menzies 'Post-War International Relations' and Menzies responding to Copland, 'Change-Over to Peace' in *Post-War Reconstruction*, pp. 12, 31–2. Carr, E.H., *The Conditions of Peace* (Macmillan, 1942), pp. 112, 118, 164, 253.

18. Carr *Conditions of Peace*, pp. 165–6.

19. Menzies 'Post-War International Relations', p. 16. On Carr's transnationalism see *Conditions of Peace*, p. 273.

20. Williams *Failed Imagination*, pp. 124–5.

21. On the links between economic control, the militarisation of society and international conflict see L. Robbins, *Economic Planning and International Order* (Macmillan, 1937), pp. 95–6, 327; Lippmann, W., *The Good Society* (George Allen & Unwin, 1937), pp. xi–xii, 3, 89–90; Mitrany, D., *The Functional Theory of Politics* (Martin Robertson, 1975), pp. 36–7, 79; Mitrany, D., 'International Consequences of National Planning', *Yale Review* (1947), 38, pp. 18–31; Hayek, F.A., *The Road To Serfdom* (Dymock's, 1944), p. 171; Phelan, E.J., *The I.L.O. and Reconstruction*, Report by the Acting Director of the International Labour Office to the Conference of the International Labour Organisation, New York, October 1941, pp. 8–9; Anderson, J., 'The Servile State', *Australasian Journal of Psychology and Philosophy* (1943), 21, pp. 115–32, pp. 124–5; Oakeshott, M., 'The Political Economy of Freedom' in *Rationalism in Politics and Other Essays* (Liberty Press, 1991), pp. 400–1. First published in 1949.

22. Hayek *Road to Serfdom*, pp. 193, 202–4, 206n.

23. Ibid., pp. 212–14.

24. Ibid., p. 216.

25. Ibid., p. 218.

26. Vernadsky, W.I., 'The Biosphere and the Noösphere', *American Scientist* (1945), 33, pp. 1–12, pp. 5–6. Vernadsky had warned in 1922:

> The time is not far away when man will take atomic energy into his hands…Does man know how to use this power, to direct it to good and not to self-destruction?…Scientist must not close their eyes to the possible consequences of their work…They must consider themselves responsible for the consequences of their discoveries.

Quoted in L.S. Wittner, *One World or None: A History of the World Nuclear Disarmament Movement Through 1953* (Stanford University Press, 1993), p. 4.

27. Ibid., p. 8.

28. Ibid.

29. Ibid.

30. Ibid., pp. 9–10.

31. Ibid., p. 1.

32. Zimmern, L.A., *Must the League Fail?* (Martin Hopkinson, 1932), p. 15.

33. Sewell, J.P., *Unesco and World Politics: Engaging in International Relations* (Princeton University Press, 1975), p. 94.

34. Ibid., p. 87. See also P. Parkinson, 'Review of Julian Huxley, Scientific Research and Social Needs', *Australian Quarterly* (December 1934), 115. John Dewey observed in 1948 that the 'destructive use made of the fission of the nucleus of an atom has become the stock-in-trade of the assault upon science'; science was being blamed for 'present evils'. See Dewey in the introduction to the 1948 edition of *Reconstruction in Philosophy* (Beacon Press, 1957), pp. xxiii, xxiv, xxxvii. Dewey was writing in defence of science and against proposals to bring it under institutional control.

35. Sewell *Unesco*, p. 114.

36. Huxley, J., *Unesco: its Purpose and its Philosophy* (Public Affairs Press, Washington D.C., 1947), p. 7 and J. Huxley, 'The Future of Unesco', *Discovery*, 7 February 1946, pp. 72–3 quoted in Sewell *Unesco*, p. 112.

37. Huxley *Unesco*, pp. 7, 38 and Sewell *Unesco*, p. 115.

38. Sewell *Unesco*, pp. 107–8 and Huxley *Unesco*, p. 8.

39. Sewell *Unesco*, p. 114. The last quotation from Huxley appears in L. Vitray, 'UNESCO: Adventure in Understanding', *Free World*, November, 1946, pp. 23–8, esp. p. 24.

40. Sewell *Unesco*, p. 116.

41. Ibid., p. 132.

42. Morgenthau, H.J., *Politics Among Nations: The Struggle for Power and Peace* (Alfred A. Knopf, 1973), pp. 260, 509–12, 515. Fifth Edition, Revised. First published in 1948.

43. Lothian quoted in Menzies 'Post-War International Relations', pp. 16–17.

44. Williams, in *Failed Imagination*, writes that the United Nations was grounded in a 'realism based on the realities of power modified by a belief that liberal internationalism might be a powerful leavening force, an ultimate global interdependence'. Zimmern, A., 'International Law and Social Consciousness', *Transactions of the Grotius Society* (1935), 20, pp. 25–44, esp. p. 40. Alfred Zimmern criticised Scelle on this score.

45. Goodrich, L.M. and E. Hambro, *Charter of the United Nations: Commentary and Documents*, Second Edition (World Peace Foundation, 1946), p. 19.

46. Morgenthau *Politics Among Nations*, pp. 325–6.

47. Harris, E.E., *One World or None: Prescription for Survival* (Humanities Press, 1993), p. 87. One of the most famous contributions to the writings on world government at this stage was by the journalist Emery Reves who called for a 'sovereign source of law' to be 'set up over and above the clashing social units'. Reves, E., *The Anatomy of Peace* (Harper, 1945), p. 121. Quoted in C. Hamer, *A Global Parliament: Principles of World Federation* (Oyster Bay Books, 1998), pp. 42–3.

48. Perry, R.B., *One World in the Making* (Current Books, 1945), p. 13; Wilkie, W.L., *One World* (Cassell, 1943), pp. 1–2. Wendell Wilkie was a former Republican presidential candidate. Published during the war *One World* sold two million copies. See Wittner *One World or None*, p. 45.

49. Perry *One World*, pp. 20–3,

50. Ibid., pp. 13–14, 40–3, 143.

51. Ibid., pp. 21, 75–7. Bowman, I., *The New World Problems in Political Geography* (The World Book Company, 1921). Bowman was a key American representative at the Paris Peace Conference.

52. Ibid., 90–6.

53. Ibid., p. 63.

54. Ibid., pp. 193, 202–3, 242–4.

55. Ibid., pp. 242–4, 262, 265.

56. Clark, R.W., *Einstein: The Life and Times* (Hodder and Stoughton, 1973) pp. 337–8, esp. p. 342. Note that as a novice professor at the University of Berlin in 1914 Einstein had co-written with four other scholars a *Manifesto to Europeans* which lamented the enormous disruption to cultural life precisely at a time when 'progress in technology and communications clearly suggest that we recognize the need for international relations which will necessarily move in the direction of a universal,

world-wide civilization'. The *Manifesto* called for a 'League of Europeans' to 'guard its soil, its people and its culture'. Nathan, O. and H. Nordern, *Einstein on Peace* (Schocken Books, 1968), p. 4. Quoted in Hamer *Global Parliament*, p. 41.

57. Bergson and Jackh cited in Clark *Einstein*, pp. 346–7.
58. Ibid., pp. 338, 352.
59. Einstein cited in ibid., pp. 346, 348.
60. Ibid., p. 34.
61. Freud, S., *Civilization, Society and Religion* (Pelican, 1985), pp. 346–7, 351, 355, 358, 362.
62. Clark *Einstein*, p. 349.
63. Ibid., pp. 353–5.
64. Ibid., pp. 337, 349.
65. Quoted in ibid., pp. 551–2.
66. Ibid., p. 555. The Committee was formed in May 1946. See Wittner *One World or None*, p. 60.
67. Wittner *One World or None*, p. 61.
68. Ibid, pp. 553–4. On the Baruch plan see Wittner *One World or None*, p. 63. Wittner notes of the Russian scientists responses: 'Given the dangers of public disagreement with this stand, which paralleled official Soviet policy, it was hardly surprising that no voices were raised in the defense of Einstein or world government', p. 114. On the State Department's and President Truman's attitudes to world federation see pp. 268–71.
69. Ibid., p. 554.
70. Hutchins, R.M., *Preliminary Draft of a World Constitution* (University of Chicago Press, 1948), pp. v–vi.
71. Ibid., pp. 3, 44.
72. Hutchins *World Constitution*, pp. 62–3, 83 and Wittner *One World or None*, p. 59.
73. Hutchins *World Constitution*, pp. 5–6, 29–33.
74. On the world government movement of the late 1940s, Unesco's polling and Gary Davis's impact see Wittner *One World or None*, pp. 71, 95, 113–14, 118–37 and Hamer, *Global Parliament*, pp. 43–5. Hamer notes that the Unesco polls found majority support for world government in France, Italy, the Netherlands, Norway, West Germany and Britain. It was rejected in Australia, Mexico and the United States. For Nehru's comments see Wittner *One World or None*, p. 307.
75. See Hamer *Global Parliament*, p. 164. The quotes from Niebuhr come from J. Schell, *The Abolition* (Alfred A. Knopf, 1984) and R. Niebuhr, 'Illusions of World Government', *Foreign Affairs* (1949), 27, p. 379–88.
76. Harris *One World*, pp. 87–8.
77. Wittner *One World or None*, pp. 162, 293, 371.
78. See Hamer *Global Parliament*, pp. 46–9.
79. Clark, G., 'World Peace Through World Law' in B.L. Sanders and A.C. Durbin, *Contemporary International Politics: Introductory Readings* (John Wiley & Sons, 1971), pp. 352–62. Taken from G. Clark and L.B. Sohn, *World Peace Through World Law* (Harvard University Press). Note that Sohn co-authored the 2nd, 1960 and 3rd, 1966, editions. The first edition was published in 1958. For biographical details see Hamer *Global Parliament*, pp. 43, 56. Clark had already proposed a world federal government in October, 1945. See Wittner *One World or None*, p. 66.
80. Bloomfield, L.P., 'Arms Control and World Government', *World Politics*, 1962, 14, pp. 633–45 in Sanders and Durbin *Contemporary International Politics*, pp. 384–6.
81. Bloomfield 'Arms Control', p. 390.
82. Fromm, E., *The Fear of Freedom* (Routledge, 1960), p. 159. First published in 1942. Fromm, E., 'Universal Controlled Disarmament' from E. Fromm *May Man Prevail: An Inquiry into the Facts and Fictions of Foreign Policy* (Garden City, 1961) reproduced as 'A Proposal for Peace' in Sanders and Durbin, pp. 377–81. Freud *Civilization*, p. 357.

83. Lippmann, W., 'The Country is Waiting for Another Innovator,' *Life* (20 June 1960), 48, p. 114 in C. Rossiter and J. Lare (eds), *The Essential Lippmann: A Political Philosophy for Liberal Democracy* (Vintage, 1965), pp. 70–4.

84. Lippmann, W., 'Explorer and Sputnik', *Today and Tomorrow* (4 February 1958), in Rossiter and Lare *Essential Lippmann*, pp. 66–70.

85. Lippmann, W., 'The Shortage of Education', *Atlantic Monthly* (May 1954), CXCIII), p. 35, in Rossiter and Lare *Essential Lippmann*, pp. 29–32, 66–70, 74.

86. Lippmann, W., 'The Portent of the Moon', *Today and Tomorrow* (10 October 1957) in Rossiter and Lare *Essential Lippmann*, pp. 66–70.

87. Excerpts from W. Lippmann, *The Public Philosophy* (Little Brown, 1955), Chapters 9 and 10. Reproduced in Rossiter and Lare *Essential Lippmann*, pp. 181–5, 208–11.

88. Lippmann 'Shortage of Education', p. 31, and 'Waiting for Another Innovator', p. 74.

89. Sorokin , P., *The Crisis of Our Age* (E.P. Dutton & Co., 1957), pp. 1–3.

90. Ibid., p. 4.

91. Frankel, C., *The Case For Modern Man* (Harper & Brothers, 1955), pp. 1–2, 5, 7, 16, 18, 142.

92. Ibid., pp. 14, 18, 22, 25–6, 39, 119.

93. Ibid., p. 140.

94. Brooks, J., *The One and the Many: The Individual in the Modern World* (Harper & Row, 1962), pp. xiii, 35–8.

95. Ibid., pp. 61–3, 310.

96. Ibid., p. 155.

97. Ibid., pp. 61–3.

98. Ibid., pp. 12, 151.

99. Ibid., pp. 136, 138–9, 152.

100. Ibid., pp. 138, 150, 152–3, 156.

101. Ibid., pp. 7–8, 20, 45, 48–9, 55–6, 126, 136–7.

102. Barraclough, G., *An Introduction to Contemporary History* (Penguin, 1967), p. 235. See also D. Bell, *The End of Ideology: On the Exhaustion of Political Ideas in the Fifties* (Collier, 1962), pp. 13, 402–6. Revised Edition. Bell opened with the statement:

> These essays, in the main, deal with the social changes in the America of the fifties. It was a decade marked by extraordinary changes in the class structure, particularly in the growth of the white-collar class and the spread of suburbia; by the 'forced' expansion of the economy, which belied earlier predictions o f stagnation; by the creation of a permanent military establishment and a bedrock defense economy; and by the heightening tensions of the Cold War. In consequence, we have had the problem, abroad of defining ourselves to Indians, Africans, Arabs, *et al.*, and, at home, a preoccupation with 'self' and 'status' that has brought to the fore not only psychoanalysis but the mirror of popular sociology. The 'restless vanity' of which de Tocqueville spoke...has been replaced by an anxious inferiority, fearful of censure and desperately eager to please.

Bell reflected on the decline in belief in the West of socialist ideology as well as in pure market liberalism and a convergence on the desirability of the welfare state, the mixed economy and political pluralism. At the same time Bell expresses unease with the rise of ideological thinking in countries in Asia, South America and Africa, some of which were upholding Russia and China as models of development. He distinguished the ideologies emerging in the South ('the ideologies of industrialization, modernization, Pan-Arabism, color, nationalism...Pan-Africanism') from those which flourished in the West in the nineteenth century. Inadvertently revealing his own parochialism, he stated:

The ideologies of the nineteenth century were universalistic, humanistic, and fashioned by intellectuals. The mass ideologies of Asia and Africa, are parochial, instrumental, and created by political leaders. The driving forces of the old ideologies were social equality and, in the largest sense, freedom. The impulsions of the new ideologies are economic development and national power. And if this involves the wholesale coercion of the population and the rise of new elites to drive the people, the new repressions are justified on the ground that without such coercions economic advance cannot take place rapidly enough.

Bell complained that even some Western liberals had come to embrace the doctrine of economic development. Going on to note the enthusiasm of the 'new Left' for the idea of revolution he stated that the test of its 'intellectual maturity' lay with the attitude it would adopt to the ideologies being promoted by Cuba and new states in Africa and Asia.

103. Harrington, M., *The Accidental Century* (Macmillan, 1965), pp. 13, 120.
104. Ibid., pp. 32, 51–3, 68.
105. Ibid., pp. 29–30, 43.
106. Ibid., pp. 16, 29–31, 33–6.
107. Ibid., pp. 38, 80, 136–7.
108. Marcuse, H., *One Dimensional Man* (Routledge, 1964), pp. x, 13.146–50.
109. Ibid., pp. 152–3. The quotation from Bachelard appears in G. Bachelard, *L'Activité rationaliste de la physique contemporane* (Presses Universitaires de Paris, 1951), p. 7.
110. Marcuse *One Dimensional Man*, p.ix.
111. Ibid., p. 12.
112. Ibid., pp. 3, 14, 144–6, 220.
113. Rosen, S., *Nihilism: A Philosophical Essay* (Yale University Press, 1968), pp. xiii, 72.
114. Ibid., p. 112.
115. Ibid., pp. 112–16.
116. Ibid., pp. 105, 118.
117. Ibid., pp. xiv–xv, xviii.
118. Ibid., p. 235.
119. Ibid., p. 232.
120. Muir, R., *Political Geography: A new introduction* (Macmillan, 1997), pp. 164, 223.
121. Anshen, R.N., in the introduction to K. Boulding, *The Meaning of the Twentieth Century: The Great Transition* (George Allen & Unwin Ltd, 1965), pp. xii–xvi.
122. Boulding, *Meaning of the Twentieth Century*, pp. 16, 135, 191–2.
123. McCormick, J., *Reclaiming Paradise: The Global Environmental Movement* (Indiana University Press, 1991), pp. 67–8, 51. Muir *Political Geography*, p. 213.
124. Modelski, G., *Principles of World Politics* (Free Press, 1972) p. 10. See also 'Treaty on the Principles Governing the Activities of States in the Exploration and Use of Outer Space, Including the Moon and Other Celestial Bodies' in I. Brownlie (ed.), *Basic Documents in International Law* (Clarendon Press, 1995), pp. 209–16.
125. Sprout, H. and M., 'The Ecological Perspective on International Politics', in C.W. Kegley and E.R. Wittkopf, *The Global Agenda: Issues and Perspectives* (Random House, 1984), pp. 324, 326.
126. Quoted in McCormick, *Reclaiming Paradise*, p. 77.
127. Ophuls, W., *Ecology and the Politics of Scarcity: Prologue to A Political Theory of the Steady State* (W.H. Freeman, 1977), pp. 216–19.
128. Ibid., pp. 155, 227, 244.
129. Harris *One World*, pp. 88, 122.
130. Ibid., p. 73.
131. Hamer *Global Parliament*, pp. 58–9. Mendlovitz, S.H. (ed.), *On the Creation of a Just World Order: Preferred World for the 1990s* (Free Press, 1975), pp. xv, 4–5. See also R. Falk, *This Endangered Planet: Prospects and Proposals for Human Survival* (Random

House, 1971), pp. 18–19. See also R. Falk, *A Study of Future Worlds* (Free Press, 1982).
132. Saul Mendlovitz in his introduction to Mendlovitz *On the Creation of a Just World Order*, p.xvi.
133. On Falk see Hamer *Global Parliament*, p. 60. For Falk's caution about unrealism see his introduction to L. Beres and H. Targ, *Reordering the Planet* (Allyn and Bacon, 1974), p. v.
134. From A.J. Dolman, *Resources, Regimes, World Order* (Pergamon Press, 1981), pp. 10–73 reproduced in Kegley and Wittkopf *The Global Agenda*, pp. 378, 381, 386–7.

CHAPTER 6

1. Modelski, G., *Principles of World Politics* (Free Press, 1972) pp. 10, 42, 49.
2. Ibid., pp. 320, 353–4.
3. Bull, H., 'The State's Positive Role In World Affairs', *Daedalus* (1979), 108, pp. 111–23, esp. p. 111.
4. Ibid., p. 118.
5. Ibid., p. 114.
6. Ibid., p. 120. Richard Falk concurs that there are many, especially in the South, who are 'suspicious' of 'grandiose proposals emanating from the existing Western power centers'. As evidence he cites R. Kothari, *Footsteps into the Future: Diagnosis of the Present World and a Design for an Alternative* (Free Press, 1976), pp. xix–xxiii and A. Mazuri, *A World Federation of Cultures: An African Perspective* (Free Press, 1976), pp. 1–15.
7. Bull 'State's Positive Role', pp. 120, 123.
8. Wittner, L.S., *One World or None: A History of the World Nuclear Disarmament Movement Through 1953* (Stanford University Press, 1993), p. 159.
9. Brown, L.R., *Redefining National Security*, Worldwatch Paper 14, October 1977 reproduced in C.W. Kegley and E.R. Wittkopf, *The Global Agenda: Issues and Perspectives* (Random House, 1984), pp. 340–5.
10. Independent Commission on Disarmament and Security Issues, *Common Security: A Blueprint for Survival* (Simon and Schuster, 1982), pp. 138–9, 175–8, esp. p. 164.
11. Ibid., p. 162–3.
12. Ibid., p. 172.
13. World Commission on the Environment and Development, *Our Common Future* (Oxford University Press, 1987), p. 27.
14. Ibid., p. 310.
15. The quoted words are borrowed from *Romeo and Juliet*, Act II, sc. iii.
16. Mische, P.M., 'Ecological Security and the Need to Reconceptualize Sovereignty', *Alternatives* (1989), 14, pp. 389–427, esp. pp. 391, 394, 396.
17. Lasch, C., *The Minimal Self: Psychic Survival in Troubled Times* (Picador, 1984), p. 64.
18. Ibid., pp. 16, 65, 110–11.
19. Ibid., pp. 16–17, 270.
20. Ibid., p. 17.
21. Boulding, K.E., *The World as a Total System* (Sage, 1985), p. 131.
22. Bell, D., 'Climate of Fear: A Symposium', *Encounter* (1987), 69, p. 14 and D. Bell, *The End of Ideology: On the Exhaustion of Political Ideas in the Fifties* (Collier, 1962), p. 393.
23. Bell 'Climate of Fear', p. 3.
24. Kennet, W., 'Do We Not Bleed?' in *Encounter* p. 17.
25. Bell 'Climate of Fear', p. 3. See also D.J. Enright, 'Assenting to the Devil', p. 5 and M. Bradbury, 'A Century's Exhausted', p. 20 in *Encounter*.

26. McNeil, p. 13 and Steiner, p. 4 in *Encounter*.

27. Hurrell, A., 'A Crisis of Ecological Viability? Global Environmental Change and the Nation State', *Political Studies* (1994), XLII, pp. 146–65, esp. p. 148.

28. Ibid., p. 165.

29. Wirth, T.E., 'The Road from Rio – Defining a New World Order', *Colorado Journal of International Environmental Law and Policy* (1993), 4, p. 37.

30. Kovar, J., 'A Short Guide to the Rio Declaration', *Colorado Journal of International Environmental Law and Policy* (1993), 4, pp. 119–40, esp. pp. 124–5; Getches, D.H., 'Foreword: The Challenge of Rio', *Colorado Journal of International Environmental Law and Policy* (1993), 4, pp. 1–18, esp. p. 12; Chandler, M., 'The Biodiversity Convention: Selected Issues of Interest to the International Lawyer', *Colorado Journal of International Environmental Law and Policy* (1993), 4, pp. 141–75, esp. p. 145–6.

31. Kovar 'Rio Declaration', pp. 119, 122.

32. Dowdeswell, E., 'Sustainable development, security and the United Nations', *Irish Studies in International Affairs* (1996), 4, pp. 27–8.

33. Ibid.

34. On the move to international environmental controls see: N. Brown, 'Planetary Geopolitics', *Millennium*, 1990, 19, pp. 447–60, esp. p. 460; Brecher, J., Brown Childs, J. and J. Cutler, 'Introduction: Globalization-from-Below', *Global Visions: Beyond the New World Order* (Black Rose, 1993), p. xix.

35. Bush, G., 'Toward a New World Order', address before a Joint Session of Congress, Washington DC, 11 September 1990, *Dispatch*, US Department of State, 17 September 1990, p. 91. Bush, G., 'The U.N.: World Parliament of Peace', address to the UN General Assembly, New York, 1 October 1990. *Dispatch*, US Department of State, 8 October 1990, p. 152. Clinton, W., 'Confronting the Challenges of a Broader World', address to the UN General Assembly, New York, 27 September 1993, cited in H. Kissinger, *Diplomacy* (Simon & Schuster, 1994), pp. 804–5.

36. Huntington, S., 'The Clash of Civilizations?', *Foreign Affairs*, 1993, 72, pp. 22–49; Walzer, M., 'Modern Tribalism', *Dialogue* (1993), 99, pp. 14–19 and R.E. Harkavy, 'Images of the Coming International System', *Orbis* (1997), 41, pp. 569–90.

37. Zolo, D., *Cosmopolis: Prospects for World Government*, trans. D. McKie (Polity Press, 1997), p. 155.

38. Bush is cited and criticised in D.J. Scheffer, 'Toward a Modern Doctrine of Humanitarian Intervention', *University of Toledo Law Review* (1992), 23, pp. 279–80n.

39. Mandelbaum, M., 'Foreign Policy as Social Work', *Foreign Affairs* (1996), 75, pp. 16, 18. See also W.E. Odom, 'How to Create a True World Order', *Orbis* (Spring 1995), p. 157. On the Clinton administration's caution see: Howard, M., 'The World According to Henry: From Metternich to Me', *Foreign Affairs* (1994), 73, p. 135; Berdal, M.R., 'Fateful Encounter: The United States and UN Peacekeeping', *Survival* (1994), 36, pp. 30–50; Malone, D., 'Haiti and the International Community: A Case Study', *Survival* (1997), 39, p. 135.

40. Carlsson, I., 'Time for a New Order in World Affairs', Lecture given by Ingvar Carlsson at the Center for International and Comparative Studies, Northwestern University, Chicago, 23 October 1996, pp. 1–2, The Commission on Global Governance, Articles and Speeches by the Co-Chairman and Commission Members, http://www.cgg.ch/articles.htm.

41. Commission on Global Governance, *Our Global Neighbourhood* (Oxford, 1995), pp. 10–11. See also Carlsson *World Affairs*, pp. 2–3.

42. Barnett, M.N., 'Bringing in the New World Order: Liberalism, Legitimacy and the United Nations', *World Politics* (1997), 49, pp. 526–51.

43. Latham, R., *The Liberal Moment: Modernity, Security and Making of Postwar International Order* (Columbia, 1997), pp. 5, 9.

44. Hayek, F.A., *The Road to Serfdom* (Dymock's, 1944), p. 217.

45. Scholte, J.A., *International Relations of Social Change* (Open University Press, 1993), p. 73.

46. Commission on Global Governance, *Our Global Neighbourhood*, pp. 11, 248.

47. Commission on Global Governance, 'A Global Common Future: Preparing for the 21st Century', Address by Sir Shridath Ramphal at a Conference on Sustainable Development in the 21st Century – Iceland's Role, Reykjavik, Iceland, 13 September 1996, http://www.cgg.ch/articles.htm, p. 1.

48. Urquhart, B., 'The UN from Herbert Lehman to the New Stone Age', 27th Annual Herbert H. Lehman Memorial Lecture, Lehman College, 9 April 1996, The Commission on Global Governance, Articles and Speeches by the Co-Chairman and Commission Members, http://www.cgg.ch/articles.htm, pp. 2–4.

49. See J.A. Scholte, 'The Globalization of World Politics', in J. Bayliss and S. Smith (eds), *The Globalization of World Politics: An Introduction to International Relations* (Oxford University Press, 1997), pp. 21–2 and P.L. van den Berghe, 'Parasitism and Corruption: State Behavior in the Throes of Deepening Global Crisis', *Politics and the Life Sciences* (1994), 13, pp. 29–30. 'The transboundary nature of environmental problems presents a major problem to political sovereignty...the globalizing effect of economic integration has substantially eroded national economic sovereignty.'

50. James, A., *Sovereign Statehood: the Basis of International Society* (Allen & Unwin, 1986), p. 24; Jackson, R.H., *Quasi-states: Sovereignty, International Relations and the Third World* (Cambridge University Press, 1990), p. 46.

51. Van den Berghe 'Parasitism', pp. 29–30. Yuwa Wong, 'Impotence and Intransigence: State Behavior in the Throes of Deepening Global Crisis', *Politics and the Life Sciences* (1994), 13, pp. 3–14, esp. p. 11.

52. Tennberg, M., 'Risky Business: Defining the Concept of Environmental Security', *Cooperation and Conflict* (1995), 30, pp. 239–58, esp. pp. 247–9.

53. Camilleri, J. and J. Falk, *The End of Sovereignty? The Politics of A Shrinking and Fragmenting World* (Edward Elgar, 1992), pp. 172, 177, 185, 192.

54. Kobrin, S.J., 'Back to the Future: Neomedievalism and the Postmodern Digital World Economy', *Journal of International Affairs* (1998), 51, pp. 361–2. See also Elkins, D.J., *Beyond Sovereignty: Territory and Political Economy in the Twenty First Century* (Toronto University Press, 1995), p. 113. Singer, J.D., 'The Evolution of Anarchy Vs. the Evolution of Cooperation', *Politics and the Life Sciences* (February 1994), Vol. 13, pp. 26–8.

55. Hassner, P., 'Beyond Nationalism and Internationalism: Ethnicity and World Order', *Survival*, 35 (1993), pp. 49–65, p. 53. See also Elkins *Beyond Sovereignty*, p. 41.

56. Prins, G., 'Politics and the Environment', *International Affairs* (1990), 66, pp. 711–30, pp. 723–4.

57. Bull *State's Positive Role*, p. 111.

58. Richard Falk, 'The Making of Global Citizenship', in Brecher, Brown Childs and Cutler *Global Visions*, p. 39; and Falk, R., *Humane Governance: Toward a New Global Politics.* (Polity Press, 1995), p. 205.

59. Falk *Humane Governance*, pp. 6, 9, 36, 86.

60. Falk *Humane Governance*, pp. 36, 81, 90. Note that Falk also found the Commission's discussion of global governance 'confusing'. Falk, R., *Human Rights Horizons: The Pursuit of Justice in Globalizing World* (Routledge, 2000), p. 260. For his most recent discussion of the positive and negative impacts of globalization see pp. 184–5.

61. Falk, R., *Explorations at the Edge of Time* (Temple Press, 1992).

62. Falk *Humane Governance*, pp. 3, 81.

63. Laski, H., 'The Personality of Associations', *Harvard Law Review* (1916), p. 425.

64. Bergson, H., *Creative Evolution*, trans. A. Mitchell (University Press of America, 1983), pp. 248–9, 307, 314, 342–3. First published in 1911.

65. Deleuze, G. and F. Guattari, *A Thousand Plateaus: Capitalism and Schizophrenia* (Athlone Press, 1988), trans. B. Massumi. pp. 365, 367.

66. Deleuze and Guattari *A Thousand Plateaus*, pp. 361–7, 373–5, 407.

67. Ibid., pp. 360, 386.

68. This is Bergson's expression. See Bergson *Creative Evolution*, pp. 208–11. See Deleuze and Guattari, *A Thousand Plateaus*, pp. 236–9, 352–4, 483–4, 573.

69. Deleuze and Guattari *A Thousand Plateaus*, p. 5.

70. Ibid., pp. 360, 386.

71. Ibid., p. 2.

72. Pick, D., *War Machine: The Rationalisation of Slaughter in the Modern Age* (Yale University Press, 1996), p. 259 and Deleuze and Guattari *A Thousand Plateaus*, p. 60.

73. Baudrillard, J., *Les Stratégies fatales* (Bernard Grasset, 1983), reproduced in J. Baudrillard, *Selected Writings*, Mark Poster (ed.) (Polity Press, 1988), pp. 190–1.

74. Baudrillard, J., *Simulations* (Semiotext[e], 1983), p. 59, trans. P. Foss, P. Patton and P. Beitchman.

75. Baudrillard *Selected Writings*, p. 202.

76. Baudrillard *Simulations*, p. 58.

77. Ibid., pp. 60–3.

78. Ibid., pp. 64–6.

79. Baudrillard, J., *The Gulf War Did Not Take Place* (Power Publications, 1995), trans. P. Patton. First published in French 1991. Christopher Norris, uncannily echoing the criticisms of James and Bergson in the early twentieth century, asserted that Baudrillard's study of the Gulf War revealed 'the depth of ideological complicity that exists between such forms of extreme anti-realist or irrationalist doctrine and the crisis of moral and political nerve'. Norris, C., *Uncritical Theory: Postmodernism, Intellectuals and the Gulf War* (Lawrence and Wishart, 1992), pp. 27, 29. Quoted in Patton's introduction to *The Gulf War*, p. 15.

80. Deleuze and Guattari *A Thousand Plateaus*, p. 62.

81. Ibid., p. 119.

82. Von Clausewitz, C., *On War* (Princeton University Press, 1982), p. 605. First published in 1832.

83. Walker, R.B.J., *Inside/Outside: international relations as political theory* (Cambridge University Press, 1993), p. 183. See G. Deleuze, *Bergsonism*, trans. H. Tomlinson and B. Habberjam (Zone Books, 1988), p. 91.

84. Walker *Inside/Outside*, pp. 2, 4–7, 10. 22, 95–8, 101, 102, 119–20, 128–9, 133, 155, 161–6, 176–8, 180, 193; Walker, R.B.J., 'From International Relations to World Politics', in J.A. Camilleri, A.P. Jarvis and A. J. Paolini (eds), *The State in Transition* (Lynne Reinner, 1995), p. 28; Walker, R.B.J., 'International Relations and the Concept of the Political', in K. Booth and S. Smith (eds), *International Relations Theory Today* (Polity Press, 1995), pp. 314–15. Walker's choice of phrase echoes Bergson. See *Creative Evolution*, p. 197.

85. Deleuze and Guattari *A Thousand Plateaus*, pp. 371–3. See also Walker *Inside/Outside*, pp. 5, 96, 129, 178; Walker *International Relations*, p. 314; Kuehls, T., *Beyond Sovereign Territory: the space of ecopolitics* (University of Minnesota Press, 1996), pp. 11–15, 37–40, 130.

86. Kuehls *Beyond Sovereign Territory*, pp. 37–42.

87. Chesneaux, J., 'Ten Questions on Globalization', *Pacifica Review* (1994), 6, pp. 92–3.

88. This expression, which I have adapted, comes from R. Rorty, *Contingency, Irony, and Solidarity* (Cambridge University Press, 1989), p. xiii. 'Their strategy [historicist thinkers] has been to insist that socialization...goes all the way down.'

89. See also Kuehls *Beyond Sovereign Territory*, pp. 15, 92–3, 130. Kuehls writes that:

> thinking society beyond borders does not necessitate creating some kind of international governing body to encompass this global human population, but might suggest a smooth or rhizomatic social space...Thinking society beyond both

> sovereign territorial boundaries and species boundaries means taking into serious consideration the ambiguity, contingency, and diversity of life.

90. These images and ideas are drawn from James, W., *Essays in Radical Empiricism and A Pluralistic Universe*, R.B. Perry (ed.), pp. 274–6, 283. See also James, W., *Pragmatism* (Longmans, Green & Co, 1907), p. 79.

91. Laski, H., *A Grammar of Politics* (Allen and Unwin, 1925), p. 250.

92. James, W., *Will to Believe and other Essays in Popular Philosophy* (New York, 1897), p. 201; *Holmes-Laski Letters: The Correspondence of Mr. Justice Holmes and Harold J. Laski 1916–1935*, M. DeWolfe Howe (ed.), foreword by F. Frankfurter, 2 vols, (London, 1953) Vol. 1, pp. 691, 697 (22 December 1924 and 6 January 1925) and Vol. II, p. 1205 (7 February 1927). See also H. Laski, 'Law and the State', *Economica* (1929), 27, pp. 267–95, esp. pp. 267, 294.

93. Jackson, R.H., 'The Evolution of International Society', in J. Baylis and S. Smith (eds), *The Globalization of World Politics: An Introduction to International Relations* (Oxford, 1997), p. 46.

94. Bull 'State's Positive Role', p. 113.

95. This is Hans Kelsen's term. See *General Theory of Law and State*, trans. A. Wedberg (Russell, 1961), p. 386.

96. Zimmern, A., 'International Law and Social Consciousness', *Transactions of the Grotius Society* (1934), 20, pp. 36–51.

97. For a discussion of this and historical examples see Baron Heyking, 'The International Protection of Minorities – The Achilles' Heel of the League of Nations', *Transactions of the Grotius Society* (1928), 13, pp. 31–51 and N. Bentwich, 'The League of Nations and Racial Persecution in Germany', *Transactions of the Grotius Society* (1934), 19, pp. 75–88.

98. Laski *Grammar*, p. 45.

99. Boutros-Ghali cited in D.J. Scheffer, 'Toward a Modern Doctrine of Humanitarian Intervention', *University of Toledo Law Review* (1992), 23, p. 283n.

100. Falk *Human Rights Horizons*, pp. 67–9.

101. See E.C. Stowell, *Intervention in International Law* (John Byrne, 1921), p. 53. See also N. Bentwich, 'The League of Nations and Racial Persecution in Germany', *Transactions of the Grotius Society* (1934), 19, pp. 75–88, esp. p. 76. On the relation of sovereignty to natural law see C.H. McIlwain, 'A Fragment on Sovereignty', *Political Science Quarterly* (1933), 48, pp. 94–106, esp. p. 98. See also E. de Vattel, *The Law of Nations* (AMS, 1863), pp. 154–9, first published in 1758, and J. Westlake, *International Law* (Cambridge, 1910), I, pp. 319–20, first published in 1904.

102. Qian, W., 'The United Nations and State Sovereignty in the Post-Cold War Era', *Pacifica Review* (1995), 7, p. 136.

103. Falk *Human Rights Horizons*, p. 70–1.

104. On this point see Laski *Grammar*, p. 260. 'We have to take the world of sense as we meet it, its losses and gains, its struggles and victories, and assume that...it is a real world in space and time. We have to treat evil as genuine and not merely an appearance capable, otherwise, of being harmonised into good.' See also James *Will to Believe*, p. 61.

CONCLUSION

1. Falk, R., *Humane Governance: Toward a New Global Politic*. (Polity Press, 1995), p. 8.

2. Bobbio, N., *Il problema della Guerra e le vie della pace* (Il Mulino, 1984) and Bobbio, N., *The Future of Democracy: a defence of the rules of the game*, trans. R. Griffen (Polity Press, 1987).

3. Zolo, D., *Cosmopolis: Proposals for World Government*, trans. D. McKie (Polity Press, 1997), pp. ix, 44.

4. Ibid., pp. 2, 53, 165.
5. Ibid., pp. 165–6.
6. De Vattel, E., *The Law of Nations* (AMS, 1863). First published in 1758. Cited in Jeremy Rabkin,'Grotius, Vattel, and Locke: An Older View of Liberalism and Nationality', *The Review of Politics* (1997), 59, pp. 302–3. On Vattel's version of intervention see P.P. Remec's *The Position of the Individual in International Law: According to Grotius and Vattel* (Martinus Nijhoff, 1960), pp. 232–3.
7. Zolo *Cosmopolis*, pp. 14, 154.
8. Cohen, M., 'Communal Ghosts and Other Perils in Social Philosophy', *Journal of Philosophy, Psychology and Scientific Methods* (1919), 16, pp. 673–90, esp. p. 689.
9. Latham, R., *The Liberal Moment: Modernity, Security and Making of Postwar International Order* (Columbia, 1997), pp. 13–14.
10. Ibid., pp. 71–2, 113. Carr, E.H., *The Twenty Years' Crisis* (Macmillan, 1951), pp. 84, 113.
11. Latham *Liberal Moment*, pp. 140, 200–3.
12. Ibid., pp. 203–10.
13. Ibid., pp. 206–7.
14. Zolo *Cosmopolis*, p. 129.
15. Ibid., pp. 148–9.

INDEX

Compiled by Sue Carlton